MATHEMATICS
FOR RETAIL BUYING

eighth edition

BETTE K. TEPPER
Fashion Institute of Technology, USA

MARLA GREENE
LIM College, USA

Fairchild Books
An imprint of Bloomsbury Publishing Inc

B L O O M S B U R Y
NEW YORK · LONDON · OXFORD · NEW DELHI · SYDNEY

Because of her encouragement, contribution, assistance, and support, I would like to dedicate this edition to my daughter, Rebecca Tepper Citron.

—Bette K. Tepper

I would like to dedicate this edition to Anne Bryan, my mentor and good friend; my colleagues at LIM College for their support over the years; and lastly, to the students, this is for you!

—Marla Greene

Fairchild Books
An imprint of Bloomsbury Publishing Inc

1385 Broadway	50 Bedford Square
New York	London
NY 10018	WC1B 3DP
USA	UK

www.bloomsburyfashioncentral.com

**FAIRCHILD BOOKS, BLOOMSBURY and the Diana logo
are trademarks of Bloomsbury Publishing Plc**

This edition published 2016
Reprinted 2017 (twice)
Seventh edition published 2014
Sixth edition published 2008
Fifth edition published 2002

Library of Congress Cataloging-in-Publication Data
Names: Tepper, Bette K. | Greene, Marla.
Title: Mathematics for retail buying / Bette K. Tepper, Marla Greene.
Description: Eighth edition. | New York : Fairchild Books, 2016. | Revised edition of Mathematics for retail buying, 2014.
Identifiers: LCCN 2015038432| ISBN 9781501315657 (paperback) | ISBN 9781501315664 (ePDF)
Subjects: LCSH: Retail trade—Mathematics. | BISAC: BUSINESS & ECONOMICS / Industries / Fashion & Textile Industry.
Classification: LCC HF5695.5.R45 T44 2016 | DDC 658.8/7001513--dc23
LC record available at http://lccn.loc.gov/2015038432
ISBN: PB: 978-1-5013-1572-5
ePDF: 978-1-5013-1566-4

Typeset by Lachina
Printed and bound in the United States of America

CONTENTS

List of Figures viii
Preface ix
Introduction xvii

CHAPTER 1: MERCHANDISING FOR A PROFIT 1
Objectives, Key Terms, and Key Concept Formulas 1

1.1 Profit Components 4
Use of Profit Calculations 4
Defining the Basic Profit Factors 5
Elements of Basic Profit Factors 7
Most Common Retail Sales Key Performance Indicators (KPIs)
      Pertaining to Sales Performance 11
Cost of Goods Sold (Also Referred to as Cost of Merchandise Sold) 12
Gross Margin 14
Operating Income (Gross Sales and Net Sales) Practice Problems 18
Cost of Goods Sold Practice Problems 23
Gross Margin Practice Problems 27
Operating Expense Practice Problems 28

1.2 Profit and Loss Statements 30
Skeletal Profit and Loss Statements 31
Final Profit and Loss Statements 33
Skeletal Profit and Loss Statement Practice Problems 37
Final Profit and Loss Statement Practice Problems 42

1.3 How to Increase Profits 45
Evaluating a Buyer 48
Case Study 1: Analyzing Profit Performance 49
Case Study 2: Controlling Expenses 50
Case Study 3: Analysis of Profit and Loss Statements 51
Case Study 4: Evaluating a Buyer 52

CHAPTER 2: RETAIL PRICING AND REPRICING OF MERCHANDISE 53

Objectives, Key Terms, and Key Concept Formulas 53

2.1   Retail Pricing and Pricing Strategies 56
The Structuring of Price Lines 56
Setting Individual Retail Prices and/or Price Lines 58
Advantages of Price Lining Strategy 59
Price Line Reports 59
The Relationship of the Basic Pricing Factors 59
Price Line Report Practice Problem 63
Retail Pricing Practice Problems 65

2.2   Basic Markup Equations Used in Buying Decisions 68
Basic Markup Percentage Equations 68
The Relationship of the Basic Pricing Factors to Profit 78
Markup Practice Problems 79
Cumulative Markup for a Purchase Practice Problems 83
Cumulative Markup Application Practice Problems 87
Additional Markup 89
Markup Cancellation 89

2.3   Repricing of Merchandise/Markdowns 90
Markdowns 90
    The Purpose of Markdowns 91
    Causes of Markdowns 91
    Timing of Markdowns 92
Markdown Calculations 93
Markdown Journalization 99
Employee Discounts 102

2.4   Point-of-Sale (POS) and Permanent (Physical) Markdowns 103

2.5   Analytical Criteria for Taking Markdowns 106
Price Change Procedures 108
The Relationship of Repricing to Profit 109
Repricing of Merchandise/Markdown Practice Problems 110
Planned and Actual Markdown Practice Problems 112
Compounding of Markdown Practice Problems 115
Point-of-Sale Markdown Practice Problems 116
Permanent Markdown Practice Problems 120
Weeks of Supply, Sell through %, and Build Practice Problems 122
Case Study 1: Pricing in Merchandising 125
Case Study 2: Justification of the Pricing Strategy 127

CHAPTER 3: BASIC MARKUP EQUATIONS USED IN MERCHANDISING DECISIONS 129

Objectives, Key Terms, and Key Concept Formulas 129

3.1 Types of Markups 131
Initial Markup Concepts 131
Calculating Initial Markup 133
Cumulative Markup 135
Maintained Markup 137
Initial Markup Concept Practice Problems 141
Calculating Initial Markup Practice Problems 142
Cumulative Markup Practice Problems 144
Maintained Markup Practice Problems 147

3.2 Average or Balancing Markup 150
Average Costs When Retail and Markup Percentage Are Known 151
Average Retail(s) When Costs and Markup Percentage Are Known 153
Average Markup Percentage When Retail and Planned Markup Percentage Are Known 155
Average Cost Practice Problems 158
Average Retail Practice Problems 160
Average Markup Percentage Practice Problems 162

3.3 Limitations of the Markup Percentage as a Guide to Profits 164
Case Study 1: Achieving a Predetermined Markup 166
Case Study 2: Ensuring Favorable Markup Results 168
Case Study 3: Balancing Markup 170
Case Study 4: Achieving Your Cumulative Markup Goal 171

CHAPTER 4: THE RETAIL METHOD OF INVENTORY 173

Objectives, Key Terms, and Key Concept Formulas 173

4.1 Explanation of the Retail Method of Inventory 176

4.2 General Procedures for Implementing the Retail Method of Inventory 178
Finding an Opening Book Inventory Figure 178
Maintaining a Perpetual Book Inventory Figure 178
Forms Used in the Retail Method of Inventory 182
Comparing Book Inventory with Planned Book Inventory 195
Maintaining a Perpetual Book Inventory Figure Practice Problems 196

4.3 Shortages and Overages 204
Causes of Shortages and Overages 205
Calculating Shortages and Overages 206
Shortages and Overages Practice Problems 208

4.4　An Evaluation of the Retail Method of Inventory　**216**
　　　Advantages of the Retail Method of Inventory　216
　　　Limitations of the Retail Method of Inventory　216
　　　Finding Cost of Goods Sold and Gross Margin with the Retail
　　　　　Method of Inventory Valuation　217
　　　The Relationship of Profit to Inventory Valuation in the Retail Method
　　　　　of Inventory　219
　　　The Effect Shortages and Overages Have on Gross Margin　220
　　　Case Study 1: Retail Method of Inventory　221
　　　Case Study 2: Controlling Shortages　222

CHAPTER 5: SIX-MONTH PLANNING AND COMPONENTS 225

　　　Objectives, Key Terms, and Key Concept Formulas　225

　　　Six-Month Seasonal Dollar Merchandise Plan　**228**
　　　The Procedure of Dollar Planning by Factor　228

5.1　Planning Net Sales　**229**
　　　Calculating Percentage of Sales Increase or Decrease When Last Year's Actual
　　　　　Sales and This Year's Planned Sales Are Known　231
　　　Calculating a Total Planned Seasonal Sales Figure When Last Year's Sales and the
　　　　　Planned Percentage of Increase Are Known　233
　　　Calculating Sales on the Basis of Sales Achieved per Square Footage　235
　　　Planning Sales Practice Problems　236
　　　Sales per Square Foot Practice Problems　240

5.2　Turnover/GMROI　**241**
　　　Determining the Turnover Figure　242
　　　Determining Gross Margin Return by Dollar Inventory　246
　　　Calculating Average Retail Stock, Turnover, and GMROI Practice Problems　251

5.3　Stock/Inventory Planning Methods　**263**
　　　Setting Individual First-of-Month Stock Figures by the
　　　　　Stock-Sales Ratio Method　263
　　　Setting Stock Figures by the Weeks of Supply Method　264
　　　Setting Beginning of the Month (BOM) Stock Figures by Basic Stock Method　266
　　　Calculating Stock-Sales Ratio Practice Problems　269
　　　Finding Weeks of Supply Practice Problems　271
　　　Using Basic Stock Method Practice Problems　273
　　　Planning Markdowns　275
　　　Planning Markups　276

5.4　Open-to-Buy and Purchase/Receipt Planning　**279**
　　　Calculating Planned Monthly Purchases at Retail　279
　　　Converting Retail Planned Purchases to Cost　280
　　　Planned Purchase Practice Problems　290

5.5   Open-to-Buy Control 296
      Explanation of Open-to-Buy Reports 299
      Calculating Retail Open-to-Buy at the Beginning of a Month 304
      Calculating Retail Open-to-Buy During the Month 304
      Calculating Retail Open-to-Buy Practice Problems 306

5.6   Six-Month Seasonal Dollar Merchandise Plan 310

5.7   Assortment/Classification Planning 314
      Case Study 1: Open-to-Buy 324
      Case Study 2: Planning for Effective Buying 327
      Case Study 3: Dollar Planning and Control 330
      Case Study 4: Formulating a Six-Month Plan 331

CHAPTER 6: INVOICE MATHEMATICS: TERMS OF SALE 333
      Objectives and Key Terms 333

6.1   Invoice Mathematics: Terms of Sale 334
      Different Types of Discounts 334
      Calculating Net Cost 337
      Net Terms 342
      Dating 342
      Anticipation 349
      Loading 349
      Shipping Terms 349
      Discount Practice Problems 351
      Dating Practice Problems 352
      Case Study 1: Terms of Sale 355
      Case Study 2: Resources Influenced by Terms of Sale 357

Glossary of Concept Formulas 359
Glossary of Terms 365
Selected Answers 375
Index 381

LIST OF FIGURES

	Introduction: Sales by Store Type, 2009–2014 **xxvi**
1.	Contribution Operating Statement 17
2.	Profit and Loss Statement 34
3.	Price Line Structure Promotional Chart 57
4.	Price Line Report by Classification 60
5.	POS Markdown Receipt 100
6.	POS Credit Slip 100
7.	Price Change 108
8.	Physical Inventory Count Sheet 177
9.	Journal of Purchase Record 183
10.	Outstanding Transfer List Form 184
11.	Shipment Summary 185
12.	Buyer's Price Change Worksheet 186
13.	Computer Price Change Entry 187
14.	Specific Departments by Classification 188
15.	Debit Memo 189
16.	Return to Vendor Authorization and Worksheet 190
17.	Daily Exception Selling Price Report 191
18.	Sales and Productivity Report by Store by Salesperson 192
19.	Weekly Sales Challenge Recap 193
20.	District Flash Sales by Store 194
21.	District Flash Sales by Group: Week 25 Ending 07/22/2013 194
22.	Shortage Report 204
23.	Calculating Gross Margin on Stock plus Purchases 217
24.	Retail 4-5-4 Calendar for 2015–2017 230
25.	Typical Conventional Department Store's Monthly Sales Distribution 234
26.	Daily Flash Sales by Store 234
27.	Worksheet for Annual Merchandise Plan 281
28.	Six-Month Merchandise Plan (by Store) 282
29.	Six-Month Merchandise Plan 283
30.	Total Corporate Six-Month Plan 284
31.	Purchase Planning 285
32.	Merchandise Statistics Report 286
33.	Open-to-Buy Monthly Report 297
34.	Open-to-Buy Report 299
35.	Six-Month Merchandising Plan for Women's Activewear 311
36.	Annual Merchandising Plan for Fashion Jewelry 312
37.	Dollar Classification Plan for Fashion Jewelry, Fall 2015: Sales/Receipts August–January 315
38.	Merchandise Assortment Plan for Fashion Jewelry 318
39.	Women's Sportswear Outlet Fall SKU Analysis 321
40.	Six-Month Merchandising Plan 325
41.	Summary of Discount Dates 348

PREFACE

"When you can measure what you are speaking about and express it in numbers, you know something about it; but when you cannot measure it, when you cannot express it in numbers, your knowledge is of a meager and unsatisfactory kind."

LORD KELVIN (1824–1901)

In the first edition of *Mathematics for Retail Buying*, we stated that operating figures, especially sales and gross margin, are the language of any retailer, regardless of the size of the store. This has not changed, and in today's highly competitive retail environment, where retailers are competing for the customers' "share of wallet," it is even more important than ever to have comprehension of the mathematical factors involved in profitable merchandising. This fundamental mathematical background gives insight into how merchandising problems are solved mathematically and perception as to why merchandising decisions are made based on analytical data. While the formulas remain constant from retailer to retailer, the numbers will vary! The most experienced and skilled merchandiser knows that mastery of mathematical techniques and figure analysis is an essential tool. Additionally, persons in related careers who comprehend the mathematics of profit will also benefit by their broader understanding of merchandising situations.

Mathematics for Retail Buying teaches the essential concepts, practices, and procedures as well as the calculations and interpretations of figures related to the many factors that produce sales and ultimately profit. The choice of material and the depth of each subject focus on that which has practical value for the performance of occupations in or associated with retail buying, planning, and merchandising. It concentrates on the mathematical concepts and their relationships to the many activities involved in achieving a profitable retail buying/selling process. The concepts provide the foundation; how they are generally applied is then described in each chapter. Actual industry application will vary based on what is right for the company or department for which you are ultimately working. Each retailer/company has different goals and reporting systems that incorporate the basic formulas. In addition to the obvious educational benefits to students of retailing, *Mathematics for Retail Buying* can serve as a guide in training junior executives and can be a constant source of reference for an assistant buyer or the merchant who operates a small, independent store. A guiding principle always to remember is that no matter how far along you are in your career, you always need to come back to the basics and understand how they work.

When contemplating the writing or revision of any retailing textbook, the question of practical value will inevitably arise. We feel the contents of *Mathematics for Retail Buying* are not only sensible but realistic because this text has been based on:

- The personal experience of the authors, who were merchandise managers and buyers for major retail organizations.

- The knowledgeable opinions of current retail executives as to the information necessary to prepare prospective retail merchandisers.

- The insights manufacturers have gained that help to provide better service and to communicate more effectively with retailers and merchandisers.

- The tested use of the material by the authors and other faculty members at many universities and colleges and by retail executives and training departments.

- The favorable comments about the value of the material in relation to career performance by many alumni who are retail executives in the industry.

The study and comprehension of the principles and techniques contained in *Mathematics for Retail Buying* will enable the student to:

- Recognize the basic and elementary factors of the buying and selling process that affect sales, gross margin, and profit.

- Understand the relationship of the profit factors and how to improve profit performance by the manipulation of these factors.

- Understand how merchandise pricing affects the bottom line.

- Become familiar with the applications of computers and computerized forms in retailing.

- Understand and apply the basic mathematical concepts used to solve real-life merchandising problems.

- Recognize the relationship between all the formulas and metrics involved in a business.

- Comprehend the standard industry terminology employed in retailing and merchandising.

In developing and changing the book for this revised Eighth Edition, we have tried to be sensitive to and concerned about comments from colleagues and students from many other colleges relating to the sequence of study units and material covered in our book. Taking these comments into account, we have restructured the chapters and increased learning materials to better prepare students to enter the retail industry, especially those students that want to apply for executive training programs.

There is a rather basic principle about the buying/merchandising process: There is no one beginning and no one end. It is a circular process—an unending, interrelated continuum within which all factors influence all other factors. Even though the chapters are interrelated, each can be used as a separate topic of study, and each can be shifted without losing the continuity of the process. The various facets of the merchandising cycle are an ongoing procedure of monitoring, analysis, and evaluation, directed to the purpose of meeting the merchandiser's objective of achieving a sales plan, a predetermined gross margin, which should, in turn, generate an appropriate net profit. This is mentioned to point out to instructors and students alike (and to merchants who use our book for in-service training purposes) that the study of retail mathematics may begin at any point on the "circle."

ORGANIZATION OF THE BOOK

In this revised Eighth Edition, the material is divided into six chapters. Each chapter covers a particular, basic mathematical factor that affects the gross margin/profits that a buyer/planner or retailer will be concerned about. The relationships among these profit factors are stressed throughout the book. The sequence within some chapters has been altered to accommodate additional and/or more detailed explanations.

The chapters of study and their subject matter are:

- Chapter 1, Merchandising for a Profit, defines, analyzes, and shows the calculations pertaining to the skeletal profit and loss statement and the components of the statement. (Previously Unit VI.)

- Chapter 2, Retail Pricing and Repricing of Merchandise, discusses and illustrates the basic pricing factors used in buying decisions and presents the calculations used when pricing merchandise initially, initial markup and cumulative markup. The section on repricing merchandise and markdowns includes compounded markdowns. Two more sections discuss point-of-sale and permanent markdowns, and the analytical criteria for taking markdowns. (Previously Unit II.)

- Chapter 3, Basic Markup Equations Used in Merchandising Decisions, explains the importance of markup to profitable merchandising and illustrates the calculations of the various types of markup (i.e., cumulative, initial, and maintained) that, when understood and implemented, achieve the desired results. (Previously Unit III.)

- Chapter 4, The Retail Method of Inventory, presents and explains this proven, reliable procedure as a mechanism and system for determining the total value of the stock-on-hand and shortages and the effect on gross margin. (Previously Unit IV.)

- Chapter 5, renamed Six-Month Planning and Components, includes the methodology of how to plan sales and inventory, including turnover and GMROI. Increased focus has been placed on the six-month planning process with an example that takes students through the steps for one department. A new assortment planning section has been added with examples. (Previously Unit V.)

- Chapter 6, Invoice Mathematics: Terms of Sale, discusses discounts and order terms that buyers are responsible for negotiating. (Previously Unit I.)

Every effort is still being made to build the contents of the book into a solid foundation for ease of understanding, and not merely to display formulas. The material has been reorganized as traditional chapters with sections and subsections while keeping the structure of a simplified outline form. Within each chapter after a major topic, a series of examples with problems and solutions is presented that tests the understanding of the fundamental principles discussed in that section. This step-by-step presentation uses brief explanations stated in basic terms and precise definitions, demonstrated clearly in examples that express the mathematical principles discussed in that section. Within each chapter, after a major topic, a series of solutions is presented that tests understanding of the fundamental principles discussed in that section. After major principles are explained, students are given practice problems to solve that mirror the various channels of distribution in the retail industry. At the end of each chapter, updated case studies illustrate practical retailing situations and common obstacles and difficulties encountered in real-life merchandising. The majority of the problems presented in this text focus on apparel and accessories as the kingdom of fashion goods is explored. Among these are problems designed for and designated as spreadsheet problems and cases, which can be calculated manually, with a calculator, or on a computerized spreadsheet. A STUDIO online learning environment replaces the CD-ROM that appeared in the prior edition and includes many of the problems and cases that pertain to the fundamental concepts of profitable retailing. These features further reinforce comprehension of the specific section.

For the revised Eighth Edition, particular attention has been paid to the comments of the various users, including their own teaching experience, as well as both of the authors, and also the comments of people in the industry interviewed for the book. New coauthor, Marla Greene, is a Clinical Associate Professor of Fashion Merchandising at LIM College in New York City, USA, and a retail professional with more than 25 years of experience as a Merchandise Manager and Buyer.

KEY LEARNING FEATURES

- The Introduction continues to connect the text contents with an overview of the growth of retailing and the mega trends of the times, accelerated by the use of computers, and the cardinal principles of successful merchandising.

- "Using Computerized Spreadsheets," at the end of the Introduction, explains the advantages and usage of spreadsheets in retail mathematics. All applicable concept problems are expressed in spreadsheet as well as traditional arithmetic format.

- Problem-solving situations throughout the text illustrate the basis for decision making.

- A list of Key Concept Formulas is included at the beginning of each chapter for immediate reference and information.

- A complete Glossary of Concept Formulas at the end of the book provides easy reference.

- Important key words continue to be highlighted throughout the book to facilitate student understanding of important key concepts.

- A Glossary of Terms, defining the highlighted terms throughout the book, facilitates student understanding of important key words and provides a convenient reference.

- Selected answers to odd number practice problems are given at the end of the book.

- The adaptation of spreadsheets to the mathematical concepts gives maximum comprehension, allowing students to solve more sophisticated problems without complicated, tedious calculations.

NEW TO THIS EDITION

- The units are now called chapters to make the text easier for students to navigate.

- The profit and loss statement and components material is together and up front in Chapter 1 (previously Unit VI) providing a foundation for subsequent chapters. This chapter now explains the criteria used to evaluate a buyer's performance.

- In Chapter 2 (previously Unit II), coverage of markup has been updated to reflect current industry standards.

- Also in Chapter 2, the topic of markdowns has been expanded to include concepts and problems on compounding; point-of-sale (POS) versus permanent markdowns and the effect each has on gross margin, as well as the analytical criteria used to determine when markdowns need to be taken; outdate; weeks of supply; and sell through percentage.

- Chapter 5, Six-Month Planning and Components, has been revised and expanded and includes an all-new section on Assortment Planning.

- Explanations are included on the relationship of basic pricing factors to profit and on the effect of merchandising policies to the pricing of goods.

- Many of the practice problems in each chapter are new or have been updated to reflect current industry practice. These problems help students comprehend material, apply industry terminology, and simulate realistic current merchandising situations.

- New case study problems at the end of each chapter demonstrate the use of material in realistic, practical merchandising situations.

- Industry terminology and data are updated and reflected in the text and problems presented.

USING THE MATHEMATICS FOR RETAIL BUYING

STUDIO™

Mathematics for Retail Buying, Eighth Edition, now includes an online STUDIO accessible via www.BloomsburyFashionCentral.com, which provides easy access to content previously provided on the CD-ROM, as well as new online study tools aligned with each chapter of the book.

With this resource, students will:

- Practice skills by computing practice problems from the text, now available digitally with formulas embedded in Excel spreadsheets.

- Enhance knowledge with additional real-world case studies and activities for each chapter.

- Study smarter with self-quizzes featuring scored results and personalized study tips.

- Review concepts with flash cards of terms and definitions and key formulas.

The Excel files available under "Studio Resources" should be downloaded and saved to the student's computer. Students have the freedom to play with the numbers in the concept problems to see how the concepts work, as well as to work the practice problems. If additional space is needed to work the problems out in Excel, go to Home > Insert and insert additional rows, columns, or even pages in the spreadsheet. Some problems do not warrant the development of a spreadsheet. Even so, the computer can be useful to do basic arithmetic calculations to solve problems.

Students can gain access to the STUDIO resources by purchasing a new textbook with bundled access code. Access is free with purchase of Book + Studio ISBN 9781501315725 or eBook + Studio ISBN 9781501315718. Students may also purchase STUDIO Access Card ISBN 9781501315701 at their campus bookstore or purchase Studio Instant Access ISBN 9781501395659 directly through Bloomsbury Fashion

Central. Redeeming the access card will give students full access to the content from the CD-ROM that was packaged with previous editions, plus material new to this edition.

TEACHING RESOURCES

To gain access to instructor resources, go to www.BloomsburyFashionCentral.com and create an account *or* log in to your account. Then visit the *Mathematics for Retail Buying*, Eighth Edition, webpage on the platform and in the instructor's module on the right-hand side of the page, select "Instructor Resources," and click "Request." Within 48 hours of requesting, instructors will receive a confirming e-mail and may access requested review/exam copies, instructor's resources, and STUDIO content via the "My Course Material" section once logged in to the platform.

- The comprehensive Instructor's Answer Manual for the entire text also includes the computations and answers to the practice problems and case studies for each chapter and has been updated to correspond to the revised edition material.

- Instructor's Materials include an Edition Correlation Guide that identifies changes from Unit to Chapter and any shifts in content to provide an easy transition to the new edition.

- *Learning with STUDIO* Student Registration Guide (PDF) and First Day of Class PowerPoint presentation (PPT) provide important information.

- PowerPoint presentations provide a framework for lecture and discussion.

- The Test Bank offers exams for each chapter.

If you have any difficulties accessing the site or downloading material, please contact Customer Service at www.bloomsburyfashioncentral.com/contact-us.

ACKNOWLEDGMENTS

The idea for this book originated with the many faculty members who helped develop some of this material to meet the needs for teaching merchandising mathematics at the various retail-oriented programs from around the country. The authors are indebted to those faculty members for their contributions, and to the many students and alumni for their constructive criticism and suggestions that were used in preparing this book. Special thanks go to the coauthor of earlier editions, Professor Newton E. Godnick. He was actively involved in sharing and participating in all phases of the original and subsequent editions. Many of his contributions are still evident in this book.

I (Marla) would like to give a special thank-you to Michael Londrigan, Dean of Academic Affairs, and Terry Burstein, Chair of Fashion Merchandising, both at LIM College, for their unequivocal support in this endeavor. In addition, I want to thank my colleagues that teach Retailing and Buying–related courses, coworkers, and Advisory

Board members at LIM College for their support and assistance in developing the new material contained in the text. I would also like to thank the National Retail Federation team, especially Allison Kroeger Zeller, for help in securing industry data. Thank you to Amanda Breccia and Joseph Miranda at Fairchild Books/Bloomsbury for their help in the entire process, and to Steve Reiss for checking the content and problems. Lastly, I thank Bette Tepper for entrusting me with updating her "baby" to better prepare students for their careers.

In revisions of this book, it was mandatory to include information conforming with generally accepted practices regarding the adaptation, preparation, and use of computerized spreadsheets to express the text's fundamental mathematical concepts, as well as the use as a management tool in the retail merchandising process. In order to present this material, it was necessary to enlist the aid, guidance, and knowledge of an expert. So we are deeply grateful and indebted to Bette's daughter, Rebecca Citron, consultant and principal of Sunnybrook Consulting, who was able to fulfill these requirements. In addition, she saw the value of summarizing Key Concept Formulas at the beginning of each chapter and including a complete Glossary of Concept Formulas at the back of the book for easy reference. She also assisted in the editing, making this textbook more readable and user friendly, adding delightful quotes to make mathematics more gratifying.

We also want to acknowledge and give special thanks to the following people for their valuable input and recommendations that were incorporated into the revision of this edition: Sheng Lu, University of Rhode Island; Shubhapriya Bennur, University of Nebraska, Lincoln; Courtney Cothren, Stephens College; Lorynn R. Divita, Baylor University; Wi-suk Kwon, Auburn University; Eun Jin Hwang, Indiana University of Pennsylvania; Charlette T. Padilla, University of Arizona; Cheryl Van Ostrand, Florida State University; Patricia Rigia, University of Bridgeport; Jung Mee Mun, Indiana State University; Joseph H. Hancock, Drexel University; and Stacie Mayo, Johnson County Community College.

BETTE K. TEPPER

MARLA GREENE

INTRODUCTION

As the retail environment continues to evolve and customers tend to be influenced more by sociological and technical developments, the retailer's ultimate goal remains constant: sell merchandise profitably. As yesterday's retailers could not anticipate the rise of new formats or channels of distribution, today's retailers cannot forecast the changes that are inevitably in store. Competition, already intense, will only increase. New markets, both domestic and global, will emerge; existing markets will evolve. How retailers adapt to this dynamic environment will be the mission for all involved in the business. Yet we can state with absolute certainty that some basic ideas will remain true: Customers will continue to have needs, and the retail industry will continue to offer rewarding and exciting career opportunities to those with the desire and ability to satisfy those needs while maintaining a solid grasp on the fundamental concepts of how profitability is achieved.

In preparation for the revised Eighth Edition of *Mathematics for Retail Buying*, much thought was given to how the text's basic mathematical concepts involved in profitable retailing—which have been and will continue to be constant, once learned and calculated to achieve a profit—could be more meaningful today. At best, retailing is volatile, and the environment continues to be exciting, stimulating, and continually changing; successful retailers constantly reinvent themselves to achieve differentiation from competition as they entice customers to their doors. The student will recognize that having learned these mathematical concepts, it is how they are applied that makes for profitable merchandising. The aim of this text is to explore in depth the mathematical concepts and procedures that achieve profitable merchandising in the retail arena. The topics integrated with the buying/selling function—such as store organization; what, when, and where to buy and vendor relations—are covered fully in other texts that focus only on those subjects. Although the practice problems and case studies cover a variety of merchandise, fashion apparel and accessories are given the greatest attention, as these are the areas in which a new trainee or assistant buyer would most likely begin when taking on the responsibility of merchandise selection. The focus still remains on the mathematical concepts and their relevancy to profitable merchandising. Formulas do not change—they remain the same from company to company. Plans and how the plans are implemented, however, will vary among retailers and within different channels.

Merchandising strategies are conceived by the retailer and executed by the buyer. The buyer knows that the basic mathematical elements involved in profitable buying must be coordinated with the concepts that are applied to the function of buying at cost, selling at retail, and producing a gross margin/profit from these activities. The most cardinal principle is that it does not matter what product you buy, or which diverse retailer offers the product, or what the industry is—be it fashion, hardware, or supermarkets—the same set of concepts and mathematical calculations are connected to the three elementary factors of retail, cost, and gross margin/profit. Their application to any product in any particular store and/or industry is identical. However, the emphasis on these elements may differ because retailers' policies may not be alike. It is understandable, for example, that the calculation of a markup percentage for a specialty store like Bergdorf Goodman and a mass market store like Target is computed identically, yet the markup percentage considered acceptable by each is different. We can better appreciate the interlinking of the retailer, or any other alternative merchandise distribution choice, with the buyer as we consider their common goals and their effect on each other's function.

By definition, retailing is the term used to describe the many activities involved in selling goods and/or services, at a profit, to the ultimate consumer. Merchandising combines having the right merchandise, in the right place, in the right quantities, at the right price, at the right time. Performed by the buyer, this task—to go into a market buying what a customer wants or needs and having it ready when it is wanted—seems simple. In practice, retail management today has become complex and increasingly sophisticated due to ever-increasing competition and the manner in which the customer is shopping (i.e., in store, online, on a tablet, on a phone, or through social media). Therefore, it is more important than ever that the buyer who fulfills the merchandising function has a basic knowledge of how the customer is buying and the mathematical factors involved in profitable merchandising. Without this background it is difficult to comprehend the operation of either a small store, a department in a large store, or a non-store–based retailer, such as a click-only retailer. This fundamental mathematical background gives insight into how merchandising problems are solved mathematically and why merchandising decisions must be based on analytics. Buyers in every major retail organization now use computer-based analytical programs and spreadsheets for analysis and profit planning. Nevertheless, the buyer's ability to understand and manipulate all the factors involved in merchandising is essential. Buyers may be challenged daily to maintain a positive sales and gross margin trend or turn around a business that is not performing to plan. In a computerized organization, the buyer can instantly retrieve a particular desired merchandising figure. However, if the data necessary to take immediate action is not available, the buyer who can compute and supply the necessary information has a decided advantage.

THE GROWTH OF RETAILING

Retailing first began in the United States with the Native American trading posts of frontier days. After 1850, such pioneers as R. H. Macy and Marshall Field established department stores. By 1900, there were department stores in all major cities, and this was the retail format recognized as the mass distributor of goods. Mail-order houses were given a substantial boost by the adoption of rural free delivery by the post office, while chain stores, established in the middle of the nineteenth century, rose to maturity in the twentieth century.

The consolidation and growth in US retailing occurred during the period between the two World Wars. After 1945, there were revolutionary changes with the appearance of planned shopping centers, which often led to direct competition among retailers. The latter part of the twentieth century saw variation in retailing format, with the inception of discounters, closeout stores, manufacturer's outlets, and warehouse clubs, to name just a few. In addition, the growth of the online and television shopping channels became convenient techniques by which to buy merchandise in a non-store environment. Another unprecedented phenomenon occurred in 1994 with the acquisition of R. H. Macy's by Federated Department Stores. This forever changed competitive strategy. Many older, well-known local stores (e.g., Filene's in Boston, Marshall Field's in Chicago, and Famous-Barr in St. Louis, to name a few) underwent name changes and are now identified as Macy's. Presently, you can find Macy's coast to coast with hundreds of locations, from the city to the suburbs, to Macys.com. Today, independent ownership of department and specialty stores has become a rare phenomenon, as ownership groups consolidate and operate their acquisitions. While many local and regional stores have disappeared, others have appeared on the scene. Competition is keen and takes many forms. Kohl's, a Midwest specialty department store, has successfully invaded the East Coast; UNIQLO, Japan's largest casual-apparel retailer, has opened stores in Manhattan, Boston, and Chicago with ambitions to become the top clothing retailer in the world; and Walmart looks for future growth from international operations in such markets as China and India. Today, retailing is not only fast paced, but it requires the ability to adapt and be flexible as the basic concepts and principles are applied.

MEGA TRENDS IN RETAILING

Retailing becomes more challenging and fast paced daily. Knowing how the fundamental mathematical elements that produce a profitable operation are affected by a variety of innovative strategies pursued by all retailers is a necessity. A survey conducted by NRFF (National Retail Federation Foundation) and Bearing Point revealed two important messages from retailers for their future—growth and differentiation. This section will allow students to better appreciate the realistic retail environment as it currently exists. The following graph shows the movement (measured by volume) by store types according to the grouping by the Bureau of the Census. The trends enumerated will affect all retailers, but how and when will be determined by each organization as it charts its own course of action. For 2014, retail's total impact to the US gross domestic product (GDP) was $2.59 trillion, which is equivalent to 16.7% of the GDP. In 2012, the retail industry added $1.2 trillion to the GDP (National Retail Federation, Retail's Impact Study, 2014).

Introduction. Sales by Store Type, 2009–2014 (Billion $)

Department Store Sales	
2009	$190.8 bil
2010	$189.3 bil
2011	$188.5 bil
2012	$182.9 bil
2013	$175.1 bil
2014	$171.6 bil

Source for Sales: U.S. Census, Monthly Retail Trade Survey

Warehouse Clubs and Superstores Sales	
2009	$356.5 bil
2010	$371.0 bil
2011	$390.6 bil
2012	$411.9 bil
2013	$421.7 bil
2014	$433.9 bil

Other General Merchandise Stores Sales (excluding Warehouse Clubs and Superstores)	
2009	$47.6 bil
2010	$50.7 bil
2011	$54.7 bil
2012	$58.2 bil
2013	$59.3 bil
2014	$62.0 bil

Electronic Shopping and Mail Order Houses Sales (not including online sales from other channels, i.e., Department or Specialty Stores)	
2009	$233.7 bil
2010	$260.6 bil
2011	$290.9 bil
2012	$322.5 bil
2013	$359.6 bil
2014	$392.4 bil

Miscellaneous Store Retailers Sales	
2009	$103.4 bil
2010	$106.5 bil
2011	$111.3 bil
2012	$113.0 bil
2013	$118.0 bil
2014	$120.4 bil

Source: U.S. Census, Monthly Retail Trade Survey

Currently, with the prevalence of multi-units, there is a major trend toward varying degrees of centralizing and organizing buying activities. The choice of how to profitably accomplish the buying/selling functions depends on such factors as fashion versus basic merchandise, number and size of store units, and so on. Regardless of the method chosen, the control of the constant flow of suitable merchandise from markets to stores can be accomplished only by understanding the specific nature of the business in the reports generated by the retailer. These reports provide accurate requirements of assortment factors that pertain to classification (grouping merchandise by common distinctive features, such as men's, women's, children's, etc.), price lines, and other assortment factors in order to achieve portions consistent with customer demands. It should be noted, however, that there are differences between merchandise classifications, store locations, and in store versus online.

The buyer continues to perform the specialized work of selection and negotiation. The buyer in all organizations makes the buying arrangements that pertain to selection of resources and product, including specifications for private branding, quantities, negotiations of cost prices, terms of sale, method of shipment, and the setting of retail prices or repricing. Deviations from these general principles are discussed with the buyer's respective divisional or general merchandise manager(s).

A significant happening took place when retailers based outside of the New York area opened offices in New York, where many best-selling clothing brands are headquartered. The retailers had a need to focus on fashion trends and increase their fashion relevance. They wanted to discover new looks quickly and incorporate them into their clothing lines. Well-known designers have shown a growing willingness to sell their clothing and household products at lower prices to a broader audience. This allows the budget-minded consumer to find clothing by Vera Wang and Chaps at Kohl's and limited-edition merchandise at H&M by designers such as Karl Lagerfeld, Stella McCartney, and Viktor & Rolf. Macy's is providing affordable luxury as it develops exclusivity with iconic names such as Tommy Hilfiger and Martha Stewart for signature lines, and JCPenney introduced exclusive product from Liz Claiborne and Nicole by Nicole Miller. New retail partnerships are also being formulated between department stores and specialty stores. Nordstrom has partnered with Topshop and Madewell and Macy's with Bluemercury, Finish Line, and Lids.

Merchandising policies are constantly shifting as retailers attempt to set themselves apart. The competitive advantage gained by optimizing assortments, products, and prices is appreciated by retailers who recognize the necessity for differentiation. The emphasis on private-label products has resulted in international sourcing. Through customer satisfaction, it is possible to achieve comparable store growth. To quote Charles Darwin, "It is not the strongest of the species that survives, nor the most intelligent, but the one most responsive to change."

In the late twentieth century, high-tech began making its mark everywhere, including retailing. Success in the contemporary retail environment relies heavily on records that are the basis for analysis, planning, decision making, and quick action. The first generation of electronic computers was started in 1951, at a time when the growth of multistore operations mandated a need for prompt, accurate, and complete data to make merchandising decisions.

Since the 1960s, data processing systems have provided retailers with an uninterrupted flow of information. In more recent years, the increased use of electronic data processing (EDP) systems by department stores and retail businesses, as well as by mass merchandising chains, has had a major impact on the management of merchandise inventories and on other areas of record-keeping. Today, because retailers locate their stores in many different geographic markets, both domestic and international, the computer not only furnishes data that identifies problems but also facilitates and accelerates the decision-making process. Computers assist retailers by providing not only merchandising functions but also information that enables them to integrate and improve merchandising, buying, customer service, store operations, and the financial management of the business.

All retailers agree about the value of computer usage in their individual stores. This powerful force that processes information accurately and promptly is particularly appreciated in the volatile retailing industry because it has resulted in much improved control and management of merchandise and finances. The network of computers that allows a continual flow of information to be electronically exchanged between retailers and manufacturers results in this control at a lower cost. Ideally, a computerized merchandising system should provide data about the physical stock that is in tandem with dollar control. Management has an almost unlimited choice concerning which programs should be instituted, maintained, or eliminated. Information available to buyers is enormous. Data can be reviewed and analyzed by store, department, vendor, style, color, and size at any point in the day, week, month, season, or year. The benefits of the retail reporting system to a particular organization is the analysis of sales, productivity, and profit.

The quick evolution of technology has become critical to a retailer's success. Retailers have made increasing capital investments in technology that touch many aspects of their operation. They include information systems that analyze and report the detailed performance of what merchandise is selling, they use historical performance to plan data to determine quantities, and they improve the efficiency of the buying process by providing better distribution of merchandise by the store based on customer profiles. Internal and external communications have changed dramatically by the prevalent use of email. Vendor partnerships through development of replenishment systems ensure that the merchandise wanted by customers is in the store when they want it. For customer relationship marketing (CRM) departments, the data collected has enabled retailers to demographically identify regional consumer preferences and thereby target their best customers, creating a more personalized relationship and ultimately capturing greater market share.

The many uncontrollable, external variable factors have encouraged retailers to invest in planning and forecasting technologies. In the 1970s, when the standardized bar code printed on tickets and labels was introduced in grocery supermarkets, it enabled merchandisers to move products quickly from distribution centers to selling floors at lower costs. Bar codes opened up a vast amount of inventory and sales data that reduced labor costs and provided a more efficient checkout process as they changed the relationship between retailers and manufacturers. The Universal Product Code (UPC) became a global bar code standard. Surveillance technology is being utilized for security and loss prevention. New software allows the creation, management, and deployment of in-store digital videos throughout the store or chain, as it gives the retailer an opportunity to learn what takes place at all points of the customer's in-store experience. It is a universal fact: Consumers are turning to technology to help them shop. E-commerce sales continue to grow exponentially, especially for retail transactions processed on smartphones and tablets. In 2008, e-commerce sales were $140 billion; by 2014, e-commerce sales had almost reached the $300 billion mark (this figure does not include mail-order sales). In 2008, e-commerce sales were approximately 3.6% of all sales, and in 2014, e-commerce represented 6.6% of all retail sales. Marketers and retailers continue to integrate new technologies to draw customers to their click sites, either via computer, tablet, or phone, trying to boost sales. Retailers, to satisfy customers' wants, can access their online stores at the in-store register and have merchandise shipped directly to a customer if that product is not available in store. In addition, a recent trend has arisen where retailers have consumers buy online and pick up in store. The objective continues to be to have what customers want, where they want it, and in precisely the right quantity, especially when the competition is just a click away.

History records past events. We know the merits and influences of the computer on the development of retailing today. The future will reveal how this or other major innovations will facilitate the degree or the speed of electronic progress.

Mathematics for Retail Buying delineates the essential concepts, practices, and procedures as well as the calculations and interpretations of figures related to the many factors that produce and affect profit. The choice of material and the depth of each subject are deliberately confined to that which has practical value for the performance of occupations in or associated with retail merchandising. The study of retail mathematics may begin at any point in the buying/selling circle. As previously mentioned, while the six chapters in this text are interrelated with the various phases of merchandising, the chapters can be studied independently or shifted without losing the continuity of the buying process. Here is an overview of the chapters and their respective roles in the buying/selling process, followed by a section on common retail terminology, an explanation of using computerized spreadsheets, and an introduction to using the online STUDIO program.

CHAPTER 1: MERCHANDISING FOR A PROFIT

The function of the retail store is to sell merchandise to consumers. The amount of merchandise sold is the store's source of operating income, commonly known as sales or sales volume. However, before merchandise can be sold, it must be bought. The basic elements of sales volume are defined, analyzed, and calculated because their effective understanding is critical to a retailer's success. A course of study in retail buying should begin with the analysis of a profit and loss statement. This statement reports a summary of the achievements of a particular department, store, or company, revealing whether or not the activities involved in operating this unit for a specific time period have been profitable. Gross margin, a buyer's measure of profitability, is of paramount importance, and understanding how to maximize this metric is the key to success for a merchant. The factors that affect gross margin include the sales generated and the cost of the goods sold incurred in buying and selling this merchandise. The buyer is the force that buys, prices, reprices, and negotiates the merchandise found in a retail store and/or the online store. These functions are the responsibilities of the buyer, who must understand the linkages of the profit elements. The fundamental relationships among the profit factors are repeated throughout the book.

CHAPTER 2: RETAIL PRICING AND REPRICING OF MERCHANDISE

This chapter presents the relationship and calculations of the basic pricing factors, the various pricing situations used in making buying decisions, the techniques involved in repricing goods (markdowns), and the effect of each on gross margin (the difference between the sales and the cost of those sales) and profit. The approach to pricing is presented from the standpoint of who sets the selling price on goods purchased for resale.

The buyer, guided by a prescribed price line structure, plans purchases and merchandise offerings that fit into this framework. The buyer sets the retail price of both initial and subsequent prices on each item purchased. Markdowns, the repricing of merchandise, are increasingly important in today's retail environment. The types of markdowns are discussed as well as the analytical criteria used to take markdowns. The effect of markdowns on the gross margin is of primary importance for the buyer.

CHAPTER 3: BASIC MARKUP EQUATIONS USED IN MERCHANDISING DECISIONS

The overall effectiveness of buying and pricing is measured by the buyer's ability to achieve a markup plan established by management, designed to produce the desired profit. As merchandise is purchased, it is neither common nor desirable to require that each item within a merchandise department be retailed with the same price or markup percentage. The results would be disastrous! Yet it is the buyer's responsibility to meet the overall target figure for profit. The buyer cannot ever forget that goods must be priced to sell. Therefore, during a season there are many considerations that affect the pricing of merchandise at the time of purchase, and many of these actually cause goods to sell at a lower price. The ability to recognize that this results in different markups allows the buyer to make the necessary adjustments. The buyer constantly has the opportunity to average high and low markups to reach the required predetermined average.

CHAPTER 4: THE RETAIL METHOD OF INVENTORY

An essential feature of retail merchandising is to determine the total value of stock-on-hand at the beginning of the retailer's fiscal month. The value of inventory is significant for planning sales, markdowns, and how much to buy in order to determine the proper valuation of inventory for profit figuring purposes. Chapter 4 discusses the retail method of inventory because it is the accepted, proven system that provides this information. We familiarize ourselves with the general procedures used in implementing this system and the calculation and records required to maintain it. A probable amount of stock-on-hand can be known at any time without counting the merchandise, and a shortage figure can easily be derived through a comparison between the actual physical inventory and the book or maintained records. The mathematical calculations involved in this method are important for the buyer to understand in order to know how he or she can plan for future months based on current business trends. The accuracy of the book inventory depends on the buyer's prompt and accurate classifying of records that pertain to price changes, receiving merchandise, and updating key reports. This system helps the buyer to constantly track the amount of stock-on-hand while protecting the gross margin (the difference between sales and the cost of those sales to be attained).

CHAPTER 5: SIX-MONTH PLANNING AND COMPONENTS

The most talked-about topic in retailing is the budget of stocks and sales, more commonly known as a six-month dollar plan. This is the subject of Chapter 5. The six-month plan is an attempt to set in advance realistic projected goals for stocks in ratio to sales, the amount and timing of markdowns, planned cumulative markup, turnover for the season, and the correct amount and proper timing of purchases. This "calendar" plans, forecasts, and controls the purchase and sale of merchandise. It is designed to protect the store's inventory investment and produce a profit as it controls the above factors. The projection of planned sales is the hub of the buying/ selling wheel, and all of the other elements are predicated on this figure. Although the estimation is based on actual past performance plus external and internal sales-related conditions, it is not an exact process. It is a process that requires making judgmental decisions, and therefore it is not always possible to predict all contingencies.

The buyer, who is responsible for interpreting and achieving the goals set, constantly monitors the sales in order to adjust the elements of the plan that rely on the amount of sales generated. The six-month dollar plan, in action, helps the buyer to keep score of whether the correct balance between sales and stocks is maintained. The procedure of planning the various elements and the calculations that produce the desired outcome give insight into why and how this technique produces a profitable operation. After a buyer creates a six-month plan in preparation for a new season, it is necessary to break down the department's business into its component parts, called merchandise classifications or categories. Assortment planning will provide the buyer with the path to create the plan for sales and purchases in the various classifications for which he or she is responsible. In any department, no two classifications sell the same in both dollars and units. It is important for the buyer to "buy correctly" in order to achieve the goals set.

CHAPTER 6: INVOICE MATHEMATICS: TERMS OF SALE

When buyers purchase merchandise, they also negotiate the terms with vendors on how the merchandise is to be shipped and paid for. This chapter discusses the various discounts and payment terms that a buyer would negotiate for and how they affect the cost of goods sold.

The practice problems, case studies, and spreadsheet solutions to be solved in *Mathematics for Retail Buying* focus mainly on situations prevalent in the women's, children's, and men's apparel and home furnishing industries because fashion is such an important factor in our economic system. It affects the major industries of retailing, manufacturing, and marketing. Practical and realistic examples follow the theories, principles, concepts, and calculations that through application test the reader's understanding of the fundamentals of each major topic discussed in that section.

TERMINOLOGY

In retailing, different terms are used interchangeably depending on the formula or how a buyer "talks" about his or her business. Therefore, we provide a list of commonly used terms that have the same meaning.

Sales/Revenues—for the most part, retailers talk sales. Both terms speak to the amount collected from consumers from the sale of merchandise.

Merchandise/Product/Goods—what a buyer is purchasing to sell to the consumer.

Inventory/Stock-on-hand—the merchandise that is available in retail stores or online for sale to the consumer.

Shortage/Shrinkage—the amount of merchandise that is missing from stock after a physical inventory is taken.

Units/Pieces/Each—buyers place orders in single costs (except for certain categories, such as socks, which may be bought in dozens) and sell for a specific single price.

Transportation/Freight/Shipping—the cost to move product from the factory to the final destination.

Purchases/Receipts—what the buyer is buying based on his or her budgets for a specific period of time.

Original retail price/Initial retail price—the first price placed on the ticket before any markdowns are taken.

New price/Sale price/Markdown price—the price that the merchandise is being sold for at that time including any markdowns or coupons.

Build/Percentage change/Trend/Acceleration—a comparison between two different points in time.

Plan/Goal/Budget—what is provided to the buyer at the beginning of a time period that the company needs to achieve.

Actual/Spent—what actually has occurred.

Categories/Classifications—the different merchandise segments within a specific department.

USING COMPUTERIZED SPREADSHEETS

Just as we have become more and more accustomed to using computers and smart devices in our everyday activities, so too it becomes apparent that the use of computerized spreadsheets in doing retail mathematics offers many advantages. Buyers use spreadsheets on a daily basis to monitor businesses and write new purchase orders. Computerized spreadsheets can make repetitive, lengthy mathematical calculations quick, easy, and accurate. Organizing data in spreadsheet format provides a visual summary of important information that is easily read and understood. They are particularly valuable when there is a large amount of data to organize and assimilate. Once spreadsheets are set up, key assumptions and/or variables can be changed in order to do quick "what if" analyses, testing various scenarios, thereby resulting in better decision making. Spreadsheets enable the user to test sensitivities such as:

- "If we make a small change in the price, how much will it impact our profitability?"

- "If we take a larger markdown, what will be the impact?"

- "What effect will it have if we reduce the markdown percentage slightly?"

Computerized spreadsheets will test your ability to understand mathematical concepts. While computerized spreadsheets will reduce your need to do basic arithmetic, it is essential to understand how the formulas work. Concept formulas must be entered absolutely correctly, and once they are properly entered your answers will always be correct. If your answers are not right, you did not enter the concept formula correctly.

In this edition of *Mathematics for Retail Buying*, solutions to the concept problems are also given, where appropriate, in both spreadsheet and the more traditional arithmetic format. Not every concept problem lends itself to preparing a spreadsheet, and only arithmetic solutions are given for those problems.

When solving the concept problems, we cannot easily show the spreadsheet formulas in the written text. When a spreadsheet is open on the computer, however, and a specific cell is highlighted, the formula that was used to compute the number appearing in that cell will appear at the top of the page in the formula bar. So that you will be able to check the concept problem spreadsheet formulas, these concept problems appear in the companion STUDIO program. These problems are solved using Microsoft Excel. With Excel, as well as other spreadsheet software, please remember that there may be multiple ways in which a particular spreadsheet can be set up and a problem solved.

USING THE STUDIO RESOURCES

The STUDIO companion to the text is a learning tool that allows the student to practice the concepts presented in an online/Excel-based capacity. Its organization mirrors that of this textbook, with each chapter having a matching folder. Thus, as one moves through the textbook, the corresponding concept problems and practice problems can be easily found. Several of the practice problems found in the text appear in the STUDIO so that you can work the problems directly.

Within the "Studio Resources" section online, you will find downloadable spreadsheets for the chapter Practice Problems. You have the freedom to play with the numbers in the concept problems to see how the concepts work, as well as to work the practice problems, but you cannot save your work in the program. If you need additional space to work the problems, in Excel go to Home > Insert and insert additional rows, columns, or even pages. Some problems do not warrant the development of a spreadsheet. Even so, the computer can be useful to do basic arithmetic calculations to solve the problem.

Remember: Be sure to save your review problems to your hard drive.
You cannot save your work in the STUDIO program!

In the future, the function in retailing of maintaining assortments appropriate for selected customers, in quantities that provide efficient use of investment, at prices that create a constant flow of merchandise while ensuring a profit focused on the buying/selling process will continue. The principles by which this will be achieved will remain constant as they adjust to the mode and tempo of life in the twenty-first century. As the retail industry evolves with new technology and ways to attract customers, retailers of all different types will be adapting and changing to consumers and how they are buying. However, the basic profit elements as we know them will continue to guide and measure success.

MERCHANDISING FOR A PROFIT

"The entrepreneur always searches for change, responds to it, and sees it as an opportunity."

PETER DRUCKER, ONE OF THE TWENTIETH CENTURY'S MOST INFLUENTIAL AND RESPECTED THINKERS ON MANAGEMENT THEORY AND PRACTICE

OBJECTIVES

- Recognize the importance of profit calculations in merchandising decisions.

- Identify components of a profit and loss statement, including the calculation of:

    - Net sales.

    - Cost of goods sold.

    - Gross margin.

    - Operating expenses.

    - Net profit.

- Complete a profit and loss statement.

- Identify types of business expenses and their impact on profit.

- Utilize profit calculations to:

    - Make comparisons between departments and/or stores.

    - Detect trends.

    - Make changes in merchandising strategy to achieve an increase in profits.

KEY TERMS

alteration and workroom costs	build/percentage change/trend	contribution
balance sheet	cash discounts	controllable expenses
billed cost	closing inventory	controllable margin

cost

cost of goods sold
(COGS)/cost of
merchandise sold

customer allowance
or markdown

customer returns

customer returns and
allowances

direct expenses

final profit and loss
statement

gross margin

gross sales

income statement

indirect expenses

inward freight

net loss

net operating profit

net profit

net sales

opening inventory

operating expenses

operating income

profit and loss
statement

reductions

retail

sales volume

skeletal profit and loss
statement

total cost of goods
purchased

total cost of goods
sold

total merchandise
handled

KEY CONCEPT FORMULAS

Cost of goods sold

$$\text{Total cost of goods sold \$} = \text{Billed cost \$} + \text{Inward freight charges \$} + \text{Workroom costs \$} - \text{Cash discount \$}$$

$$\text{Cost of goods sold \%} = \frac{\text{Cost of goods sold \$}}{\text{Net sales \$}} \times 100$$

$$\text{Cost of goods sold \$} = \text{Cost of goods \%} \times \text{Net sales \$}$$

Billed cost

$$\text{Billed cost} = \text{List price} - \text{Trade discount(s)}$$

$$\text{Billed cost} = \text{\# Units purchased} \times \text{Invoice cost}$$

Customer returns and allowances

$$\text{Customer returns and allowances \$} = \text{Total of all refunds or credits to the customer on individual items of merchandise \$} \times \text{Number of units actually returned}$$

$$\text{Customer returns and allowances \%} = \frac{\text{Customer returns and allowances \$}}{\text{Gross sales \$}} \times 100$$

$$\text{Customer returns and allowances \$} = \text{Gross sales \$} \times \text{Customer returns and allowances \%}$$

Department's net sales

$$\text{Department's net sales \% of total store sales} = \frac{\text{Department's net dollar sales}}{\text{Store's total net dollar sales}} \times 100$$

Gross sales

$$\text{Gross sales} = \begin{array}{c}\text{Total of all the prices} \\ \text{charged to consumers} \\ \text{on individual items}\end{array} \times \begin{array}{c}\text{Number of units} \\ \text{actually sold}\end{array}$$

$$\text{Gross sales \$} = \frac{\text{Net sales \$}}{(100\% \ - \ \text{Customer returns and allowance \%})}$$

Net cost

$$\text{Net cost \$} = \text{Billed cost \$} \ - \ \text{Cash discount \$}$$

$$\text{Net cost \$} = \text{List price \$} \ - \ \begin{array}{c}\text{Trade} \\ \text{discount(s) \$}\end{array} \ - \ \text{Cash discount \$}$$

Net sales

$$\text{Net sales \$} = \text{Gross sales \$} \ - \ \text{Customer returns and allowances \$}$$

Build/percentage change/trend

$$\begin{array}{c}\text{Build/percentage} \\ \text{change/trend}\end{array} = \frac{\text{This year sales} \ - \ \text{Last year sales}}{\text{Last year sales}} \times 100$$

$$= \frac{\text{This year sales} \ - \ \text{Planned sales}}{\text{Planned sales}} \times 100$$

Gross margin

$$\text{Gross margin} = \text{Net sales} \ - \ \text{Total cost of goods sold}$$

$$\text{Gross margin \$} = \text{Gross margin \%} \times \text{Net sales \$}$$

$$\text{Gross margin \%} = \frac{\text{Gross margin \$}}{\text{Net sales \$}} \times 100$$

Operating expenses

$$\text{Operating expenses} = \text{Direct expenses} \ + \ \text{Indirect expenses}$$

$$\text{Operating expenses \$} = \text{Operating expenses \%} \times \text{Net sales \$}$$

$$\text{Operating expenses \%} = \frac{\text{Direct and indirect expenses in dollars}}{\text{Net sales \$}} \times 100$$

Net profit

$$\text{Net profit} = \text{Net sales} \ - \ \text{Cost of goods sold} \ - \ \text{Operating expenses}$$

$$\begin{array}{c}\text{Net operating profit} \\ \text{or net profit}\end{array} = \text{Gross margin} \ - \ \begin{array}{c}\text{All operating} \\ \text{expenses}\end{array}$$

$$\text{Net profit \$} = \text{Net profit \%} \times \text{Net sales \$}$$

$$\text{Net profit \%} = \frac{\text{Net profit \$}}{\text{Net sales \$}} \times 100$$

The function of the retail store is to sell merchandise to consumers. The amount of merchandise sold is the store's source of operating income, commonly known as sales or sales volume. However, before merchandise can be sold, it must be bought. In this opening chapter, the basic elements of sales volume are defined, analyzed, and calculated because their effective understanding is critical to a retailer's success.

1.1 Profit Components

Why is the study of the calculation of profit necessary? An individual involved in retailing will inevitably have many opportunities to become involved with the concept of profit. An employee of a private organization should be aware of profit. For example, many companies offer a profit-sharing plan, which is now a frequent form of incentive in many industries. An individual may invest personal funds in publicly owned corporations. To an employee of a publicly owned corporation, profit is a significant goal in the sale of shares. Since the beginning of the twentieth century, the US government has requested that all entrepreneurs declare profits or losses of all business ventures. Profits are taxed. Competent accounting methods require a statement of net profit before and after taxes.

Because one of the major responsibilities of a merchandiser in retailing is to attain a profit for the department[1] store, or retail business being supervised, it is logical to recognize that this can be achieved only by knowing the elements of profit, their calculation, and their importance.

USE OF PROFIT CALCULATIONS

The merchandising executive uses the calculation of profits to:

1. Exchange data and compare stores to determine relative strengths and weaknesses.

2. Indicate the direction of the business and whether it is prosperous, struggling for survival, or bankrupt.

3. Provide a statement for analysis so that knowledgeable changes in management or policy can be made.

4. Improve the profit margin by using this analysis.

This chapter examines the basic profit elements, defines them, shows their relationships to one another in profit and loss statements, and describes methods practiced to manipulate these elements to improve profits.

---

1. Department (Merchandise Department): A grouping of related merchandise for which separate expense and merchandising records are kept for the purpose of determining the profit of this grouping. It is not merely a physical segregation.

DEFINING THE BASIC PROFIT FACTORS

The function of the retail store is to sell merchandise to consumers at a profit. These sales are the store's source of operating income. Before merchandise can be sold, however, it must be bought. Even in a computerized organization in which financial personnel may preset programs and spreadsheets, the buyer is ultimately responsible for creating a merchandise assortment. This selection occurs after planning and predicting what, when, where, and how much to buy, and what to pay for these purchases. **Cost** is the amount the retailer pays for these purchases. **Retail** is the price at which stores offer merchandise for sale to the consumer.

Because the buyer buys and prices the merchandise offered for sale in a retail store, the buyer must have the ability to understand and manipulate five basic profit factors: **Operating income**, also known as **net sales** or **sales volume**, indicates in dollars how much merchandise has been sold. **Cost of goods sold (COGS)** (also referred to as **cost of merchandise sold**) shows the amount paid for the goods sold. This results in **gross margin**, in which the total cost of goods is subtracted from the net sales. **Operating expenses** refer to those expenses, other than the cost of the goods, incurred in the buying/selling process. When all the operating expenses are deducted from the gross margin figure, the result is called **net operating profit** or **net profit**.

To properly compare profits among retailers, it is necessary to know how expenses are treated. In accounting, there are acceptable variations in how expenses are recorded. In this text, expenses are listed individually or referred to merely as operating expenses. In performing the calculations necessary to answer the practice problems that apply to the profit concepts and principles, the focus is on adjusting the proper element to the appropriate basic profit factor. For example, cash discount is an adjustment to the cost-of-goods factor. When there is other net income that does not result directly from the everyday operation of the retail business, it is added to or subtracted from net operating profit to get "net profit before taxes." This income does not result from the everyday operation but rather reflects financial or nontrading earnings and deductions.

Gross sales is the entire dollar amount received for goods sold during a given period before any reductions are taken. Gross sales can also be thought of as the total sales based on the initial or regular retail price. This total sales figure is calculated by multiplying the retail price of the individual items of merchandise by the number of pieces actually sold to consumers before any reductions are taken. The accurate calculation of gross sales, however, must also take into account adjustments due to returns and price reductions. Stores typically give customers the privilege of returning merchandise. When merchandise is returned to stock and the customer receives a cash refund or a charge credit, these returns of sales are called **customer returns**. This process is now automatic for stores with sophisticated computer systems. In addition, if a customer receives a price reduction, it is known as a **customer allowance or markdown**. These two adjustments are referred to collectively as **reductions** or **customer returns and allowances**. When customer returns and allowances are subtracted from gross sales, the resulting total is the net sales figure. Thus, **net sales** are the sales total after all reductions and customer returns and allowances have been deducted from gross sales. Net sales represent the amount of sales a retailer collects from the customer from the sale of merchandise that actually remains sold. When retailers calculate profit, the net sales figure is the more significant because a firm can realize a profit only on goods that remain sold at the retail price. For this reason, the term "sales volume" is always a net sales figure.

Merchandisers must determine and balance the retail price for the items they purchase for sale to customers with, among other factors, how much they can afford to pay a vendor for merchandise. Cost of goods sold is simply the cost of the merchandise that has been sold during a given time period. This concept is simple, but the actual calculation is complex because other necessary adjustments must be made to the cost or purchase price that appears on the bill or invoice (vendor's bill). These adjustments are transportation costs, also known as **inward freight**, which is the amount a vendor may charge for transporting merchandise to the designated premises of the retailer; **alteration and workroom costs**, which is a charge made to a selling department when it is necessary to treat merchandise so that it will be in condition for sale (i.e., ticketing, hanging, assembling, etc.); and **cash discounts**, which is a percentage deducted from the invoice cost that vendors may grant for the payment of an invoice within a specified period of time.

Gross margin is the difference between net sales and the total cost of goods sold. It is a figure that indicates the buyer's ability to purchase the "right" merchandise, negotiate the "right" cost and credit terms, and put the "right" retail price on these purchases. Gross margin is the measure of the buyer's profitability. Therefore, to maximize gross margin, it is a buyer's responsibility to drive sales and negotiate the best possible cost. In order to secure the lowest total cost of goods sold, the buyer will need to work with vendors to obtain the lowest billed cost on merchandise, negotiate substantial discounts on purchase orders, or find a way to lower shipping costs. If gross margin goals are not achieved, buyers are challenged to negotiate additional assistance from vendors.

In addition, the retailer must maintain a place of business from which the goods are sold, and to maintain this place, it must incur operating expenses. Operating expenses usually fall into two major categories and are charged to a merchandise department to determine the net profit for that department. Expenses that are specific to a given department, and which would cease if that department were discontinued, are called **direct expenses**. These include salaries of the buyer, assistant buyer, and salespeople; departmental advertising; selling supplies; and customer delivery expenses. Store expenses that exist whether a department is added or discontinued are **indirect expenses**. These include store expenses that are prorated to all selling departments on the basis of their sales volume, such as store maintenance, insurance, and salaries of top management.

The operating expenses, which refer to those expenses, other than the cost of the goods incurred in the buying/selling process, are deducted from the gross margin, resulting in net operating profit or net profit.

ELEMENTS OF BASIC PROFIT FACTORS

Each of the basic profit factors needs to be dissected because each consists of elements that contribute to profit. The calculations involved highlight the meaning and importance of each factor. The fifth factor (net profit) and its elements will be explored in Section 1.2. We explore the other four factors here.

Sales (Operating Income)

Gross Sales

Gross sales are the total *initial* dollars received for merchandise sold during a given period.

Gross sales \$ = $\dfrac{\text{Total of all the initial prices charged}}{\text{to consumers on individual items}}$ × $\dfrac{\text{Number of units}}{\text{actually sold}}$

CONCEPT

During the week (Sunday–Saturday), a toy department sold 30 dolls (Group A) priced at $15 each, 25 dolls (Group B) priced at $25 each, and 5 dolls (Group C) priced at $30 each. What were the gross sales for the dolls for that week?

PROBLEM

Item	Quantity	Unit retail price	Income
Dolls (A)	30	$15	$450
Dolls (B)	25	$25	$625
Dolls (C)	5	$30	$150
Gross Sales			$1,225

SOLUTION: *Spreadsheet format*

30 dolls @ $15 each	=	$450
25 dolls @ $25 each	=	625
5 dolls @ $30 each	=	150
Total gross sales	=	$1,225

SOLUTION: *Arithmetic format*

Customer Returns and Allowances

Customer returns and allowances are elements of the operating income profit factor because the customer receives either a complete refund of the purchase price or a reduction of the selling price of the product. Thus, the retailer must make a corresponding deduction from the gross sales figure because these transactions result in some cancellation of sales and inventory value. This dollar figure is usually expressed as a percentage of gross sales.

Although these transactions may seem insignificant, they are considered a daily happening in the buying/selling process, and they should be scrutinized and evaluated. If returns and allowances are excessively numerous, they can ultimately affect profit because it is costly to sell, process returns, and, hopefully, resell the same merchandise. The causes of returns should be examined, and an attempt should be made to reduce them to a reasonable percentage, which is the yardstick used for comparison. In addition, reductions or markdowns to the selling price are commonplace in retailing. They are used by buyers to drive sales. Markdowns will be addressed in more detail in Chapter 2.

CONCEPT

$$\begin{array}{c} \text{Customer returns} \\ \text{and allowances \$} \end{array} = \begin{array}{c} \text{Total of all refunds or credits} \\ \text{to the customer on individual} \\ \text{items of merchandise \$} \end{array} \times \begin{array}{c} \text{Number of units} \\ \text{actually returned} \end{array}$$

PROBLEM

On Saturday, the junior petite department refunded $98 for one leather jacket, $75 each for two wool skirts, and $55 each for two knit tops. Other returns for the week amounted to $400, and the weekly total of markdowns given was $1,687. What was the dollar amount of customer returns and allowances for Saturday? For the week?

SOLUTION:
Spreadsheet format

Item	Quantity	Unit retail	Customer returns and allowances
Leather jackets	1	$98	$98
Wool skirts	2	$75	$150
Knit tops	2	$55	$110
Saturday total			$358
Other weekly returns			$400
Weekly customer allowances/markdowns			$1,687
Total customer returns and allowances and reductions			$2,445

SOLUTION:
Arithmetic format

$98	×	1 Leather jacket		=	$98
$75	×	2 Wool skirts		=	150
$55	×	2 Knit tops		=	110
		Customer returns for Saturday		=	$358
+		Total weekly customer returns		=	400
+		Total weekly customer allowances/markdowns		=	1,687
		Customer returns and allowances (for week)		=	$2,445

Customer returns and
allowances percentage $=$ Dollar sum of customer returns and allowances
expressed as a percentage of gross sales

$$\text{Customer returns and allowances \%} = \frac{\text{Customer returns and allowances \$}}{\text{Gross sales \$}} \times 100$$

Last week, the junior petite department had gross sales of $20,375. Customer returns and allowances for the week totaled $2,445. What was the combined percentage of allowances and merchandise returns for the week?

PROBLEM

$$\text{Customer returns and allowances \%} = \frac{\$2,445 \text{ Customer returns and allowances}}{\$20,375 \text{ Gross sales}} \times 100$$

Customer returns and allowances % $=$ 12%

SOLUTION

Conversely, the dollar sum of customer returns and allowances can be computed when the gross sales and customer returns and allowances percentage are known.

Dollar sum of customer
returns and allowances $=$ Gross
sales $\$$ $\times$ Customer returns
and allowances %

CONCEPT

Last week, the junior petite department reported gross sales of $20,375, with customer returns and allowances of 12%. What was the dollar amount of customer returns and allowances?

PROBLEM

Dollar sum of customer
returns and allowances $=$ $20,375 Gross sales $\times$ 12% Customer
returns and allowances

SOLUTION

Dollar sum of customer returns and allowances $=$ $2,445

Net Sales

Net sales are the sales total for a given period after customer returns and allowances have been deducted from gross sales.

Net sales $\$$ $=$ Gross sales $\$$ $-$ Customer returns and allowances $\$$

CONCEPT

A shoe department sold $65,000 worth of merchandise. Customer returns and allowances and reductions were $16,250. What were the net sales of this department?

PROBLEM

SOLUTION

Net sales   = $65,000 – $16,250

Net sales   = $48,750

In retailing, the operating income is known as net sales. The net sales figure, also called sales volume, is used to designate the size of a particular store or merchandise department. For example, last year Department #37 had a sales volume of $1,000,000. Net sales are the barometer of success versus the plan for a day, week, month, quarter, season, or year.

Retailers use net sales to measure a department's performance or productivity. It is common practice to calculate the percentage of sales that an individual department has contributed to the store's or company's net sales. This type of analysis allows a retailer to compare a particular department of one store with other departments or stores within the company, as well as to compare this selected department's sales with industry figures.

CONCEPT

The individual department's net sales are expressed as a percentage of the store's total net sales.

$$\text{Department's net sales \% of total store sales} = \frac{\text{Department's net sales \$}}{\text{Store's total net sales \$}} \times 100$$

or

$$\text{\% of total store sales} = \frac{\text{Department's net sales \$}}{\text{Company's total net sales \$}} \times 100$$

PROBLEM

The costume jewelry department had net sales of $900,000. For the same period, total store sales were $45,000,000. What is the costume jewelry department's net sales percentage of the total store's net sales?

SOLUTION

Department's net sales = $900,000

Total store net sales = $45,000,000

$$\text{Department's net sales \% of total store sales} = \frac{\$900,000}{\$45,000,000} \times 100$$

Department's net sales % of total store sales = **2%**

Because net sales are determined by the adjustment of customer returns and allowances to gross sales, it is also possible through this relationship to calculate, when desired, a gross sales amount—provided that an amount of the dollar net sales and the percentage of customer returns and allowances are known.

$$\text{Gross sales} = \frac{\text{Net sales}}{(100\% - \text{Customer returns and allowance \%})}$$

The net sales of Department #39 were $460,000. The customer returns and allowances were 8%. What were the gross sales of the department?

Net sales   = $460,000

$$\text{Gross sales} = \frac{\text{Net sales}}{100\% \text{ (Gross sales)} - 8\% \text{ Customer returns and allowances}}$$

$$\text{Gross sales} = \frac{\$460,000}{92\%}$$

Gross sales   = $500,000

MOST COMMON RETAIL SALES KEY PERFORMANCE INDICATORS (KPIS) PERTAINING TO SALES PERFORMANCE

Sales versus Plan and Last Year Sales

The first performance indicator for sales is the comparison of actual sales for the period versus sales plan for that period—for example, this week versus plan sales for this week, sales for the month versus plan sales for the month, and sales year-to-date (YTD) versus plan sales YTD. Are sales sufficient to cover expenses and leave a profit?

Buyers will have to calculate the comparison of how the sales are actually performing for the time period. This formula is called **build/percentage change/trend**.

The formula compares current sales versus the planned sales or two different points in time. The formulas are:

$$\text{Build/percentage change/trend} = \frac{\text{This year sales} - \text{Last year sales}}{\text{Last year sales}} \times 100$$

$$\text{Build/percentage change/trend} = \frac{\text{This year sales} - \text{Planned sales}}{\text{Planned sales}} \times 100$$

Same Store or Comparable Store Sales

This refers to sales this week or month versus the same period last year, or sales YTD for last year only, comparing stores open for at least one year. Store openings or closings do not impact this comparison. The fact that each company handles online and mobile channel sales in different ways must be taken into consideration when making comparisons. With the rise of the omni-channel retail format, e-commerce sales may be considered a "store" for a retail corporation.

Sales per Square Foot

This figure is calculated by dividing the dollar gross sales figure by the square footage of selling space. Retailers can improve return on the total space their stores or departments occupy by:

    a.   Allocating more space to selling.

    b.   Increasing sales from existing space.

    c.   Selling more profitable items.

Sales per Linear Foot

This figure measures the selling space by linear feet and is used mainly by food and cosmetics retailers.

Inventory Turnover

Inventory turnover refers to the number of times, usually in one year, that the average inventory is sold.

Sell through Percentage

This is calculated by dividing the number of items sold by the number of items bought and multiplying by 100.

The mathematics required to calculate these performance indicators will be examined in appropriate chapters that pertain to each topic.

COST OF GOODS SOLD (ALSO REFERRED TO AS COST OF MERCHANDISE SOLD)

The control of the cost of goods sold is crucial to profitability. The buyer, who decides what merchandise to buy, also makes decisions regarding the cost, transportation, and credit terms as they relate to these purchases. In actual practice, to determine the accurate **total cost of goods sold**, there must be a complete calculation to represent the **total cost of goods purchased**, which begins with an invoice or **billed cost**, to which the following factors are adjusted:

Calculation of Total Cost of Goods Sold

Billed Cost

This is the purchase price that appears on the invoice (i.e., vendor's bill). Buyers may need to calculate the total billed cost for the merchandise they are purchasing. The calculation is as follows:

Total billed cost = # Units purchased × Invoice cost

This formula is also used when calculating cumulative markup, which is discussed in Chapter 2.

PLUS

Inward Freight or Transportation Costs

This is the amount that a vendor may charge for delivery of merchandise. Inward freight or transportation costs plus billed cost is called the billed delivered cost.

PLUS

Alteration and Workroom Costs

It is accepted practice to treat this figure as an additional cost, as the alteration cost applies only to merchandise that has been sold and any workroom costs apply to all purchases.

MINUS

Cash Discounts

Discounts are a negotiated price concession given to a buyer by a vendor. This is usually a percentage of the total *billed* cost and *MUST* be converted into a *dollar* amount. This discount is *NOT* taken on the transportation cost. This is a normal operating process for a buyer to secure the best possible cost price.

Vendors may grant these discounts for payment of an invoice within a specified time. For example, a vendor may offer a 2% cash discount (deducted from the billed cost) if payment is made within a designated time period. The discounts are offered in the form of a percentage and are deducted from only the billed cost, but the dollar discount earned is used in the calculation of the total cost of sales. For example, a 2% cash discount given on a billed cost of $1,000 translates into a $20 cash discount or deduction:

$1,000 Billed cost × 2% Cash discount = $20 Cash discount

CONCEPT

Total cost of goods sold $ = Billed cost $ + Inward freight charges $ + Workroom costs $ − Cash discounts $

PROBLEM

An activewear department, for the first month of the period, had billed costs of merchandise amounting to $80,000, inward freight charges of $2,000, negotiated cash discounts of 7.5%, and workroom costs of $500. Calculate the total cost of merchandise purchased.

Billed costs	=			$80,000
+ Inward freight	=	+		2,000
Billed delivered cost	=			$82,000
+ Workroom costs	=	+		500
Gross merchandise costs	=			$82,500
– Cash discount (7.5% × $80,000)	=	–		6,000
Total cost of goods sold	=			$76,500

GROSS MARGIN

The difference between the total *amount* of goods sold (net sales) and the total *cost* of the goods sold is the gross margin. It is calculated for a given period of time by subtracting the total cost of goods from the net sales for the period under consideration. It is a critical profit factor because it can be an indicator of the final results, and it is frequently known as gross profit. This figure must be large enough to cover operating expenses and allow for a reasonable profit. If the difference is not large enough to cover operating expenses, a **net loss** will result. It is a yardstick to measure the performance of a buyer.

Gross margin is important in both dollars and percentage. Both need to be looked at together and related back to actual net sales versus plan net sales. The percentage is frequently shown on merchandising reports in order to allow buyers to compare plan versus actual gross margin dollars as well as percentage, that is, what should be collected versus what is collected.

CONCEPT

$$\text{Gross margin \$} = \text{Net sales \$} - \text{Total cost of goods sold \$}$$

$$\text{Gross margin \%} = \frac{\text{Gross margin \$}}{\text{Net sales \$}} \times 100$$

PROBLEM

A department had net sales of $300,000, with the total cost of goods sold at $180,000. Determine the gross margin dollars and percentage.

SOLUTION

Net sales	=		$300,000
– Total cost of goods sold	=	–	$180,000
Gross margin	=		$120,000

$$\text{Gross margin \%} = \frac{\$120,000}{\$300,000} \times 100 = 40\%$$

Operating Expenses

Because the expenses of operating a business determine whether or not a net profit is achieved, the control and management of operating expenses are of major concern. For the purpose of analysis, the expenses incurred by the retailer (e.g., maintenance of store space, salaries, etc.) are classified to measure the performance of the designated function or activity. There are various approaches to classifying these items and, although there are many different kinds of expenses, each can be easily identified. However, there is variation in the format used to record them. Traditionally, operating expenses fall into two major categories and are charged to a merchandise department to determine its net profit. These major categories are direct and indirect expenses.

Direct Expenses

Direct expenses exist only within a given department and cease if that department is discontinued. These might include salespeople's and buyers' salaries, buyers' traveling expenses, advertising, selling supplies, delivery to customers, and selling space. For the purpose of expense analysis in retailing, the amount of floor space occupied that generates a given department's sales volume is allotted by the square foot and charged directly to that department, even though there is no cash outlay. Each expense and/or the total direct expenses are expressed as a percentage of net sales. For example, if the net sales of a department are $100,000 and $3,500 is spent on advertising, the percentage of advertising expenses would be $3,500 ÷ $100,000, or 3.5%.

Indirect Expenses

Indirect expenses are store expenses that will continue to exist even if the particular department is discontinued. These might include store maintenance, insurance, security, depreciation of equipment, and salaries of senior executives. Many indirect expenses are distributed among individual departments on the basis of their sales volume (e.g., if a department contributes 1.5% to the store's total sales, the indirect expenses charged to this department are 1.5%).

Operating expenses = Direct expenses + Indirect expenses

<table>
<tr><td>A children's department has net sales of $300,000, and indirect expenses are 10% of net sales. Direct expenses are:</td><td>PROBLEM</td></tr>
</table>

- Selling salaries = $24,000
- Advertising expenses = $6,000
- Buying salaries = $12,000
- Other direct expenses = $18,000

Find the total operating expenses of the department in dollars and as a percentage.

SOLUTION | Indirect expenses (10% × $300,000) = $30,000

Direct expenses:

Selling salaries	=	24,000
Advertising expenses	=	6,000
Buying salaries	=	12,000
Other	=	18,000
Total dollar operating expenses	=	$90,000

$$\text{Operating expense \%} = \frac{\$90{,}000 \text{ Operating expenses}}{\$300{,}000 \text{ Net sales}} \times 100$$

Operating expense % = 30%

Controllable and Noncontrollable Expenses

There are additional expenses that further complicate expense assignments. Many, but not all, direct expenses are **controllable expenses**. For example, the rent for Branch Store Y is directly related to this store, but it is not under the control of the present store manager because this expense was previously negotiated. Utilities are another example of a direct expense to a store, but an indirect expense to a particular department. The rates are not controllable, but the utilization is.

Store associates' hours are also considered to be controllable. These hours are subject to change based on whether that particular store is meeting its sales goals for the week or month. If stores are exceeding their sales plans, the manager may be given more hours to allocate among the associates. If stores are not meeting their plans, unfortunately, sales associates' hours are decreased and the salaried management team will be responsible for covering the store.

Because retailers do not always agree on the handling of expenses, some firms use the contribution technique to evaluate the performance of a buyer or store manager. **Contribution**, also known as **controllable margin**, includes those expenses that are direct, controllable, or a combination of direct and controllable (e.g., selling salaries). Contribution is the amount the department contributes to indirect expenses and profit, as seen in Figure 1.

In learning situations, it is more important to identify expense items and to understand the control, management, and relevancy to profit of those expenses than to make the accounting decision as to which expense is direct, indirect, controllable, or noncontrollable. To eliminate the confusion of how to classify and charge a particular expense item, in this text, expenses are listed individually or are referred to simply as operating expenses.

Figure 1. Contribution Operating Statement

		Dollars	Percentages	
Net Sales		$500,000	100.0%	
(minus) **Cost of Merchandise Sold**		− $266,000	− 53.2%	
		$234,000	46.8%	
(minus) **Direct Expenses**				
Payroll	$73,000			
Advertising	$13,000			
Supplies	$7,000			
Travel	$5,000			
Other	$12,000			
		− $110,000	− 22.0%	$\left(\dfrac{\$110,000}{\$500,000}\right)$
Contribution		$124,000	24.8%	$\left(\dfrac{\$124,000}{\$500,000}\right)$
(minus) **Indirect Expenses**		− $106,500	− 21.3%	$\left(\dfrac{\$106,500}{\$500,000}\right)$
Operating Profit		$17,500	3.5%	

Operating Income (Gross Sales and Net Sales) Practice Problems

1. Customer returns and allowances for Department #620 came to $4,500. Gross sales in the department were $90,000. What percentage of merchandise sold was returned?

2. For Family Department Stores, gross sales for the year were $369,000 and total reductions were $79,704. What is the reduction % for Family Department Stores for the year?

3. If gross sales for Store A are $1,150,000 and reductions are $245,000, what are the net sales?

4. The gross sales for Store B were $876,500. The customer returns and allowances were 10%.

    a. What was the dollar amount of returns and allowances?

    b. What were net sales?

NS
− COGS
GM
− OE
Profit

5. If gross sales for Main Street Men's Store were $298,000 and the reduction % was 15%, calculate the following:

    a. The dollar amount of reductions.

$$\$44,700$$

    b. The net sales.

$$\$253,300$$

6. The net sales of Department X were $46,780. The customer returns were $2,342. What were gross sales?

$$X - 2342 = 46780$$

$$\boxed{\$49122}$$

7. The gross sales of Store C were $2,500,000. The customer returns and allowances were $11,360. What were net sales?

$$2500000 - 11360 =$$

8. The net sales of Department Y were $36,000. The customer returns and allowances were 10%. What were gross sales?

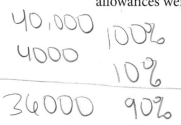

40,000 100%
4000   10%
36000 90%

$$X - 3600$$
$$36000 =$$

$$= \$40,000$$

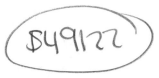

$$\times \quad 100\%$$
$$= \quad 10\%$$
$$36000 \quad 90\%$$

$$36000 \times .9 = 40,000$$

Gross Sales − returns = net sales

9. After Mother's Day this year, the loungewear department had customer returns of 10.5%. The department's net sales amounted to $635,380. As the buyer reviewed last year's figures for the same period, the customer returns were 12.5%, with gross sales of $726,149.

   a. Compute the department's performance in dollars and percentages for this year and last year, in regard to gross sales, customer returns, and net sales.

   b. Compare this year's results to last year's performance. Discuss the performance from a profit viewpoint.

10. The hosiery department's net sales are $30,000 and the total store net sales are $1,200,000. What is the hosiery department's % to total sales?

11. The towel department represents 4% of total store sales, which are $4,500,000. What are the net sales planned for the towel department?

12. Total store sales are $15,000,000. Missy sportswear sales are $6,000,000 and junior sportswear sales are $2,800,000. What is the percentage of sales for each department?

13. Casual sneaker sales represent 4.5% and athletic shoe sales represent 3.2% of total store sales. If the total store sales are $900,000, what are the dollar sales for each department?

CS: $40,500

AS: $28,800

14. For this year, Store G's sales volume was $550,000,000. The juniors' dress department had net sales of $8,250,000, and the misses' dress department had net sales of $24,750,000. What were the net sales percentages of each department to the total store?

15. Branch Store H had total sales of $30,000,000. The small leather goods department's sales were 1.9% of Store H's total sales. The handbag department's sales were 2.1% of the total branch sales. What were the dollar net sales for each department?

Slg: $570,000

H: $630,000

16. Discussion Problem: Explain why a merchant should be alarmed if customer returns are excessive. How does a merchant determine what is an excessive percentage of returns? What can be done by the department itself to correct a problematic rate of returns?

17. The customer returns for the Fall season were 10% on gross sales of $900,000. For the Spring season, gross sales were $850,000, and customer returns were $70,000. What was the percentage of customer returns for the entire year?

Cost of Goods Sold Practice Problems

18. The missy tops buyer is placing an order for T-shirts. The buyer will be purchasing 10,000 units of solid T-shirts at a billed cost of $10.75 per unit and 8,400 units of printed T-shirts at a billed cost of $11.50 per unit. Calculate the total billed cost for the T-shirt order.

19. The girls' buyer placed an order for the following merchandise:

    120 sweaters with a billed cost of $7.75 each

    180 knit tops with a billed cost of $4.50 each

    150 leggings with a billed cost of $6.25 each

    Calculate the total billed cost for this order.

20. Marjorie's Baby Store placed an order for infant blankets that totaled $4,800. Discounts earned were $480, and shipping charges were $100. What is the total cost of goods sold for this order?

    4800 +100 (-480) =

    $4420

21. The kitchen textiles buyer placed an order for 12,000 holiday motif towels at a billed cost of $1.70 each. The shipping charges on the order amounted to $300. The buyer negotiated a cost discount of 12%. What is the cost of goods sold for this order?

    12000 × 1.7 = $20400
                  −2448
                  ‾‾‾‾‾
                  17952
                  + 300
                  ‾‾‾‾‾
    $ 18252

    20 400
    12%
    $300

22. The petite sportswear buyer placed the following order:

- 36 pants costing $10.75 each $= 387$
- 48 pants costing $15.50 each $= 744$ } $1551
- 24 pants costing $17.50 each $= 420$

Shipping charges (paid by the store) were 6% of the billed cost. Find:

a. The dollar amount of shipping charges.

$93.06

b. The delivered cost of the total order.

$1644.06

23. A specialty store placed an order for the following merchandise:

600 pants with a billed cost of $29.00 each

500 pants with a billed cost of $32.00 each

There was an 8% discount secured for the order. Shipping charges were $1,670 of the total order. The merchandise needed to be ticketed, and the store incurred a $150 workroom cost.

a. What is the total billed cost for the order?

b. What is the discount in dollars?

c. What is the cost of goods sold for this order?

24. A luggage buyer purchased 72 attaché cases that cost $40 each. The cash discount earned was 2%, and the store paid inward freight of $95. Find the total cost of the merchandise on this order.

25. A gift shop has workroom costs of $575. The billed cost of merchandise sold amounted to $59,000, with cash discounts earned of $1,180 and freight charges of $650. Find the total cost of the merchandise.

26. A specialty dress shop made purchases amounting to $3,700 at cost, with 8% cash discounts earned, workroom costs of $100, and no inward freight. Determine the total cost of the merchandise.

27. A sporting goods buyer placed the following order:
    - 18 nylon backpacks costing $22 each   = 396
    - 12 two-person tents costing $54 each   = 648   } 1374
    - 6 camp stoves costing $55 each   = 330

    Shipping costs paid by the store were $60, and a cash discount of 1% was taken. Find:

    a. Billed cost on the total order.

    $1374

    b. Total delivered cost of the merchandise.

    $1420.26

28. Discussion Problem: Explain why control of inward freight costs and work-room (alterations) costs is vital. Can a merchandiser help to control these factors? If so, how? Why is cash discount calculated on billed cost?

Gross Margin Practice Problems

29. Calculate the gross margin in dollars and percentage for the shoe department given the following:

    Net sales   = $510,000

    Cost of goods sold = $315,200

30. Calculate the gross margin in both dollars and percentage for the swim department if net sales are $1,150,000 and cost of goods sold is $638,400.

    $511,600

    44.5%

31. Calculate the gross margin in dollars and percentage for the home department if:

    Net sales   = $140,000

    Billed cost of merchandise = $84,000

    Cost discount   =   7.5%

    Shipping charges   = $240

    84000
    6300
    +240
    _____
    77,940
       ↓
    140000 — 77940 = $62,060

    net sales
    − cogs
    _____
    140,000
    − 84,000
    _____
    $56,000

    62,060 = 44.3%

Operating Expense Practice Problems

32. Analyze the following information:

JOHNSTON CANDY COMPANY

Operating expenses	This Year	Plan	Last Year
Advertising	$24,300	$27,700	$28,500
Sales salaries	$75,100	$75,300	$74,000
Misc. selling costs	$8,300	$8,500	$8,300
Total	$107,700	$111,500	$110,800
Net sales	$1,140,000	$980,000	$900,000

Find the following:

a. What is the percentage of advertising expenses for each year?

b. What is the percentage of sales salary expenses for each year?

c. What is the percentage of miscellaneous selling costs for each year?

d. What is the yearly percentage of total operating expenses shown?

e. What is the percentage change of operating expenses for this year to plan and this year to last year?

f. What is the percentage change of net sales for this year to plan and this year to last year?

33. Analyze the following information:

	This Year (TY)	Plan	Last Year (LY)
Net sales	$495,000	$517,500	$450,000
Advertising costs	$82,000	$80,000	$86,000
Salaries	$96,000	$90,000	$91,000

Find the following:

a. What are the total expenses in $ and % for TY, Plan, and LY?

b. What is the comparison (build) of sales for TY versus Plan and TY versus LY?

1.2 PROFIT AND LOSS STATEMENTS

Businesses must keep accurate records of sales income, merchandise costs, and operating expenses to calculate profit. In retailing, one of the most important financial records is the **profit and loss statement**. Income and expenses are summarized in the form known in retailing as a profit and loss statement (for other types of organizations, this statement is frequently called an **income statement**). This statement, prepared periodically by the department, store, or organization, summarizes the basic merchandising factors that affect profit results, showing the difference between income and expenses. Generally, the accounting department keeps a continuous record of sales income and expenses. At set intervals, this statement is analyzed to determine whether these transactions have resulted in a profit or loss. (The interval might be a year, three months [quarter], or six months [season].) If income exceeds expenses, the result is profit. If expenses exceed income, the result is a loss. Thus, it is a summary of the business transactions during a given period of time expressed in terms of making or losing money. It is used to measure profitability, as it evaluates the results of current performance and allows for comparison of present and possible future trends.

In the calculation of a profit and loss statement, there is emphasis on an exact and rigid order of the factors included. Although adding and subtracting the appropriate figures can determine a correct profit result, the standard arrangement provides an analytical picture that allows a determination of the store's strengths and weaknesses and facilities comparisons with other counterparts. The buyer must critically examine these figures and then make a determination of causes from these results. A profit and loss statement should not be confused with a **balance sheet**, which shows the assets, liabilities, and net worth of a business.

Because this is a retailing text, the profit and loss statement will not be analyzed as a bookkeeping procedure, but in terms of how a merchant can use the data it contains to improve a merchandising operation. It is a fundamental merchandising concept that one of a buyer's chief responsibilities is to ensure that a store or department earns a profit on the merchandise sold specifically during the accounting period under consideration. For the most part, buyers will not have control on expenses; therefore, gross margin is their fiscal responsibility to monitor profitability.

Profit and loss statements can show the performance of a department, division, branch, or the entire organization. The basic format of a profit and loss statement is as follows:

Net sales

– Cost of goods sold

= Gross margin

– Operating expenses

= Net profit or loss

SKELETAL PROFIT AND LOSS STATEMENTS

A **skeletal profit and loss statement** does not spell out all transactions in detail, but it is a quick method to determine, at any particular time, a given department's profit or loss. It contains the five major components of a profit and loss statement and is expressed in *both* dollars and as a percentage.

Net sales	=		$300,000	100%
– Cost of goods sold	=	–	180,000	60%
= Gross margin	=		$120,000	40%
– Operating expenses	=	–	105,000	35%
= **Net profit**	=		$15,000	5%

The value of a profit and loss statement is that it can be used to compare previous statements or to compare a company's figures to industry-wide figures to help improve profit or adjust any of the other factors mentioned in the example. Therefore, it is vital to think in terms of percentages as well as dollar amounts. For example, a buyer's statement that a net profit of $2,869 was earned during a given business period has no real meaning unless the dollar amount for each of the other contributing factors is also stated. The profit figure could be phenomenally high or dismally low by industry standards, depending on the dollar net sales volume of the department. Unless the figures for all other factors are available, it is impossible to determine which departmental operations excelled or faltered. The only meaningful way to compare departmental performances is to compare the respective results expressed as a percentage of the net sales volume. From this information, the deduction can be made that profit will vary upward or downward as one or more of the three major factors (i.e., net sales, cost of goods sold, or operating expenses) change.

$$\text{Cost of goods sold \%} = \frac{\text{Cost of goods sold \$}}{\text{Net sales \$}} \times 100$$

$$\text{Gross margin \%} = \frac{\text{Gross margin \$}}{\text{Net sales \$}} \times 100$$

$$\text{Operating expenses \%} = \frac{\text{Direct and indirect expenses \$}}{\text{Net sales \$}} \times 100$$

$$\text{Net profit \%} = \frac{\text{Net profit \$}}{\text{Net sales \$}} \times 100$$

The juniors' sportswear department in Store A had net sales of $160,000; the cost of goods sold was $88,000, and operating expenses were $64,000. The juniors' sportswear department in Store B, for the same business period, had net sales of $260,000, the cost of goods sold was $135,200, and operating expenses were $109,200. Which store earned a higher net profit percentage?

SOLUTION

	Store A		Store B	
Net sales	$160,000	100%	$260,000	100%
– Cost of goods sold	– 88,000	– 55%	– 135,200	– 52%
Gross margin	$72,000	45%	$124,800	48%
– Operating expenses	– 64,000	– 40%	– 109,200	– 42%
Net profit	$8,000	5%	$15,600	6%

As a basis for comparison, the percentage figures give the clearest picture. Upon examination of this skeletal profit and loss statement, the reader can see that the junior sportswear department in Store A spent 55¢ of every dollar of sales on the cost of merchandise sold, while Store B spent 52¢. Respectively, Store A spent 40¢ and Store B spent 42¢ of every dollar of sales on operating expenses. Gross margin, net profit, and individual transactions can be more accurately compared when these figures are recorded in a complete profit and loss statement. Also, all other figures in the skeletal profit and loss statement are then expressed as a part or a percentage of net sales. Conversely, when the respective results for cost of goods sold, gross margin, operating expenses, or net profit are expressed as a percentage of net sales, the dollar amounts of each factor can be determined.

CONCEPT

Cost of goods sold $ = Cost of goods sold % × Net sales $

Gross margin $ = Gross margin % × Net sales $

Operating expenses $ = Operating expenses % × Net sales $

Net profit $ = Net profit % × Net sales $

PROBLEM

The junior sportswear department in Store A had net sales of $160,000. The cost of goods sold was 55%, gross margin was 45%, operating expenses were 40%, and net profit was 5%. What were the dollar amounts of each?

SOLUTION

Net sales	=	$160,000	
– Cost of goods sold	=	– 88,000	($160,000 × 55%)
Gross margin	=	$72,000	($160,000 × 45%)
– Operating expenses	=	– 64,000	($160,000 × 40%)
Net profit	=	$8,000	($160,000 × 5%)

FINAL PROFIT AND LOSS STATEMENTS

A **final profit and loss statement** shows the basic profit factors developed in detail so that every transaction is clearly seen. The skeleton format discussed earlier shows the basic factors—that is, sales and cost of goods and expenses—and provides a quick method of monitoring profit or loss, but it is also necessary to have more detailed information on these basic factors to detect weaknesses that need strengthening or to illuminate strengths that bear repetition.

Thus, a final profit and loss statement includes additional information pertaining to stock levels. Bearing in mind that profit occurs only when the merchandise sold remains sold, the retailer must be able, from an accounting viewpoint, to determine the value of inventory or merchandise sold. Generally, retailers use an accounting method known as the retail method of inventory (see Chapter 4), in which the retail stock figure at the end of the accounting period provides the basis for determining the cost value of stock. An **opening inventory** figure refers to the retail value of the merchandise in stock at the beginning of the accounting period. It is established by a physical count of the merchandise in stock at current retail prices; this figure is then converted to a cost amount. The **closing inventory** figure is the amount of merchandise in stock at the end of the period under consideration. The opening inventory, at cost, is added to the cost of new net purchases and transportation charges (inward freight) to determine an amount known as **total merchandise handled**. Total merchandise handled is the sum of merchandise at cost available for sale. To determine the cost of only the merchandise that was sold, the final profit calculation requires a total merchandise handled amount. It can be determined at cost or at retail. The gross cost of goods sold can be calculated when the closing inventory at cost is subtracted from the total merchandise handled amount.

Opening inventory at cost		$100,000
+ Billed costs on new purchases	+	$500,000
+ Inward freight	+	$1,000
Total merchandise handled at cost	=	$601,000
– Closing inventory at cost	–	$159,000
Gross cost of goods sold	=	$442,000

EXAMPLE

With this information, it is now possible to determine the net cost of goods sold by the other adjustments (e.g., cash discounts).

Figure 2. Profit and Loss Statement

Profit Factors		Cost		Retail	%
Income from Sales					
	Gross Sales			$450,000	
−	Customer Returns & Allowances			− $25,000	
	Net Sales			$425,000	100%
Cost of Goods Sold					
	Opening Inventory		$52,000	$100,000*	
	New Net Purchases	$258,000			
+	Inward Freight	+ $2,000			
		$260,000			
+	Total Cost of Goods		$260,000		
	Total Merchandise Handled at Cost		$312,000		
−	Closing Inventory at Cost		− $65,000		
	Gross Cost of Goods Sold		$247,000		
−	Cash Discounts		− $13,000		
	Net Cost of Goods Sold		$234,000		
+	Alteration & Workroom Costs		+ $1,000		
	Total Cost of Goods Sold		$235,000	− $235,000	55.3%
GROSS MARGIN				$190,000	44.7%
Operating Expenses					
	Total Direct Expenses		$101,250		
	Total Indirect Expenses		$67,500		
	Total Operating Expenses			$168,750	39.7%
	Net Profit			$21,250	5.0%

* $100,000 represents the opening inventory figure (determined by physical count), from which $52,000, the opening cost inventory figure, is derived by applying a markup percentage.

Figure 2 illustrates a final profit and loss statement, which is an amplification of the skeletal profit and loss statement. The basic profit factors (that is, sales, cost of goods sold, and expenses) are developed in detail so that each transaction is clearly seen. To analyze the results, each factor must be presented in a standard accounting arrangement. The final profit and loss statement is the only way to make a valid comparison among departments or stores because the detailed information supplied by this statement is necessary to compute the cost of goods actually sold. For a better understanding of the detailed final profit and loss statement shown in Figure 2, refer to the following definitions.

- **INCOME FROM SALES** is divided into such categories as:

  - **Gross sales** ($450,000): The retail value of total initial sales.

  - **Customer returns and allowances** ($25,000): The total value of cancellation of sales by customer credit, refund, or partial rebate.

  - **Net sales** ($425,000): The figure derived by subtracting customer returns and allowances from the gross sales of a period. It is the dollar value of sales that "stay sold."

- **COST OF GOODS SOLD** is divided into such categories as:

  - **Opening inventory at retail** ($100,000): The amount of merchandise at the beginning of a period, counted and recorded at the current selling price.

  - **Opening inventory at cost** ($52,000): The figure derived from the retail figure by applying a markup percentage to the total merchandise handled.

  - **New net purchases** ($258,000): The **billed cost** of merchandise purchased. It is the gross purchases minus returns and allowances to vendors.

  - **Inward freight** ($2,000): The cost of transporting goods to the premises.

  - **Total cost of goods** ($260,000): The combination of the cost of merchandise purchased and inward freight.

  - **Total merchandise handled at cost** ($312,000): The sum of the opening inventory ($52,000) plus the total cost of goods ($260,000).

  - **Closing inventory at cost** ($65,000): The figure derived from the retail inventory figure that represents the merchandise in stock at the end of an operating period.

  - **Gross cost of goods sold** ($247,000): The total merchandise handled at cost ($312,000) less the closing inventory at cost ($65,000 cost).

  - **Cash discounts** ($13,000): Adjustments made to the cost of goods sold from paying bills in a specified time.

  - **Net cost of goods sold** ($234,000): The gross cost of goods sold ($247,000) minus cash discounts ($13,000).

  - **Alteration and workroom costs** ($1,000): The cost of preparing goods for resale. It is another adjustment to the cost of goods sold.

  - **Total cost of goods sold** ($235,000 or 55.3%): The figure that results when the gross cost of goods sold ($247,000) is adjusted by subtracting cash discounts ($13,000) and adding alteration and workroom costs ($1,000).

- **Gross margin** ($190,000 or 44.7%): The difference between net sales ($425,000) and total cost of goods sold ($235,000). This is often called gross profit.

- **OPERATING EXPENSES** are divided into such categories as:

  - **Total direct expenses** ($101,250): Expenses that come into being with a department and cease if it is discontinued.

  - **Total indirect expenses** ($67,500): Expenses that continue even if a department is discontinued.

  - **Total operating expenses** ($168,750): Direct ($101,250) and indirect ($67,500) expenses combined.

- **NET (OPERATING) PROFIT** ($21,250 or 5%): The result of the relationship among sales, cost of goods, and expenses. When the gross margin is larger than the operating expenses, a net profit is achieved.

For problems 34 and 35, set up skeletal profit and loss statements in both dollars and percentage given the information in each problem.

34.

Net sales	$240,000
Cost of goods sold	$100,800
Expenses	$125,000

35.

Net sales	$1,290,000
Gross margin	$554,700
Profit	$104,000

36. The children's department has net sales of $96,000, cost of goods sold for the department is 54%, and expenses were 28% of sales. Set up a profit and loss statement in dollars and percentage for the department.

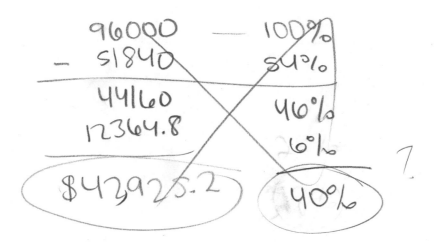

$$
\begin{array}{ll}
96000 & 100\% \\
-\ 51840 & 54\% \\
\hline
44160 & 46\% \\
12364.8 & 6\% \\
\hline
\$43925.2 & 40\%
\end{array}
$$

37. A buyer has the following information:

Gross margin $535,000

Gross margin   25%

Expenses $575,000

Set up a skeletal profit and loss statement in both dollars and percentage.

38. Set up a skeletal profit and loss statement in both dollars and percentage if your year-end profit is $7,800, the profit percentage is 3.9%, and your yearly cost of goods sold is $120,000.

127 800   100%
120,000   94%
7800   3.9%

39. Note the following figures:

Net profit   2.5%

Gross margin $7,000

Operating expenses $6,600

Find:

   a. The cost of goods in dollars.

   b. The percentage of operating expenses.

40. The net profit in an appliance department for the Spring/Summer period was $20,000, which represented 2% of net sales. Operating expenses totaled $480,000. Find:

   a. The dollar amount of gross margin.

   b. The net sales figure.

41. The linen department had net sales of $80,000. There was a 2% loss, and the gross margin was 46%. Determine the operating expenses of the department and express the result in dollars and as a percentage.

80,000   100%
43,200   54%
36800   46%
38400   48%
(1,600)   (2%)

42. Calculate the percentage of operating expenses for a home furnishings department that has the following figures:

Gross sales	$476,000
Customer returns	$4,000
Advertising costs	$10,000
Salaries	$101,000
Miscellaneous expenses	$6,160
Utilities	$9,000
Insurance	$11,000
Rent	$70,000

43. Set up a skeletal statement that shows the following figures as dollars and as a percentage:

Net profit $	$5,500
Net profit %	2.5%
Operating expenses	47.5%

44. Suppose that the estimated net sales for the coming year are $100,000, estimated cost of merchandise purchases is $52,000, and the total estimated operating expenses are $43,000. The buyer's goal is a net profit of 5%. Determine the percentage of gross margin on sales needed to achieve this desired profit.

45. Using the following figures, set up a skeletal profit and loss statement that shows each factor in dollars and as a percentage.

Net sales	$85,000
Net profit	$1,700
Cost of goods sold	$45,000

46. What is the profit or loss in dollars if gross sales are $218,000, customer returns and allowances are $3,000, cost of goods sold is 55%, and operating expenses are 41%?

47. Complete a profit and loss statement for Store C, given the following information:

Net sales	$1,300,000
Billed cost of merchandise	$680,000
Cost discounts	10%
Shipping charges	$10,400
Salaries	$260,000
Advertising	$125,000
Other expenses	$114,000

Handwritten annotations: 68000; 1300000; 622400; 677600; 499000; 178600; COGS; exp; 499000

48. Discussion Problem: In measuring gross margin performance, which is more significant: the dollar amount or the percentage figure? Why?

49. Find the net profit or loss as a percentage and the gross margin as a dollar amount.

Gross sales	$200,000
Customer returns and allowances	$15,000
Opening inventory at cost	$38,000
Billed cost of goods	$99,000
Inward freight	$5,000
Cash discount	$6,000
Closing inventory at cost	$36,000
Payroll	$48,000
Occupancy	$28,000
Wrapping and packing	$1,200
Utilities	$2,000
Delivery	$2,800

GS   200,000
R+A   15000
_____
NS   185,000

OI +38000
COGS +99000
D -6000
F +5000
CI -36000
_____
100,000

NS 185000   100%
COGS 100,000
GM 85,000
-OE 82000
_____
P   3000

50. Construct a profit and loss statement using the following departmental figures and show the dollar amounts for net sales, total cost of goods sold, gross margin, expenses, and profit.

Gross sales	$82,000
Customer returns and allowances	$4,000
Inward freight	$2,000
Workroom costs	$1,000
Opening inventory at cost	$17,000
Closing inventory at cost	$14,000
Purchases at cost	$36,000
Cash discounts	8%
Advertising	$5,000
Rent	$12,000
Salaries	$17,000
Miscellaneous expenses	$2,500

Handwritten: } net sales = 78,000

Handwritten: 8% → of purchases

Handwritten calculations:

COGS
+ 17000
+ 2000 + 1000
+ 36000
- 8% (2880)
- 14000
———
39120

exp
5000
12000
17000
2500
———
36500

78000   100%
- 39120
———
38880
- 36500
———
$2,380 → 3.1%

51. Construct a final profit and loss statement from the following figures and calculate the major factors as percentages and dollar amounts.

Opening inventory	$74,200
Gross sales	$248,000
Advertising	$15,000
Miscellaneous expenses	$18,000
Purchases at cost	$120,000
Closing inventory	$78,000
Customer returns	$25,800
Salaries	$26,000
Transportation charges	$8,000
Rent	$39,000
Cash discounts	3%

248000
25800
———
222200

NS 222200   100%
COGS 120600   5.4%
GM 101600   4.6%
exp 98000   4.4%
P   3600   1.6%

exp
15000
18000
26000
39000
———
98000

COGS
+74200
+120000
-78000
+8000
-3600
———
120600

1.3 How to Increase Profits

Realistically, it is impossible to list everything a retailer needs to know to merchandise at a profit because the factors that govern profitability are variable and net profits do not represent any fixed sum. The results achieved by a retailer illustrate that the amount of profit can be different for different organizations and is rarely, if ever, constant. In every organization, the actual figures will change annually, but the information required for analysis will remain constant.

After reviewing a profit and loss statement, however, to determine how each of these factors affects profit, certain measures can be taken to improve profits. Because these three factors (sales, cost of goods sold, and operating expenses) are interrelated, the adjustments made must keep all three factors balanced in relationship to one another. Fundamentally, profits can be improved through the following three approaches:

1. Increase sales with only a proportionate increase in the cost of the merchandise and little or no increase in expenses.

2. Decrease the cost of merchandise sold without a decrease in sales, which should result in a larger gross margin.

3. Lower or reduce expenses.

The following example shows the application and effect of each approach. For the accounting period under consideration, a merchant estimated sales at $100,000, merchandise purchases at $70,000, and total operating expenses at $25,000. If the merchant wants to increase the previous 5% net profit, which approach should he or she take?

Actual Estimated Performance:

EXAMPLE

		Dollars		Percentages
Sales		$100,000		100%
– Cost of goods sold		– 70,000		– 70%
Gross margin	=	$30,000	=	30%
– Operating expenses		– 25,000		– 25%
Net profit	=	$5,000	=	5%

Approach 1:

Increase sales with only a proportionate increase in cost of goods sold and little or no increase in expenses.

		Dollars		Percentages	
Sales		$110,000		100%	(Increased sales)
– Cost of goods sold		– 75,900		– 69%	(Decreased % of cost of goods sold)
Gross margin	=	$34,100	=	31%	(Increased $ and % of gross margin)
– Operating expenses		– 28,050		– 25.5%	(Increased $ and % of operating expenses)
Net profit	=	$6,050	=	5.5%	(Increased net profit)

Approach 2:

Decrease the cost of goods sold without decreasing sales, which is equivalent to a larger gross margin.

		Dollars		Percentages	
Sales		$100,000		100%	(Constant)
– Cost of goods sold		– 69,500		– 69.5%	(Decreased cost of goods sold)
Gross margin	=	$30,500	=	30.5%	(Larger gross margin)
– Operating expenses		– 25,000		– 25%	(Same expenses)
Net profit	=	$5,500	=	5.5%	(Increased net profit)

Approach 3:

Lower or reduce expenses.

		Dollars		Percentages	
Sales		$100,000		100%	(Constant)
– Cost of goods sold		– 70,000		– 70%	(Constant)
Gross margin	=	$30,000	=	30%	(Constant)
– Operating expenses		– 24,500		– 24.5%	(Reduced expenses)
Net profit	=	$5,500	=	5.5%	(Increased net profit)

Mathematically, the preceding example demonstrates three possible approaches to increasing profits. It shows that the manipulation of any one of the three basic profit elements studied (sales, cost of goods, and expenses) will produce different profit results.

In the real retailing arena, each approach can be accomplished only by applying specific merchandising strategies that focus on the particular initiative under scrutiny. Unless there are major management policy changes, it would be counterproductive to attempt changing all three elements at the same time. The three approaches remain the same, but the order of importance may change for any particular period under consideration.

There are many merchandising and retailing texts that examine, in depth, the principles and techniques concerning optimizing sales, decreasing cost of goods, and lowering expenses. Some of the common effective strategies used (not necessarily in order of importance) are:

1. Increasing sales:

   - Price merchandise competitively.

   - Analyze regional customer preferences to achieve proper assortment.

   - Respond quickly to product performance.

   - Minimize out-of-stock items.

   - Control amount and timing of markdowns.

2. Decreasing cost of goods:

   - Sell a larger proportion of higher-markup goods.

   - Develop and maintain vendor relationships that result in advantageous actions concerning new market developments, shipping preferences, and competitive pricing.

   - Qualify for greater quantity discounts, cash discounts, lower shipping terms, and so on.

   - Develop private brands that offer one-of-a-kind merchandise and exceptional value at negotiable costs.

3. Lowering or reducing expenses:

   - Practice "lean retailing," today's motto. The emphasis is not on which expenses can be further reduced, but on optimizing all the functions that pertain to the buying/selling process, from receiving room to sales floor.

   - Maximize selling floor space with improved presentations to facilitate "easy" selling.

   - Forecast and plan all sales promotion activities to produce maximum results and effectiveness.

   - Look for innovative ideas to improve customers' in-store experiences.

EVALUATING A BUYER

Management evaluates the performance of a buyer on objective results. The common measurements used, expressed in figures, are:

1. Sales Results: Measured in dollars and indicates how well the merchandise purchased has been accepted, priced, and sold. This is reflected in the net sales achieved. Increase is the major consideration. Buyers are expected to achieve planned sales goals based on reasonable appraisal of both outside and inside conditions and trends. In addition, sales can be measured by units or by number of sales transactions and sales per square foot of selling space.

2. Inventory Results: Refers to the amount of merchandise in stock as shown by stock turn (sales for that period divided by the average stock for that period). This goal is set by management and compared to industry standards. It indicates the use of capital investment. The control of merchandise shrinkage or shortage is another criterion of the buyer's performance.

3. Margin Results: Achieved by pricing merchandise at a profitable initial markup (aggregate original retail prices minus aggregate invoice costs) and realizing a planned gross margin (final selling price minus cost of goods sold, including cash discounts and alteration costs). This occurs after performing the specialized task of selecting vendors and negotiating costs and other terms of sale that are included in the total cost of merchandise delivered and sold, when subtracted from the net sales achieved.

4. Net Operating Profit Results (gross margin minus all expenses chargeable to the selling department): Evaluated properly at the level when management has chosen an expense plan that designates expenses, which can be attributable to the department's operation and are subtracted from the gross margin results.

The mathematics required to achieve these desired results will be studied in appropriate chapters that pertain to each topic. Once studied and mastered in application, success cannot be far away.

In addition to these criteria expressed by figures, buyers can be assessed on their daily buying, pricing, and stock control activities when improvement is shown over a period of time, resulting in developments that generate increased profits.

CASE STUDY 1
ANALYZING PROFIT PERFORMANCE

The ABC Development Company was selected to manage a major new mall. This mall would be surrounded by a large, medium-income residential neighborhood composed of private homes and townhouses ranging from $350,000 to $1,000,000.

In order to select the appropriate store type that would be successful in this area, management researched the profitability of different types of stores. The following information was collected:

Store Type	Profits		Profits to Sales	
	This Year	Last Year	This Year	Last Year
Department stores	$1,580,722	$1,470,655	3.5%	3.3%
Mass merchandisers	$2,033,300	$1,896,700	2.8%	2.8%
Specialty stores	$568,774	$555,579	4.4%	4.4%
Discounters	$432,774	$335,336	3.4%	3.4%
Off-price stores	$32,073	$24,143	5.4%	5.4%
Miscellaneous	$461,537	$478,326	2.3%	2.3%
Total	$5,109,180	$4,760,739	3.0%	3.0%

Using the preceding data:

a. Calculate the dollar profit percentage change from this year to last year.

b. Calculate the net sales for last year and this year.

c. Which store type had the most significant profit change?

d. What store type would you recommend? Why?

e. Discuss the possible causes of profit percentage change from last year to this year.

CASE STUDY 2
CONTROLLING EXPENSES

The housewares department in a specialty store had net sales of $1,500,000. The direct expenses during the period under consideration were:

Buying salaries	$125,000
Selling salaries	$275,000
Advertising	$90,000
Receiving and marking	$15,000
Wrapping and packing	$10,000

The gross margin achieved during this time was 34.0%. After reviewing this performance, management decided that expenses must be reduced. The manager was given the choice of either reducing the advertising budget to a maximum of $50,000 or eliminating a salesperson, which would reduce selling salaries by $50,000.

Which plan of action would you choose? Why? Explore the two options mathematically, and then state your choice. Justify your decision. Discuss the impact your strategy will have on net profit.

CASE STUDY 3
ANALYSIS OF PROFIT AND LOSS STATEMENTS

Ms. Kane, the china and glass buyer of Crystal Clear, Inc., was asked to present a yearly profit and loss statement in skeletal form to the divisional merchandise manager. In addition, she wanted to prepare a summary of comments that included a comparison of her performance this year with that of her major competitor, China Seas, Ltd. Ms. Kane obtained the following information from Crystal Clear's statistical department:

Gross sales	$135,000
Alteration and workroom costs	$1,000
Opening inventory at cost	$49,500
Closing inventory at cost	$61,000
New purchases at cost	$77,500
Inward freight	$1,500
Cash discounts	4%
General overhead	$11,000
Advertising	$9,000
Salaries	$20,000
Rent	$8,600
Customer returns and allowances	$15,000

Ms. Kane obtained, from outside research, profit and loss data on her competitor, China Seas, which had the following results for the same year:

Profit	6% or $7,350
Operating expenses	40%

Ms. Kane then prepared a skeletal profit and loss statement for her department and for that of her competitor, China Seas. On completion of this task, she compared the two statements. Based on this study, where and how did Ms. Kane determine that she could take action that would give immediate results and have an impact on the department's profitability? Support the suggested action mathematically.

CASE STUDY 4
EVALUATING A BUYER

Refer to the following year-end factors for a buyer for a missy swimwear department:

	This Year	Plan	Last Year
Average inventory $	$22,600	$20,700	$23,200
Sales $	$49,900	$45,200	$44,600
Cost of goods $			
Gross margin $	$24,300	$23,600	$22,600
Gross margin %			

Analyze the following:

1. Calculate the cost of goods in dollars for This Year, Plan, and Last Year.

2. Calculate the gross margin percentage for This Year, Plan, and Last Year.

3. For this year the buyer negotiated terms of a 10% order discount; the average billed cost on the swimwear was $40.00. The majority of the merchandise arrives in stores for April. The majority of sales for swimwear occur in June and July. After analyzing the gross margin dollars and percentage achieved versus Plan, what can the buyer do in order to achieve the planned gross margin dollars and percentage?

RETAIL PRICING AND REPRICING OF MERCHANDISE

## CHAPTER 2

"Ideas are a dime a dozen.
People who put them into action are priceless."

2002 GEMS OF EDUCATIONAL WIT & HUMOR (PARKER PUBLISHING 1994)

OBJECTIVES

- Identify activities that retailers can use to maximize profits.

- Understand price lining and pricing strategy, and identify the types of price zones.

- Recognize and identify the three basic pricing elements and how they relate to one another.

- Calculate markup as dollar amounts and percentages for individual items and groups of items.

- Establish retail prices.

- Ascertain the types of price adjustments and confirm their importance as merchandising decisions.

- Calculate markdowns as dollar amounts and percentages.

- Understand the differences between point-of-sale (POS) and permanent (physical) markdowns.

- Understand the criteria for the determination of taking markdowns (outdate, weeks of supply, sell through percentage, build).

- Delineate the procedures for making price changes.

- Recognize the impact of pricing and repricing decisions on profit, including the journalization of markdowns.

KEY TERMS

additional markup	employee discount	gross markdown
build	everyday low price (EDLP)	markdown (MD)
cost complement		
cumulative markup	everyday value price (EDVP)	markdown cancellation

markdown journalization	permanent (physical) markdown	price zone
markdown percentage	point-of-sale (POS) markdown	promotional price zone
markup (MU)		retail price
markup cancellation	prestige price zone	retail reduction
markup percentage	price line	sell through percentage (ST %)
net markdown	price lining	volume price zone
outdate	price range	weeks of supply (WOS)

KEY CONCEPT FORMULAS

Cost (Markup Formulas)

$$\text{Cost \$} = \text{Retail \$} - \text{Markup \$}$$

$$\text{Cost \%} = \frac{\text{Cost \$}}{\text{Retail \$}} \times 100$$

$$\text{Cost \%} = \text{Retail \%} - \text{Markup \%}$$

$$\text{Cost \%} = 100\% - \text{Markup \%}$$

$$\text{Cost \$} = \text{Retail \$} \times (100\% - \text{Markup \%})$$

Markdown

$$\text{Markdown \$} = \text{Original or present retail price \$} - \text{New retail price \$}$$

$$\text{Markdown \$} = \text{Percentage off} \times \text{Present retail price \$}$$

$$\text{Total markdown \$} = \text{First total \$ markdown} + \text{Second total \$ markdown}$$

$$\text{Planned markdowns \$} = \text{Net sales \$} \times \text{Markdown \%}$$

$$\text{Markdown \%} = \frac{\text{Markdown \$}}{\text{Net sales}} \times 100$$

$$\text{Markdown \%} = \frac{\text{Markdown \$}}{\text{Total dollar sales of group's final selling prices}} \times 100$$

$$\text{Markdown cancellation} = \text{Higher retail \$} - \text{Markdown price \$}$$

$$\text{Net markdown \$} = \text{Gross markdown \$} - \text{Markdown cancellation \$}$$

Markup

$$\text{Markup \$} = \text{Retail \$} - \text{Cost \$}$$

$$\text{Markup \% on retail} = \frac{\text{Markup \$}}{\text{Retail \$}} \times 100 \ \text{ or } \ \frac{\text{Retail \$} - \text{Cost \$}}{\text{Retail \$}} \times 100$$

$$\text{Markup \% on cost} = \frac{\text{Markup \$}}{\text{Cost \$}} \times 100 \ \text{ or } \ \frac{\text{Retail \$} - \text{Cost \$}}{\text{Cost \$}} \times 100$$

Cumulative retail markup % on entire purchase $= \dfrac{\text{Total markup \$}}{\text{Total retail \$}} \times 100$

or

Cumulative retail markup % on entire purchase $= \dfrac{\text{Total retail \$} - \text{Total cost \$}}{\text{Total retail \$}} \times 100$

Retail

Retail \$ = Cost \$ + Markup \$

Retail % = Cost % + Markup %

Retail \$ $= \dfrac{\text{Cost \$}}{\text{Cost \%}}$

or

Retail \$ $= \dfrac{\text{Cost \$}}{(100\% - \text{Markup \%})}$

Sell Through Percentage

Sell through % $= \dfrac{\text{Units sold in a week (Sunday–Saturday)}}{\text{Beginning units on hand for a week (Sunday)}} \times 100$

Weeks of Supply

Weeks of supply $= \dfrac{\text{Beginning units on hand for a week (Sunday)}}{\text{Units sold in that week (Sunday–Saturday)}}$

Every business aims to yield the largest possible total profit. One way a retail buyer attempts to secure maximum profits is through the skillful pricing of goods offered for sale. Price is a strong motivation in consumer buying habits and can be a competitive advantage for a retailer in today's challenging environment. It is very frequently the only way to attract customer patronage when merchandise assortments are comparable, if not identical. A buyer must consider salability, consumer demand, and history of what that item sold for previously when determining a pricing strategy. Because many factors influence pricing, it can be considered an art as well as a science.

In large industrial organizations, the actual pricing decisions are generally the responsibility of management. In large retail stores, the actual pricing of merchandise is determined by individual departmental buyers or a comparable person designated by the particular organizational structure. Top management, however, does formulate the basic price policies of the store, such as the implementation of a policy of price matching on all items. Although the retailer establishes the price of individual items as they are offered for sale, ultimately the total of all purchases must realize maximum gross margin and profits. In the final analysis, the volume of sales as an aggregate figure must be great enough not only to cover the costs of goods sold but also to provide a profit. Pricing, therefore, is an integral part of merchandising that requires training and skill.

2.1 RETAIL PRICING AND PRICING STRATEGIES

Pricing refers to **price lining**, which is the practice of predetermining the retail prices at which an assortment of merchandise will be carried. A retail buyer selects and offers to the consumer a merchandise assortment at a specific price point, or pricing strategy of **price lines**, such as $15, $20, and so on.

THE STRUCTURING OF PRICE LINES

In retailing, the different channels of distribution will set different pricing strategies. Differences exist between how department stores, "store is the brand"/specialty stores, mass market stores, fast fashion stores, and off-price retailers price the merchandise that is being sold to the consumer. Pricing will be determined by the retail format, the store's image, and the gross margin and profit goals that need to be met. Different types of retailers have different markup, gross margin, and profit goals that need to be attained, and the actual price product is sold at impacts the bottom line. A buyer creates a stock assortment by considering what vendors and private labels are carried and the depth of assortment offered at the various price points. The number of price lines, and those particular price lines in the assortments, can help reflect the desired character that management wishes to project. The emphasis of stock by price lines depends on the composition of the consumer segment that management wishes to attract. Pricing strategies that retailers use include:

Good/Better/Best

EDLP/EDVP (Everyday Low Price/Everyday Value Price)

High/Low

Price Zones: High Volume/Medium Volume/Low Volume

In terms of a good/better/best strategy, retailers can have brand name and private label merchandise in the same department or classification. Private labels will usually be the opening or good price point, priced lower than the brand names in the department, which are the better or best priced merchandise. Private labels for a retailer have become a promotional vehicle to attract customers' attention and bring them into the store. The missy sportswear department may sell T-shirts for $20.00–$50.00, which is the **price range** for that classification. Most customers generally prefer to concentrate their purchases either at one price line or at several that are relatively close to one another.

Everyday low price (EDLP) or **everyday value price (EDVP)** is primarily used by mass market retailers to provide "the value" to the customer. Department stores have recently begun to implement this strategy on select key item styles in selected departments. These products may have a different pricing ending ($49.98 vs. $50.00) and may be excluded from markdowns and coupons.

Figure 3. Price Line Structure Promotional Chart

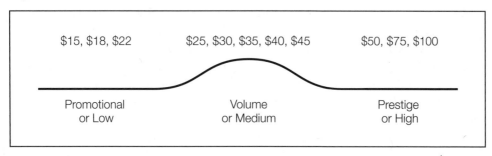

High/low pricing strategies are being used by most retailers. Prices are established at the high end and then promoted with a lower price to entice the customer to buy. Retailers use this as a tool for private labels as well as brands, but brands control when their product is to be marked down. A retailer may, for example, establish a pair of denim jeans to retail at an initial price of $69.00, but then promote the jeans to $49.99.

Price zone refers to a series of pricing strategies that are likely to appeal to one group of the store's customers. When more than two price lines are stocked, a price zone situation exists. The price zones can be referred to as **volume price zone** (medium volume), **promotional price zone** (low volume), and **prestige price zone** (high volume). Figure 3 illustrates three possible price zones for a price range from $15 to $100.

In general, the promotional price zone refers to the lower priced product lines carried and can be key item basic oriented. These items may be available at multiple retailers, and the best price the retailer prices the merchandise for may be the competitive advantage for that retailer. The medium volume price zone is the middle price lines, where a majority of sales occur; these are usually fashion basics with a wide customer appeal. The prestige price zone refers to the highest price lines carried in a department, which "tone up" the assortment. These are the most fashion-oriented items and can be lower in volume of sales. This distribution curve typically occurs within a price range, regardless of the price lines.

In economics, the central idea is use, which is closely associated with the idea of choice and value. Without going into the realm of the psychology of the concept, it is easy to understand that before anything is consumed, somebody must choose to use it. The choices made determine the relative value. Price reflects these uses and choices. Some of the influences on the pricing strategies within the merchandising framework are store type and policy—for example, department stores versus "off-price" stores, and the choice of fashion versus staple goods in addition to customer demand as it relates to the supply-demand theory and competition.

The mathematical skill of the buyer helps to produce an assortment balanced in variety, breadth, and depth by retail price lines, while negotiating the best possible cost price assists in maximizing markup. The increase in markup will assist in covering any markdowns taken and meeting gross margin and profit goals. The success of optimizing the sale of merchandise depends on sound pricing and repricing principles. It is one of the customer selection factors that affects the ultimate sale or rejection of merchandise. Although pricing goods for resale is the sole responsibility of the buyer, divisional merchandise managers will monitor the amount of markdowns taken in order to ensure that the overall gross margin and profit goals are achieved. The policies used to price merchandise throughout the organization can also reflect the store image that is chosen to lure the appropriate customer to the "right" store. Retailers who project a prestigious image featuring high-quality merchandise and exclusivity will focus on prestige high-priced lines. Competitive pricing will be used by some when they concentrate on easily identifiable brand goods and want to offer comparable merchandise; discount or off-price retailers will price merchandise at a discounted or lower price than the manufacturers' suggested retail price in order to provide the consumer with additional savings. However, all retailers on occasion may offer merchandise at lower prices than normal for promotional purposes.

SETTING INDIVIDUAL RETAIL PRICES AND/OR PRICE LINES

The pricing of individual items and the establishment of price lines also require experience and skill. When pricing merchandise as it is bought, a buyer must always consider its salability in terms of its retail price, remembering that the aggregate of all prices must be high enough to cover merchandise costs, operating expenses, a fair profit return, possible reductions, shortages, and discounts to employees. Variations in pricing occur because there are some noncontrollable factors that influence pricing decisions, such as the volatility of ready-to-wear. The basic factors influencing the setting of the retail price that a buyer must consider in pricing are:

- Wholesale costs.

- Competition.

- Price maintenance policies of manufacturers, such as "suggested" retail prices.

- Markdown history.

- Handling and selling costs.

- Store policies, such as off-price policy.

- Nature of the goods, such as markdown risk in fashion goods.

- Correlation among departments.

- Supply and demand factors.

- Gross margin and profitability goals.

ADVANTAGES OF PRICE LINING STRATEGY

The practice of offering merchandise for sale at a limited number of predetermined price points creates several merchandising problems, but the practice is prevalent because the advantages are numerous and significant. The advantages of developing a pricing strategy is that it:

- Simplifies customer choice, which facilitates selling.

- Enables the store to offer wide assortments at best-selling prices.

- Focuses promotions and advertising.

- Allows buyers to negotiate quantity discounts and better wholesale billed costs.

- Reduces the size of stock, resulting in more favorable stock turnover and decreased markdowns.

- Simplifies stock control.

- Decreases marking costs.

- Provides a basis for stock-sales control of customer preferences by price.

PRICE LINE REPORTS

Reports by price line make possible an analysis of an entire department's sales trends. The control over planning and purchasing a stock that reflects customer demand is improved by knowledge of net sales. The information regarding stock-on-hand, outstanding orders, receipts, transfers, and markdowns, as well as the stock-sales ratio for each group, aids present and future buying decisions.

Figure 4 shows a typical report of price line by classification and presents a complete selling history by dollars and units of merchandise by classifications or groupings. Only two price lines are included here due to space. The practice problem following this section shows the value and application of this report analysis.

THE RELATIONSHIP OF THE BASIC PRICING FACTORS

Merchandising, or the act of buying and selling, is performed by the retailer, who selects and buys merchandise that is offered for resale to the consumer. To make a profit, the retail merchandiser must set the proper price on the merchandise. Although the profitable pricing of selected individual items cannot always be done by applying a mathematical formula, the three basic elements involved in the pricing of all goods are the cost of the merchandise, the **retail price**, and the difference in value between them, which is referred to as **markup (MU)**. The cost of goods is related to what was discussed in Chapter 1. Markup is the amount that is added to the cost price of merchandise to arrive at a retail price. This amount must be large

Figure 4. Price Line Report by Classification

(1) Code No.	(2) Code Description	(3) Store	(4a) Net Sales Units This Week Ending 02/07	(4b) One Week Ago Ending 01/31	(4c) 2 Weeks Ago Ending 01/24	(4d) Last 4 Weeks Ending 01/10	(4e) Season to Date 02/07	(5) On Hand Units	(6) On Order Units	(7a) MTD Receiving	(7b) MTD Transfer	(7c) Markdown $	(7c) Markdown %	(7d) Net Sales $	(7d) Net Sales %	(7e) Inventory $	(7e) Stock Sales Ratio	(7f) Open Order	(7g) Inventory + On Order	Code No.
96	JEANS																			96
	$15.01 – $20.00	01					48	51	120											
		05					34	15	84											
		08					31	13	48											
		10					13	1	48											
		14					26	24	48											
		15					25	25	60											
	TOTAL UNITS						177	129	408											
96	TOTAL DOLLARS						3142	2310	6528											
96	JEANS																			96
	$20.01 – $29.00	01	4	1		5	5	5	5–											
		05	3			3	3	3	3–											
		08	2	1		3	3	3	3–											
		10	4	1		5	5	5	5–											
		14	2	1		3	3	3	3–											
		15	1	3		4	4	4	4–											
	TOTAL UNITS		16	7		23	23	23	23–											
96	TOTAL DOLLARS		464	203		667	667	667	667–											
96	JEANS																			96
	PRICE LINE–ALL	01	6	3	1	11	391	199	120					1	30	28	20	19	47	
		05	3		3	8	325	66	84					1	19	8	9	13	21	
		08	2	5	1	8	259	111	48					1	12	14	24	8	21	
		10	4	2	3	12	188	14	48					1	25	1	1	8	9	
		14		2	6	9	238	100	48						7	14	41	8	21	
		15	2	4	1	11	285	76	60						7	11	32	10	20	
	TOTAL UNITS		17	16	15	59	1686	566	408											
96	TOTAL DOLLARS		468	320	188	1099	23005	7656	6528					5	100	75	16	65	140	
96	CLASS TOTALS																			90
	PRICE LINE–ALL	01	108	154	302	884	7673	2394	1192					11	28	264	24	140	404	
		05	67	131	93	362	3475	1636	958	16				8	20	172	22	109	281	
		08	30	121	67	258	3054	1136	906					3	7	112	41	107	219	
		10	65	118	65	317	2680	1072	708	12				7	18	107	15	79	186	
		14	49	56	72	225	2609	1162	796					5	12	114	24	91	205	
		15	69	92	86	327	3610	1319	792	14				6	16	135	22	87	222	
	TOTAL UNITS		388	672	685	2373	23101	8719	5352	42										
90	TOTAL DOLLARS		3965	6019	5385	20605	239725	84680	77191	42				40	100	905	23	612	1516	
99	INVALID CODES																			99
	PRICE LINE–ALL	01		1	1	1	3	52	530	29						62–		80	18	
		05	1–	1–	2	3–	33–	84	378			13				5–	62	58	53	
		08			1–		31–	35	378									58	59	
		10		3		4	20–	53	378			24					2	58	58	
		14	1–	1–	1–	3–	84	70–	378			63				10–	25	58	48	
		15			1–	2	19–	29	378							7–		58	51	
	TOTAL UNITS		2–	1–		2	16–	183	2420											
99	TOTAL DOLLARS		62–	10–	37–	330–	4875–	3751	37204	29	638–			1–	100	84–	133	372	288	

1 = Code Number: Designates code within a classification. Example: Code 96.

2 = Code Description: Description of codes separated by price lines. Example: Jeans are separated as $15.01–$20.00. Totals include:

  a = By Code: Example: Under STD (season-to-date) for all price lines in the code both by units and dollars, 1,686 total units, $23,005 total dollars.

  b = By Classification: Example: Under STD (season-to-date), all codes and all price lines, both in units and dollars, 23,101 total units, $239,725 total dollars.

  c = By Department: All classifications, codes, and price lines both in units and dollars. (Not shown.)

3 = Store: Designates by store, each store. Example: 01.

4 = Net Sales Units: Permits analysis of unit sales. This category is divided into the following sections:

  a = This Week Ending: Net units sold for the week ending indicated. Example: 02/07.

  b = One Week Ago Ending: Net units sold for the week previous to the date of this report. Example: 01/31.

  c = Two Weeks Ago Ending: Shows the net sales for the week, two weeks previous to the date of this report. Example: 01/24.

  d = Last Four Weeks Ending: An accumulated statistic of net units sold over the total last four weeks. Example: 01/10.

  e = Season to Date: A cumulative statistic of units and/or dollars from the beginning of the season's accounting period to present date. Example: 02/07.

5 = On-Hand Units: Net units on hand as of the date of the report. Example: Code 96, Store 01—51 units.

6 = On-Order Units: Numbers that are shown are obtained from an order file of the purchase order. Example: Store 01—Jeans $15.01–$20—120 units.

7 = Dollars to the Nearest Hundred: Financial figures that reflect the actual value of the indicated transactions. This category is divided into the following sections:

  a = MTD Receiving: Net receipt to inventory, month-to-date.

  b = MTD Transfers: Cumulative transfers between stores during the current month.

  c = MTD Markdown: Cumulative markdowns processed for the current month in both dollars and percentages.

  d = MTD Net Sales: Cumulative dollar sales for the current month, by price line for each store, plus the percentage of the total company's business equaling 100% for each total.

  e = Inventory: The stock-sales ratio is calculated by Stock-sales ratio = Current dollar inventory ÷ Net sales previous week. This can be looked on as "weeks supply." Example: 20 stock-sales ratio means if a particular price line continues to sell at the rate of last week's sales and nothing new is received, it will sell out in 20 weeks.

  f = Open Order: Dollar value of the outstanding orders.

  g = Inventory and On Order: Total liability calculated by adding the on-hand to the on-order figures.

enough to cover the cost of the merchandise; the expenses incurred to sell it; and the markdowns, shortages, and employee discounts, which reduce the value of total purchases as well as the gross margin/profit. Finally, the price must also generate profit for the retailer. The aim of proper pricing can be expressed by the following:

$$
\left.
\begin{array}{l}
\text{Cost of goods} \\
+ \quad \text{Markup} \\
= \quad \text{Retail price}
\end{array}
\right\}
\quad
\begin{array}{l}
\text{Expenses, gross margin/profit,} \\
\\
\text{markdowns, shortages, and employee discounts}
\end{array}
$$

If one knows any two of the basic pricing factors (cost of goods and markup), the third (retail price) can be calculated both in dollar amounts and/or in percentage relationships. The following formulas show the relationship, in dollars, of the three basic pricing elements.

Calculating Retail When Cost and Dollar Markup Are Known

Retail $ = Cost $ + Markup $ CONCEPT

A retailer buys a crop top for $10 cost and has a markup of $15. What is the retail price?   PROBLEM

Cost $	=	$10
+ Markup $	= +	15
Retail $	=	$25

SOLUTION

Calculating Dollar Markup When Retail and Cost Are Known

Markup $ = Retail $ – Cost $ CONCEPT

A retailer buys a crop top for $10 cost and decides to price it for $25. What is the dollar markup on this item?   PROBLEM

Retail $	=	$25
– Cost $	= –	10
Markup $	=	$15

SOLUTION

Calculating Cost When Retail and Dollar Markup Are Known

CONCEPT	Cost \$ = Retail \$ – Markup \$
PROBLEM	What is the cost of an item that retails for \$25 and has a dollar markup of \$15?

SOLUTION

$$
\begin{array}{rcr}
\text{Retail \$} & = & \$25 \\
- \quad \text{Markup \$} & = & - \quad 15 \\
\hline
\textbf{Cost \$} & = & \$10
\end{array}
$$

Although retailers pay for and sell merchandise in dollars, knowing the relationship of the three basic pricing elements (i.e., retail, cost, markup) in both percentages and dollars is useful to the merchandiser. Frequently, the retailer thinks in terms of dollars only for the retail price, and this will vary by the different type of retailer. For example, a department store may sell T-shirts at \$29.00, an off-price retailer could sell them for \$14.99, and a fast fashion retailer may sell the T-shirt for \$19.90. Cost prices may vary between vendors, and that is where a buyer needs to be cognizant of the markup percentage goals the retailer needs to achieve. In determining the dollar cost of an article to be purchased, a buyer must balance the retail price the customer is willing to pay with the particular markup percentage required by management.

Calculating Initial or Individual Markup Percentages When Dollar Cost and Retail Are Known

While it is important to understand how to calculate markup dollars, most buyers see the markup percentage on their retail reports and purchase orders. Therefore, to solve for the markup percentage for an item or the initial markup for an item, a buyer will calculate the individual or initial markup (IMU) percentage.

CONCEPT

$$
\text{Markup \%} = \frac{\text{Markup \$}}{\text{Retail \$}} \times 100
$$

$$
\text{Markup \%} = \frac{\text{Retail \$} - \text{Cost \$}}{\text{Retail \$}} \times 100
$$

PROBLEM

What is the markup percentage of a crop top that costs \$10 and retails for \$25?

SOLUTION

$$
\text{Markup \%} = \$15 \text{ Markup} \quad \text{or} \quad (\$25 \text{ Retail} - \$10 \text{ Cost})
$$

$$
= \frac{\$15 \text{ Markup}}{\$25 \text{ Retail}} \times 100
$$

$$
\textbf{Markup \%} = 60.0\%
$$

Price Line Report Practice Problem

1. Answer the following questions based on the data in Figure 4.

    a. What is the price line with Code 96 that generates the majority unit and dollar sales?

    b. Which store has the best performance for Class Totals, Code 96? How many units were sold STD (season-to-date)?

    c. Which two stores contributed 49% of the MTD (month-to-date) sale in Code 96 Jeans?

    d. In the Jeans $15.01–$20.00 price lines, which store requires a "rush" delivery of its order so that it can stay "in business" with this price line in this classification? How many units does this store have on hand?

e. Consider the Inventory and On-Order figures for 96 Class Totals—Price Line—All. Which two stores require adjustments to an order because of the relation between their stock-sales and their MTD net sales percentage? What adjustments should be made?

f. For each store, calculate the percentage increase or decrease in sales from the previous week to the current week. Which store has shown the largest increase?

g. What reasons might explain a decline in sales from one week to the next?

h. Since January 24, which stores show a continuous decline in sales of this merchandise classification?

i. Why must changes be made in merchandising strategies at these stores?

j. What changes in merchandising strategies would you suggest?

Retail Pricing Practice Problems

Solving for Retail Price

2. A merchant buys a sweatshirt for $15 and has a dollar markup of $14.95. What is the retail price?

3. If the men's buyer purchases pants at a cost of $32.00 and has a markup of $35.00, what will be the retail price for each pair of pants?

4. The girl's buyer purchases leggings at a cost price of $4.80 and the markup is $7.20. What is the retail price for the leggings?

5. If the electronics buyer purchases televisions at a cost price of $375.00 and the markup is $224.99, what is the retail price for the televisions?

Solving for Cost Price

6. What is the cost of a set of golf clubs that retails for $250 and has a markup of $157?

7. The missy sweater buyer retails cotton sweaters for $49.99, and the markup is $29.24. What is the cost price of each sweater?

8. A pair of denim jeans retails for $199.00, and the markup is $107.50. What is the cost price?

9. A man's belt retails for $59.00, and the markup is $37.00. What is the cost price?

Solving for Markup Dollars and Markup Percentage

10. The toddlers' department buyer purchases coats that cost $30 each and prices them at $65 each. What is the dollar markup on this item?

11. Calculate the markup dollars for a tie if the cost is $23.60 and the manufacturer's suggested retail price is $59.00.

12. What is the markup percentage on a jacket that costs $49.75 and retails for $125?

13. If a necklace retails for $36.00 and the cost is $10.80, what is the markup in dollars and percentage at retail for the necklace?

14. If a private label missy T-shirt retails for $19.99 and the cost is $7.20, what is the markup for the T-shirt in both dollars and percentage at retail?

15. If a pair of brand name leather boots has a retail price of $149.00 and the cost is $70.00, what is the markup for the boots in both dollars and percentage at retail?

2.2 Basic Markup Equations Used in Buying Decisions

Markup, as defined in this text, applies to an individual item, a group of equations and their relationship to other pricing factors of items, or entire merchandise stock of a department or a store, and it can be expressed in either dollars or percentages. For comparison and analysis, it is the markup percentage (rather than the dollar amount) that is significant. To understand the effect of markup on buying decisions, it helps to know the basic markup equations.

BASIC MARKUP PERCENTAGE EQUATIONS

Markup percentages can be computed as a percentage of the retail or cost price. Because the retail method of inventory is prevalent in large stores, it is more common to calculate the markup percentage on the retail price. The cost method of calculating markup may still be used by some retailers.

Calculating Markup Percentage on Retail Using the Retail Method of Inventory

CONCEPT

$$\text{Markup \% on retail} = \frac{\text{Markup \$}}{\text{Retail \$}} \times 100$$

PROBLEM

What is the markup percentage on an item when the markup is $15 and the retail is $25?

SOLUTION

$$\text{Markup \% on retail} = \frac{\$15 \text{ Markup}}{\$25 \text{ Retail}} \times 100$$

$$= 60.0\%$$

Calculating Markup Percentage on Cost

CONCEPT

$$\text{Markup \% on cost} = \frac{\text{Markup \$}}{\text{Cost \$}} \times 100$$

PROBLEM

What is the markup percentage on cost when the markup is $15 and the cost is $10?

Markup % on cost $\quad = \quad \dfrac{\$15 \text{ Markup}}{\$10 \text{ Cost}} \quad \times \quad 100$

$\qquad\qquad\qquad = \quad 150\%$

(Note: Markup percentage calculated on cost is higher than markup percentage calculated on retail.)

Generally, the retail calculation of markup is more acceptable because retailers also figure expenses and profits as a percentage of retail sales. Thus, they tend to consider price lines, stocks, and customer demands in retail values when making plans, and the calculation of markup on retail price is consistent with this approach. In this book, discussions and problems on markup will use the retail basis for all further calculations.

The retailer faces numerous purchase-planning and merchandise-pricing problems when buying goods for resale. To achieve maximum profits, the same estimated initial (original) markup percentage is not applied to all purchases. The buyer is given a markup plan but realizes that unexpected situations may cause deviations, as goods bought to sell to the consumer are selected from different manufacturers. Therefore, manipulation of the markup and sales volume will ultimately provide the largest possible dollar profit. Calculations of the various buying and pricing situations that may occur in merchandising are expressed in formulas that must be understood by all retail merchandisers.

Markup plans vary by retail channel of distribution and product classifications. Mass market stores may work on a lower markup, as their sales volume compensates for this, allowing them to maintain their gross margin goals. Private label merchandise generally has a higher markup, as the branded name costs are eliminated. Apparel and fashion accessories generally have a higher markup, whereas furniture, appliances, and electronics have a lower markup.

Keystone markup, a term used by some entrepreneurial retailers, is 50% markup based on the retail price. Stated another way, keystone markup would be doubling the cost. For department and specialty stores, using keystone markup may not be a profitable model based on the amount of markdowns taken to drive sales. If retailers use a keystone markup as their planned markup and take 50% markdowns, there would be no markup and/or profit left. For example, a buyer buys a sweater for $50 cost and retails it for $100. If the sweater does not sell (for various reasons to be discussed in markdowns) at the original retail price, and the buyer now sells the sweater at 50% off, then the retailer will be selling at $50, which is the cost price, resulting in zero markup. The buyer will need to negotiate a better cost price with the manufacturer or get assistance with the markdown to secure any gross margin dollars necessary.

Retail $	$100	Sale retail $	$50
– Cost $	$50	– Cost $	$50
= Markup $	$50	= Markup $	0
Markup %	$\frac{\$50}{\$100} \times 100 = 50\%$		

Calculating Cost and Retail Prices When Markup Percentage Is Known

One of the primary functions of a buyer's job is to price product. The buyer is provided with his or her departmental or classification markup percentage plans. From history, the buyer will know what price the merchandise will sell for and can determine the retail price of product. Therefore, if the buyer knows the retail price for which the product will sell and the markup percentage is known, the buyer can calculate the maximum cost that can be paid for the product. He or she can then negotiate with vendors to secure the best possible cost price. In addition, if the buyer knows the markup percentage plan and a vendor has provided the cost prices, the buyer can then calculate the retail selling price.

To fully understand the relationship among the three basic elements in terms of percentages, it should be noted that the retail of the basic equation is always 100%, and the dollar cost and markup can be converted from dollars to percentage by expressing each as a part of the retail.

Therefore, you can state the formula as:

CONCEPT

MU % = Retail % – Cost %

MU % = 100% – Cost %

Cost % = 100% – MU % (also known as the **cost complement**)

PROBLEM

If the retail price for a crop top is $25.00, the markup dollars are $15.00, and the markup percentage is 60.0%, what are the cost dollars and percentage?

SOLUTION

	Dollars	Percentages
Retail	$25.00	100.0%
– Markup	– $15.00	– 60.0%
= Cost =	$10.00	40.0%

The markup formulas that buyers use day in and day out are presented next.

Solving for Retail Price

CONCEPT

$$\text{Retail \$} = \frac{\text{Cost \$}}{\text{Cost \%}}$$

$$\text{Retail \$} = \frac{\text{Cost \$}}{100\% - \text{MU \%}}$$

PROBLEM

If a vendor charges the buyer $10.00 for a crop top and the markup plan is 60.0%, at what price will the buyer retail the crop top?

SOLUTION

$$\text{Retail \$} = \frac{\text{Cost \$}}{\text{Cost \%}}$$

$$\text{Retail \$} = \frac{\$10.00}{100\% - 60.0\%} = \frac{\$10.00}{40.0\%}$$

$$\text{Retail \$} = \$25.00$$

Solving for Cost Price

PROBLEM

A buyer needs to sell a crop top at $25.00 retail and the planned markup percentage is 60.0%. What is the maximum cost price that the buyer can buy the crop top from a vendor for?

SOLUTION

Cost $ = Retail $ × Cost %

Cost $ = $25.00 × (100% − 60.0%)

Cost $ = $25.00 × 40%

   = $10.00

Individual or initial markup, as defined in this text, applies to an individual item or the initial price of an item. **Cumulative markup** is the markup for a group of items or the entire merchandise stock of a department or a store. Both can be expressed in either dollars or percentages. For comparison and analysis, it is the markup percentage (rather than the dollar amount) that is significant. To understand the effect of markup on buying decisions, it helps to know the basic markup equations and their relationship to other pricing factors.

Cumulative Markup

When the individual cost and the individual retail do not change, but the number of purchased pieces varies, the markup percentage is the same whether it is calculated for one piece or for the entire quantity purchased. The following calculations illustrate this principle.

PROBLEM

What is the markup percentage on a purchase of 12 pieces that cost $5.70 each and are retailed at $15.00 each?

SOLUTION

Individual retail	=	$15.00
Individual cost	=	− 5.70
Markup	=	$9.30
Markup %	=	$\dfrac{\$9.30 \text{ Markup}}{\$15.00 \text{ Retail}} \times 100$
Retail markup % **on individual item**	=	62.0%

While:

SOLUTION:
Spreadsheet format

	Unit retail	Volume	Total retail
Retail	$15.00	12	$180.00
Cost	$5.70	12	$68.40
Markup $ on total			$111.60
Retail markup %			62.0%

SOLUTION:
Arithmetic format

Total retail	=	$180.00	(12 pieces × $15.00)
− Total cost	=	− 68.40	(12 pieces × $5.70)
Markup $ on entire purchase	=	$111.60	
Markup %	=	$\dfrac{\$111.60 \text{ Markup}}{\$180.00 \text{ Retail}} \times 100$	
Retail markup % on entire purchase	=	62.0%	

As a buyer evaluates a particular item, the history of what that item or a similar item sold for as well as the markup percentage on the individual piece will generally be used to determine its salability. Once an order is placed, however, the markup percentage will be calculated on the basis of the entire quantity to be purchased. Buyers do not just buy one style at the same cost and same retail. The department(s) or categories that they are responsible for contain many styles that are purchased at different costs and will sell at different retail prices. They may also buy the same merchandise category from different vendors at different costs. Therefore, the total markup for all items purchased must be calculated, that is the cumulative markup (CMU) percentage.

Calculating Markup Percentage on a Group of Items with Varying Costs or Retail Prices (i.e., Order Writing)

In the final analysis, purchases are evaluated on an overall basis. The following variations on markup formulas illustrate this concept in that the markup percentage is calculated on the total amounts ordered, rather than on an individual basis, so that the total purchase can be evaluated.

CONCEPT

$$\text{Cumulative markup \% on entire purchase} = \frac{\text{Total markup \$}}{\text{Total retail \$}} \times 100$$

or

$$\text{Cumulative markup \% on entire purchase} = \frac{\text{Total retail \$} - \text{Total cost \$}}{\text{Total retail \$}} \times 100$$

Calculating Markup Percentage When Writing Orders Placed for a Variety of Items and Prices

Currently, some stores use computer-generated purchase-order systems and automated replenishment systems. Although the mechanics of order writing can vary, determining the markup percentage on the entire purchase always requires a calculation of the total cost and total retail to determine the overall percentage on the purchase.

$$\text{Total retail \$} = \text{\# Units purchased} \times \text{Retail price \$ per unit}$$

$$\text{Total cost \$} = \text{\# Units purchased} \times \text{Cost price \$ per unit}$$

A buyer is placing an order for 100 pieces of a cable knit sweater at a cost of $20.00 that will retail for $49.00 and 200 pieces of a lace-trimmed V-neck sweater at a cost of $22.00 that will retail for $59.00. What is the cumulative markup percentage on this entire purchase?

PROBLEM

	Unit retail	Units purchased	Total retail	Unit cost	Units purchased	Total cost	Markup $	Markup %
Cable knit sweater	$49.00	100	$4,900.00	$20.00	100	$2,000.00		
Lace-trimmed V-neck sweater	$59.00	200	$11,800.00	$22.00	200	$4,400.00		
Total			$16,700.00			$6,400.00	$10,300.00	61.68%/61.7%

Total retail

 100 Cable knit sweaters × $49.00   = $4,900.00

 200 Lace-trimmed V-neck sweaters × $59.00   =   + $11,800.00

 Total retail $16,700.00 $16,700.00

– Total cost

 100 Cable knit sweaters × $20.00   = $2,000.00

 200 Lace-trimmed V-neck sweaters × $22.00 =   + $4,400.00

Total cost $6,400.00 $ 6,400.00

Markup $ on entire purchase   = $10,300.00

Markup %   = $$\frac{\$10{,}300 \text{ Total markup}}{\$16{,}700 \text{ Total retail}} \times 100$$

Retail markup % on entire purchase   =   61.68%/61.7%

Calculating Markup Percentage with Varying Retail Prices of Either a Classification or a Group That Has the Same Cost

A buyer bought 150 handbags that cost $22.50 each. The buyer then retailed satchels, 50 pieces, for $60 each, hobos, 75 pieces, for $65 each, and the balance, totes, for $70 each. What is the markup percentage on this purchase?

	Unit retail	Units purchased	Total retail	Unit cost	Total cost	Markup $	Markup %
Satchels	$60.00	50	$3,000.00	$22.50	$1,125.00	$1,875.00	62.5%
Hobos	$65.00	75	$4,875.00	$22.50	$1,687.50	$3,187.50	65.38%/65.4%
Totes	$70.00	25	$1,750.00	$22.50	$562.50	$1,187.50	67.86%/67.9%
Total		150	$9,625.00		$3,375.00	$6,250.00	64.94%/64.9%

SOLUTION:
Spreadsheet format

Units		Unit retail		Total retail
Satchels, 50 pieces ×		$60	=	$3,000
Hobos, 75 pieces ×		$65	=	$4,875
Totes, 25 pieces ×		$70	=	+ $1,750
Total retail				$9,625 $9,625
– Total cost				
150 pieces ×		$22.50	=	$3,375
Total cost				– $3,375
Markup $ on entire purchase			=	$6,250

SOLUTION:
Arithmetic format

Markup % $= \dfrac{\$6,250 \text{ Total markup}}{\$9,625 \text{ Total retail}} \times 100$

Retail markup % on entire purchase = 64.94%/64.9%

Calculating Markup Percentage on Merchandise with Varying Costs at the Same Retail Price

A jewelry buyer is buying a Mother's Day earring promotion that will retail for $24.99. The group consists of 1,000 pieces with the following costs:

Studs: 200 pieces at $7.50 cost

Hoops: 500 pieces at $6.00 cost

Drops: 300 pieces at $7.00 cost

What is the markup percentage on this group?

PROBLEM

SOLUTION:
Spreadsheet format

	Unit retail	Units purchased	Total retail	Unit cost	Total cost	Markup $	Markup %
Studs	$24.99	200	$4,998.00	$7.50	$1,500.00	$3,498.00	70.0%
Hoops	$24.99	500	$12,495.00	$6.00	$3,000.00	$9,495.00	76.0%
Drops	$24.99	300	$7,497.00	$7.00	$2,100.00	$5,397.00	72.0%
Total			$24,990.00		$6,600.00	$18,390.00	73.59%/73.6%

SOLUTION:
Arithmetic format

Total retail

1,000 pieces × $24.99   = $24,990

Total retail   = $24,990

– Total cost

200 pieces × $7.50   = $1,500

500 pieces × $6.00   = $3,000

300 pieces × $7.00   =   + $2,100

Total cost $6,600   – $6,600

Total markup $ on entire group   = $18,390

Markup %   = $\dfrac{\$18{,}390 \text{ Total markup}}{\$24{,}990 \text{ Total retail}} \times 100$

**Retail markup %
on entire purchase**   =   73.59%/73.6%

A way to double-check that the cumulative markup for the order is correct is that the end result has to be somewhere in the middle of the lowest and highest individual markup percentages. It will not be a direct average unless all factors (units, cost, and retail) are identical.

Cumulative Markup Applications

CONCEPT

Buyers are given a planned CMU % and a receipt plan for purchases that are based on retail value of inventory. Using versions of the total retail and total cost formulas, you can solve for an individual retail price and cost price for a specific buy.

PROBLEM

The handbag buyer wants to spend $24,000 at retail for May receipts. The departmental CMU % is 65.0%. The minimum number of handbags in each store is 400. Solve for the retail price per handbag and the cost price per handbag.

First, solve for the retail price of each handbag:

Total retail $ = # Units × Individual retail price $

$24,000 = 400 × Individual retail price $

$$\text{Individual retail price} = \frac{\$24,000}{400}$$

Individual retail price = $60.00

Second, solve for the cost price:

Cost $ = Retail $ × Cost %

Cost $ = $60.00 × (100% – 65.0%)

Cost $ = $60.00 × 35.0% = $21.00

When a buyer places an order for merchandise, the retail value may or may not be on the purchase order. Therefore, the total cost value of the order needs to be converted to a retail value because the budget is maintained based on retail value of inventory. If the buyer has already placed orders against his or her plan/budget (open-to-buy), the buyer can calculate the balance left to spend or see if he or she has overspent. If the balance is positive, there is money left to spend. If the balance is negative, the buyer has overbought.

A buyer has $100,000 at retail to spend at retail for a summer T-shirt promotion. The buyer has already spent $20,000 at cost. The planned MU % is 60.0%. Is there any money left for the buyer to spend, and if so, how much?

First, convert the cost spent to retail value:

$$\text{Retail } \$ = \frac{\text{Cost } \$}{\text{Cost } \%}$$

$$\text{Retail } \$ = \frac{\$20,000}{100\% - 60\%} = \frac{\$20,000}{40\%}$$

Retail $ spent = $50,000

Second, calculate the balance left to spend:

Retail plan/budget – Retail spent = Balance over/under

$100,000 – $50,000 = $50,000 left to spend

THE RELATIONSHIP OF THE BASIC PRICING FACTORS TO PROFIT

Retail stores buy and sell. All of the buying and selling activity is in terms of price. There is great interest in the relationship between the buying price and the selling price because the difference between these two largely determines profit. The size of this margin between the cost and the selling price, referred to as markup, not only has to include markdowns, shortages, expenses, and profit, but also affects the amount of gross margin achieved. Management generally plans a reasonable, realistic figure to meet this objective, but it must be controlled and monitored constantly, like "locking the barn before the horse is stolen."

Fundamentally, there are two elements in this scenario: the cost of the goods and the retail selling price of these goods. The cost of the merchandise bought can and is negotiated by the buyer. Therefore, in an intensely competitive retail climate, it is more important than ever to "buy right." It has been said that "merchandise well bought is half sold." National brands will have a set manufacturer's suggested retail price (MSRP) and will negotiate cost prices on a retailer-by-retailer basis. Private labels/brands are becoming more prevalent, and emphasis must be placed on a thorough and complete knowledge of domestic and foreign market conditions and offerings in order for the buyer to secure the best possible cost price. Achieving the markup goal is dependent on the buyer negotiating the lowest cost price from vendors. Negotiating a lower cost price will increase the markup percentage without having to raise the retail price. The retail price—governed by price lining principles, store policies, and so on—that is initially placed on merchandise offered for sale is the variable factor. The pricing of merchandise must be a consideration at the time of purchase, whether the merchandise is bought as an individual item or to build an assortment. Pricing will influence the purchase or rejection of merchandise by both the buyer and the consumer. In fashion goods versus staple goods, pricing will be further influenced by the risk factor of acceptability in addition to other pertinent considerations. The manipulation of selling prices (both initially and for markdowns) requires skill and experience for its impact on profit to be recognized. Any change from the initial retail price will automatically change the markup achieved; therefore, these changes, generally downward, must also be planned and controlled in order to achieve the gross margin necessary for a profitable operation.

Markup Practice Problems

16. Fill in the blank spaces for parts (a)–(g) in the following table.

	Cost $	Retail $	Markup $	Markup %
a.	$150.00	$349.99		
b.	$30.00/dzn		$4.00	
c.		$36.00	$21.00	
d.		$100.00		64.0%
e.	$18.20			72.0%
f.		$240.00		53.6%
g.	$90.00			55.0%

Calculate the cost price given the retail and the planned MU %:

17. A pair of sneakers will be ticketed with a retail price of $89.00 and the markup % is 54.0%. What is the cost price for the sneakers?

18. Calculate the cost price a specialty store buyer will pay for a pair of earrings with a suggested retail of $28.00 and a 67.5% markup.

19. What is the maximum cost a buyer can pay for a coat that will sell for $270.00 with a markup of 55.0%?

20. A buyer for an off-price retailer wants to sell one-piece swimsuits at a retail of $39.99. The planned markup is 60.0%. What is the cost price the buyer should negotiate for?

21. You are the jewelry buyer for a large mass market chain. For the Holiday season you are planning a boxed jewelry "Gifts to Go" promotion for $14.99. The markup for the promotion is planned at 39.0%. What is the maximum cost price that you will pay for the boxed jewelry?

22. A toy buyer planned a special sale of dolls to retail at $25 each. If the overall markup on the purchase was 46%, what was the cost per doll?

23. Given the following departmental markups and average retails per department, what is the maximum cost that the buyer can pay?

   a. Sneakers, 58.4% markup; Retail price $69.00.

   b. Men's ties, 61.7% markup; Retail price $39.00.

   c. Boy's apparel, 67.9% markup; Retail price $24.00.

Calculate the retail price given the cost and the planned MU %:

24. If a buyer purchases a 40-piece boxed set of dishes for $25.00 and the planned MU % is 50%, what will be the suggested retail for the dishes?

25. An eye shadow compact costs $20.40, and the markup is 40.0%. What is the retail price of the compact?

26. The men's tie buyer purchases ties at a cost of $7.20 each, and the markup is 64.0%. What is the retail price for each tie?

27. A buyer will purchase handbags at a cost of $37.75, and the planned MU % for the department is 62.0%. What is the minimum retail price for each handbag? What possible retail price for each handbag might be used if you were the buyer of a department store? An off-price retailer?

28. If the cost of a swimsuit is $26.50 and the MU % is 61.5%, what is the retail price for which you can sell the swimsuit? What pricing strategy should the store use if you are a fast fashion retailer?

29. If a graphic T-shirt costs $6.95 and the MU % is 53.4%, what is the retail price for the T-shirt? What would the pricing strategy be?

Cumulative Markup
Practice Problems

30. The coat buyer is buying 5,400 activewear jackets at $43.00 cost per piece. The jackets will retail at $109.00. What is the cumulative markup percentage for the buy?

31. A buyer purchased 50 assorted leather briefcases that cost $79.50 each and establishes retail prices based on the style as follows:

    - 25 zip-top briefcases to retail for $175 each.
    - 10 messengers to retail for $150 each.
    - 15 backpacks to retail for $125 each.

    Find the cumulative markup percentage on this purchase.

32. An off-price outerwear buyer negotiated a special purchase from a manufacturer who had availability on 1,500 pieces of different styles of raincoats at one low price of $25 each. The buyer decides to establish retail prices as follows for the different styles:

    - 500 units of ponchos to retail at $49.99 each.
    - 500 units of trench coats to retail at $54.99 each.
    - 500 units of anoraks to retail at $59.00 each.

    What markup percentage is realized on this purchase?

33. The handbag buyer is buying in an assortment of handbags for Mother's Day that will sell for $90.00 each. The buyer is buying 2,400 satchels that cost $27.00 each and 1,800 hobos that cost $31.00 each. What is the markup percentage for the handbag buy?

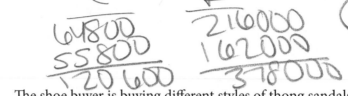

34. The shoe buyer is buying different styles of thong sandals that will retail for $49.00. The styles the buyer is going to purchase are 1,200 units of metallic-colored sandals that have a cost price of $21.50 each and 3,000 units of printed thong sandals that have a cost price of $18.00 each. What is the markup percentage for this buy?

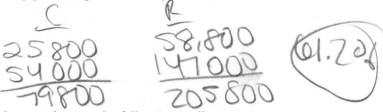

35. The pant buyer is buying the following twill pants:

Vendor A: 6,000 pants at $24.75 cost to retail at $54.00

Vendor B: 7,200 pants at $21.00 cost to retail at $49.00

   a. Calculate the IMU $ and IMU % for Vendor A.

   b. Calculate the IMU $ and IMU % for Vendor B.

   c. Calculate the CMU % for the total buy.

36. The infant's buyer is buying one-piece sleepers from different vendors to retail at $12.00. The buy is as follows:

Vendor A: 600 sleepers at a cost of $4.20

Vendor B: 480 sleepers at a cost of $5.30

    a. Calculate the IMU $ and IMU % for Vendor A.

    b. Calculate the IMU $ and IMU % for Vendor B.

    c. Calculate the CMU % for the total buy.

37. The sweater buyer is buying 12,000 cashmere crew neck and 8,000 V-neck sweaters at a cost of $31.50. The buyer plans to retail the sweaters as follows:

Crew neck to retail at $79.00

V-neck to retail at $89.00

    a. Calculate the IMU $ and IMU % for the crew neck.

    b. Calculate the IMU $ and IMU % for the V-neck.

    c. Calculate the CMU % for the total cashmere buy.

38. The activewear buyer is buying a new fashion group for a discount retail chain. The buy is as follows:

1,500 hoodies at $22.50 cost to retail at $59.99

1,800 pants at $17.75 cost to retail at $49.99

2,700 striped T-shirts at $10.25 cost to retail at $24.99

1,200 tank tops at $5.75 cost to retail at $14.99

    a. Calculate the CMU % for this order.

    b. If the buyer's markup plan for the month is 65.6%, what will the buyer need to do?

39. The jewelry buyer wants to spend $15,000 at retail. The department maintains a 56.7% markup. The buyer needs a minimum of 600 pairs of earrings to cover each branch with an adequate assortment.

   a. What should be the retail price per pair?

   b. What should be the cost per pair?

40. The home buyer has a budget of $60,000 for February receipts. The minimum amount of sheet sets in each store is 1,200. The departmental CMU % is 58.0%.

   a. What is the retail price per sheet set?

   b. What is the cost price that the buyer needs to pay for the sheet sets?

41. For a Fall pump promotion, the buyer wants to spend $419,940 at retail. The buyer needs to buy 6,000 pairs of shoes. If the planned MU % is 55.8%, find:

    a. The retail price per pair of shoes.

    b. The cost price per pair of shoes the buyer will need to pay.

42. The sportswear buyer wants to spend $84,000 at retail. Orders for $18,000, at cost, have already been placed. If the planned markup percentage to be achieved is 52.0%, how much, in dollars, does the buyer have left to spend at retail?

43. For a monthly T-shirt buy, you will be spending $22,560 at retail. Orders for $7,980 at cost have been placed. The planned MU % is 71.5%. What is left in retail dollars for you to place?

44. For a men's pants buy, you will be spending $300,000 at retail. Orders for $105,000 at cost have been placed. The planned MU % is 58.0%. What is left in retail dollars for you to place?

ADDITIONAL MARKUP

An **additional markup** is a type of price adjustment that raises the price of merchandise already in stock. It increases the original retail price placed on the merchandise. It is taken after, and in addition to, the original (initial) markup. Although it is not a common type of adjustment, a provision must be made when an upward change of the retail prices of existing inventories is necessary. For example, an upward change of wholesale costs, especially for basic product, might necessitate the immediate upward revision of retail prices on existing inventory.

MARKUP CANCELLATION

Markup cancellation is a downward price adjustment that offsets an original inflated markup to a markup that is more normal. It is used to adjust the markup on a purchase in accordance with the original intent and is not used to manipulate stock values. Currently, it is controlled by law, which dictates the time period allowed from receipt to reduction of the purchase, as well as the size of the markup resulting from this practice. It is justified when quoting "comparable value" prices used in promoting goods. For example, a resource offers a retailer gloves at $7, which is lower than the normal cost of $10. This item may be presently in stock and retailing for $22. During the permitted time, the gloves costing $7, which originally retailed at $22, are reduced to $14. This lowered price appears to the public as a markdown, yet results in a markup that is close to normal. The $8 difference between $22 and $14 is the markup cancellation.

2.3 REPRICING OF MERCHANDISE/ MARKDOWNS

The dynamic nature of merchandising makes the repricing of goods in retailing universal. Price adjustments are made primarily to decrease the original retail price placed on merchandise in order to increase sales and create demand for product. These changes in prices must be properly recorded to:

- Achieve an accurate book inventory figure used in the retail method of inventory.

- Plan initial (original) markup goals when pricing goods.

- Control and manage the amount received in an attempt to merchandise at a profit and meet the gross margin goals established.

The repricing of goods for sale is constant, the causes are numerous, and the skill required is considerable. It is rare that a retailer makes an upward adjustment to the retail price. The reasons to increase the selling price of product would be due to an increase in manufacturing costs for the product for the next season or a normal increase in price on a basic replenishment style. Often a buyer is forced to make a downward retail price change on a significant portion of sales. In a profit and loss statement, the downward differences frequently have a group heading of retail reductions that include:

- Markdowns—both point-of-sale and permanent.

- Coupons.

- Employee discounts.

Although all retail reductions have an impact on gross margin, they are, for the most part, considered a necessity. Their study is of major importance, for only with complete understanding of their use can the retailer turn them into a dynamic and advantageous merchandising tool.

MARKDOWNS

The most common and important type of price adjustment is technically called a **markdown (MD)**. It is the lowering or reducing of any retail price on one item or a group of items. For example, a sweater that was originally priced at $80 when it was received in the store may be reduced to $59.99 to drive sales. This price adjustment is called a markdown because the retail value of the merchandise is lowered. The difference between the new selling price ($59.99) and the former price ($80) is $20.01. The amount by which the retail value has been lowered is called the markdown and is the meaningful figure to the merchandiser. The buyer expresses markdowns as a percentage of net sales of all goods sold during a week, month, quarter, season, or year. Frequently, the merchandiser needs to calculate the markdown percentage that is necessary to sell a group of items. When this occurs, the markdown is still expressed as a percentage of the net sales figure.

Markdowns are an important tool in merchandising. They are recognized as a means of promoting and increasing sales volume, yet they have an impact on gross margin and profit and therefore must be controlled. Markdowns vary depending on the type of merchandise and conditions. In order to use them advantageously, there must be an analysis of the purpose of the markdown, the causes, the timing, and the repricing principles.

The Purpose of Markdowns

Markdowns are "a cure, not a curse." This necessary merchandising tool can be used to good advantage if the retailer realizes the objectives of markdowns. The major aims of price reductions are:

- To drive sales on a store, department, or class level.

- To stimulate the sale of merchandise to which customers are not responding satisfactorily.

- To attract customers to stores by offering "sales."

- To meet competitive prices/price matching.

- To free up open-to-buy money to bring in the new season's merchandise already on order and to purchase new merchandise that is selling.

- To create special "promotions" or sales (e.g., Mother's Day, Holiday sales).

- To clear fashion merchandise that has a short life cycle.

- To increase sales on merchandise not selling at an acceptable sell through rate.

- To drive traffic to the stores or website.

- For end-of-season clearances.

Buyers are given a markdown plan in both dollars and percentage. Buyers will have to project the amount of markdowns taken and the projected sales increase (build) they will achieve in order to be allowed to take the markdown. After the markdown is taken, they will need to compare the actual markdowns taken to the plan to see if the markdown achieved the desired results, an increase in sales.

Causes of Markdowns

By analyzing all the possible causes of markdowns, a merchandiser can make an effort to minimize them. The most common causes (not in order of importance) are:

- Buying errors, which include:
  - Overbuying in quantities.
  - Poor timing in ordering goods.
  - Receiving and accepting merchandise that has been shipped late.
- Pricing errors, which include:
  - Poor timing of markdowns.
  - Setting the initial price too high.
  - Not being competitive in price for same goods.
  - Not taking timely markdowns.
  - Calculated risks of carrying "prestige" merchandise.
  - Unbalanced buying, or accepting of merchandise that is sized contrary to order.
- Selling errors, which include:
  - Poor stock keeping.
  - Failure to display merchandise properly or advantageously.
  - Uninformed salespeople.
- Special sales from stock, which include:
  - Off-price promotions.
  - Multiple sales (e.g., buy one, get one for 50% off).
  - Broken assortments. This is product that has been on the selling floor for a substantial period of time and selected styles/sizes/colors, possibly 1–2 pieces, are remaining.
  - Necessary price adjustments.
  - Remainders from special sales.

Timing of Markdowns

Your first markdown is your least costly and most profitable; it needs to be a smart markdown. One of the reasons for this is that a buyer should have sufficient markup to cover costs and expenses. Timely in-season markdowns present customers with a good assortment of products to choose from. Retailers and buyers need customers to buy more than one item when they are shopping. If the markdowns are taken in season, "wear now," the customer can find that matching top and bottom or two to three tops in different colors. In-season markdowns will reduce end-of-season clearance markdowns, which are more costly. Accurate timing of markdowns can help reduce the amount of the markdown needed to sell the merchandise. It is suggested that merchandise be analyzed and reduced when:

- Merchandise becomes "slow selling."

- Customer demand is sufficient to sell the merchandise with a minimum price reduction.

- Consumer interest in the merchandise in stock diminishes because of the arrival of a new fashion or product of a lower price elsewhere.

The Amount of Markdown

Good judgment is required to determine the price at which items can be cleared quickly. The pricing of goods is a major factor in the control of markdowns. It is difficult to generalize on the amount of the markdown to be taken because the "right" price depends on:

- The reasons for the reduction.

- The nature of the merchandise.

- The time of the selling season (the proper moment during the selling season).

- The quantity on hand.

- The original (initial) markup.

- History of like item pricing and customer response to that price.

Because the purpose of a markdown is to sell the merchandise quickly, the size of the markdown must be large enough to produce the desired results. Some rules to be considered in repricing are:

- The first markdown should be sharp enough to move a considerable amount of the goods.

- The markdown should be sufficiently large to attract customers who rejected the merchandise at its original price.

- The price may be reduced sufficiently to appeal to the next price zone customer.

MARKDOWN CALCULATIONS

Calculating the Dollar Markdown

To find the dollar amount of markdown taken when there is a group of items, it is customary to first determine the difference per piece between the present and new retail prices and then to determine the total cost of the markdown.

On an Individual Item

CONCEPT

Original or present retail $ – New retail $ = Markdown $

PROBLEM

A cashmere pullover that was not selling as well as planned was reduced from $198 to $169. What is the dollar markdown?

SOLUTION

Original or present retail		$198
– New retail	–	169
Markdown $		$29

On a Group of Items

CONCEPT

Original or present retail $ – New retail $ = Markdown $

Markdown $ × Units taken = Total markdown $

PROBLEM

A buyer reduces 93 calculators from $15 to $10. What is the total markdown in dollars?

SOLUTION

Original or present retail		$15		
– New retail	–	10		
Markdown $		$5 per piece		
Total markdown $	=	$5 markdown	×	93 pieces
Total markdown $	=	$465		

Using Percentage "Off" Method

However, retailers frequently advertise markdowns as a percentage off the current retail price, for example, "25% off the selling price," so a different calculation is needed.

CONCEPT

Markdown $ = Percentage off × Present retail price $

PROBLEM

A store advertises 25% off on a group of 50 chairs currently retailed at $100 each. What is the total dollar markdown?

Percentage off   =   25% × $100 Retail

Markdown $ = $25 per chair

Total markdown $ = $25 markdown × 50 pieces

Total markdown $ = $1,250

Compounding of Markdowns

Buyers may need to take an additional reduction in the price of product when the first markdown no longer results in the planned sales necessary to sell through the product. You may see signs on a fixture in a department or specialty store to take an additional 25% off product that has already been marked down 25%–40%.

The use of storewide coupons or extra dollar off promotions has become prevalent in retailing today. In order to push sales, retailers entice customers by offering extra percent off or dollar off coupons or markdowns on top of any previous markdowns taken. This results in a lower retail price being paid for the customer and higher markdowns for the retailer but can increase sales exponentially.

These extra discounts must be calculated by the buyer and planned for. One note of caution: The customer may believe that the markdowns are added together, but they are not. The first markdown is taken off the initial price, and the second markdown is based on the first markdown retail price.

Calculating Total Dollar Markdown When a Second Markdown Is Taken (Dollars Off First Markdown and Dollars Off Second Markdown)

Total markdown $ =   First total $ markdown + Second total $ markdown

The men's clothing buyer had a group of 50 jackets priced at $225 each that was selling very slowly. To stimulate sales of these jackets, the buyer reduced the price of the jackets in that group to $175. At this price, 40 pieces were sold in a short time. At a later date, the remaining pieces needed a further reduction to clear them from stock. The buyer reduced them to $100 each, and at that price they all sold out. What was the total dollar markdown taken?

	Original price	Markdown price	Markdown per piece	Number of items	Dollar markdown
1st markdown on group	$225.00	$175.00	$50.00	50	$2,500.00
2nd markdown on group	$175.00	$100.00	$75.00	10	$750.00
Total markdown					$3,250.00

First Markdown on Group

Original retail price		$225
− First markdown price	−	175
Amount of markdown per piece	=	$50
× Number of jackets	×	50
First $ markdown	=	$2,500 $2,500

PLUS

Second Markdown on Group

First markdown price		$175
− Second markdown price	−	100
Amount of markdown per piece	=	$75
× Number of jackets	×	10
Second $ markdown	=	$750 + 750
Total markdown $ on this group	=	$3,250

Calculating Total Dollar Markdown When a Second Markdown Is Taken (Percent Off First Markdown and Percent Off Second Markdown)

A collection of twill pants with an original retail price of $100 was promoted for 25% off. There was a coupon in the circular for an additional 20% off. What is the total markdown taken if 200 pants were sold?

	Original price	Markdown %	Markdown per piece	New retail price	Markdown $
1st markdown on group	$100	25%	$25.00	$75.00	
2nd markdown (coupon) on group	$75.00	20%	$15.00	$60.00	
Total markdown $ per unit × 200 Units sold			$40.00 ×	200 Units sold =	$8,000.00

First Markdown on Group

SOLUTION:
Arithmetic format

Original retail price		$100
− First percent off markdown (25%)	−	$25
New retail price	=	$75
− Second percent off markdown (20%)	−	$15
= New retail price	=	$60

Total markdown = $25 + $15 = $40 × 200 Units sold = $8,000.00

Calculating Planned Dollar Markdown When Markdown Percentage and Net Sales Are Known

Once an estimated net sales figure for an accounting period has been projected and the markdown percentage allowed is known, the total amount of markdown in dollars can be determined. Because markdowns are taken in dollars off the retail price, a buyer's thinking and decisions in merchandising markdowns alternate, according to circumstances, from percentages to dollars, and vice versa.

Planned markdown $ = Planned net sales $ × Planned markdown %

CONCEPT

The sales in the men's footwear department were planned for $560,000, and the markdown percentage was planned at 35%. Find the dollar amount of markdowns that would be permitted.

PROBLEM

Total planned markdown $ = $560,000 Net sales × 35% Planned markdown %

Total planned markdown $ = $196,000

SOLUTION

Calculating Actual Dollar Markdown When Markdown Percentage and Net Sales Are Known

After a given time period, whether a specific promotion or a month, quarter, season, or year, buyers will need to compare the actual amount of markdowns taken to the planned markdowns. The concept is the same as the preceding concept using the Actual net sales $ and Markdown %.

Actual markdown $ = Actual net sales $ × Actual markdown %

CONCEPT

The sales in the men's footwear department actually totaled to $700,000, and the actual markdown percentage was 40%. Find the actual dollar amount of markdowns that occurred.

PROBLEM

| SOLUTION | Total actual markdown $ $=$ $700,000 Net sales $\times$ 40% Actual markdown % |
| | **Total actual markdown $** $=$ $280,000 |

Comparing Planned Markdowns to Actual Markdowns

A comparison is necessary in order to determine whether the markdown was over or under the plan and whether the markdown achieved the intended goal. If the actual markdowns taken are greater than the planned markdowns, the resulting number will be negative. In the industry, this is referred to as "in the hole" or "overspent." If the actual markdowns taken are less than the planned markdowns, the result will be positive. Ultimately, the goal is to drive sales, which will be the deciding factor whether being over or under the markdown dollar plan was successful. If sales increased enough to cover the markdown, generally, in today's retail environment, that is a good thing!

| CONCEPT | Over/under markdown $ $=$ Planned markdown $ $-$ Actual markdown $ |

| PROBLEM | In the previous men's footwear example, compare the actual markdown dollars incurred to the markdown dollars planned by the buyer. |

| SOLUTION | Over/under markdown $ $=$ $196,000 $-$ $280,000 |
| | Over/under markdown $ $=$ $-$84,000, or $84,000 over the planned markdowns |

In this case the buyer is over the planned markdowns as the result is a negative number.

Calculating Markdown Percentage

Markdowns taken are expressed as a percentage of the net sales for an accounting period. It is important to control and plan markdowns within a store. **Markdown percentages** can be calculated for an entire department, vendor, or classification, as shown in the following calculations.

| CONCEPT | $\text{Markdown \%} = \dfrac{\text{Markdown \$}}{\text{Net sales \$}} \times 100$ |

| PROBLEM | In March, Department #33 had net sales of $50,000. The markdowns taken for March totaled $16,500. What was the markdown percentage for March? |

| SOLUTION | $\textbf{Markdown \%} = \dfrac{\$16,500 \text{ Markdown}}{\$50,000 \text{ Net sales}} \times 100$ |
| | $= 33.0\%$ |

MARKDOWN JOURNALIZATION

It is important to understand that there is a difference in what the customer takes into consideration and realizes when product is marked down versus what it costs a retailer. Markdowns are a depreciation or devaluation of the retail value of inventory. Once product is reduced in value and a markdown is taken, the retailer is not collecting those inventory dollars set by the original price. Retailers need to account for this depreciation in value and the markdown percentage that appears on the open-to-buy and six-month planning reports. This is referred to as **markdown journalization**. A markdown will always journalize higher due to the fact that retailers are not collecting the full retail value of inventory.

Relating this back to the profit and loss statement, the gross sale was based on the original or initial price of product. Once reductions are taken (i.e., markdowns), the retailer does not collect that price; hence the markdown becomes the actual retail selling price or net sales of the product. (Reminder: Gross sales – Reductions = Net sales.)

CONCEPT

$$\text{Markdown \% to the customer} = \frac{\text{Markdown \$}}{\text{Original retail price \$}} \times 100$$

$$\text{Markdown \% journalization} = \frac{\text{Markdown \$}}{\text{Actual retail price \$}} \times 100$$

PROBLEM

A women's denim buyer is running a Fall promotion on denim jeans. Denim jeans that have a regular retail price of $120.00 will be promoted at $80.00. Calculate the markdown percentage for the customer and the markdown percentage journalized by the buyer.

SOLUTION

Original retail $ – New retail $ = Markdown $

$120.00 – $80.00 = $40.00

$$\text{Markdown \% to the customer} = \frac{\text{Markdown \$}}{\text{Original retail price \$}} \times 100$$

$$\text{Markdown \% to the customer} = \frac{\$40.00}{\$120.00} \times 100 = 33.3\%$$

$$\text{Markdown \% journalization} = \frac{\text{Markdown \$}}{\text{Actual retail price \$}} \times 100$$

$$\text{Markdown \% journalization} = \frac{\$40}{\$80} \times 100 = 50.0\%$$

Calculating Markdown Cancellations

It is easier to describe a markdown cancellation than to define it. When the markdown price is raised to a higher retail price, it is considered a cancellation of a markdown. Cancellations may occur after special sales from stock if the remaining merchandise is repriced upward. The restoration of a markdown price to the former retail price is a **markdown cancellation**. The calculation is included to indicate the arithmetic and mechanics involved in reviving the selling price upward.

Currently, markdown cancellations are much less common because most large stores electronically program temporary markdowns into the cash register. This means of recording the markdown as the reduced offering when an item is being sold is called a **point-of-sale (POS) markdown**. It eliminates the need to mark the goods with the reduced price, and, subsequently, to re-mark the goods to the original price. Figure 5 shows a sales slip recording the purchase of a pair of comfort shoes selling for $52, less 30%. The $15.60 is an example of a POS markdown. Figure 6 is a credit slip indicating the return of sale merchandise and shows how the $15.60 markdown is canceled. POS markdowns are explained in more detail in the next section.

Figure 5. POS Markdown Receipt   **Figure 6.** POS Credit Slip

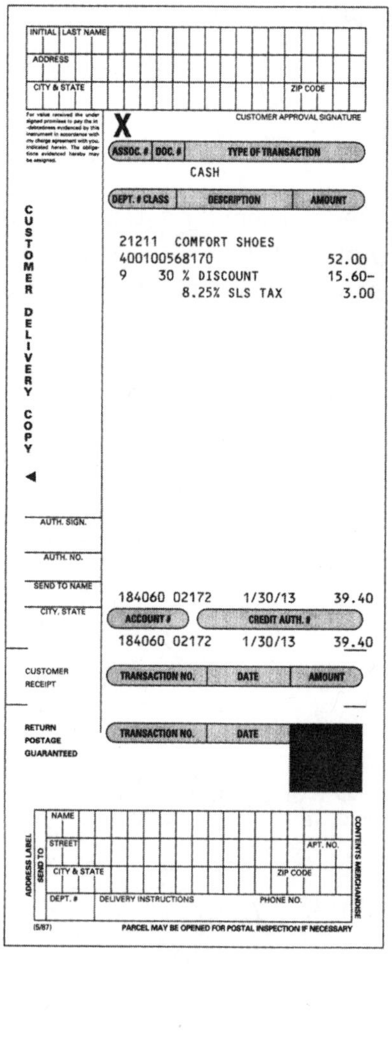

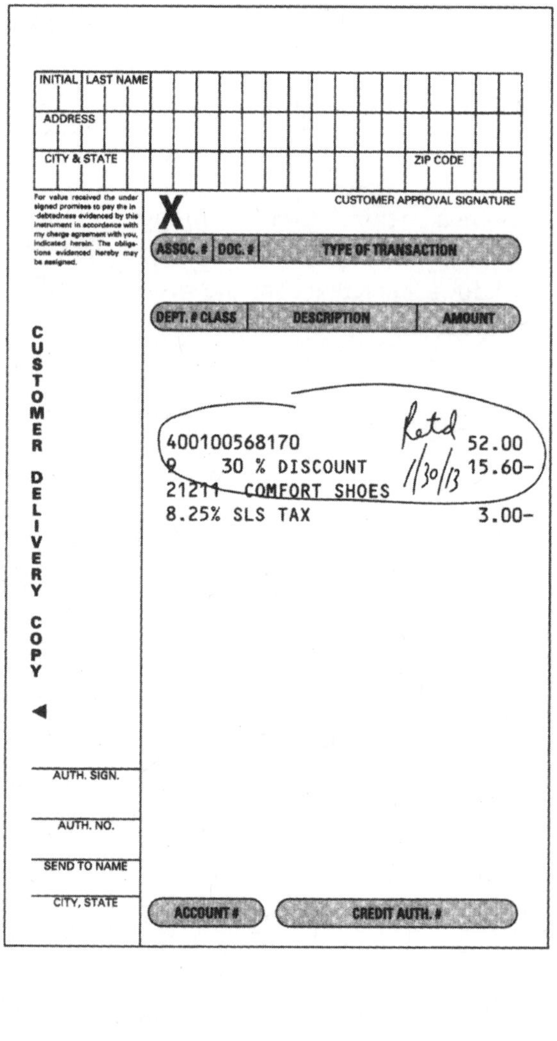

Markdown cancellation   =   Higher retail price   –   Markdown price

After a one-day sale, a buyer marked up the remaining 12 pieces to the original price of $50, which had been reduced to $43 for the special event. What was the amount of the markdown cancellation?

Markdown cancellation   = $50   Higher retail price

   – $43   Markdown price

= $7   Difference per piece

=   12 pieces   × $7

Markdown cancellation   = $84

Calculating Net Markdown

When a reduction in price is made originally, it is called the **gross markdown**. The difference between gross markdown and markdown cancellation is called the **net markdown** figure, or the amount of the permanent markdown.

Net markdown   =   Gross markdown   –   Markdown cancellation

A buyer reduces each of the 75 pieces from $50 to $43 for a one-day sale. After the sale, the remaining 28 pieces were marked up to the original price and were sold out at that price.

What was the gross markdown in dollars?

What was the markdown cancellation?

Find the net markdown in dollars.

	Original price	New price	Change per piece	Number of pieces	Markdown $
Original MD	$50	$43	$7	75	$525 Gross
MD cancellation	$43	$50	$7	28	$196 Cancellation
Net MD					$329 Net

Determine gross markdown.

Individual markdown   = $50   – $43

or markdown per piece   = $7 per piece

=   75 Pieces   × $7 Markdown

Gross markdown   = $525

SOLUTION:
*Arithmetic format
continued*

Determine markdown cancellation.

Markdown cancellation		=	$43 to $50
		=	$7 per piece
		=	28 Pieces $\times$ $7 Markdown cancellation
Markdown cancellation		=	$196

Determine net markdown.

Gross markdown		=	$525
– Markdown cancellation		=	<u>– 196</u>
Net markdown		=	$329

EMPLOYEE DISCOUNTS

It is common practice for a retail store to give its employees a reduction off a retail price. This type of retail reduction is called an **employee discount**. As noted previously, this is another type of price adjustment that must be recorded, because it lowers the value of merchandise. This reduction is generally stated as a percentage off the retail price (e.g., a 30%–50% discount). It must be recorded by the statistical department of the accounting division for accuracy of the book inventory figure under the retail method of inventory. The cumulative amount of employees' discounts is usually shown on the profit and loss statement under the general heading of "**retail reductions**."

PROBLEM

Store X grants its employees a 20% discount on all merchandise purchased. If a salesperson buys an item that retails for $16.95, what is the employee discount in dollars? What is the amount paid for the item?

SOLUTION

Retail price of item	=	$16.95
Discount allowed	=	20%
	=	$16.95 $\times$ 20% .
Employee discount	=	$3.39
Employee's price	=	$16.95 – $3.39
	=	$13.56

or

| | = | $16.95 – (0.20 $\times$ 16.95) |
| | = | $13.56 |

2.4 Point-of-Sale (POS) and Permanent (Physical) Markdowns

There are two types of markdowns: point-of-sale (POS) and permanent (physical) markdowns. Each of these markdowns affects the gross margin differently and buyers need to understand the implications that each has on profitability.

Point-of-sale (POS) markdowns are the most common type of markdown retailers use today. POS markdowns are temporary. They can change weekly, daily, or even hourly (think of the Black Friday sales). Merchandise can revert back to the current retail selling price and be reduced to a new price at a later date or time. POS markdowns can be dollars off or a percentage off the current retail selling price. Some examples of POS markdowns are signs in store windows that state, "Buy one, get one at 50% off" or "Take an additional 25% off entire stock." Or they can be coupons found in a circular or sent to customers by e-mail or text message. The benefit of taking POS markdowns is that the markdown is journalized and gross margin is affected only when the merchandise is sold.

CONCEPT

Total POS markdown $ = Individual markdown $ × Units sold

PROBLEM

The activewear buyer is planning a New Year's "Get Fit" sale. On December 31, all $69.00 leggings will be promoted at $49.99 and on New Year's Day, all $69.00 leggings will be promoted at 40% off. Here is what sold on each day:

December 31, 480 leggings

New Year's Day, 600 leggings

Calculate the total point-of-sale markdown dollars, total sale dollars, and markdown percentage for the sale.

SOLUTION

a. Total markdown $ for the POS promotion

Retail price $ – New retail $ =	MD $ ×	Units sold =	Total MD $
$69.00 – $49.99 =	19.01 ×	480	$9,124.80
Retail price $ × MD % =	MD $ ×	Units sold =	Total MD $
69.00 × 40% =	27.60 ×	600	$16,560.00
Total MD $ =			9,124.80 + 16,560 = $25,684.80

b. Total sales $ for the POS promotion

New retail $ ×	Units sold =		Total sales $
49.99 ×	480		$23,995.20
Original retail $ − MD $ =	New retail $ ×	Units sold =	Total sales $
69.00 − 27.60 =	41.40 ×	600	$24,840
Total sales =			23,995.20 + 24,840 = $48,835.20

c. The markdown % for the POS promotion

$\dfrac{\text{MD \$}}{\text{Net sales \$}} \times 100 =$	MD %
$\dfrac{25,684.80}{48,835.20} \times 100 =$	52.59%/52.6%

Permanent (physical) markdowns, though not as common as POS, are still used by retailers. When a buyer takes a permanent markdown, the merchandise price is changed immediately, thereby reducing the inventory value. The ticketed price of merchandise is changed with a new price ticket, a red line, a green line, or whatever method a retailer uses to change the price on the ticket. Once merchandise is permanently marked down, it cannot be marked up again. Since the ticketed price is changed, permanent markdowns are changed to a dollar value. Percentage off is not used on the actual merchandise ticket. Permanent markdowns tend to be more costly for a buyer, as the markdown is journalized immediately. Inventory is devalued once the price is changed, thereby affecting all units that are in stock at the point when the markdown is taken. Most permanent markdowns occur after POS markdowns have been taken and inventory has been sold down. In order to calculate the total permanent markdown, a buyer needs to understand how many units are on hand and create a sell down chart. Another difference occurs in calculating total sales. As this product has been decreased in value, the markdown price becomes the starting price for any additional markdowns.

CONCEPT

Total permanent markdown $ = Individual markdown $ × # Units on hand

PROBLEM

The dress buyer is *permanently* marking down Fall velvet dresses. The buyer purchased 1,000 dresses and only 100 sold at the regular price of $150.00. The first permanent markdown was to $129.99 and 200 sold. The second permanent markdown was taken to $99.99 and 500 sold.

Calculate the total markdown dollars for the dresses, the total sales dollars, and the markdown percentage.

First, you need to create a sell down chart:

1,000 Units purchased to sell at $150.00
− 100 Units sold at regular price $150.00
= 900 Units on hand to permanent MD to $129.99
− 200 Units sold at $129.99
= 700 Units on hand to permanent MD to $99.99
− 500 Units sold at $99.99
= 200 Units remain on hand

Total permanent markdown $ for the dresses:

Retail price $ − New retail $ =	MD $ ×	Units on hand =	Total MD $
150.00 − 129.99 =	20.01 ×	900	$18,009.00
129.99 − 99.99 =	30.00 ×	700	$21,000.00
Total MD $ =			18,009 + 21,000 = $39,009.00

Note: The next markdown would start at $99.99, the new retail price. With shortage and inaccurate counts, merchandise does not sell out totally.

Total retail sales $ for the dresses:

Retail $ ×	Units sold =	Total sales $
150.00 ×	100	$15,000.00
129.99 ×	200	$25,998.00
99.99 ×	500	$49,995.00
Total sales =		15,000 + 25,998 + 49,995 = $90,993

Total markdown % for the dresses:

$\dfrac{\text{MD \$}}{\text{Net sales \$}} \times 100 =$	MD %
$\dfrac{39{,}009}{90{,}993} \times 100 =$	42.87%/42.9%

2.5 ANALYTICAL CRITERIA FOR TAKING MARKDOWNS

Most buyers buy for a large number of stores in many locations. They are not in every store every day and cannot just look at a sales floor to determine if a markdown needs to be taken or not. They must use analytical criteria for determining the right time to take a markdown. The criteria that are used are outdate, weeks of supply (WOS), sell through percentage (ST %), and build.

The **outdate** is the last date merchandise should be available for sale to a customer. Merchandise has a limited life span, especially fashion product. A buyer sets an outdate for fashion product when the product is received, and sales are monitored on a week-to-week basis to see if the store will be out of that product before the outdate or after. Basic merchandise is replenishable, and an outdate is not usually set for this type of product unless the vendor is discontinuing a style.

Buyers must decide the last date for merchandise to be on the selling floor. For example, if you are purchasing holiday-themed product (merchandise with snowmen, snowflakes, wreaths, etc.), the last date you will sell that product is January 1. For summer product (swimwear, shorts, short sleeve tees), especially in the northern parts of the country, the last date for sale is normally Labor Day.

Weeks of supply (WOS) tells a buyer how many weeks of product you have left to sell out completely. WOS is calculated weekly and based on the current trend of product sales. WOS is monitored against the outdate. If you have too many weeks of product left that will surpass the outdate, it may be wise for a buyer to take a markdown on that product to accelerate sales. WOS is normally calculated in units. A buyer needs to sell through the units of product in inventory. If you take markdowns, the value of the inventory will change, and if you calculate WOS in dollars, it will be a different result based on the amount and type of markdown taken.

Once you sell product, it is removed from your inventory. Therefore, when calculating weeks of supply and sell through for subsequent weeks, you start with the units remaining after sales occur.

CONCEPT

$$\text{Weeks of supply} = \frac{\text{Beginning units on hand for a week (Sunday)}}{\text{Units sold in that week (Sunday–Saturday)}}$$

PROBLEM

You started a season with 1,000 wallets to retail at $39.00. In the first week, you sold 50 wallets. In the second week, you sold 80 pieces when you took a POS markdown to $29.99. Calculate the WOS for the first week and the second week.

SOLUTION

$$\text{WOS week 1} = \frac{1,000}{50} = 20.0 \text{ Weeks of supply}$$

Start week 2 with 1,000 Units on hand – 50 Units sold = 950 Units at the beginning of week 2.

$$\text{WOS week 2} = \frac{950}{80} = 11.875/11.9 \text{ WOS}$$

Sell through percentage (ST %) tells a buyer how fast or slow merchandise is selling. Like weeks of supply, sell through percentage is calculated on a weekly basis and given in units. It is based on the current selling trend and gives the buyer a "snapshot in time." Sell through percentage should not be confused with turnover (turn). Turn is a productivity measure and is calculated over a longer period of time. Turn is discussed in Chapter 5.

CONCEPT

$$\text{Sell through \%} = \frac{\text{Units sold in a week (Sunday–Saturday)}}{\text{Beginning units on hand for a week (Sunday)}} \times 100$$

PROBLEM

A small leather goods buyer starts a season with 1,000 wallets to retail at $39.00. In the first week, the retailer sold 50 wallets. In the second week, the retailer sold 80 pieces when the buyer took a POS markdown to $29.99. Calculate the sell through % for the first and second weeks.

SOLUTION

$$\text{Sell through \% week 1} = \frac{50}{1,000} \times 100 = 5.0\%$$

$$\text{Sell through \% week 2} = \frac{80}{950} \times 100 = 8.4\%$$

The last analytical criteria used is **build**, which retailers also refer to as percentage change, acceleration, or trend. Build provides the comparison as a percentage change in what was sold from week to week. If you take markdowns, you need to project the increase in sales you expect to achieve by taking the markdown. Remember, markdowns are taken to increase sales; therefore, it is important to analyze build to determine whether the intended sales goal was met. For markdowns, you are selling units at different prices, and build will also be calculated in units. It is a basic percentage change formula comparing two different points in time. Builds achieved can be over 100% or can be negative, meaning you sold less than the week before.

CONCEPT

$$\text{Build \%} = \frac{\text{This week unit sales} - \text{Last week unit sales}}{\text{Last week unit sales}} \times 100$$

PROBLEM

Calculate the build for the wallets in the previous example between week 1 and week 2.

SOLUTION

$$\text{Build \%} = \frac{80 - 50}{50} \times 100$$

$$\text{Build \%} = \frac{30}{50} \times 100 = 60.0\%$$

There is a vital relationship between weeks of supply and sell through percentage that is important and valuable for a buyer to understand. WOS and ST % have an inverse relationship. Therefore, these formulas tell a buyer when it is time to take a markdown on product and when it may be time to reorder product that is selling. If WOS is too long or too high and merchandise will be in stock past the outdate set, that means the ST % is slow and a buyer should take a markdown to increase sales and reduce inventory. If WOS is too short or too low and you will sell out of product before the outdate, that means the ST % is fast and a buyer should consider reordering that product if it can be received and sold in a timely manner.

PRICE CHANGE PROCEDURES

An efficient system of reporting and recording price changes is important for the following three reasons:

- Facilitation of the review of price adjustments.

- Accurate calculation of inventory records.

- Identification of shortages.

Figure 7 illustrates a computer printout of a buyer-authorized price change. It instructs individual stores to change the retails on certain merchandise, where to change them (i.e., store location), if the change is permanent or temporary, what the new retails should be, and the reason for repricing. Presently, most systems do not require that the store count the merchandise, only remark it, because, financially, the perpetual inventory system has already made the adjustment.

Figure 7. Price Change

Run Date: 02/28/13		Price Change						Report No: Page: 12
Run Time: 22:29:30								

BUYER 02   DEPT NO: 02

P/C NO: 2331916   P/C TYPE: 01 MARKDOWN-PERMANENT, TOTAL STYLE   ORIGINATING LOCATION: 02 ENTRY DATE: 02-27-13

EFFECTIVE DATE: 03/04/13   REASON: 02 REPRICING CLEARANCE

DOCUMENT NO:

APPLICABLE LOCATIONS: 01 02 03 05 07 08 09 11 12 13 14 15 16 17 18 19 20 21 23 24 25 26
SPECIAL INSTRUCTIONS: REPRICING

CLASS	VENDOR	STYLE	UPC	OLD RETAIL	NEW RETAIL	CURR TKT RETAIL	NEW TKT RETAIL	DESCRIPTION
41	1	6028	400100964255	11.00	7.00	11.00	7.00 ( )	LG CIRCULAR STRETC
41	1	6140	400101350996	6.00	4.00	6.00	4.00 ( )	CHANNEL CIRCLE STR
41	1	6143	400101365136	6.00	4.00	6.00	4.00 ( )	STRETCH MATTE META
41	1	9106	400101338239	11.00	7.00	11.00	7.00 ( )	½" MESH
41	1	9107	400101109839	14.00	9.00	14.00	9.00 ( )	MESH BELTS
41	1	9115	400101338246	13.00	9.00	13.00	9.00 ( )	ROLLED MESH
41	28	1602	400101479789	10.00	7.00	10.00	7.00 ( )	STUD BELT
41	28	1730	400101479796	10.00	7.00	10.00	7.00 ( )	STUD BELT
41	117	1305	400101271024	9.00	6.00	9.00	6.00 ( )	1¼" W/SILVER 3
41	117	1359	400101207726	5.00	3.00	5.00	3.00 ( )	¾" CROCO SILVER

THE RELATIONSHIP OF REPRICING TO PROFIT

Every price change has an impact on gross margin and net profits. Because the elimination of price adjustments in retailing is impossible, stores must classify each type of adjustment separately so that it can be analyzed, planned, and controlled. Markdowns, the major type of price changes, reduce the retail price, causing a decrease in gross margin that is further reflected in a decrease and/or elimination of profit. As discussed earlier, point-of-sale and permanent markdowns affect the gross margin differently. With certain merchandise or classifications, the markdown risk is frequently anticipated. It is offset by planning a higher initial (original) markup. Unfortunately, profit cannot always be preplanned because there are business forces and economic trends that do not permit easy solutions to such problems (e.g., nonacceptance of a newly introduced fashion or style, change in competition, etc.).

If you look at the top of the profit and loss statement versus the markup formula, there is an important association. Remember, Gross sales – Reductions = Net sales. Net sales is always equal to 100%. In the markup formula, retail equals 100%; therefore, a correlation can be made as follows:

Net sales	100%	Retail	100%
– Cost of goods sold %		– Cost %	
= Gross margin %		= Markup %	

Therefore, if *no markdowns* are taken, gross sales and net sales would be the same, and gross margin % and markup % would, for all intents and purposes, *be equal*. As soon as markdowns *are taken*, gross margin % may be reduced (depending on sales achieved) and *will not equal* markup %.

Repricing of Merchandise/Markdown Practice Problems

Basic Markdown Practice Problems

45. The men's shirts buyer for the Best Department Store is taking a mark-down on short sleeve denim shirts for Father's Day. All $99.00 shirts will be markdown to $69.99. Calculate the markdown dollars for the shirts.

46. The swimwear buyer for an off-price retailer is taking a clearance mark-down on the balance of inventory for swim cover-ups that were originally priced at $29.99 to $19.98. What are the markdown dollars for each cover-up?

47. The bedding buyer is running a promotion on sheet sets for a back-to-school sale. All twin size sheet sets will be promoted at 33% off. The sheet sets regularly retail at $69.00. What are the markdown dollars and the new retail price for the sheet sets?

48. The boy's buyer is taking a markdown on licensed T-shirts. All licensed T-shirts that have a suggested retail of $24.00 will be promoted at 20% off. Calculate the markdown dollars and the sale price for the licensed shirts.

49. Fill in the blanks for parts (a)–(d) in the following table:

Regular price --	Markdown price =	MD $ ×	Units sold =	Total MD $	MD % to customer = MD $ × 100 / Original price
a. $30.00	$19.99	10.01	1,275	12762.75	33.4 %
b. $149.00	$109.99	39.01	480	18724.80	26.2 %
c. $199.00	$149.98	49.02	350	17157	24.6 %
d. $69.00	$29.95	39.05	720	28116	56.6 %

sales

50. Fill in the blanks for parts (a)–(d) in the following table:

Regular price ×	Percentage off =	MD $ ×	Units sold =	Total MD $	New retail price
a. $24.00	25%		1,800		
b. $39.00	30%		500		
c. $59.99	15%		190		
d. $120.00	40%		750		

Planned and Actual Markdown Practice Problems

51. For November, a suit buyer took markdowns totaling $24,700. During this month, the net sales for the department amounted to $50,000. What was the markdown percentage for November?

52. The shoe department's Spring season markdown dollar plan is $187,000, and the planned net sales for Spring are $580,000. Calculate the markdown percentage for the Spring season in shoes.

53. The gift department took markdowns in December of $11,000, and its December sales were $27,500. What is the markdown percentage for the gift department in December?

40%

54. The junior sportswear buyer planned sales for the month amounting to $700,000. The markdown percentage was planned at 36.5%. What were the planned markdown dollars?

55. The yearly planned sales for men's are $365,000, and the planned markdown % for the year is 42.0%. Calculate the planned markdown dollars for the year in men's.

56. For October, the coat department did $26,800 in sales and took 30% markdowns. What are the markdown dollars for the coat department in October?

57. If the girls' department Fall season actual sales were $59,000, and the actual markdown percentage was 29.5%, calculate:

    a. The actual markdown dollars for the Fall season in girls'.

    b. If the planned markdown dollars for Fall in girls' was $21,000, is the buyer over or under the markdown plan?

58. The handbag department's planned markdown percentage for last year was 37.6%, and the planned sales were $750,000. If actual markdowns totaled $295,000, was the buyer over or under the markdown plan, and by how much in dollars?

59. In July, a towel buyer took markdowns totaling $18,000. During this month, the net sales for the department were $34,000. If the net sales plan was $36,000 and the original markdown plan for this month called for 58% markdowns, was the actual markdown taken over or under the original plan, and by how much in dollars? What was the actual markdown percentage?

60. The seasonal plan for a shoe department shows planned sales of $753,000, with planned markdowns of 56.4%.

    a. What is the planned dollar amount of markdowns?

    b. If the actual markdowns are $450,000 on actual sales of $800,000, are the actual markdowns taken more or less than planned? By how much? What is the actual markdown percentage?

61. What reasons could cause a buyer to be over markdowns in a given time period?

Compounding of Markdown
Practice Problems

62. For a one-day sale the entire stock of cashmere sweaters with an original retail of $99.00 will be promoted at $20.00 off. In addition, customers will be able to use an additional 15% off coupon. Calculate the final selling price for the cashmere sweaters.

63. The entire stock of $59.00 velour activewear will be promoted during Thanksgiving weekend as a POS promotion at 40% off. There will be a coupon in the paper for an additional 10% off. If the customer uses the coupon, calculate:

    a. The final selling price for the velour activewear.

    $$59 \times .6 = 35.4 \times .9 = \boxed{\$31.86}$$

    b. The actual markdown % to the customer.

    $$\$27.14 / 59\% = 46\%$$

    c. The markdown journalized by the retailer.

64. The sandal buyer is planning a Memorial Day sale event on all $79.00 sandals. The sandals will be promoted at $60.00. There will be a coupon in the sale circular for customers to take an additional 25% off their purchase. What will be the final selling price for the sandals? What is the markdown percentage that the customer actually receives and the retailer journalizes?

65. The men's tie buyer planned a Father's Day promotion on ties. The POS price point promotion was $24.99. Here is what sold during the promotion:

40 ties with an original retail of $35.00

50 ties with an original retail of $40.00

Calculate the following:

    a. Total markdown in dollars for the promotion.

    b. Total sales dollars generated for the promotion.

    c. Total markdown percentage for the promotion.

66. The missy top buyer ran a point-of-sale promotion on denim shirts for Columbus Day weekend at $69.99. Here is what was sold during the sale:

    270 shirts with an original retail of $99.00   *69.99*

    180 shirts with an original retail of $89.00   *69.99*

    Calculate the following:

    a. Total markdown $ for the sale.

450 × 69.99
———————
31495.5

= 29.01 × 270 = 7837.7
= 19.01 × 180 = 3422
———————
$11255.

35.7%

b. Total sales $ generated for the sale.

$31,495.50

c. Markdown % for the sale.

35.7%

67. For Mother's Day, the handbag buyer planned a point-of-sale promotion at 25% off for straw handbags. Here is a record of what sold during the promotion:

100 handbags with an original retail of $49.00

200 handbags with an original retail of $39.00

36.75   100 × 49   4900
29.25   200 × 39   7800
                     12700

Calculate the following:

a. Total markdown in dollars for the promotion.

$3175

100 × 12.25 = 1225
200 × 9.75 = 1950
              3175

b. Total sales generated for the Mother's Day event.

3675   100 × 36.75
5850   200 × 29.25
9525

c. Total markdown percentage for the Mother's Day sale event.

33.3%

68. The shoe buyer ran a point-of-sale promotion on ballet flats for a Spring Sale weekend at 30% off. Here is what was sold during the sale:

600 ballet flats with an original retail of $79.00

720 ballet flats with an original retail of $69.00

Calculate the following:

    a. Total markdown $ for the sale.

    b. Total sales $ generated for the sale.

    c. Markdown % for the sale.

69. The shoe buyer ran a POS promotion during the Thanksgiving weekend on ankle boots that had a regular retail price of $129.00. On Black Friday, these boots were promoted at $79.99 and 600 pairs sold. On Saturday and Sunday, the boots were on a POS promotion at 40% off and 500 pairs sold. Calculate the following:

    a. Total markdown $ for the POS promotion.

    b. Total sales $ for the POS promotion.

c. The markdown % for the POS promotion.

d. If the buyer projected to take $49,000 in markdown $, was the buyer over or under his or her projection and by how much?

70. The handbag buyer bought 960 printed handbags to retail at $60.00. At the regular retail price, only 60 handbags sold. The buyer took a 25% off POS markdown and 150 handbags sold. The buyer took another POS markdown to $34.99 and 200 handbags sold. Calculate the following:

   a. Markdown $ for this sale.

   b. Sales $ generated for the sale.

   c. Markdown % for this sale.

   d. If planned markdown dollars were $8,000, does the buyer have more or less markdowns to spend and by how much in dollars?

Permanent Markdown Practice Problems

71. The missy sweater buyer bought V-neck sequin-trimmed sweaters to retail at $49.99. The buyer purchased 360 sweaters. At the full price, 40 pieces sold. A permanent markdown was taken to $39.99 and 120 pieces sold. Another permanent markdown was taken to $29.99 and 150 pieces were sold. Calculate the following:

     a. Total markdown $ for this sweater sale.

     b. Total sales generated for the sweater sale.

     c. Total markdown % for the sweater sales.

72. The dress buyer bought 150 "little black dresses" to retail at $90.00. At this price only 30 were sold. The buyer then took a permanent markdown to $69.99. At $69.99, 50 dresses were sold. The buyer then took another permanent markdown to $49.99 and 50 more were sold. Calculate the following:

     a. Total markdown $ for this sale.

b. Total sales $ generated.

c. Total markdown % for this sale.

73. The sunglass buyer bought 7,200 pairs of sunglasses for summer to retail for $49.00. At full price, 2,150 pieces were sold. The buyer took a permanent markdown to $29.99 and 2,975 pieces were sold. A second permanent markdown was taken to $19.99 and 1,600 were sold. Calculate the following:

    a. Total permanent markdown $ for the sunglasses.

    b. Total retail sales $ for the sunglasses.

    c. Total markdown % for the sunglasses.

74. A buyer purchases 1,200 sandals from a vendor to retail at $89.00. In the first week, the buyer sold 30 pairs at regular price.

    a. Calculate the WOS and ST % for week 1.

    b. The second week, the buyer sold 40 pairs at regular price. Calculate the WOS and ST % for week 2. What was the build in unit sales for week 2 from week 1?

    c. The third week, the buyer took a POS markdown to $69.99 and sold 65 pairs. Calculate the WOS and ST % for week 3.

    d. What is the markdown % to the customer and what is the markdown % to the retailer (journal)?

    e. Calculate the build in unit sales from week 3 to week 2.

75. You are buying 300 sweaters from two vendors to retail at $50.

    a. If you sold 20 sweaters in week 1, calculate the WOS and ST % for week 1.

    b. If you sold 30 sweaters in week 2 with a POS markdown retail of $40, calculate the WOS, ST %, build, and markdown % to the customer and to the journal.

    c. In week 3, you sold only 25 pieces at $40. Calculate the WOS, ST %, and build.

    d. In week 4, you took a POS markdown to $25 and sold 60 pieces. Calculate the WOS, ST %, build, and markdown % to the customer and to the journal.

76. For Spring, you purchased 640 pairs of men's fashion denim jeans that retail at $149.00.

    a. In the first week, you sold only 25 pieces. Calculate the WOS and ST % for week 1.

b. In week 2, the decision was made to take a POS markdown to $99.99 and you sold 55 pieces. Calculate the WOS, ST %, build, and markdown to the customer and to the journal.

77. Discussion Problem: Markdowns are a normal and positive element of merchandise planning. The markdown factor may be used advantageously by a buyer in an effective departmental operation. What factors should be carefully scrutinized, and why?

CASE STUDY 1
PRICING IN MERCHANDISING

In mid-October, a key vendor offers a missy top department store buyer a group of long sleeve crew neck knit tops that it had previously purchased. The vendor has 4,800 units of assorted knit tops available that it can sell to the buyer for a reduced cost price of $6.00; the regular cost price of the tops was $9.00. The buyer previously priced these tops at $29.00. In order to secure the reduced cost price, the buyer has to buy the entire 4,800 unit availability. The vendor has the following color assortment:

Striped knit tops, 2,400 units

Solids of black and ivory, 1,440 units

Paisley print knit tops, 960 units

The vendor can ship this assortment and it will be in store by the end of October.

The buyer previously purchased the same tops that started selling in mid-September; approximately four weeks of sales have been recorded. Here is a recap of what was received and what was sold in the four-week time period:

Color/print	Units purchased	Units sold in 4 weeks	Average units sold per week	Units on hand mid-October
Stripes	10,000	2,700	675	7,300
Solids	15,000	4,500	1,125	10,500
Paisley	7,200	1,400	350	5,800

As these are long sleeve knit tops, the buyer set an outdate for November 30 (approximately seven weeks from mid-October).

Before the vendor discussed the availability with the buyer, there was a promotion planned on the tops for an Election Day sale at $24.99. The buyer has reviewed the selling and feels the purchase would ultimately be advantageous because increased departmental activity will lead to improved sales. The buyer's planned markup percentage for November is 64.0%. To make the correct decisions, the following questions must be answered:

a. If the buyer takes advantage of this special purchase, what would the markup for the entire purchase be based on the regular retail price?

b. What should the knit tops be promoted at for Election Day? Will $24.99 be a significant incentive for customers to buy multiple units, or should the buyer restrategize the pricing for the event? What promotions would you recommend?

c. Based on current selling trends, if the buyer takes in the extra merchandise, will he meet the end-of-November outdate for the product?

Decide what course of action the buyer should pursue and mathematically justify your suggestions as you apply the principles of pricing and repricing.

CASE STUDY 2
JUSTIFICATION OF THE PRICING STRATEGY

You are a fashion jewelry buyer for a major specialty store. On November 1, one of your vendors has immediate availability for boxed jewelry pins and earrings that will enhance your holiday "gifts-to-go" assortment. The vendor has 12,000 units of boxed jewelry at a cost of $4.25 per unit if the entire quantity is purchased. If not, the cost is $7.50 per unit. To properly assess this offering, you must consider the following factors that will be helpful in making the appropriate decision:

a. There are many different styles in the assortment and some have a "winter" theme that may not sell in the "hot" climate stores.

b. You already have purchased from other resources 15,000 units of boxed jewelry for the gifts-to-go setup at a cost of $5.00.

c. This classification (boxed jewelry) has enjoyed stronger sales this season than in previous years. The "healthy" position of this classification is such that this offering could contribute to an unexpected sales increase for the entire department.

d. An analysis of the selling reports and the "on order" of this category shows that the condition of the present inventory may be inadequate to cover the conservative, realistic anticipated sales for November and December.

Because of the strong sales of this classification, the buyer would like to take advantage of this offering and use a strategy in pricing this group that will generate a markup above the required departmental 62.5% to afford a successful post-Christmas clearance sale. The buyer begins to make more basic calculations and considerations that will justify the final course of action to be taken.

Plan 1. If the normal departmental 62.5% markup were applied in pricing this group, what would be the retail price per box at a cost of $4.25 each?

Usually, the boxed jewelry that costs $5.00 carries a 75% markup. Using this as a guideline, what would be the retail price per pair of pins and earrings?

Plan 2. What would be the markup realized if the entire group were purchased and integrated into the $15.00 price line?

Plan 3. There is a Gift for Christmas ad planned for December 1 that features other gift-to-go items priced at $9.99 to $14.99. This merchandise represents exceptionally good value and quality. Should the boxed jewelry be combined with this particular promotion?

Plan 4. Immediately on delivery, should the buyer integrate half of the entire amount of boxed jewelry into the regular price strategy based on the 75% usual markup and include the balance in the December 1 ad?

State the possible negative and/or positive results for each suggested option. Recommend or develop a pricing strategy, and justify your recommendations mathematically.

BASIC MARKUP EQUATIONS USED IN MERCHANDISING DECISIONS

CHAPTER 3

"Strategy without tactics is the slowest route to victory. Tactics without strategy is the noise before defeat."

SUN TZU, ANCIENT CHINESE MILITARIST, PHILOSOPHER, STRATEGIST, AND AUTHOR OF *THE ART OF WAR* (CIRCA 500 B.C.)

OBJECTIVES

- Identify the types of markups and the use of each in making merchandise decisions.

- Calculate initial markups, cumulative markups, and maintained markups.

- Recognize the need to balance markups among different items of merchandise.

- Balance markups for diverse situations.

- Recognize and understand both the dollar amounts and percentages of markup needed to evaluate the impact of merchandising decisions.

KEY TERMS

average cost	final selling price	initial or original retail
average retail	gross margin	maintained markup (MMU)
averaging or balancing markups	initial cumulative markup	new retail price
billed cost	initial, mark on, or original markup	retail reductions
cumulative markup		vendor analysis

Key Concept Formulas

Initial markup %

$$\text{Initial markup \%} = \frac{\text{Gross margin \% } + \text{ Retail reductions \%}}{100\% + \text{ Retail reductions \%}}$$

$$\text{Initial markup \%} = \frac{\text{Gross margin \$ } + \text{ Retail reductions \$}}{\text{Sales \$ } + \text{ Retail reductions \$}} \times 100$$

$$\text{Initial markup \%} = \frac{\begin{array}{c}\text{Gross} \\ \text{margin}\end{array} + \begin{array}{c}\text{Alteration} \\ \text{costs}\end{array} - \begin{array}{c}\text{Cash discount} \\ \text{earned}\end{array} + \begin{array}{c}\text{Retail} \\ \text{reduction}\end{array}}{\text{Sales (100\%) } + \text{ Retail reductions \%}}$$

Cumulative markup % $= \dfrac{\text{Cumulative markup \$}}{\text{Cumulative retail \$}} \times 100$

Gross margin %

$$\text{Gross margin \%} = \frac{\text{Net sales \$ } - \text{ Total cost of goods sold \$}}{\text{Net sales \$}} \times 100$$

or

$$\text{Gross margin \%} = \frac{\text{Gross margin \$}}{\text{Net sales \$}} \times 100$$

$$\frac{\text{Gross}}{\text{margin \%}} = \frac{\text{Maintained markup } + \text{ Cash discounts } - \text{ Alteration costs}}{\text{Net sales}} \times 100$$

Maintained markup %

$$\text{Maintained markup \%} = \frac{\text{Net sales } - \text{ Gross cost of goods sold}}{\text{Net sales}} \times 100$$

$$\frac{\text{Maintained}}{\text{markup \%}} = \frac{\text{Gross margin } - \text{ Cash discounts } + \text{ Alteration costs}}{\text{Net sales}} \times 100$$

$$\frac{\text{Maintained}}{\text{markup \%}} = \text{Initial markup \% } - \text{ Retail reduction \% } \times \begin{array}{c}(100\% - \text{ Initial} \\ \text{markup \%})\end{array}$$

$$\text{Purchase balance} = \begin{array}{c}\text{Total planned} \\ \text{(pieces, retail, cost, or markup \%)}\end{array} - \text{ Purchases to date}$$

Retail reduction % $= \dfrac{\text{Initial markup \% } - \text{ Maintained markup \%}}{\text{Sales (100\%) } - \text{ Initial markup \%}}$

Chapter 3 examines the significance of pricing and repricing, as well as factors such as gross margin that influence the retailer/buyer when setting retail prices. As discussed in Chapter 2, one of the factors to consider when determining the retail prices of merchandise will be based on the markup deemed appropriate by the buyer. Markup, which is simply the difference between retail prices placed on merchandise and the cost of this merchandise, has an effect on the:

- Price at which product will be sold to generate the desired sales volume.
- Markdowns that can be taken.

- Gross margin it can achieve.
- Profits it can produce.

As a result, markup must be planned, always monitored, and, if necessary, adjusted. Because basic markup calculations in both dollars and percentages are used in buying decisions as they relate to a single item or a group of items, the buyer responsible for a particular department is involved with the markups planned and obtained. These markups are constantly reviewed because the desired gross margin depends on how successfully they are achieved.

To better understand the various markups indigenous to the retailing business, the term "retail price" must be clarified. The first price placed on merchandise for resale is the **initial** or **original retail**. The price received when an item sells (which may be different) is the **final selling price** or **new retail price**. The original, initial, or first retail placed on merchandise is the price the retailer hopes to realize, and the final selling price is the price actually received for the merchandise. (For example, a raincoat costing $55 is retailed at $200 when received in the store, but eventually sells for only $120.) The initial retail price is often higher than the price at which the merchandise ultimately sells, because price reductions (markdowns) may be necessary before the goods are sold.

3.1 TYPES OF MARKUPS

INITIAL MARKUP CONCEPTS

Initial markup, also known as "**mark on**" or "**original markup**," is the difference between the **billed cost** of merchandise and the original or first retail price placed on a given item or group of items. When freight charges are known, they are added to the billed cost when calculating initial markup. Certain vital factors and common practices must be considered in determining the initial markup; the following considerations cannot be ignored:

- Plan in advance an initial markup for merchandise when it is received to ensure a favorable gross margin figure that will cover expenses and provide a reasonable profit.

- Initial markup for any item should consider the buyer's total monthly/ seasonal cumulative markup plans. When orders for merchandise are placed, the initial markup needs to be calculated to ensure that it is within the planned markup. When negotiating cost pricing with a vendor, the buyer needs to calculate the retail price and then check that it falls within the markup plans.

- Recognize that the gross margin figure can fluctuate because it is the result of many merchandising decisions, for example, markdowns, shortages, and employee discounts. Buyers will need to review their monthly purchase journals to check that orders placed actually achieve the desired markup. Any discrepancy in markup due to a potential cost pricing change needs to be reviewed and corrected in order to meet the planned cumulative markup goal.

- Negotiate for and take advantage of any cash discounts offered to retailers in the purchase of merchandise.

For a department, an **initial cumulative markup** is planned on a monthly and/or seasonal basis, can be expressed in either dollar figures or percentages, and is usually reported as a percentage on open-to-buy and sales reports. In most large retail corporations, buyers are given their markup goals, which are determined by history and company goals and set by the general and divisional merchandise managers in conjunction with the planning team. This cumulative initial markup goal is the guide that will need to be checked against aggregate initial markups obtained in pricing new merchandise purchases.

In addition, it is essential to know that the initial cumulative markup planned for a month/season must take into consideration the markups on new purchases as well as any merchandise remaining in stock. The gross margin figure for the month/season is dependent on the markups achieved on the entire inventory available for sale. Thus, in planning an initial markup, the gross margin and/or profit goal, planned reductions, planned expenses, and planned sales must be projected first.

An initial markup is expressed as a percentage of the aggregate original retail price placed on the merchandise, not on the price at which the merchandise sold. The price at which the merchandise sold is expressed as sales plus reductions. For example, if sales are planned at $1,000,000 and all retail reductions at $350,000, the goods that eventually sell at $1,000,000 must be introduced into stock at $1,350,000, with the desired markup expressed as a percentage of this total. This seasonal planned markup percentage can be calculated, and the concept can be expressed by a formula.

Establishing an Initial Markup

To better appreciate the establishment of an initial markup, examine the methods commonly used to institute a seasonal markup, and the calculations (in both dollars and percentages) as they appear in the chart and steps that follow. (The figures listed in the chart are for illustration only; they do not represent actual retail figures.)

GIVEN		Dollars	Percentages
	Planned sales	$1,000,000	100.0%
	Estimated expenses	$320,000	32.0%
	Price reductions	$350,000	35.0%
	Profit	$50,000	5.0%

METHOD

Step 1: Forecast the total sales for the season or the year ($1,000,000).

Step 2: Estimate the required expenses ($320,000) and price reductions ($350,000) needed to reach the sales plan.

Step 3: Set a profit goal—operating profit or department contribution ($50,000).

Step 4: Add the estimated expenses ($320,000) to the price reductions ($350,000) and profit ($50,000) to determine the dollar markup ($720,000).

		Dollars		Percentages
	Estimated expenses	$320,000		32.0%
+	Price reductions	+ $350,000	+	35.0
+	Profit	+ $50,000	+	5.0
	Dollar markup	= $720,000	=	72.0%

Step 5: Determine the original retail price ($1,350,000) by adding the planned reductions ($350,000) to the planned sales ($1,000,000).

		Dollars		Percentages
	Planned sales	$1,000,000		100.0%
+	Price reductions	+ $350,000	+	35.0
	Original retail price	= $1,350,000	=	135.0%

Step 6: Compute the markup percentage by dividing the dollar markup ($720,000) found in Step 4 by the original price ($1,350,000).

		Dollars		Percentages
	Markup	$720,000		72.0%
÷	Original retail price	÷ $1,350,000	÷	135.0%
	Initial markup %	= 53.3%	=	53.3%

CALCULATING INITIAL MARKUP

The formula for calculating an initial markup percentage on goods purchased shows the amount of markup necessary to achieve a desired profit. As already discussed, this markup should cover cost of merchandise, expenses, reductions, and profits. These projections can be based on past results or calculated mathematically on the basis of anticipated sales, reductions (primarily markdowns), and expenses. The equation to determine an initial markup percentage can spell out each factor (i.e., expenses + profits + markdowns + stock shortages + employee discounts), or it can be simplified (i.e., expenses + profits = **gross margin** [the bottom portion of the skeletal profit and loss statement], and markdowns + stock shortages + employee discounts = **retail reductions**). Because gross margin and retail reduction figures are more significant in planning than the analysis of expenses, shortages, and other factors, the second, simplified equation is more often used.

Finding Initial Markup Percentage When Gross Margin Percentage and Retail Reduction Percentage Are Known

CONCEPT

$$\text{Initial markup \%} = \frac{\text{Gross margin \%} + \text{Retail reductions \%}}{100\% + \text{Retail reductions \%}}$$

PROBLEM

A store has a gross margin (GM) of 37.0% (32.0% expenses + 5% profit) and retail reductions (markdowns, shortages, and employee discounts) of 35%. What is the initial markup percentage?

SOLUTION

$$\text{Initial markup \%} = \frac{\underset{\text{(32.0\% Expenses} + 5\% \text{ Profit)}}{37.0\% \text{ GM}} + \underset{\text{(markdowns, shortages, employee discounts)}}{35\% \text{ Retail reductions}}}{100\% \text{ Sales} + 35\% \text{ Retail reductions}}$$

$$= \frac{72.0\%}{135\%}$$

Initial markup % = 53.3%

Finding Initial Markup Percentage When Gross Margin and Retail Reductions in Dollars Are Known

CONCEPT

$$\text{Initial markup \%} = \frac{\text{Gross margin \$} + \text{Retail reductions \$}}{\text{Sales \$} + \text{Retail reductions \$}} \times 100$$

PROBLEM

A store plans sales of $1,000,000 and retail reductions of $350,000, and it requires a gross margin of $370,000 (i.e., expenses, $320,000, profit $50,000). What should be the initial markup percentage?

SOLUTION

$$\text{Initial markup \%} = \frac{\$370,000 \text{ (GM)} + \underset{\text{(Retail reductions)}}{\$350,000}}{\$1,000,000 \text{ Sales} + \underset{\text{(Retail reductions)}}{\$350,000}} \times 100$$

$$= \frac{\$720,000}{\$1,350,000}$$

Initial markup % = 53.3%

Finding Initial Markup Percentage When Cash Discounts and Alteration Costs Are Known

As shown in Chapter 1, the cost of goods sold is adjusted by alteration and workroom costs and cash discounts. Therefore, these factors (if and when alteration/workroom costs exist) are essential in calculating retail markups. Because markup covers alteration and workroom costs, these factors are added to gross margin. Because cash discounts reduce the cost of goods sold, which affects the final markup obtained, they are subtracted from gross margin.

CONCEPT

$$\text{Initial markup \%} = \frac{\text{Gross margin} + \text{Alteration costs} - \text{Cash discount earned} + \text{Retail reduction}}{\text{Sales (100\%)} + \text{Retail reductions \%}}$$

PROBLEM

The desired gross margin of a store is 37.0%, and the retail reductions are 35%; the cash discounts earned are 15%, and the alteration costs are 2%.

SOLUTION

$$\text{Initial markup \%} = \frac{37.0\% \text{ Gross margin} + 2\% \text{ Alteration costs} - 15\% \text{ Cash discounts} + 35\% \text{ Retail reductions}}{100\% \text{ (Sales)} + 35\% \text{ Retail reductions}}$$

$$= \frac{59.0\%}{135.0\%}$$

Initial markup % = 43.7%

CUMULATIVE MARKUP

Although an initial markup may be calculated for individual items, the initial markup on merchandise received is more commonly reported on a monthly basis, season-to-date (STD), or for the year. The markup for all merchandise based on current pricing is called "cumulative markup," which is the markup percentage figure generally used by retailers to calculate the markup for new product being received and all merchandise on the selling floor. In Chapter 2, cumulative markup was discussed as the markup for any new items written on a purchase order for a given buy. **Cumulative markup** is also the markup percentage achieved on all goods available for sale from the beginning of a given period. It is the markup percentage obtained on the accumulated inventory at the beginning of the given period, plus the markup of all new purchases received STD. This is the markup that is reflected on the buyer's merchandising reports. The cumulative markup in dollars equals the difference between the invoiced cost of the merchandise (including transportation) before cash discounts have been adjusted and the cumulative original retail prices of all merchandise handled (Opening inventory + Net purchases) during a given period of time. Permanent markdowns enter into the calculation since the original retail price has been lowered and the inventory is now valued at the markdown price. POS markdowns do not enter into the calculation of the cumulative markup percentage. The concept is simply stated by saying:

CONCEPT

$$\text{Cumulative markup \%} = \frac{\text{Cumulative markup \$}}{\text{Cumulative retail \$}} \times 100$$

PROBLEM

On February 1, a boys' clothing department has an opening inventory of $200,000 at retail with markup of 59.0%. On July 31, the new purchases season-to-date (STD) amounted to $1,350,000 at retail with a 64.0% markup. The buyer's planned markup is 63.0%. Find the cumulative markup percentage achieved.

SOLUTION

The given information is in bold, and the other items are calculated from the basic markup formulas. Each calculation is identified with the steps of the procedure.

	Cost	Retail	Markup %
Opening inventory	$82,000	**$200,000**	**59.0%**
+ Purchases STD	+ 486,000	**+ 1,350,000**	**64.0%**
Total merchandise handled	$568,000	$1,550,000	63.4%

Step 1: Find the cost value of the retail opening inventory.

Cost	=	Retail × (100% – Markup %)
	=	**$200,000** × (100% – **59%**)
	=	**$200,000** × 41%
Cost	=	$82,000

Step 2: Find the total cost value of all purchases season-to-date.

Cost	=	Retail × (100% – Markup %)
	=	**$1,350,000** × (100% – **64%**)
	=	**$1,350,000** × 36%
Cost	=	$486,000

Step 3: Find the total retail value of total merchandise handled.

Total retail value = $200,000 + $1,350,000

Total retail value = $1,550,000

Step 4: Find the total cost value of total merchandise handled.

Total cost value = $82,000 + $486,000

Total cost value = $568,000

Step 5: Find the cumulative markup on total merchandise handled.

Cumulative retail (Step 3)   = $1,550,000

Cumulative cost (Step 4)   =   – 568,000

Cumulative markup (Step 5)   = $982,000

Cumulative markup %   = $\dfrac{\$982,000 \text{ Cumulative markup}}{\$1,550,000 \text{ Cumulative retail}} \times 100$

Cumulative markup %   =   63.4%

The new purchases required a 64.0% markup to achieve a 63.4% cumulative markup, because the merchandise of the opening inventory came into the period with only a 59% markup against the plan of 63.0%.

At this point, it must be understood that both the initial and cumulative markups are on merchandise purchased. Initial markup percentage refers to those markups obtained when pricing new merchandise purchases. Cumulative markup percentage is the amount of markup on all the merchandise available for sale, whether it is new purchases or stock-on-hand at the beginning of the period. The cumulative markup percentage is the initial markup percentage calculated from the beginning of the season to any given later date (e.g., the end of the season or year).

MAINTAINED MARKUP

A maintained markup that is controlled helps buyers to analyze results to date and is similar to the calculation of the gross margin. Before maintained markup is explained, however, it is essential to know that although gross margin and a maintained markup are related, they are not identical. Gross margin is the difference between net sales and the cost of merchandise sold, adjusted by subtracting cash discounts and adding alteration and workroom costs (i.e., total cost of merchandise sold) and freight. **Maintained markup** (MMU) is the difference between net sales and the cost of merchandise sold without the credits of cash discounts and without the addition of alteration and workroom costs (i.e., gross cost of merchandise sold) and freight. If these differences are not considered in calculations, the gross margin and maintained markup figures will be the same. For both, the net sales figure reflects the final selling prices received for the goods sold and the margin actually realized when the goods are sold. The relationship between gross margin and maintained markup is revealed clearly in the following example:

	Net sales	$1,000,000
	Cost of goods sold	$220,000
+	New purchases	+ $645,000
+	Inward freight	+ $14,000
	Total merchandise handled	$879,000
–	Closing inventory	– $280,000
	Gross cost of merchandise	$599,000
–	Cash discounts earned	– $32,000
	Net cost of merchandise sold	$567,000
+	Alteration/workroom costs	+ $10,000
	Total cost of merchandise sold	= $577,000
	Gross margin	= $423,000

CONCEPT

$$\text{Gross margin \%} = \frac{\text{Net sales} - \text{Total cost of goods sold}}{\text{Net sales}} \times 100$$

$$= \$1,000,000 \text{ (Sales)} - \$577,000 \text{ (Total cost of goods sold)}$$

$$= \$423,000 \text{ Gross margin}$$

$$= \frac{\$423,000 \text{ Gross margin}}{\$1,000,000 \text{ Net sales}} \times 100$$

Gross margin % = 42.3%

While:

CONCEPT

$$\text{Maintained markup \%} = \frac{\text{Net sales \$} - \text{Gross cost of goods sold \$}}{\text{Net sales \$}} \times 100$$

$$= \frac{\$1,000,000 \text{ Net sales} - \$599,000 \text{ (Gross cost of goods)}}{\$1,000,000 \text{ Net sales}}$$

$$= \frac{\$401,000 \text{ Maintained margin}}{\$1,000,000 \text{ Net sales}} \times 100$$

Maintained markup % = 40.1%

Because the difference between gross margin and maintained markup is the amount of cash discounts and alteration and workroom costs, this relationship can also be expressed (using the same figure) as the following concept.

<table>
<tr><td>Gross
margin %</td><td>=</td><td>$\dfrac{\text{Maintained markup + Cash discounts – Alteration costs}}{\text{Net sales}}$</td><td>× 100</td><td>**CONCEPT**</td></tr>
</table>

$$= \frac{\$401{,}000 \text{ MMU} + \begin{array}{c}\$32{,}000 \\ \text{Cash discounts}\end{array} - \begin{array}{c}\$10{,}000 \\ \text{Alteration costs}\end{array}}{\$1{,}000{,}000 \text{ Sales}} \times 100$$

$$= \frac{\$423{,}000}{\$1{,}000{,}000} \times 100$$

Gross margin %   =   42.3%

<table>
<tr><td>Maintained
markup %</td><td>=</td><td>$\dfrac{\text{Gross margin \$ – Cash discounts \$ + Alteration costs \$}}{\text{Net sales}}$</td><td>× 100</td><td>**CONCEPT**</td></tr>
</table>

$$= \frac{\begin{array}{c}\$423{,}000 \\ \text{Gross margin}\end{array} - \begin{array}{c}\$32{,}000 \\ \text{Cash discounts}\end{array} + \begin{array}{c}\$10{,}000 \\ \text{Alteration costs}\end{array}}{\$1{,}000{,}000 \text{ Sales}}$$

$$= \frac{\$401{,}000}{\$1{,}000{,}000} \times 100$$

Maintained markup %   =   40.1%

Although maintained markup is the markup actually achieved on the sale of the merchandise, gross margin is the better indicator. Retailers more commonly use gross margin rather than maintained markup to measure buyers' profitability. Gross margin and/or maintained markup is generally calculated for a department or, frequently, for **vendor analysis**, which is an investigation of the profitability of each vendor's products sold. It is not customary to plan a maintained markup, because it is the result of merchandising activities. The initial markup must be planned in advance so that the desired final or maintained markup goal is achieved. In addition, maintained markup must be large enough to cover expenses and provide a profit, while, as previously explained, the initial markup must be high enough to anticipate and also cover all possible retail reductions (i.e., markdowns, shortages, and employee discounts). However, once the initial markup and retail reductions are planned, the probable maintained markup can be projected.

Finding Maintained Markup Percentage When Initial Markup Percentage and Retail Reductions Percentage Are Known

CONCEPT

$$\text{Maintained markup \%} = \text{Initial markup \%} - \text{Retail reduction \%} \times (100\% - \text{Initial markup \%})$$

PROBLEM

A department planned an initial markup of 49.8% and retail reductions of 15%. What is the maintained markup?

SOLUTION

$$\text{Maintained markup \%} = 49.8\% - 15\% \times (100\% - 49.8\%)$$

$$= 49.8\% - 15\% \times 50.2\%$$

$$= 49.8\% - 7.53\%$$

Maintained markup % = 42.27% or 42.3%

Finding Retail Reductions Percentage When Initial Markup Percentage and Maintained Markup Percentage Are Known

CONCEPT

$$\text{Retail reduction \%} = \frac{\text{Initial markup \%} - \text{Maintained markup \%}}{\text{Sales (100\%)} - \text{Initial markup \%}}$$

PROBLEM

The department planned an initial markup of 49.8% and wanted to achieve a maintained markup of 42.3%. What should be the amount of retail reductions?

SOLUTION

$$\text{Reduction \%} = \frac{49.8\% \text{ Initial MU} - 42.3\% \text{ MMU}}{\text{Sales (100\%)} - 49.8\% \text{ Initial MU}}$$

$$= \frac{7.5\%}{50.2\%}$$

Reduction % = 14.9%

The same factors have been used deliberately to show the calculations of both initial and maintained markups so that the relationship can be fully appreciated. The maintained markup concepts can also be expressed in dollars, and the procedure for calculation is identical. A particular merchandising situation, however, may require the focus to be on dollars rather than percentages (e.g., merchandising fast-turnover goods).

1. A lingerie buyer determines that the department has net sales of $750,000, expenses of $315,000, and total reductions of $75,000. This buyer also wants to attain a net profit of 4.5%. Find the initial markup percentage.

2. A department shows a gross margin of 41% (37.9% expenses + 3.1% profit) and lists retail reductions (i.e., markdowns, shortages, and employee discounts) of 43%. What is the initial markup percentage?

3. A chain of specialty shops plans sales of $1,500,000 and retail reductions of $260,000. It needs a gross margin of $805,000 (i.e., expenses $550,000, profit $255,000). What should be the initial markup percentage?

4. In a small leather goods department, the markdowns, including employee discounts, were 38.7%, stock shortage was 2.8%, and the gross margin was 46.6%. Determine the initial markup percentage.

Calculating Initial Markup
Practice Problems

5. A retailer in a boutique jewelry store has estimated expenses of 39%, markdowns at 15%, and stock shortage at 6.3%. A profit of 4% is desired. Calculate the initial markup percentage required.

6. The intimate apparel buyer wants to determine an initial markup percentage for the robe classification. The buyer knows that the gross margin is 44%, markdowns are at 31.4%, and shortages are at 0.6%. Calculate the initial markup percentage.

7. A gross margin of 49.4% is targeted by a gift department. Retail reductions are 16% and cash discounts are 4%, with alteration costs of 1%. Find the initial markup percentage.

8. A buyer plans, for the period, net sales of $1,500,000, with a 49% gross margin. The acceptable markdowns are 42%, with employee discounts at 1%, and planned shortages of 2.5%. Cash discounts to be earned are estimated at 12%, and alteration costs are 0.5%. What initial markup percentage is needed to achieve the desired results?

9. Determine the initial markup percentage from the following data:

Gross margin	=	46.8%
Markdowns	=	35.0%
Employee discounts	=	1.5%
Cash discounts to be earned	=	15.0%
Alteration costs	=	0.5%

10. The petite sportswear buyer plans seasonal net sales of $2,000,000, with a gross margin of 48%, markdowns (including employee discounts) estimated at 32.9%, planned shortages at 2.1%, cash discounts to be earned planned at 6%, and alteration costs at 1%. Calculate the planned initial markup percentage.

Cumulative Markup Practice Problems

11. A sleepwear buyer has an opening stock figure of $180,000 at retail, which carries a 62% markup. On March 31, new purchases since the start of the period were $990,000 at retail, carrying a 64% markup. Find the cumulative markup percentage on merchandise handled in this department to date.

12. The slipper department showed an opening inventory of $80,000 at retail, with a markup of 48%. The purchases for that month amounted to $30,000 at cost, which were marked in at 52%. The initial markup planned for this department was 50.5%.

    a. Determine the season-to-date cumulative markup percentage for the department.

    b. Was the department markup achieved on target? If not, what factors caused a deviation?

13. A belt department had an opening inventory of $95,000 at retail, with a 55.8% markup. Purchases during November were $64,000 at cost and $142,000 at retail. Determine:

    a. The cumulative markup percentage.

    b. The markup percentage on the new purchases.

14. During the Fall season, a retailer determined that in order to meet the next season's planned sales, the total amount of merchandise required next season was $360,000 at retail, with an initial markup goal of 52%. At the beginning of the next season, the merchandise on hand (opening inventory) came to $80,000 at retail, with a cumulative markup of 49% on these goods. For the coming season, what initial markup percentage does the buyer need to achieve on any new purchases?

15. In preparation for a foreign buying trip, a buyer determines that a 55.4% markup is required on purchases that will amount to $560,000 at retail. While on this trip, the following purchases are made:

	Cost	Retail
Resource A	$20,000	$45,000
Resource B	$50,000	$125,000
Resource C	$70,000	$170,000

What markup percentage is needed on the balance of the purchases?

Maintained Markup Practice Problems

16. A men's shop with an initial markup of 53% had markdowns of 12%, employee discounts of 2.5%, and shortages of 1.5%. What was the maintained markup percentage?

17. A sporting goods store has an initial markup of 44.5%. The expenses are 31%, markdowns are 12%, cost of assembling bicycles, and so on (i.e., workroom costs), are 6%, and shortages are 1%. What was the maintained markup percentage?

18. The Closet Shop had the following operational results:

Net sales	=	$125,000
Billed cost of new purchases	=	$64,000
Inward freight	=	$1,000
Alteration costs	=	$2,000
Cash discounts	=	$7,000

    Find:

    a. The maintained markup in dollars and percentages.

    b. The gross margin in dollars and percentages.

19. The jewelry department has an initial markup of 55.6%, with total retail reductions of 15%. There are no alteration costs or cash discounts. What is the maintained markup percentage and the gross margin percentage?

20. A children's store has sales of $500,000, with markdowns of 14.5% and shortages of 2%. The initial markup was 51.7%. What was the maintained markup percentage?

21. The T-shirt department buyer determined that the department's initial markup should be 51.5%. The buyer also wanted to attain a maintained markup of 45%. Under this plan, what retail reduction (in percentage) would be allowed?

22. A boutique had planned a gross margin of 49%, with total retail reductions of 18%. At the end of the period, the maintained markup attained was actually 48.8%.

      a. Find the initial markup percentage needed to achieve the planned gross margin of 49%, with total retail reductions of 18%.

      b. Find the actual amount of markdowns (in percentages) taken.

Prove your calculations and explain your findings. What may have caused the maintained markup percentage to vary from the planned gross margin target?

3.2 Average or Balancing Markup

A buyer's skill is truly tested by the ability not only to buy "the right goods, at the right time, in the right amounts," but also to achieve a predetermined markup percentage over a month, quarter, season, or year. Failure to reach this goal can have an adverse effect on profits, and sometimes can determine whether or not a profit is generated at all. Ultimately, as short-term buying decisions are made, the merchandiser must know how any deviations from the markup objective will affect the long-term performance.

In the actual pricing of goods in retailing, it is seldom possible to obtain the same markup on all categories of merchandise, all classifications, all price lines, or all items carried within a particular department. In the world of retailing, deviations from the planned seasonal markup will occur. These differences can be the result of competition, variations in special promotional merchandise offered by resources, special buying arrangements, private brands/labels, imports, and other factors that depend on the buyer's judgment. Thus, to realize the planned markup necessary for a profitable operation, below-average markups should be balanced by above-average markups. **Averaging markups** (also called **balancing markups**) means adjusting the proportions of goods purchased at different markups to achieve the desired aggregate markup, either for an individual purchase or for a certain buying period. In merchandising the purchases, the buyer builds a "cushion" or lowers the markup, depending on the situation. This practice is prevalent in the fashion and fashion-related industries.

There are diverse pricing policies that are determined by an industry or by the specific retailer. Some of these factors are odd pricing (e.g., $89.99 instead of $90); multiple-unit pricing (e.g., 1 for $7.00 or 3 for $15.00 as in the case of socks); loss leaders, in which an item is sold below the retailer's cost; high/low pricing, in which high everyday prices are combined with "specials"; or low leader pricing on featured items advertised weekly. Each retailer must evaluate the usefulness of each type of pricing service. The appropriate cumulative markup originates from effective averaging of many purchases.

When solving problems that illustrate how markups are averaged or balanced, it is helpful to remember that:

- On a day-to-day basis, buyers strive to achieve a projected markup by the averaging process.

- Appropriate cumulative markups result from the effective averaging of many purchases for a given time period, usually a month or quarter, and the effects of this averaging on the entire inventory.

- Basic markup equations are applied to given information to calculate the figures required for solutions.

- Solutions can be calculated readily when:

    - It is understood what information is missing.

    - The given information is determined.

    - The calculations required for the solution (based on the given information) are identified.

The next section's problems and solutions employ the preceding principles in two ways; that is, the steps necessary for the calculations are listed in sequence, and the results of these calculations are arranged in a diagram. It should be understood that an average markup is always determined by working with a total cost figure and a total retail figure. Spreadsheets simplify the calculating of averages.

AVERAGE COSTS WHEN RETAIL AND MARKUP PERCENTAGE ARE KNOWN

Determining the **average cost**, a merchandising technique, involves one retail price with two or more costs. It is common to have one retail line that consists of merchandise with varying wholesale costs. The merchandiser must be able to calculate the proportion of merchandise at different cost amounts that can carry the same retail price and still achieve the desired markup percentage. To understand this, it is essential to realize that the merchandiser is attempting to proportion the varying costs to achieve the desired markup percentage, because the aggregate results are the buyer's major concern.

PROBLEM

For a special sale, a men's tie buyer plans to promote a $25 tie. Consequently, the buyer purchases 500 ties and wants to achieve a 60% markup. An order for 100 ties that cost $11.00 each is also placed by this same buyer. What will be the average cost of the remaining pieces?

SOLUTION:
Spreadsheet format

Given information is in bold, and the other items are calculated.

	# Ties	Unit price	Total retail	MU %	Unit cost	Total cost
Special sale	**500**	**$25.00**	$12,500.00	**60%**		$5,000.00
Purchased	**100**				**$11.00**	$1,100.00
Balance	400				$9.75	$3,900.00

SOLUTION:
Arithmetic format

Given information is in bold, and the other items are calculated from the basic markup formulas. Each calculation is identified with the steps of the procedure.

Step 1: Find the total planned retail.

500 Pieces × **$25 Retail** = $12,500 (Total planned retail)

Step 2: Find the total cost of total planned retail using a planned markup percentage.

Total cost	=	Retail × (100% − Markup %)
	=	$12,500 × (100% − 60%)
	=	$12,500 × 40%
Total cost	=	$5,000

Step 3: Find the cost of purchases to date.

100 Pieces × **$11.00** = $1,100 (Cost of purchases to date)

Step 4: Find the purchase balance in units and dollars.

Purchase balance	=	Total planned figures − Purchases to date
	=	(500 Pieces cost $5,000) − (100 Pieces cost $1,100)
	=	(400 Pieces cost $3,900)

	Total pieces	Total $ cost	Total $ retail	MU %
Total plan	500 (1)	$5,000 (2)	$12,500	60%
− Purchases to date	− 100 (3)	− $1,100 (3)		
Purchase balance	400 (4)	$3,900 (4)		

Step 5: Find the average cost of purchase balance.

Average cost of purchase balance = $ Cost on balance

        Purchase balance   *Number of units*

= $3,900 (Purchase balance cost) ÷ 400 Pieces (Purchase balance pieces)

= $9.75 each is the average cost of the remaining pieces

AVERAGE RETAIL(S) WHEN COSTS AND MARKUP PERCENTAGE ARE KNOWN

In merchandising, a buyer must be able to manipulate markups because purchases are made on similar or different items that have two or more costs, and the buyer may want to determine an **average retail** that will achieve the desired markup percentage. Furthermore, the buyer may make purchases that have not only two or more costs but also two or more retails. These situations require the proper proportion of varying retails to achieve the planned markup percentage, because a buyer is always concerned with the aggregate results. The following problems illustrate the averaging processes.

For Mother's Day, the handbag buyer wants to advertise a select group of handbags at a single retail price. The handbag vendor the buyer is working with offers the following assortment: 500 satchels at a cost of $17.35 each, 300 hobos at a cost of $18.75 each, and 200 totes at a cost of $18.50 each. The buyer's markup goal for the event is 55.0%. What is the retail price that the buyer can sell the handbags for?

Given information is in bold, and the other items are calculated from the basic markup formulas.

Handbags	# Suits	Unit cost	Total cost	MU %	Total $ retail	Average retail per handbag
Satchels	**500**	**$17.35**	$8,675			
Hobos	**300**	**$18.75**	$5,625			
Totes	**200**	**$18.50**	$3,700			
Total	1,000		$18,000	**55%**	$40,000	$40.00

Given information is in bold, and the other items are calculated from the basic markup formulas. Each calculation is identified with the steps of the procedure.

Step 1: Find the total cost and total units of purchase.

	500 Satchels @ $17.35	=	$8,675.00
+	**300 Hobos @ $18.75**	=	+ 5,625.00
+	**200 Totes @ $18.50**	=	+ 3,700.00
	Total	=	$18,000.00 Total cost

Step 2: Find the total retail from the planned markup percentage.

$$\text{Total retail} \quad = \quad \frac{\text{Cost}}{(100\% - \mathbf{55\%})}$$

$$= \quad \frac{\$18,000}{45\%}$$

$$\text{Total retail} \quad = \quad \$40,000$$

	Total pieces	Total $ cost	Total $ retail	MU %
Total plan	1000 (1)	$18,000 (1)	$40,000 (2)	55%

Step 3: Find the average retail for each piece.

$$\text{Average retail} \quad = \quad \frac{\text{Total retail}}{\text{Total units purchased}}$$

$$= \quad \frac{\$40,000 \text{ (Total retail)}}{1,000 \text{ (Total units purchased)}}$$

$$\textbf{Average retail} \quad = \quad \$40.00$$

The jewelry buyer bought 1,500 pairs of hoop earrings that cost $6.00 each and will retail for $24.00. They will also be purchasing 1,000 pairs of chandelier earrings at a cost of $7.50 each. An overall markup of 75.0% is needed. What is the retail price for each pair of chandelier earrings to achieve the planned markup percentage?

Given information is in bold, and the other items are calculated from the basic markup formulas.

	# Earrings	Unit cost	Total cost	MU %	Unit retail	Total retail
Hoop earrings	**1,500**	**$6.00**	$9,000.00		**$24.00**	$36,000.00
Chandelier earrings	**1,000**	**$7.50**	$7,500.00		$30.00	$30,000.00
Total	2,500		$16,500.00	**75.0**		$66,000.00

Given information is in bold, and the other items are calculated from the basic markup formulas. Each calculation is identified with the steps of the procedure.

Step 1: Find the total cost and total units.

$$\mathbf{1,500} \text{ Hoop earrings @ } \mathbf{\$6.00} \quad = \quad \$9,000.00$$

$$+ \quad \mathbf{1,000} \text{ Chandelier earrings @ } \mathbf{\$7.50} \quad = \quad \$7,500.00$$

$$2,500 \text{ Earrings} \quad = \quad \$16,500.00$$

Step 2: Find the total retail from the planned markup percentage.

$$\text{Total retail} = \frac{\text{Cost}}{(100\% - \textbf{75.0\%})}$$

$$= \frac{\$16,500}{(100\% - \textbf{75.0\%})}$$

$$= \frac{\$16,500.00}{25.0\%}$$

$$\text{Total retail} = \$66,000.00$$

Step 3: Find the total on the established retail price.

1,500 Hoop earrings × **\$24 each** = \$36,000

Step 4: Find the purchase balance in units and dollars.

$$
\begin{aligned}
\text{Purchase balance} \quad &= \quad \text{Total planned figures} - \text{Total established retail figures} \\
&= \quad 2{,}500 \text{ Earrings @} \quad \$66{,}000.00 \text{ (Total \$ retail)} \\
&- \quad \underline{1{,}500 \text{ Earrings @} \quad \$36{,}000.00 \text{ (Established retail)}} \\
&\quad\quad 1{,}000 \text{ Earrings} \quad\quad \$30{,}000.00
\end{aligned}
$$

Step 5: Find the average retail of the purchase balance.

$$\text{Average retail of purchase balance} = \frac{\text{Purchase balance \$ retail}}{\text{Purchase balance number of units}}$$

$$= \frac{\$30,000.00}{1,000 \text{ Earrings}}$$

Average retail for each remaining piece $=$ $\$30.00$

AVERAGE MARKUP PERCENTAGE WHEN RETAIL AND PLANNED MARKUP PERCENTAGE ARE KNOWN

Realistically, a profit goal can be realized only when a buyer is able to determine the markup percentage that must be obtained on present or future purchases to balance out the markup percentage that has already been achieved on past purchases. This involves the proportioning of markup percentages on goods so that the aggregate results produce the desired, planned markup percentage.

A coat buyer plans to buy \$200,000 at retail for different coat styles for October in store. This buyer requires a 54% markup. The first purchase is for 500 coats costing \$64.00, with a planned retail of \$129.00. What markup percentage should the buyer obtain on the balance to attain the planned markup goal of 54%?

PROBLEM

	# Coats	Unit cost	Total cost	MU %	Unit retail	Total retail	Markup $
1st purchase	**500**	**$64.00**	$32,000	**50.4%**	**$129.00**	$64,500	$32,500
Balance			$60,000	55.7%		$135,500	$75,500
Total			$92,000	54.0%		**$200,000**	

SOLUTION: *Spreadsheet format*

Given information is in bold, and the other items are calculated from the basic markup formulas.

SOLUTION: *Arithmetic format*

Given information is in bold, and the other items are calculated from the basic markup formulas; each calculation is identified with the steps of the procedure.

Step 1: Find the total cost of the total planned retail from the planned markup percentage.

Total cost = Retail × (100% – Markup %)

= **$200,000** × (100% – **54%**)

= $200,000 × 46%

Total cost of purchase = $92,000

Step 2: Find the total cost and retail of purchases to date.

500 Coats @ **$64.00** = $32,000 Total cost of purchases to date

500 Coats @ **$129.00** = $64,500 Total retail of purchases to date

Step 3: Find purchase balance at cost and retail.

Purchase balance at cost = Total planned cost – Cost of purchases to date

= $92,000 (Planned total cost) – $32,000 (Cost of purchases to date)

= $60,000 (Cost of purchase balance)

Purchase balance at retail = Total planned retail – Retail purchases to date

= **$200,000** (Planned total retail) – $64,500 (Total retail purchases to date)

Total retail of purchases balance = $135,500

	Total $ cost	Total $ retail	MU %
Total plan	$92,000	$200,000	54%
Purchase to date	$32,000 (2)	$64,500 (2)	
Purchase balance	$60,000 (3)	$135,500 (3)	

Step 4: Find the markup percentage on purchase balance.

Dollar markup = Retail − Cost

= $135,500 (Purchase balance retail) − $60,000 (Purchase balance cost)

= $75,500 (Markup on purchase balance)

Markup % $= \dfrac{\text{Markup \$}}{\text{Retail}} \times 100$

$= \dfrac{\$75,500 \text{ (Markup on purchase balance)}}{\$135,500 \text{ (Retail on purchase balance)}} \times 100$

Markup % = 55.7%

23. A buyer plans to purchase 7,200 pairs of socks for a pre-Christmas sale. The unit retail price is planned at $7.50, and the markup goal for the purchase is 59%. The buyer purchases 4,800 pairs at the Sock Company showroom, at a cost of $3.15 each.

      a. What is the maximum total cost the buyer can pay for the balance of the total purchase?

      b. What will be the average cost per pair for the socks (2,400 socks) yet to be purchased?

24. A separates buyer—who operates on a 61% markup—needs 300 skirts to retail at $79 each and 600 blouses to retail at $49 each. If this buyer pays $20.75 for each blouse, how much can be spent for each skirt, without deviating from the target markup percentage?

    $ 8259/300 =
              27.53

25. A buyer who needs $10,000 worth of merchandise at retail for a house-wares department has written orders for $2,875.50 at cost. The planned departmental markup percentage is 53.5%. How much (in dollars) is left to spend at cost?

26. A December promotion of 1,500 crystal bud vases to retail at $40 each is planned. The buyer requires a 48.5% average markup and has made an initial purchase consisting of 1,200 units costing $23 each. What is the cost to be paid on each remaining unit? Comment on the buyer's "predicament" if you detect one.

27. A buyer for the exclusive Britique Shop purchased 100 cashmere pullover sweaters at $31 each and priced them at $90 retail. Also planned is a purchase of 72 chunky knit wool sweaters to retail at $120 each. Departmental goal markup is 67.5%. How much can be paid for each chunky knit wool sweater?

Average Retail Practice Problems

28. An off-price buyer purchases closeouts of 400 pairs of men's jeans, 280 pairs costing $24 each and 120 pairs costing $27 each. If a 54% markup is targeted, what would be the average unit retail price on the jeans?

29. A buyer purchased 120 bandeau swimsuits at $32 cost and placed a $79 retail on them. Sixty string bikinis are also purchased at $26 each. What would be the retail price on the bikinis if a 60% markup is desired on the combined purchase?

30. A men's accessories buyer purchases 10,000 neckties from a manufacturer at the low cost price of $16 per tie. Noticing that the ties are of two types, 6,200 solids and 3,800 stripes, the buyer decides to attempt some creative merchandising. If each solid tie is retailed at $45, what minimum retail price should be placed on each striped tie if an average markup of 68% is desired?

31. An outerwear buyer confirms an order reading as follows:

    a. 145 trench raincoats costing $39 each.

    b. 75 anorak rain jackets costing $28 each.

If a retail price of $85 is placed on the trench coats, and a markup average of 55.5% is sought, what retail price must the anorak rain jackets carry?

32. A buyer plans to purchase jackets at a 58% markup with a retail value of $18,500. If the buyer acquires 100 jackets at $54.75 each and retails them at $125 each, what markup percentage must now be obtained on the balance of the purchases in order to achieve the desired markup percentage?

33. A buyer who needs $23,000 worth of goods at retail for May has a planned markup of 59.5%. May orders to date total $4,500 at cost and $9,800 at retail. What markup percentage must now be obtained on the balance of the purchases for May to achieve the planned markup percentage for the month?

34. The men's outerwear buyer, who needs a 51% average markup for a Columbus Day promotion, is planning to buy $9,500 worth of merchandise at retail for October. To date, 100 motorcycle jackets costing $23.40 each have been purchased, with a plan to retail them at 48% markup. What markup percentage is needed on the balance of the purchase to attain the average markup percentage?

35. A suit buyer who plans sales of $75,000 at retail during April has an average markup goal of 54%. An order is placed with the B&C Sportswear Company for April delivery in the amount of $5,975 at cost and $11,000 at retail. What markup percentage must be made on the balance of the April purchases to achieve the planned markup?

36. A housewares buyer plans a $15,000 promotion of decorative stepstools to retail at $25 each at a 48% markup. A local manufacturer supplies 500 stools for $14 each. What markup percentage must be obtained on the remainder of the planned purchase to reach the markup goal?

37. For a Spring Sale event, a buyer plans to purchase 250 floral print dresses to retail for $79.99 each. A 56% markup is needed on the total purchase. From one of the buyer's best resources, 110 dresses were purchased that cost $37.50 each. The buyer knows, however, that the costs will have to be averaged on the balance of other purchases from alternate resources in order to achieve a 56% markup on the entire group.

   a. What must be the average cost per dress on the balance of the purchases if the buyer is to attain the planned markup percentage?

   b. What markup percentage did the buyer attain on the first purchase of 110 dresses?

   c. What markup percentage did the buyer have to get on the balance of the purchases to realize the overall needed markup?

3.3 LIMITATIONS OF THE MARKUP PERCENTAGE AS A GUIDE TO PROFITS

From the discussions on markup and its relationship to profit, it is understood that markup can be calculated in both dollars and percentages. A markup percentage is a useful guideline in establishing a markup high enough to cover expenses, provide for reductions, and still realize a profit.

In the calculation of all types of markup, the focal point is generally on the markup, especially cumulative markup percentage because it is particularly meaningful for analysis and comparison. However, under certain conditions, attention must be given to the dollar markup. Expenses are paid in dollars and profit is invested, reinvested, or taken to the bank in dollars. During periods of declining sales, a markup percentage initially deemed appropriate may be insufficient for a profit because a certain markup percentage is based on a specific estimated sales figure. There is a correlation between these two figures. For example, a buyer achieves sales of $300,000 and attains the required initial markup of 52% that would be large enough to cover expenses of $136,000 and markdowns of $12,000, and allow a profit of $8,000. In dollars and percentages this calculation would be:

		Dollars		Percentages
Sales		$300,000		100%
− Cost of goods sold		− 144,000		− 48%
Initial markup		= $156,000		52%
Expenses $136,000 ⎫ Markdowns + $12,000 ⎬ Total profit ⎭		− 148,000 $8,000		− 49.3% 2.7%

If sales declined 10% to $270,000, the 52% markup may not yield a profit. As sales decline, the fixed nature of expenses will not decline proportionately to the sales, if at all, and it is not always possible to lower markdown reductions, which may increase to stimulate lagging sales. This type of situation can result in a loss despite the establishment of what seemed a satisfactory markup percentage. The results are illustrated in the following example:

With the same 52% markup, only $140,400 would be available to cover the expenses of $136,000 and the markdowns of $12,000.

	Dollars	Percentages
Sales	$270,000	100%
− Cost of goods sold	− 129,600	− 48%
Initial markup	= $140,400	52%
Expenses $136,000 ⎱ Markdowns + $12,000 ⎰	− 148,000	− 54.8%
	− $7,600 (Loss)	− 2.8%

Conversely, as sales increase, the markup percentage can decline even though the dollar markup is maintained at an adequate level. The astute retailer recognizes that the dollar markup figure cannot be ignored while attempting to achieve a fixed markup percentage.

CASE STUDY 1
ACHIEVING A PREDETERMINED MARKUP

Miss Jay Tee is the shoe buyer for a fashion specialty store located in the trendy "Near North Side" of Chicago. It is October 1, and she is scheduled for a European buying trip on October 25, during which she will place orders for Spring delivery. Her Spring six-month plans are complete and have been approved by management.

Before leaving on her buying trip, she reviews her current operational figures to evaluate her position for the forthcoming last quarter of the year (i.e., November, December, January). They are:

- Merchandise on hand (BOM, or beginning of the month) November 1: $1,300,000 with a 51.5% cumulative markup.

- Closing inventory (BOM) February 1: $400,000.

Planned sales:	November	December	January	Total sales
	$500,000	$550,000	$250,000	$1,300,000

- Planned markdown to be taken in November, December, January: $80,000, or 6.2%.

- Estimated shortages for this period: 2.0%.

- Gross margin (no cash discounts or alteration costs): 48.1%.

Based on this information, Miss Tee does some calculations and determines that she still has $506,000, at retail, to spend for this quarter.

It is customary for Miss Tee to devote several days at the beginning of her trip to scout the market to obtain extremely desirable current seasonal goods, available for immediate shipment, at advantageous prices that will stimulate pre-Christmas sales and that will generate sales in the slow-selling month of January, traditionally associated with only clearance and/or highly competitively priced merchandise.

On October 25, she arrives in Florence, Italy, and as she covers the boot resources, she finds there is an abundance of the current season's merchandise—available for immediate shipment—because of cancellations by importers and retailers. This situation has been caused by sluggish economic and business conditions. One of her best key resources has in stock 4,000 pairs of leather boots in this season's avant-garde styling with balanced sizes and colors. Fifty percent of the resource's offering are the same styles as 500 pairs currently in stock, selling reasonably well at $200 retail. Providing she agrees to buy the complete group, the final landed cost negotiated is $50 per pair. Despite the fact that she considers this merchandise to be a superb value at this sensational cost, she is hesitant about buying such a large quantity so late in the selling season. However, she receives an email from her assistant informing her that the boots are moving quickly and sales have increased due to very cold, wintery weather conditions. She decides to buy this offering before a competitor has an opportunity to do so. Her strategy considerations are:

- Retailing the group.

- Shipping for present selling.

- Integrating this purchase with present stock.

- Obtaining the necessary markup percentage.

She commits herself to the purchase, returns to her hotel, and diligently works to map out the delivery and pricing factors. Her first decision is to start shipping some of these goods so that they are available as soon as possible for November selling. Therefore, despite the expense, she immediately sends 1,000 pairs by air because it is fast and it serves her purpose. This mode of transportation increases the delivered cost of the 1,000 pairs from $50 to $55 a pair, and the retail is set at $150.

After making this decision, she turns her attention to the 500 pairs in stock currently selling at $200 a pair. Because markdown money is available, Miss Tee wants to begin to reduce the higher-priced boots while there is traffic. She can afford to reduce these 500 pairs from $200 to $150, taking a larger than usual first markdown, because the markup of the 1,000 pairs (that will sell simultaneously) is so above average.

On the balance of the 3,000 pairs, she divides half for December selling and retails them for $125. The remaining 1,500 pairs she reserves for her annual Blizzard Promotion scheduled in January. For this event, her boot sales rely solely on merchandise that creates "riots." She has not yet set a retail price on the 2,500 pairs for the January sale because she would like to price them at levels that are somewhat low, but that will not kill the required markup for the season. However, she calculates that a 54.4% markup is needed on the entire purchase so that her seasonal markup target will be met.

Prepare a merchandising plan for class discussion and, in doing so, consider the following:

- Do you agree with the merchandising techniques Miss Tee uses in this particular purchase? Explain why or why not, and justify your position mathematically.

- Advise Miss Tee of the retail price you would establish on the 1,500 pairs of boots targeted for the January promotion, keeping in mind that all of her objectives should be satisfied.

CASE STUDY 2
ENSURING FAVORABLE MARKUP RESULTS

You have been hired by a group of investors to buy and merchandise accessories for their small chain (four stores) of infant apparel shops. This new classification is to complement and reflect their prestigious, unique merchandise assortments, which are targeted for the young, upper-income mother and/or grandparents looking for the "unusual." This new classification was introduced in the Fall/Winter period and was well received by their clientele. Although the projected sales goal was met, the profit performance was more than disappointing.

After analysis of each market segment and location, your focus will be on the combined merchandise selection factors that form the basis of your ultimate selections suitable for your particular customer group.

The pricing factor is one of the elements that is of major importance and is not only significant but also observable. Because of the relationship of pricing to gross margin, management has planned and set certain gross margin guidelines and limitations to ensure that the store achieves a more satisfactory gross margin. These figures are to be achieved while accomplishing the projected sales. As an incentive, you have been promised an additional bonus if you provide gross margin results that are an improvement over the following expected guidelines:

Gross margin	47.4%	(43.4% expenses, 4% profit)
Sales	$600,000	
Markdowns	$660,000	(10%)
Shortages	$612,000	(2%)
Opening inventory	$150,000	
Closing inventory	$200,000	

You are confident that with appropriate planning and forecasting you will be able to attain the results management wants, and the phantom bonus mentioned could become a reality for you.

Situation 1. A key factor in gross margin control is the pricing of merchandise. Since management already established a 47.4% gross margin, will advance planning of an initial markup help ensure a favorable gross margin? Yes or no? Why? Should you be able to determine the gross margin or maintained markup having calculated the initial markup? What is to be gained by determining these two figures?

Situation 2. During the course of the season, you know the cumulative markup percentage is another important profit factor because it represents the markup on the merchandise on hand at the beginning of the season, as well as the purchases during this period. You notice that the opening inventory of $150,000 carried a 52.0% markup. What, if any, effect will this have on the markup percentage required of the new purchases in order to achieve the cumulative markup of 53% for the season?

Situation 3. Although you will focus on obtaining the desired markup percentage, you will also have to pay attention to the dollar markup. Why? Because these (sales, markdowns, shortages) are projections (which could prove erroneous). Compute and compare how the dollar markup could give different results if the actual reductions increased to 13%. Should you aim for a higher initial markup in order to build a "cushion" to account for the unpredictable?

CASE STUDY 3
BALANCING MARKUP

In preparation for a buying trip, a buyer determined a 54% markup was required on all purchases, which amounted to $750,000 at retail. On completion of the trip, the buyer reviewed the orders placed. At the end of the season, a vendor analysis revealed the following sales results:

	Cost	Initial retail	Final retail
Resource A	$25,000	$50,000	$50,000
Resource B	40,000	85,000	83,000
Resource C	60,000	135,000	130,000
Resource D	55,000	135,000	135,000
Resource E	75,000	170,000	167,000
Resource F	90,000	175,000	165,000
Total	$345,000	$750,000	$730,000

Compute the following:

a. Initial markup percentage for each resource.

b. Final markup percentage achieved for each resource.

c. Compare the anticipated markup percentage of the entire purchase to the actual markup percentage achieved.

d. Which vendor(s) markup percentage performance was superior to the overall markup percentage and by how much?

CASE STUDY 4
Achieving Your Cumulative Markup Goal

You are the buyer for Missy Weekend Wear (casual) outlet store. For April in store, you have already purchased a coordinate group, modern contrast. The total cost for the order is $476,735. The total retail spent is $1,339,542. Therefore, the cumulative markup % is 64.4%. As the buyer, you still need to place an order for key item T-shirts for April. These T-shirts will retail for $16.99, and you need to buy 48,944 units. The total open-to-buy for the month is $2,171,101.

Your planned cumulative markup % for April is 68.5%. Please calculate the markup percentage that you must achieve on any remaining open-to-buy to achieve the planned cumulative markup % for April. If the vendor states that the cost for the T-shirts will be $5.00, what other actions could you take to achieve the planned markup percentage?

THE RETAIL METHOD OF INVENTORY

## CHAPTER 4

"What's measured improves."

PETER DRUCKER

OBJECTIVES

- Gain knowledge and understanding of the retail method of inventory.

- Differentiate between physical inventory and book inventory.

- Identify and describe information and procedures necessary to implement the retail method of inventory.

- Calculate book inventory figures at cost.

- Recognize and identify the causes of shortages and overages.

- Calculate shortages and overages based on inventory figures.

- Evaluate the advantages and limitations of the retail method of inventory.

KEY TERMS

average dollar per sale or transaction (ADT)	maintained book inventory	purchase record
book inventory	opening book inventory	retail method of inventory
charge-back to vendors	overage	return to vendor (RTV)
closing book inventory	perpetual inventory	shortage/shrinkage
closing physical stock/ inventory	physical inventory	transfer
debit memo form	price change form	units per sale or transaction (UPT)
	price changes	

Key Concept Formulas

Book inventory

$$\begin{array}{c} \text{Book} \\ \text{inventory} \\ \text{at retail} \end{array} = \begin{array}{c} \text{Physical} \\ \text{inventory} \end{array} + \begin{array}{c} \text{Net retail} \\ \text{purchases} \\ \text{(Total merchandise} \\ \text{handled)} \end{array} + \begin{array}{c} \text{Other} \\ \text{stock} \\ \text{additions} \end{array} - \begin{array}{c} \text{Net} \\ \text{sales} \end{array} - \begin{array}{c} \text{Markdown} \\ \text{differences} \end{array} - \begin{array}{c} \text{Other} \\ \text{deductions} \\ \text{from stock} \end{array}$$

$$\begin{array}{c} \text{Book} \\ \text{inventory} \\ \text{at cost} \end{array} = \begin{array}{c} \text{Opening} \\ \text{retail book} \\ \text{inventory} \end{array} \times \left(100\% - \begin{array}{c} \text{Cumulative} \\ \text{markup \%} \\ \text{achieved on} \\ \text{stock} \end{array} + \text{Purchases} \right)$$

Shortage or overage

$$\begin{array}{c} \text{Shortage} \\ \text{(or overage) \$} \end{array} = \text{Closing book inventory at retail \$} - \begin{array}{c} \text{Physical inventory count} \\ \text{at retail \$} \end{array}$$

$$\text{Shortage \%} = \frac{\text{Shortage \$}}{\text{Annual net sales \$}} \times 100$$

$$\text{Planned dollar shortage} = \begin{array}{c} \text{Planned shortage} \\ \text{percentage} \end{array} \times \text{Planned net sales \$}$$

To control and guide the operations of a retail organization, it is essential to keep records. Records are the working tools that provide information on the profitability of a business or for making everyday decisions (e.g., what types of merchandise are needed, when and how much is needed, etc.). Of particular concern to management and buyers is inventory control.

Inventory (product, merchandise) is what the retailer sells to the consumer. Successful merchandising requires that the size of inventories offered to the consumer be large enough to satisfy customer demand but that the dollar investment be controlled to maximize profitability. This can be accomplished only by having a frequent indication of stock-on-hand. The retail merchandiser who is concerned with the question "How much can I sell?" must know how much to buy to maintain this satisfactory relationship between the amount of sales volume and the size of stocks carried. Today the increased use of computer information systems by department stores, small retail businesses, and most merchandising chains has a major impact on the management of merchandise inventories and other areas of record-keeping.

In large retail stores, it would be inconvenient and prohibitive in terms of cost to constantly determine the value of the amount of stock-on-hand by taking an actual count. However, because this balance of sales to stocks is vital, a system of accounting that determines the probable amount of stock-on-hand at any given time—without physically counting the goods—has been devised. The retail method of inventory is a system of accounting that values merchandise at current retail prices, which can be converted by markup formula to cost value. Although the computer turns available information into electronic documents, for illustrative purposes in the study of the retail method of inventory, the actual types of records connected with this method are shown here in order to appreciate the data required by this accounting system. The information required is critical, not the means of collection.

The **retail method of inventory** is a calculation of how much stock should be on hand at the end of the retail accounting month based on the previous month's starting point subtracting any reductions to the stock and adding any new additions to inventory. Retailers normally calculate this in retail value of inventory, the price on the merchandise tickets, and then may convert it to a cost basis. The conversion of the closing inventory at retail to a cost figure is calculated by the determination of the cumulative markup percentage on the total merchandise handled as described in Chapters 2 and 3. To understand the retail method of inventory, it is vital to realize that it operates on the theory that the merchandise in stock is always representative of the total merchandise handled to date (i.e., stock plus new purchases). It allows an acceptable cost value of the book inventory to be established so that gross margin can be determined periodically.

It is common practice for large stores to "think at retail" because net sales (100%) are the primary basis for the analysis of all the relationships of expenses to sales and are the ultimate determining factors that show whether the merchandising endeavors result in a profit or a loss. Gross margin, which is the difference between cost of goods sold and net sales, is also expressed as a percentage of net sales (Chapter 1). Consequently, the danger of failing to make the correct percentage comparisons is eliminated because these percentages are all calculated on the same base (i.e., net sales), which is a retail figure. The dollar value of the inventory owned must also be expressed as a retail figure to predetermine the desired relationship of these two factors (i.e., sales to stocks). In the process of buying and selling to yield a more satisfactory profit, retailers can compare and contrast their merchandising departments to determine which product categories/vendors are trending up in sales and profitability and which are not. They compare such factors as net sales produced (a retail figure); the relationship of retail stock to net sales (figures used to attain the needed proportion); the pricing of merchandise expressed as a percentage based on the retail; and the percentage of reductions (markdowns taken to sell through the product). Finally, when filing income taxes, insurance claims, and so on, the current retail price of the merchandise is the significant valuation.

These examples illustrate the importance of the maintenance of a perpetual retail inventory figure. Though inventory figures are not always perpetually derived, they can be obtained as often as is desirable, usually every week or month.

4.1 Explanation of the Retail Method of Inventory

The retail system of merchandise accounting permits the retailer to determine the value (at retail) of the stock-on-hand at frequent and periodic intervals without taking constant physical counts. However, it must be noted that periodic—generally semiannual—physical counts (i.e., inventories) are taken at the current retail prices of the merchandise on hand. To control stocks and determine the profitability of individual departments, the retail method of accounting is applied separately for each department or store. The retail method of inventory valuation involves:

- Taking a physical inventory count to determine the total retail value of a particular department.

- Determining the cumulative markup percentage on the total merchandise handled (sum of opening inventory plus the total purchases).

- Deriving the cost value of the closing inventory from the retail by using the cumulative markup percentage achieved on the total merchandise handled. Subsequently, this valuation is used to find the cost of goods sold to establish the gross margin.

This system requires the collection and analysis of data pertaining to any movement of merchandise from the time it is bought until it is sold to the consumer. The retail method of inventory requires maintaining a book inventory at retail, as well as other records that permit the calculation of the cost of total merchandise handled during the period. This, in turn, allows constant calculation of the gross margin amount, including the possible protection of profitability. All additions to and reductions from stock must be recorded in retail dollar values. The computation from "statistical records" or book figures of the amount of merchandise that should be on hand at retail is called a **book** or **maintained book inventory**.

At the beginning of the accounting period under consideration, a **physical inventory** count is taken at the current retail price of the goods owned. It is common that when large stores take semiannual physical count of stocks and record the value at retail, the date of receipt of merchandise into stock is also recorded.

Figure 8 illustrates the information generally recorded during a physical count. This form, as well as the subsequent forms used in this chapter, merely demonstrates what information is required by the retail method of inventory. Today's retailer, whether checking a price, handling a point-of-sale transaction, or tracking the receipt of inventory, relies on some type of data-collection technology to suit the needs of the company. The system of collecting the data may be different, but the data required will be identical.

Figure 8. Physical Inventory Count Sheet

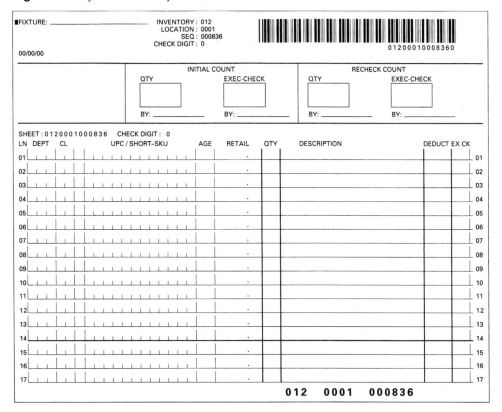

When taking a physical inventory using this method, it is not necessary to list the cost price of each individual item. The physical count of each individual item, at the current retail price stated on its ticket, is recorded, and the total retail figure (e.g., $100,000) is the actual amount of goods accounted for at the time the semiannual count is made. There will be product that is sold at the original retail price, but some product may have been permanently marked down, which has caused a change in the retail value of merchandise (refer to permanent markdowns in Chapter 2). Therefore, the total inventory value will be an aggregate of the current retail value of the merchandise in that department or store. If warranted, this count can be made more often. This actual physical count figure is then used as the **closing physical stock (inventory)** figure for that accounting period. If the physical inventory value is less than the book inventory, the difference is called a **shortage (shrinkage)**. When the physical inventory value exceeds the book inventory, that difference is called an **overage**.

4.2 GENERAL PROCEDURES FOR IMPLEMENTING THE RETAIL METHOD OF INVENTORY

FINDING AN OPENING BOOK INVENTORY FIGURE

When the "retail method" system is first installed, a complete physical count at retail (see Figure 8) is taken for each merchandising department. (Note: This physical count reflects the retail value of the inventory at aggregate retail prices.) The retail value of the goods counted is used as the **opening book inventory** figure. This is the same figure as the closing physical stock figure of the previous accounting period. Inventory counts continue to be taken semiannually at the current retail prices of the goods. (Remember, closing physical inventory at retail equals the opening book inventory at retail for the next period.)

MAINTAINING A PERPETUAL BOOK INVENTORY FIGURE

A book inventory indicates the amount of stock in dollars that has been determined from records, rather than from an actual count. During the time period between the semiannual physical counts just described, many other merchandising transactions occur.

Additions to inventory occur regularly via the following transactions:

- Merchandise is purchased and received from vendors/manufacturers. This can be new merchandise or reorders for basic replenishment product. Retailers signify merchandise ordered using the terms "purchases" and "receipts" interchangeably.

- Customers return merchandise.

- Transfers from other stores.

Reductions to reduce inventory occur due to:

- Merchandise being sold to customers.

- Markdowns and employee discounts are taken on merchandise.

- Product is transferred to other stores that are selling that product at a faster rate.

- Merchandise is transferred to the outlet divisions of stores.

- Merchandise is returned to vendors based on agreements made between the buyers and vendors.

Every such transaction, and any other kind of merchandise movement, is accompanied by paperwork in the form of computerized receipts, sales checks, return-to-vendor forms, orders, and so on. The retail organization's statistical department or the accounting division records every transaction and adds to or reduces the "book stock" accordingly. For example, sales to customers or transfers to other divisions reduce the "book stock" (also known as **perpetual** or maintained book **inventory**) by the dollar amount corresponding to the retail value of the goods sold or transferred. The records must be current and accurate so that a retail book inventory figure is always available during an accounting period, usually on a monthly basis. For some product categories, in high traffic times, this may be calculated on a week-to-week basis (e.g., toy department from Black Friday to Christmas). Any additions to or reductions from stock must be recorded as the current retail prices and reported to the statistical department. In other words, every change that affects the stock value must be recorded.

In a multistore operation, a constant inventory figure is maintained for a particular department in each store. This inventory figure is evaluated not only on an individual store basis but also on a department's overall operation. The main reasons for calculating a physical book inventory are that:

- The determination of stock shortage whenever physical inventory is taken can prevent or lessen losses by taking prompt action.

- The accurate determination of stock-on-hand periodically maintains the proper relationship between sales and stock, as merchandise purchases are controlled in ratio to ample stocks.

- The estimation of profits at any given time allows the timely correction of any adverse conditions.

- Possible insurance claims can be maximized by providing acceptable, accurate records of inventory validation.

The following is an example of a department for a branch store, which should serve to illustrate the "addition or reduction" of the value of the merchandise in stock. All these changes must be recorded to ensure accuracy.

Additions or Increase of retail value			Reductions or Decrease of retail value			EXAMPLE
	Purchases (total retail value of merchandise received)	$35,000		Net sales	$28,000	
			+	Transfers out at retail	+ 2,000	
			+	Returns to vendor	+ 3,000	
+	Transfers in at retail	+ 5,000	+	Employee discounts	+ 500	
	Total stock additions	$40,000	+	Markdowns taken	+ 9,000	
				Total stock reductions	$42,500	

Calculating a Book Inventory Figure at Retail

A retail book inventory is determined by:

- Taking a periodic physical count at retail to determine a closing physical stock figure.

- Establishing the physical count amount as the opening retail book inventory.

- Adding all new additions (e.g., purchases/receipts, customer returns, transfers in) at retail to determine the total merchandise handled at retail.

- Subtracting all retail reductions (e.g., net sales, markdowns, returns to vendors, transfers out) from the retail total merchandise handled to find the **closing book inventory** for the current month at retail. This closing book inventory will become the starting book inventory for the next month. Then additions and subtractions will be made to this inventory figure to find the subsequent month's inventory. This is an ongoing process until the next physical inventory count is taken.

CONCEPT

Closing book inventory at retail = Opening physical inventory + retail additions (purchases, transfers in, customer returns) – retail reductions (sales, markdowns, returns to vendors, transfers to)

PROBLEM

On January 31, the physical count of the infants' department in Branch #15 revealed an inventory of $90,000. On February 1, the opening retail inventory of this department was $100,000. February retail purchases amounting to $50,000 were received. The net sales for February were $20,000, the markdowns taken were $15,000, transfers to outlet stores were $2,000, and returns to vendors were $5,000. What was the closing retail book inventory for this period under consideration?

SOLUTION

	Opening book retail inventory (Feb. 1)			$100,000
+	Retail purchases (February)		+	50,000
	Total merchandise handled (Retail additions)			$150,000
	Net sales	$20,000		
+	Markdowns	+ 15,000		
+	Returns to vendor	+ 5,000		
+	Transfers to outlet store	+ 2,000		
	Total retail reductions	= $42,000	–	42,000
	Retail book inventory		=	$108,000

Calculating a Book Inventory at Cost

A book inventory at cost is determined by:

Step 1: Converting the opening retail book inventory to a cost inventory figure by using the cumulative markup percentage achieved on the stock plus purchases during the previous accounting period.

Step 2: Adding all new purchases at cost, plus freight (on cost only), to the cost opening inventory figure to determine the total merchandise handled at cost.

Step 3: Finding the cumulative percentage on total merchandise handled.

Step 4: Converting the closing book inventory at retail to a closing book inventory at cost, by using the cumulative markup percentage that has been calculated from the difference between the total merchandise handled at retail and the total merchandise handled at cost.

CONCEPT

Calculate a book inventory at cost if the markup percentage on the previous season's inventory is 60% and the cost of the new purchases is $20,000. (The same figures are used as in the previous problem illustrating the determination of a book inventory figure at retail.)

PROBLEM

Step 1: Convert opening book retail inventory to cost inventory figure, using the cumulative markup percentage achieved on stock plus purchases (total merchandise handled) for the previous accounting period.

SOLUTION

$$\begin{aligned} \text{Opening cost inventory} &= \underset{\text{(Opening retail book inventory)}}{\$100,000} \times (100\% - \text{Cumulative markup \%}) \\[2mm] &= \underset{\text{(Opening retail book inventory)}}{\$100,000} \times (100\% - 60\% \text{ Cumulative markup \%}) \\[2mm] &= \$100,000 \times 40\% \\[2mm] &= \$40,000 \end{aligned}$$

Step 2: Add all new purchases plus freight to opening inventory at cost. Given:

	$20,000	(New purchases at cost)
+	1,000	Freight at cost
	$21,000	New purchases including freight
+	40,000	(Opening inventory at cost)
	$61,000	Total merchandise handled at cost

Step 3: Find cumulative markup percentage on total merchandise handled.

	Cost	Retail
Opening inventory	$40,000	$100,000
+ Purchases	+ 21,000	+ 50,000
Total merchandise handled	$61,000	$150,000

$$\text{Cumulative MU \%} = \frac{\begin{array}{c}\text{\$150,000 Retail of total}\\\text{merchandise handled}\end{array} - \begin{array}{c}\text{\$61,000 Cost of total}\\\text{merchandise handled}\end{array}}{\text{\$150,000 Retail}}$$

$$= \frac{\text{\$89,000 MU}}{\text{\$150,000 Retail}} \times 100$$

Cumulative markup % = 59.3%

Step 4: Convert closing book inventory at retail to closing book inventory at cost by using the cumulative markup percentage.

Closing book inventory at retail = $108,000

Closing book inventory at cost = $108,000 × (100% − 59.3%)

= $108,000 × 40.7%

= $43,956.00

FORMS USED IN THE RETAIL METHOD OF INVENTORY

Today a retailer's records are often supplemented and/or obtained through the store's (or organization's) computer system (e.g., POS markdowns). How the information is recorded is a matter of choice or monetary necessity, but the loss of records or the failure to record the proper information that shows the increase or decrease in the value of the stock will result in an inaccurate stock valuation of the book inventory. There are many forms to help the retailer accurately record this valuable information. Each form serves a particular function, but not all retailers use identical forms. The forms in this section illustrate and allow you to become familiar with the function of each record (some or all of which may be entirely part of a computerized operating system) required to appreciate or depreciate the value of a stock. Today, with the widespread use of automated merchandising systems, the information necessary to maintain an accurate recording of transactions is adopted and tailored to each retailer's needs.

Purchase Record (Also Called Purchase Journal, On-Order Report, Bankbook, Flow Sheet, or Checkbook)

Figure 9 is a **purchase record**, which provides a record of the billed or invoiced costs, transportation charges, cash discounts, retail amounts, and percentages of markup for each individual purchase. The names of the vendors, dates of invoices, and invoice numbers are also entered. Each department checks this record periodically to ensure

Figure 9. Journal of Purchase Record

DIV 04

VENDOR NAME GREEN & CO.

S T	DEPT. NO.	VENDOR NO.	APRON NO.	INV. NO.	INV. DATE	REC. DATE	RETAIL	INV. AMT.	MU %	TRANS.	DISCOUNT	ANTIC.	VENDOR FRT.	NET
2	310100	616920	14020	004803	3/01/13	3/10	115	62.10	46.00	.00	1.86	.00	.00	60.24
8	310100	616920	48049	004805	3/08/13	3/10	126	69.10	45.16	.00	2.07	.00	.00	67.03
8	310100	616920	48049	004806	3/08/13	3/10	76	41.80	45.00	.00	1.25	.00	.00	40.55
8	310100	616920	48049	004807	3/08/13	3/10	773	395.05	48.89	.00	11.85	.00	.00	383.20
2	310100	616920	14936	004984	3/16/13	3/17	360	197.87	45.04	.00	5.94	.00	.00	191.93
2	310100	616920	14936	004985	3/16/13	3/17	619	387.23	37.44	.00	11.62	.00	.00	375.61
3	310100	616920	49226	005069	3/19/13	3/22	317	174.50	44.95	.00	5.24	.00	.00	169.26
3	310100	616920	49226	005070	3/19/13	3/22	417	229.54	44.95	.00	6.89	.00	.00	222.65
2	310100	616920	AJ742	074230 SU	4/05/13			.00		.00	17.65–	.00	.00	17.65
	TOTALS FOR VENDOR 616920						2,603	1,557.19		.00	29.07	.00	.00	1,528.12

that the department is being charged or credited with merchandise either entering or leaving a department and that these amounts are intended for only that department. This report also shows the department classification, vendor, style, and price receipts in units for the total store as well as individual branches. The negative units represent returns to vendors, units not received, or corrections made on orders placed. The purpose of the report is to allow buyers to examine receipts entered into the computer against copies of the purchase order. Discrepancies are then reported so that appropriate adjustments can be made to reflect accurate inventory levels. If merchandise is not received, a buyer must check with a vendor to see if the retailer will be receiving that product. If for some reason the vendor is not shipping the entire amount ordered, that merchandise must be canceled out of the buyer's systems. If merchandise received is greater than what was ordered, then buyers need to accurately reflect this additional product in their purchase records.

Transfer of Goods

A **transfer** of merchandise involves the movement of goods. When the merchandise leaves a department, the transfer is out; conversely, when the merchandise is received, the transfer is in. When merchandise is transferred from one store to another (e.g., a branch), an Outstanding Transfer List Form is used to record the number of units transferred, unit cost, total cost, unit retail, and total retail. Merchandise may also be transferred from the full line store to a store's outlet store division. This record is used to indicate the change of ownership of merchandise. Figure 10 (Outstanding Transfer List Form) illustrates the detailed information that an automated merchandising system can furnish on interstore transfers (e.g., reasons for transfers, size, color, etc.).

Figure 10. Outstanding Transfer List Form

OUTSTANDING TRANSFER LIST AS OF OCT 08, 2013				DATE OCT 09, 2013						PAGE: 1		
						TIME 5:31 PM						
1) BY FROM STORE — WITH DETAILS												
FROM STORE	TO STORE	TRANSFER NUMBER TYPE	TRANSFER DATE	SKU NO.	STYLE NO.	COL	SIZE	QTY	PRICE	RETAIL AMOUNT	COST AMOUNT	TRANSFER REASON
001	002	000002 1	OCT 08, 2013	0015149	SW10	030	XS	4	22.55	90.20	40.00	001 Slow Moving
				0015156	SW10	030	S	4	22.55	90.20	40.00	
				0015164	SW10	030	M	5	22.55	112.75	50.00	
				0015172	SW10	030	L	3	22.55	67.65	30.00	
				0015189	SW10	030	XL	2	22.55	45.10	20.00	
003	001	000001 1	OCT 07, 2013	0014555	200XT	020	R - 40	3	440.00	1,320.00	825.00	003 Fast Moving
				0014563	200XT	020	R - 42	3	440.00	1,320.00	825.00	
				0014571	200XT	020	R - 44	3	440.00	1,320.00	825.00	
				0014589	200XT	020	R - 46	3	440.00	1,320.00	825.00	
				0014662	200BK	020	T - 38	1	440.00	440.00	275.00	
				0014670	200BK	020	T - 40	1	440.00	440.00	275.00	
				0014688	200BK	020	T - 42	1	440.00	440.00	275.00	
				0014696	200BK	020	T - 44	1	440.00	440.00	275.00	
				0014704	200BK	020	T - 46	1	440.00	440.00	275.00	

Figure 11 (Shipment Summary) lists the amount of cartons received by number and their condition. The carrier and the store's designated person countersign receipt of goods.

Figure 11. Shipment Summary

SHIPMENT SUMMARY
Carrier Stop 5174000100

Expected : 80
Good : 81
Damaged : 0
Total Received : 81
Outbound : 0

RECEIVED   RECEIVED

Carton Number	Carton Condition	UPC/SKU	Damaged
517420471869	GOOD		
517420470798	GOOD		
517420471834	GOOD		
517420471654	GOOD		
517420469402	GOOD		
517420469375	GOOD		
517420466477	GOOD		
517420465036	GOOD		
517420467748	GOOD		
517420468473	GOOD		
517420462871	GOOD		
517420463742	GOOD		
517420463718	GOOD		
517420462894	GOOD		
517420466889	GOOD		
517420462994	GOOD		
517420462012	GOOD		
517420466556	GOOD		
517420463602	GOOD		
517420464100	GOOD		
517420466982	GOOD		
517420464261	GOOD		
517420455898	GOOD		
517420467245	GOOD		
517420464751	GOOD		
517420462991	GOOD		
517420462808	GOOD		
517420463340	GOOD		

SIGNATURES   SIGNATURES

_C. _____   _____
(Store Associate)   (Driver)

**** PLEASE FILE SIGNED STORE COPY IN CURRENT MONTH OF 6 MONTH RETENTION FILE. ****

Price Change Forms

All retail **price changes** that are required to merchandise must be recorded on **price change forms**. Among the changes necessary to record are:

- The number of units.

- The old retail price per unit.

- The new retail price per unit.

- The difference per unit.

- The total amount of difference.

Today it is common that temporary price changes (e.g., one-day sale items) are recorded by a cash register at the time of the purchase. As described in Chapter 2, this is called a point-of-sale (POS) markdown. When a consumer pays for a purchase, the preprogrammed cash register records the new or lower retail, which corresponds exactly with the prescribed reduction posted on signs displayed with the merchandise. Only permanent markdowns are recorded separately on computerized forms illustrated by Figures 12 and 13. Figure 12 is a worksheet that requires the listing of any or all price changes. Figure 13 shows the permanent or temporary price change information that has been entered onto a computer screen. Figure 14 lists specific departments by classification, resource, description, current and new prices, and percentage off original price.

Figure 12. Buyer's Price Change Worksheet

All of these price change reports are computerized and available to buyers online. There are very few manual forms used by a buyer today, but the information found on these examples would be the same as that found on the computerized versions.

Figure 13. Computer Price Change Entry

```
DATE: OCT 09, 2013
                         PRICE CHANGE ENTRY
=====================================================================

   COMPANY 01  GROUP 0001  TYPE 1  FUNCTION 1  DATE 10/09/13  EFFECTIVE DATE FR: 10/10/13
                          (New)    (Price Change)             EFFECTIVE DATE TO: 12/31/13


   1) AUTHORIZATION      :123456
   2) ENTRY TYPE         :1        MARKDOWN
   3) BUYER NO           :001      Michael Wood
   4) REASON             :001      Slow Moving
   5) EFF. DATE FROM     :10/10/13        6) EFF. DATE TO            :12/31/13
   7) REGION FROM        :000             8) REGION TO               :000
   9) STORE FROM         :000            10) STORE TO                :000
  11) REM-1: Permanent price change      13) PRODUCE TICKETS (Y/N)   :Y
  12) REM-2: Effective for all stores    14) COUNT INVENTORY         :N


 LINE  SEASON  DEPT  CLS  PR  LN COST  PT  COOR  GR  STYLE  CHANGE   TO RETAIL
                                                           % AMT     PRICE
 001    FROM    L    01                                     10.00
        TO      L    02
 EXCLUDE STYLES:      12056      12654      13101      141256
```

Figure 14. Specific Departments by Classification

SSI
PRICE CHANGE AUTHORIZATION
RED TICKET
EFFECTIVE DATE 07/05/2013

STORE: 5147
DATE: 06/29/2013
503-RMPRCHA

STORE GROUP 5174 BARKHAMSTED
5200 CHILDRENS

DEPT	NAME	CLASS	BRAND	VPN	DESCRIPTION	COLOR	CURRENT PRICE	NEW PRICE	% OFF ORIG	TAKEN BY
5070	BOY'S 8–20 SEPARATES	ACTIVEWEAR	AMC KIDS	S6B8844	RVRS MESH SHORT	20 GREY	$7.19	$4.32	73	——
						400 BLUE	$16.00	$9.60	40	——
						410 NAVY	$16.00	$9.60	40	——
						600 RED	$16.00	$9.60	40	——
5070	BOY'S 8–20 SEPARATES	ACTIVEWEAR	AUTHENTIC GRAPH	S6B8158	MESH MUSCLE TEE	40 SILVER	$7.19	$4.32	73	——
5070	BOY'S 8–20 SEPARATES	DRESSWEAR	BRUNO BOYS	B122739	SM PLAID MICRO	410 NAVY	$16.00	$9.60	40	——
						300 GREEN	$24.00	$14.40	40	——
						450 LIGHT/PASTEL BLUE	$10.79	$6.48	73	——
5070	BOY'S 8–20 SEPARATES	DRESSWEAR	BRUNO BOYS	B124116	STRIPE MICRO	400 BLUE	$10.79	$6.48	73	——
						800 ORANGE	$24.00	$14.40	40	——
5070	BOY'S 8–20 SEPARATES	DRESSWEAR	BRUNO BOYS	B124676	CHECK MICROFIBR	300 GREEN	$24.00	$14.40	40	——
5070	BOY'S 8–20 SEPARATES	KNITS	DELTA	DG4848	HEAR NO EVIL TEE	BLACK	$14.00	$8.40	40	——
5070	BOY'S 8–20 SEPARATES	KNITS	DELTA	DG4855	GROUNDED FOR LIFE	HEATHER GREY	$14.00	$8.40	40	——
5070	BOY'S 8–20 SEPARATES	KNITS	DELTA	DG4862	SISTER FOR SALE TEE	400-ROYAL	$14.00	$8.40	40	——
5070	BOY'S 8–20 SEPARATES	PANTS	JAZZMAN SPORTSW	B3Q127	CAMDEN JEAN	400 BLUE	$13.19	$7.92	73	——
						410 NAVY	$29.99	$17.99	40	——
5070	BOY'S 8–20 SEPARATES	PANTS	LEE BOYS	5675344	BACKSTACK JEAN	400 BLUE	$30.00	$18.00	40	——
5071	BOY'S 8–20 COLLECTS.	LEVI	LEVI STRAUSS	309930819	PAINTER HUSKY	400 BLUE	$32.00	$19.20	40	——
5206	INFANT BOY APPAREL	PLAYWEAR	AMC KIDS	0318853156	STRPGIRFAPLQ CRP	400 BLUE	$12.00	$7.20	40	——
				B1707						——
5206	INFANT BOY APPAREL	PLAYWEAR	AMC KIDS	S6B-1707	STRPFROGAPLQ CRP	400 BLUE	$12.00	$7.20	40	——
5209	INFANT GIRL APPAREL	PLAYWEAR	AMC KIDS	S6G-1705	PRNT FLRL CRPR	810 MEDIUM ORANGE	$12.00	$7.20	40	——

Charge-Back to Vendors

A **debit memo form,** shown in Figure 15, records the return of merchandise from the retailer to the vendor, which may occur for a variety of reasons. It displays the number of pieces or units, the name of the item, and both cost and retail prices. Typically, a worksheet, as illustrated by Figure 16, is used to record the **return to vendor (RTV)** information before it is verified by the person packing the merchandise. This ensures that the actual debit memo is legible and correct. As with other retail accounting forms, debit memos are now computerized.

Figure 15. Debit Memo

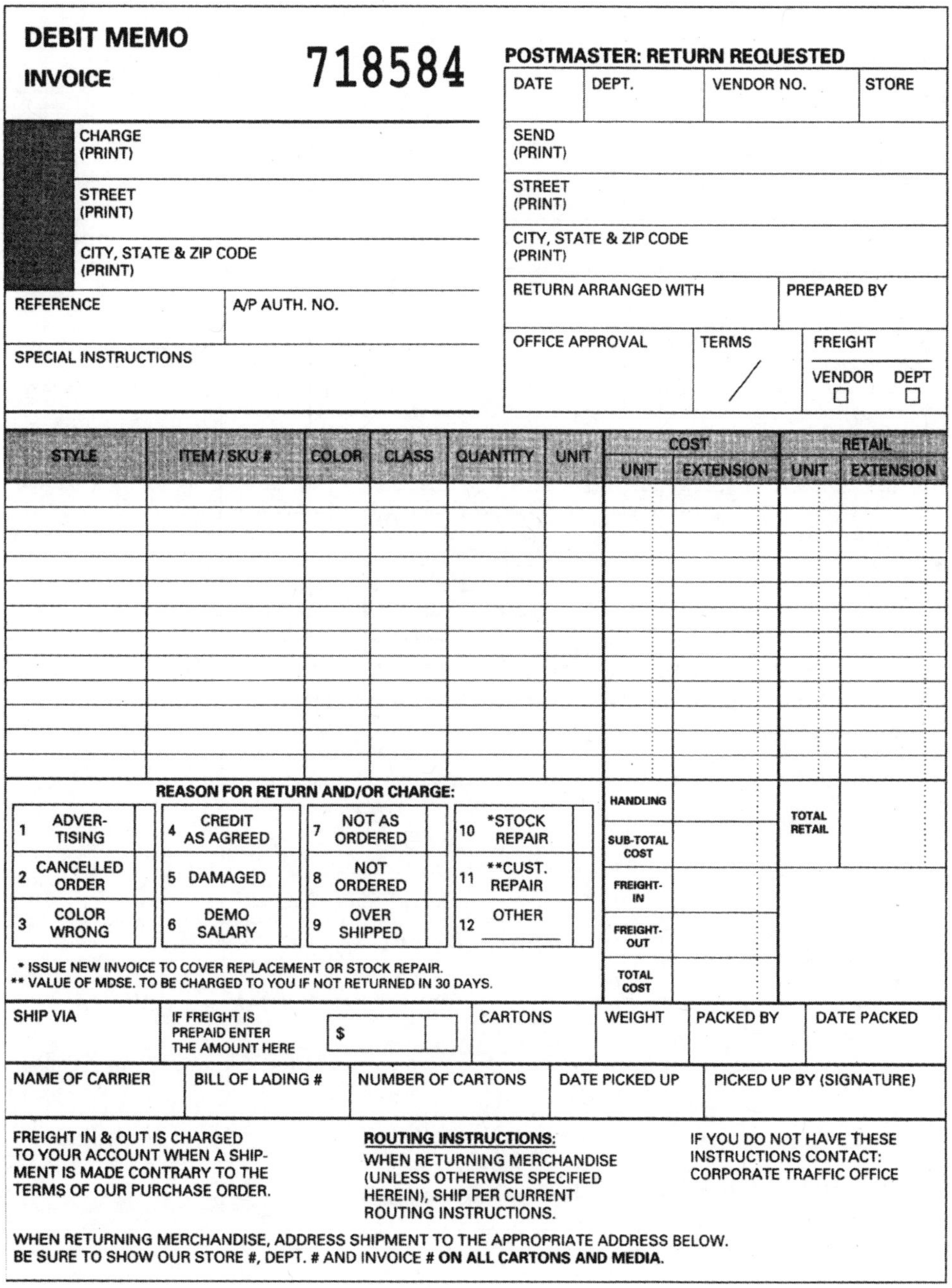

DEBIT MEMO
INVOICE 718584

POSTMASTER: RETURN REQUESTED

DATE	DEPT.	VENDOR NO.	STORE

CHARGE (PRINT)
STREET (PRINT)
CITY, STATE & ZIP CODE (PRINT)
REFERENCE | A/P AUTH. NO.
SPECIAL INSTRUCTIONS

SEND (PRINT)
STREET (PRINT)
CITY, STATE & ZIP CODE (PRINT)
RETURN ARRANGED WITH | PREPARED BY
OFFICE APPROVAL | TERMS | FREIGHT: VENDOR ☐ DEPT ☐

STYLE	ITEM / SKU #	COLOR	CLASS	QUANTITY	UNIT	COST UNIT	COST EXTENSION	RETAIL UNIT	RETAIL EXTENSION

REASON FOR RETURN AND/OR CHARGE:

1 ADVERTISING	4 CREDIT AS AGREED	7 NOT AS ORDERED	10 *STOCK REPAIR
2 CANCELLED ORDER	5 DAMAGED	8 NOT ORDERED	11 **CUST. REPAIR
3 COLOR WRONG	6 DEMO SALARY	9 OVER SHIPPED	12 OTHER

* ISSUE NEW INVOICE TO COVER REPLACEMENT OR STOCK REPAIR.
** VALUE OF MDSE. TO BE CHARGED TO YOU IF NOT RETURNED IN 30 DAYS.

HANDLING
SUB-TOTAL COST
FREIGHT-IN
FREIGHT-OUT
TOTAL COST
TOTAL RETAIL

SHIP VIA | IF FREIGHT IS PREPAID ENTER THE AMOUNT HERE $ | CARTONS | WEIGHT | PACKED BY | DATE PACKED

NAME OF CARRIER | BILL OF LADING # | NUMBER OF CARTONS | DATE PICKED UP | PICKED UP BY (SIGNATURE)

FREIGHT IN & OUT IS CHARGED TO YOUR ACCOUNT WHEN A SHIPMENT IS MADE CONTRARY TO THE TERMS OF OUR PURCHASE ORDER.

ROUTING INSTRUCTIONS: WHEN RETURNING MERCHANDISE (UNLESS OTHERWISE SPECIFIED HEREIN), SHIP PER CURRENT ROUTING INSTRUCTIONS.

IF YOU DO NOT HAVE THESE INSTRUCTIONS CONTACT: CORPORATE TRAFFIC OFFICE

WHEN RETURNING MERCHANDISE, ADDRESS SHIPMENT TO THE APPROPRIATE ADDRESS BELOW.
BE SURE TO SHOW OUR STORE #, DEPT. # AND INVOICE # ON ALL CARTONS AND MEDIA.

Figure 16. Return to Vendor Authorization and Worksheet

RETURN TO VENDOR AUTHORIZATION AND WORKSHEET   № 627893

Instructions: (Please print legibly)
                              Department Manager   DM No. _____

1) Dept. Mgr. prepares Worksheet
2) Complete Worksheet including quantities and extensions
3) Completely prepare D.M. from information
   on Worksheet except for merchandise
   quantities AND extensions.
   (D.M. Room will do this.)
4) Do Not put in cost figures.

Dept._____ Store _____ Prepared by _____ Date _____

Mfr. name _____ Freight paid by dept. _____ vendor _____
                                                                    CHECK ONE

Vendor no. _____

Return arranged with _____ Sticker needed   Yes _____   No _____

Special instructions _____Terms _____

Reason_____

Item / SKU No.	Class	Style	Size	Color	Qty.	Units	Cost Unit	Cost Ext.	Retail Unit	Retail Ext.
CHARGE TO: Name / Address / City State Zip					SEND TO: Name / Address / City State Zip					
Total										

ON DMS OVER $400 RETAIL

COMPLETE THE FOLLOWING:
                                           D.M. ROOM COMPLETES
ACCTS. PAYABLE AUTH. NO. _____   D.M. # _____
                                           Date _____
                                           Total $ Amount _____
                                           Packed by_____
                                           Checked by_____

*IF BSR MERCHANDISE IS INVOLVED, INFORMATION MUST BE PROVIDED TO THE BSR OFFICE BY STYLE, SIZE AND COLOR.

17-930-061 (REV. 6/91)

Sales Reports

Today's automated business systems offer sophisticated reporting for processing and auditing sales. In addition to full accounting sales summaries, Figures 17 and 18 show information that can be provided to improve sales performance. Figure 17, Daily Exception Selling Price Report, highlights daily sales for items sold at prices other than current retail (e.g., markdown price). Salesperson performance is then analyzed by week with the use of a Sales and Productivity Report, as illustrated in Figure 18. Sales associates are given goals to sell a specified amount of **units per sale or transaction (UPT)** and **average dollars per sale or transaction (ADT)**. UPT is based on the average number of units sold by the associate divided by the number of transactions. In Figure 18, George Brown sold 2.3 units per sale for the week, whereas Mark Lewis sold 1.7 units per sale. The higher number is better and is dependent on the product being sold. ADT is the retail sales an associate secures divided by the number of transactions. Both are important retail analytics to indicate productivity. Figure 19, Weekly Sales Challenge Recap, reports by department the actual and goal sales by units. Figure 20, District Flash Sales by Store, records for the week the daily dollar sales by individual store, recapping the performance and the changes in both dollars and percentages by week, month, and year-to-date. Figure 21, District Flash Sales by Group, offers the same information by merchandise grouping.

Figure 17. Daily Exception Selling Price Report

STORE NO.	SALES BILL NUMBER	CLERK	STYLE	SEASON	DESCRIPTION	COLOR	SIZE	QTY	PRICE PER UNIT CURRENT	PRICE PER UNIT ACTUAL	TOTAL EXTENDED DIFFERENCE	% M/DOWN
001	103256	0018	SW50A	M	Cotton V-Neck Sweater	030	- S	1	45.00	32.00	13.00	29
	103273	0026	SK1715	M	Cotton Pants	030	- L	2	64.00	50.00	28.00	22
					STORE DAILY TOTAL						41.00	24
002	204312	0042	SC1210	M	Wool Sweater	010	- M	1	95.00	75.00	20.00	21
	204317	0042	200XT	M	2 Pces Dress Suit	020	R - 40	1	440.00	390.00	50.00	11
					STORE DAILY TOTAL						70.00	13

DAILY EXCEPTION SELLING PRICE REPORT   DATE OCT 09, 2013   PAGE: 1
TIME 9:10 AM
DATE OF SALE: OCT 08, 2013
MINIMUM PRICE DIFFERENCE REQUIRED: 10.00%

APPROVED BY: _____

Figure 18. Sales and Productivity Report by Store by Salesperson

SALES AND PRODUCTIVITY REPORT BY STORE BY SALESPERSON

WEEK ENDING OCT 08, 2013

DATE OCT 09, 2013 TIME 9:44 AM PAGE 1

REGION: 001 EAST COAST
STORE: 001 BOSTON

SALESPERSON NO NAME	DOLLAR SALES	DOLLAR RETURNS	DOLLAR NET SALES	% STORE	UNITS SOLD	% STORE	UNITS/ SALE	DOLLARS/ SALE	AVG. SALE/ UNIT	GROSS PROFIT	EMPL WAGES	HRS WORKED	% WAGES/ SALES	SALES/ HOUR	EMP $ PURCH
0018 George Brown															
THIS WEEK	4,200	76	4,124	35.0	84	40.0	2.3	113	49	2,288	600	40	14.6	103	0
THIS PERIOD	17,255	430	16,825	34.5	246	27.8	1.6	109	58	8,457	2,432	162	14.5	104	300
THIS YEAR	149,765	3,450	146,315	35.3	2,826	38.8	1.7	88	52	74,620	22,565	1500	15.4	98	1,450
0026 Mark Lewis															
THIS WEEK	3,155	65	3,090	26.2	59	28.1	1.7	88	52	1,623	495	40	16.0	77	105
THIS PERIOD	12,112	255	11,857	24.3	211	23.8	1.9	106	56	6,260	2,150	160	18.1	74	105
THIS YEAR	107,270	2,380	104,890	25.3	1,687	23.2	1.3	81	62	51,396	18,915	1525	18.0	69	600
TOTAL STORE															
THIS WEEK	12,465	216	12,249	100.0	210	100.0	2.1	122	58	5,980	1,702	180	13.9	68	352
THIS PERIOD	50,981	1,250	49,731	100.0	886	100.0	1.8	101	56	25,874	8,225	715	16.5	70	625
THIS YEAR	425,236	10,205	415,031	100.0	7,281	100.0	1.6	91	57	182,870	56,111	6864	13.5	60	3,584
TOTAL REGION															
THIS WEEK	45,243	752	44,491		983		1.6	72	45	21,885	6,583	692	14.8	64	1,125
THIS PERIOD	202,853	4,223	197,630		4,184		1.7	80	47	103,882	32,581	2835	16.5	70	2,152
THIS YEAR	1,602,356	42,347	1,560,009		31,483		1.4	70	50	678,401	223,004	27154	14.3	58	12,003
TOTAL COMPANY															
THIS WEEK	124,725	2,850	121,875		2,722		1.6	72	45	58,745	19,850	2102	16.3	58	3,002
THIS PERIOD	608,124	14,987	593,137		12,584		1.6	75	47	312,715	97,100	8525	16.4	70	6,100
THIS YEAR	4,707,453	108,401	4,599,052		91,123		1.4	71	51	2,001,453	658,343	80131	14.3	57	35,111

Figure 19. Weekly Sales Challenge Recap

DATE RUN 7/11/13				STORE 174	WEEK END 7/08/13				WEEKLY SALES CHALLENGE RECAP								PAGE 1		TIME RUN 11.27.21			CTL PAGE 1029		FORM # PSIR10
					SALES FOR WEEK				SALES MTD				SALES STD				SALES YTD				MTHS	PROJECTED	SALES GOAL
ZONE	GRP	DPT	DESC	RESP	GOAL	ACTUAL	%LY	% GOAL	GOAL	ACTUAL	%LY	%GOAL	GOAL	ACTUAL	%LY	%GOAL	GOAL	ACTUAL	%LY	%GOAL	RESP	CURR MTH	NEXT MTH
3	5566	5567	Petites Active	C6	60	115		192	60	115		192	1354	1259		93.0	1354	1259		93.0	5	262	186
		5572	Pets. Classic Care	C6	466	346		74	466	346		74	13187	12017		91.1	13187	12017		91.1	5	2025	991
		5579	Petites Traditiona	C6	405	585		144	405	585		144	10178	11654		114.5	10178	11654		114.5	5	1760	1505
		5586	Womens Active	C6	17	100		588	17	100		588	362	1437		397.0	362	1437		397.0	5	75	105
		5587	Wans Classic Caree	C6	284	616		217	284	616		217	7871	10578		134.4	7871	10578		134.4	5	1237	1446
		5588	Wans Classic Casua	C6	327	485		148	327	485		148	5980	5602		93.7	5980	5602		93.7	5	1421	1131
		5590	Pets. Classic Casu	C6	395	609		154	395	609		154	9095	8459		93.0	9095	8459		93.0	5	1719	1716
		5591	Womens Traditional	C6	306	140		46	306	140		46	6716	5419		80.7	6716	5419		80.7	5	1332	700
		5755	Junior Plus	C6	186	68-		37	186	68		37	3254	2432		74.7	3254	2432		74.7	5	810	803
			SUB	C6	2446	3064		125	2446	3064		125	57997	58857		101.5	57997	58857		101.5	5	10641	8583
4	5110	5484	Wan's Opening Pric	C6	147	91		62	147	91		62	3659	3068		83.8	3659	3068		83.8	5	641	303
	5300	5300	Women's Fragrance	C6	287	79		28	287	79		28	8373	5104		61.0	8373	5104		61.0	5	1248	1069
		5304	Elizabeth Arden	C6	45	0			45	0			1420	521		36.7	1420	521		36.7	5	197	137
		5335	Men's Fragrance	C6	143	55		39	143	55		39	4143	1895		45.7	4143	1895		45.7	5	622	615
		5377	Cosmetic Accessori	C6	98	31		32	98	31		32	2159	1536		71.1	2159	1536		71.1	5	426	279
	5464	5464	Hndbgs, Sm Leather	C6	1180	0			1180	0			21809	12868		59.0	21809	12868		59.0	5	5131	3559
		5473	Costume Jewelry	C6	390	531		136	390	531		136	9753	12216		125.3	9753	12216		125.3	5	1697	791
		5482	Socks & Hosiery	C6	134	189		141	134	189		141	4485	4732		105.5	4485	4732		105.5	5	581	446
		5489	Wearable Accessori	C6	215	115		54	215	115		54	6109	4506		73.8	6109	4506		73.8	5	935	640
		5496	Fine Jewelry	C6	389	543		140	389	543		140	9459	12155		128.5	9459	12155		128.5	5	1691	1417
	5566	5576	Petites Collection	C6	106	0			106	0			2760	130		4.7	2760	130		4.7	5	461	25
	5624	5620	Missy Updated/Tren	C6	113	152		135	113	152		135	2631	3766		143.1	2631	3766		143.1	5	493	0
		5625	Missy Active	C6	458	204		45	458	204		45	10818	7707		71.2	10818	7707		71.2	5	1992	839
		5626	Missy Classic Casu	C6	1699	2840		167	1699	2840		167	37237	45090		121.1	37237	45090		121.1	5	7388	7047
		5635	Missy Classic Care	C6	1640	1449		88	1640	1449		88	42648	33140		77.7	42648	33140		77.7	5	7134	5792
		5638	Missy Traditional	C6	2020	2236		111	2020	2236		111	48098	40729		84.7	48098	40729		84.7	5	8786	5370
		5662	Missy Collections	C6	1943	1557		80	1943	1557		80	46520	35125		75.5	46520	35125		75.5	5	8451	4308
			SUB	C6	11007	10072		92	11007	10072		92	262081	224288		85.6	262081	224288		85.6		47874	32637
C	GIBBS				13453	13136		98	13453	13136		98	320078	283145		88.5	320078	283145		88.5		58515	41220

Figure 20. District Flash Sales by Store

			Sun $	Mon $	Tue $	Wed $	Thu $	Fri $	Sat $	WTD $	WTD %	MTD $	MTD %	HTD $	HTD %	YTD $	YTD %	STD%	%CHG STD
Store																			
5044	Brattleboro	TY	2838	3533	4572	3639	0	0	0	14583	-8	75	-10	764	17	764	17	38.31	0
		LY	3547	3154	4961	4122	5130	6548	5412	15784		84		654		654			1993
5070	Geneva	TY	5239	5402	8105	11797	0	0	0	30543	3	155	11	1317	-4	1317	-4	42.01	0
		LY	3124	7069	7229	12341	13951	14910	10804	29763		139		1376		1376			3135
5072	Rochester	TY	0	2155	2280	6085	0	0	0	10519	13	41	-8	451	-13	451	-13	39.61	0
		LY	0	2381	2206	4685	4056	3986	2299	9272		44		520		520			1139
5095	Johnstown	TY	8725	11018	13333	18347	0	0	0	51424	-3	249	-2	2170	-9	2170	-9	40.95	0
		LY	8951	10068	11425	22578	18798	23726	21461	53022		255		2387		2387			5299
5121	St Albans	TY	3360	3831	5176	4295	0	0	0	16661	-4	81	-7	673	-6	673	-6	36.83	0
		LY	3405	4801	4681	4437	6538	6197	7053	17324		87		718		718			1826
5129	Hornell	TY	2680	2473	3870	5861	0	0	0	14885	9	66	3	656	-1	656	-1	42.03	0
		LY	1694	2663	1799	7551	6964	6577	6149	13706		64		660		660			1561
5165	Hudson	TY	4148	5959	7125	10427	0	0	0	27660	12	155	28	1284	3	1284	3	45.66	0
		LY	4794	5280	6214	8329	8152	8101	10705	24618		121		1245		1245			2812
5170	Belmont	TY	2962	3680	4744	4410	0	0	0	15796	-8	89	-12	728	-7	728	-7	39.10	0
		LY	3115	4133	4568	5439	6454	6800	6721	17255		102		781		781			1863
5174	Barkhamsted	TY	4398	2691	2423	5008	0	0	0	14520	0	78	0	695	0	695	0	46.58	0
		LY	0	0	0	0	0	0	0	0		0		0		0			1492
5175	Carbondale	TY	3324	3192	3914	5516	0	0	0	15946	22	75	2	654	62	654	62	39.04	0
		LY	2940	3665	3147	5341	3914	4073	4582	13094		73		402		402			1674
5182	Springfield	TY	2663	3508	4481	5156	0	0	0	15809	0	68	0	588	0	588	0	35.39	0
		LY	0	0	0	0	0	0	0	0		0		0		0			1661
			Sun $	Mon $	Tue $	Wed $	Thu $	Fri $	Sat $	WTD $	%	MTD $	%	HTD $	%	YTD $	%	STD%	%CHG STD
Store																			
Dist. Total	Comp	TY	29953	38053	49204	64861	0	0	0	182071	1	910	2	7355	-5	7355	-5		
		LY	28630	39549	43083	69481	70043	76844	70604	180743		895		7771		7771			
Dist. Total	ALL	TY	40337	47444	60023	80541	0	0	0	228345	18	1131	17	9979	14	9979	14		
		LY	31569	43214	46231	72823	73956	80917	75186	193836		969		8744		8744			
Comp Store %	Dist.	TY	5	-4	14	-7	-100	-100	-100										
	Chain	TY	-6	1	-3	-13	-100	-100	-100		-7		-2		-5		-5		
		LY	-3	-2	3	76	47	39	34		22		6		7		7		
All Store %	Dist.	TY	28	10	30	11	-100	-100	-100										
	Chain	TY	2	7	4	-7	-100	-100	-100		0		5		3		3		
		LY	7	7	12	87	58	49	44		31		15		16		16		

Figure 21. District Flash Sales by Group: Week 25 Ending 07/22/2013

Group		Sun $	Mon $	Tue $	Wed $	Thu $	Fri $	Sat $	WTD $	WTD DI%	WTD Ch%	MTD $	MTD DI%	MTD Ch%	HTD $	HTD DI%	HTD Ch%	YTD $	YTD DI%	YTD Ch%
MENS	TY	4876	4715	6535	8832	0	0	0	24958	20	2	118	12	5	1119	11	4	1119	11	4
	LY	3705	4892	4541	7662	7582	8175	9379	20799			106			1009			1009		
YOUNG MENS	TY	2459	2731	2614	3920	0	0	0	11725	3	3	62	19	7	526	8	5	526	8	5
	LY	2313	2660	2647	3740	3969	5549	5000	11360			52			489			489		
SHOES	TY	3748	3668	5740	9961	0	0	0	23117	13	5	116	25	12	1041	13	1	1041	13	1
	LY	3442	4122	4695	8247	8566	9837	8187	20506			93			918			918		
CHILDRENS	TY	2908	4157	4644	7024	0	0	0	18733	-5	-10	98	8	-2	1015	17	3	1015	17	3
	LY	3588	4396	4134	7663	7369	8753	7972	19782			91			865			865		
COSMETICS/FRAGRANCES	TY	1886	2465	3289	3022	0	0	0	10663	0	7	64	0	1	524	17	5	524	17	5
	LY	2009	2506	3201	2916	4513	5269	4577	10631			64			448			448		
INTIMATE	TY	1131	1392	2508	2569	0	0	0	7599	2	-12	38	4	-9	340	15	-1	340	15	-1
	LY	743	2189	2064	2471	3219	3120	1885	7466			36			297			297		
HOME/GIFTS	TY	1295	1646	1818	2691	0	0	0	7450	33	-6	35	31	17	288	16	-2	288	16	-2
	LY	980	1168	1318	2120	2324	2038	2520	5586			27			249			249		
ACCESSORIES	TY	2279	2891	3215	4394	0	0	0	12779	8	-11	64	3	-3	676	17	7	676	17	7
	LY	2176	2689	2480	4450	4409	4951	4407	11796			62			579			579		
OUTERWEAR	TY	54	18	58	12	0	0	0	142	-45	-59	1	15	-39	86	10	-15	86	10	-15
	LY	0	61	22	177	87	69	127	260			1			78			78		
SWIMWEAR	TY	1813	1889	1920	2043	0	0	0	7665	83	20	28	22	8	82	-20	-12	82	-20	-12
	LY	697	1114	1492	884	1028	574	1336	4187			23			103			103		
SP SIZE SPORTSWEAR	TY	2953	3664	4728	6589	0	0	0	17933	28	-4	89	17	4	804	16	1	804	16	1
	LY	2142	3012	2715	6120	5989	6190	5345	13988			75			696			696		
MISSY SPORTSWEAR	TY	10697	12473	15891	21220	0	0	0	60281	41	9	292	33	13	2382	21	6	2382	21	6
	LY	6006	9137	10498	17104	16635	16144	14567	42745			219			1971			1971		
JR SPORTSWEAR	TY	3304	4675	5393	5808	0	0	0	19180	8	-4	98	9	2	843	3	-5	843	3	-5
	LY	3127	3741	4176	6638	6527	7822	7732	17682			90			821			821		
DRESSES	TY	827	1058	1469	2197	0	0	0	5551	-20	-21	25	-11	-9	211	-3	-9	211	-3	-9
	LY	620	1513	2224	2588	1703	2393	2100	6946			29			218			218		
MISCELLANEOUS	TY	106	1	200	261	0	0	0	568	446	979	3	420	660	42	568	456	42	568	456
	LY	23	13	24	45	35	34	52	104			1			6			6		
Dist. Total Comp	TY	29953	38053	49204	64861	0	0	0	182071	1	-7	910	2	-2	7355	-5	-5	7355	-5	-5
	LY	28630	39549	43083	69481	70043	76844	70604	180743			859			7771			7771		
Dist. Total All	TY	40337	47444	60023	80541	0	0	0	228345	18	0	1131	17	5	9979	14	3	9979	14	3
	LY	31569	43214	46231	72823	73956	80917	75186	193836			969			8744			8744		
Comp St. % Dist.	TY	5	-4	14	-7	-100	-100	-100												
Chain	TY	-6	1	-3	-13	-100	-100	-100												
All St. % Dist.	TY	28	10	30	11	-100	-100	-100												
Chain	TY	2	7	4	-7	-100	-100	-100												

The analysis of all this information, although not used in maintaining the retail method of inventory per se, allows for evaluation of sales as well as stock position and should result in optimizing sales performance and profit margin.

Employee Discounts

As described in Chapter 2, an employee discount is a common practice in retail stores, allowing store employees a percentage off the retail price when making purchases for themselves. It is essential to record the difference between the retail price and the price paid by the employee. The procedure and form of record used for this transaction vary widely from store to store. Typically, employee discounts are listed under "Retail Reductions" but are classified separately from markdowns, even though they are reductions in retail price.

COMPARING BOOK INVENTORY TO PLANNED BOOK INVENTORY

As discussed, buyers are given plans for several metrics to guide them. Key metrics that need to be monitored are sales, gross margin, markdowns, markup, and inventory. After buyers calculate their closing book inventory, they will need to compare that inventory level to the planned inventory given to them. If their closing book inventory is greater than the planned inventory needed, buyers will need to formulate ways to increase sales, possibly by taking additional markdowns, or they might negotiate canceling or moving out of merchandise orders written. If the buyer is below planned inventory levels, he or she needs to secure additional product. (That is what every buyer wants to do!)

Maintaining a Perpetual Book Inventory Figure Practice Problems

1. In July, a book inventory indicates an on-hand retail stock of $64,250. A physical count on that date reveals a stock of $62,875. What is the opening retail book inventory figure for the period commencing at the beginning of August?

2. Opening inventory at retail for an outerwear department is $575,000. Purchases retail for October are $290,000, net sales are $150,000, markdowns are $46,000, returns to vendors are $10,000, transfers (transfers out) to the outlet stores are $15,000, and employee discounts are $4,000. Find the closing retail book inventory at the end of October.

3. Using the following figures from an accessories department, find the closing book stock at retail.

Physical inventory taken	$850,000
Purchases retail	$168,000
Net sales	$170,000
Returns from customers	$30,000
Returns to vendors	$5,000
Markdowns	$22,000

4. The following figures are from a juniors' sportswear department in a California store for May:

Markdowns	$42,000
Purchases (retail)	$180,000
Returns to vendors	$3,500
Transfers in from Oregon store (retail)	$8,000
Transfers out to Arizona store (retail)	$4,000
Net sales	$125,000
Opening book inventory (retail)	$315,000

   a. Determine the closing book inventory for May at retail.

   b. If planned June book beginning inventory is supposed to be $319,200, what does the buyer need to do?

5. The following figures are from a small boutique, which has a 54% markup:

Opening book inventory at retail	$16,000
Net sales	$6,000
Markdowns	$2,000
Purchases (retail)	$40,000

    a. Determine the retail book inventory for the period.

    b. Convert the closing retail book inventory figure to the cost value.

6. Distinguish between physical inventory and book inventory. Which one is more likely to be affected by human error? Why? Which one has become more accurate since the advent of electronic capability?

7. Calculate the July closing book inventory for Boys' 4–7 at retail given the following:

Opening book inventory	$98,000
Net sales	$16,000
Markdowns	$4,500
Purchases	$27,500
Returns to vendor	$3,000

8. Calculate the April closing book inventory for the New York store given the following information (all figures are in retail value):

Opening book inventory	$221,000
Net sales	$27,400
Markdowns	$9,100
Purchases	$37,000
Returns to vendors	$8,100
Transfers to the New Jersey store	$1,500
Transfers from the Connecticut store	$2,700

9. Calculate the October closing book inventory if October's opening inventory at retail was $2,650, net sales were $375, markdowns for the month were $124, and new purchases were $1,195. If the October planned closing inventory was supposed to be $3,618, what would a buyer need to do to get to that inventory level?

10. Calculate August closing book BOM at retail if:

Opening book inventory is	$18,975.
Net sales are	$5,880.
Markdowns are	30.0%.
Receipts are	$8,264.

11. A lingerie department buyer was given the following data:

	Retail
Opening inventory	$2,275,000
Purchases	$550,000
Net sales	$900,000
Markdowns	$378,000

(Includes employee discounts.)

Calculate:

a. The closing book inventory at retail.

b. The closing book inventory at cost if the planned cumulative markup is 63.8%.

12. The athletic footwear department had a closing book inventory at retail of $400,000 and had achieved a 53.5% markup on total merchandise handled. Determine the closing inventory at cost.

13. Find the closing inventory at retail of a furniture department if:

	Retail
Net sales	$330,000
Opening inventory	$325,000
Markdowns	15%
Returns to vendors	$18,000
Employee discounts	$6,500
Purchases	$390,000

14. Utilize the following figures to calculate:

    a. The closing book inventory at retail.

    b. The cost value of this closing book inventory.

    c. The cumulative markup percentage on merchandise handled.

	Cost	Retail
Opening inventory	$390,500	$1,562,000
Gross purchases	$890,000	$3,000,000
Returns to vendors	$3,800	$12,000
Freight	$3,260	
Net sales		$517,000
Customer returns		$25,000
Markdowns		$193,000

4.3 SHORTAGES AND OVERAGES

Physical inventories at current retail prices are taken at the end of the accounting period usually in January or July, which are the end of the Fall and Spring retail seasons, respectively. At this same time, the "book stock" at retail is adjusted to agree with the dollar value of the physical count. Any discrepancy between the dollar value of the "book stock" and the dollar value of stock determined by the physical count of merchandise on hand is classified as a shortage (or shrinkage) or an overage. As described, shortages exist if physical inventory is lower than book inventory; overages exist if the physical count exceeds the statistical tally.

It is almost impossible to run a merchandising operation with 100% accuracy. Shortages or overages nearly always result and are actually expected to occur. The shortage or overage is commonly expressed as a percentage of the yearly net sales. Regardless of the cause, the inventory shortage is fundamentally the store's or department manager's problem and responsibility. Buyers need to know the shortage or overage amount and must be able to calculate their current inventory levels accurately in order to plan future sales, purchases, and markdowns. Keeping discrepancies to a minimum is one of the many challenges a merchant faces. For internal control purposes, it is sometimes desirable to plan shortages. This plan is also expressed as a percentage of yearly net sales. Furthermore, even though merchandise planning is devised with estimated planned shortages in mind, generally the actual shortage exceeds the expected shortage.

Figure 22, a typical shortage report, which is usually calculated at the end of the accounting period, shows typical shortage information. From the data in this report, a multistore operation can pinpoint prevention, causes, and shortage remedies and can attempt to improve the shortage results.

Figure 22. Shortage Report

DVI 10						DATE
	----------SHORTAGES IN DOLLARS----------			----------SHORTAGES IN PERCENTS----------		
STORE	CURRENT SEASON	CURRENT –1	CURRENT –2	CURRENT SEASON	CURRENT –1	CURRENT –2
00						
01	8,731	2,395	3,920	2.8	0.8	1.3
06	891-	717	1,112	0.5-	0.5	1.1
09	999-	867-	1,583	0.9-	0.9-	1.5
12	293-	668	1,518	0.3-	0.8	1.6
14	5,107	501	524	5.0	0.6	0.6
15	1,056	1,361	1,928	0.8	1.2	1.6
DIV 10	12,711	4,781	11,185	1.4	0.6	1.3

CAUSES OF SHORTAGES AND OVERAGES

As seen in the chart, shortage occurs, but it is still a small percentage of the sales, usually no more than 3%. Shortages may stem from inaccurate record-keeping and/or faulty physical counts. Another principal cause of shortages is theft, which, realistically, can never be prevented completely. Overages, however, can be caused only by faulty record-keeping. Shortages are more commonplace in retailing whereas overages rarely occur.

The common causes of shortages and overages are:

- Clerical errors in the calculation of the book and/or physical inventory, which include:

    - Failure to record sales or markdowns properly.

    - Incorrect pricing of product.

    - Errors in receiving of product.

    - Errors in charging invoices to departments.

    - Errors in recording transfers.

    - Errors in recording returns to vendor.

    - Errors in recording physical inventory.

        (Note: The computer processing of these forms has minimized these clerical errors.)

- Physical merchandise losses, which include:

    - Theft by customers and/or employees.

    - Unrecorded breakage and spoilage (especially for food retailers).

    - Salesclerks' errors in recording sales.

    - Borrowed merchandise not returned.

    - Lost or incorrect price tickets compared to what is written on a purchase order.

    - Sampling.

CALCULATING SHORTAGES AND OVERAGES

Physical Inventory Count as a Determining Factor in the Calculation of Shortages or Overages

CONCEPT

$$\text{Shortage (or overage)} = \text{Closing book inventory at retail} - \text{Physical inventory count}$$

PROBLEM

Find the shortage or overage in dollars from the following figures:

Opening inventory at retail	$22,000
Purchases at retail	$17,500
Net sales	$18,000
Markdowns	$300
Employee discounts	$600
Physical inventory, end of period	$19,200

SOLUTION

	Opening book inventory retail	=	$22,000	
+	Purchases retail	= +	17,500	
	Total merchandise handled (retail)	=	$39,500	→ $39,500
	Net sales	=	$18,000	
+	Markdowns	= +	300	
+	Employee discounts	= +	600	
	Total retail deductions	=	$18,900	→ – 18,900
	Closing book inventory at retail	=		$20,600
–	Physical inventory	=		– 19,200
	Dollar shortage	=		$1,400

Expressing the Amount of Shortages or Overages for a Period as a Percentage of Net Sales for the Same Period

$$\text{Shortage \%} \quad = \quad \frac{\text{Shortage \$}}{\text{Annual net sales \$}} \quad \times \quad 100$$

For the period under consideration, the net sales of Department #23 are $100,000. The physical count revealed a $5,000 shortage. What was the shortage percentage for this period?

$$\frac{\text{Shortage \$}}{\text{Net sales \$}} \quad = \quad \frac{\$5,000}{\$100,000} \quad \times \quad 100$$

Shortage % $\quad = \quad$ 5.0%

Estimating Dollar Shortages That Are Expressed as a Percentage of the Planned Net Sales Figure for Internal Control Purposes

$$\text{Planned dollar shortage} \quad = \quad \begin{array}{c}\text{Planned shortage}\\ \text{percentage}\end{array} \quad \times \quad \begin{array}{c}\text{Planned annual}\\ \text{net sales \$}\end{array}$$

The seasonal plan for a department showed planned sales of $350,000, with a planned shortage of 2.5%. What was the planned dollar shortage?

Planned dollar shortage	=	$350,000	Net sales
	×	2.5%	Planned shortage
Planned dollar shortage	=	$8,750	

Shortages and Overages
Practice Problems

15. Fill in the blanks in parts (a)–(c) in the following table:

	Shortage %	Shortage $	Net sales $
(a)	1.4%		$17,000
(b)		$965	$45,900
(c)		$236,800	$7,800,000

16. Calculate the planned shortage in dollars if the planned shortage % is 1.64% and the planned net sales are $1,189,000.

17. Calculate the shortage % for the jewelry department if shortage $ are $127 and net sales for the year are $4,550.

18. Net sales for the misses' sportswear department were $359,000. Physical inventory was taken and the amount is $636,000. Book inventory shows $625,648. Was there a shortage or overage, and by how much in dollars? What is the shortage or overage %?

19. Physical inventory for the shoe department was $1,975,000 with a book inventory showing $2,160,000. Net sales for shoes for the year are $6,850,000. Was there a shortage or overage? What is the shortage or overage dollar amount and percentage?

20. A costume jewelry department showed the following figures for a year:

Net sales	$125,000
Purchases (at retail)	$105,000
Opening retail inventory (Feb. 1)	$464,000
Markdowns	$40,000
Employee discounts	$2,600
Physical count (July 31)	$397,000

a. What was the shortage in dollars?

b. What was the shortage in percentage?

c. If the planned shortage was estimated at 2.5%, was the actual short-age more or less? By how much in dollars? In percentage?

21. Find the shortage or overage percentage if January figures are as follows:

Net sales	$137,000
Opening inventory (retail)	$640,000
Markdowns	$27,000
Employee discounts	$1,000
Retail purchases	$96,000
Closing physical inventory	$531,450
Net sales for the year	$1,520,000

22. Last year, the net sales in a home fashions department were $365,000. The book inventory at year-end was $67,500, and the physical inventory was $62,000. What was the shortage percentage?

23. Find the shortage or overage percentage using the following data:

Opening inventory (retail)	$1,204,000
Net sales	$342,000
Vendor returns	$4,000
Transfers to branches	$8,000
Employee discounts	$1,000
Purchases (at retail)	$495,000
Markdowns	$146,000
Closing physical inventory	$1,287,000
Yearly net sales	$2,875,000

24. If the retail book inventory at the close of the year is $1,500,000 and the physical inventory totals only $1,275,000, what will be the shortage percentage if net sales were $15,000,000?

25. The merchandise plan for Fall shows planned sales of $35,000, with an estimated shortage of 1.7%. What is the planned dollar shortage for Fall?

26. For the six-month period ending in January, your department showed the following figures:

Opening inventory (retail)	$1,262,000
Customer returns	$10,000
Returns to vendor	$6,200
Employee discounts	$3,800
Net sales	$910,000
Retail purchases	$870,000
Markdowns	60%
Transfers in	$5,100
Transfers out	$4,000
Physical inventory	$638,000
Yearly net sales	$1,654,000

a. What are the markdown dollars?

b. Determine the overage or shortage in both dollars and percentage.

27. Find the following:

    a. January closing book inventory given the following:

        January sales $323,000

        January markdowns $140,000

        January receipts $230,000

        January BOM $2,761,000

    b. If a physical inventory was taken and the actual inventory is $2,400,000. Is there a shortage or overage, and by how much in dollars?

    c. If the yearly net sales are $5,600,000, what is the shortage or overage %?

28. Describe in detail the various methods that a merchant might use to reduce excessive departmental shortage.

29. Research and Discussion: One of the major duties of any merchant is to control inventory discrepancies (e.g., excessive shortages or overages). Prepare a brief fact sheet for new assistant buyers that outlines the actions a merchant at the departmental level can take to effectively accomplish this responsibility. Briefly explain each action mentioned.

4.4 An Evaluation of the Retail Method of Inventory

ADVANTAGES OF THE RETAIL METHOD OF INVENTORY

The benefits of the retail method of inventory are that:

- It permits control over profit because the figures for markup obtained (i.e., the difference between the cost and the retail of the total merchandise handled) and markdowns taken (on which the realized gross margin depends) frequently are available, and immediate action can be taken to protect the desired profit margin.

- It simplifies the physical inventory process because the physical inventory is taken at retail prices, which is less difficult and less expensive. Additionally, because all entries are made rapidly and no decoding is necessary, the personnel do not require special training or experience.

- It provides a book inventory and, therefore, discrepancies (i.e., shortages and/or overages) in stock can be determined, shortage causes may be discovered, and preventive/corrective measures can be taken.

- It provides an equitable basis for insurance and adjustment claims.

LIMITATIONS OF THE RETAIL METHOD OF INVENTORY

The disadvantages of the retail method of inventory are that:

- It is a system of averages and therefore does not provide a precise cost evaluation of the inventory at its present cost price. This figure (i.e., cost evaluation of inventory) is calculated by applying the cost complement percentage (i.e., 100% – markup%) to the retail value of the inventory. This may result in a figure that is either greater or smaller than the invoice cost of the merchandise currently received. This is the most significant weakness of this method.

- It depends on extensive record-keeping for system accuracy.

- It is essential that all price changes be recorded.

FINDING COST OF GOODS SOLD AND GROSS MARGIN WITH THE RETAIL METHOD OF INVENTORY VALUATION

The retail method of inventory was introduced in department stores because it allowed a more simplified method to constantly monitor the all-important gross margin figure. The retail method of inventory eliminated a whole system of records formerly necessary to determine the valuation of an inventory at cost. Because the calculation of profit depends on cost data, the subsequent steps shown are taken in the calculation of a book inventory and in the determination of a continual gross margin figure. The following problem illustrates the calculation of gross margin on stock plus purchases (i.e., total merchandise handled) (see Figure 23):

Figure 23. Calculating Gross Margin on Stock Plus Purchases

	Cost	Retail	% of Sales	CMU %
Opening Inventory	$49,000 $\left(\begin{array}{c}\$100{,}000 \times (100\% - MU\ \%)\\ \$100{,}000 \times 49\%\end{array}\right)$	$100,000		51.0%
(Plus) New Purchases & Freight	+ $240,000	+ $500,000		
Total Mdse. Handled	$289,000	$600,000		51.8%
(Minus) Total Deductions		− $475,000 $\left(\begin{array}{l}\text{Sales} \quad \$425{,}000\\ + \text{Markdown} \quad \$45{,}000\\ + \text{Shortages} \quad \$5{,}000\end{array}\right)$		
(Minus) Closing Inventory	− $60,250 $\left(\begin{array}{c}\$125{,}000 \times (100\% - MU\ \%)\\ \$125{,}000 \times 48.2\%\end{array}\right)$	$125,000		
Gross Cost of Mdse. Sold	$228,750	$\begin{array}{l}\text{Net Sales} \quad \$425{,}000\\ - \text{Gross Cost of Msde.}\\ \quad \text{Sold} \quad \$228{,}750\end{array}$		
Merchandise Margin		$196,250	46.2%	
(Plus) Cash Discounts		+ $13,000		
		$209,250		
(Minus) Workroom Costs		− $1,000		
Gross Margin		$208,250	49%	

A juniors' sportswear buyer wants to calculate the gross margin figure to ascertain whether the department is "on target" and will achieve the planned gross margin goals for the season. The available season-to-date information is:

	Cost	Retail	MU %
Opening inventory		$100,000	51%
New purchases and freight	$240,000	$500,000	

SOLUTION

Step 1: Begin with a retail opening inventory figure: $100,000. The opening inventory at retail ($100,000) was determined when the stock-on-hand was physically counted at the end of the previous accounting period. The cumulative markup of 51% was achieved.

Step 2: Determine a cost opening book inventory figure:

$100,000 × (100% − 51%)

= $100,000 × 49%

= $49,000

Step 3: All new purchases ($240,000 cost, $500,000 retail) are added to the opening book inventory figures ($49,000 cost, $100,000 retail) to find total merchandise handled (TMH) figures ($289,000 at cost and $600,000 at retail), resulting in a 51.8% cumulative markup.

Step 4: The sum of $475,000 ($425,000 Total of net sales + $45,000 Markdowns + $5,000 Shortages) is subtracted from the retail figure of TMH ($600,000) to find the retail closing book inventory figure ($125,000).

Step 5: Determine a cost closing book inventory figure:

$125,000 × (100% − 51.8%)

= $125,000 × 48.2%

= $60,250

Step 6: The closing book inventory at cost ($60,250) is subtracted from TMH at cost ($289,000) to find the cost of goods sold ($228,750).

Step 7: The cost of goods sold ($228,750) is then subtracted from the net sales ($425,000) to find the merchandise margin ($196,250).

Step 8: The cash discounts ($13,000) are added to the merchandise margin ($196,250), which equals $209,250.

Step 9: The workroom costs ($1,000) are subtracted from $209,250 to find the gross margin ($208,250).

From an accounting viewpoint, in the calculation of gross margin, the cash discounts and workroom costs are adjusted after the margin on the merchandise itself (i.e., maintained markup) is determined. Nonetheless, because merchants frequently negotiate cash discounts or influence the workroom factor, their impact on the gross margin must be considered.

THE RELATIONSHIP OF PROFIT TO INVENTORY VALUATION IN THE RETAIL METHOD OF INVENTORY

The value placed on an inventory has a decided effect on profits. In this unit there is a detailed examination of the mathematical calculations and records adopted by departmentalized retailers who use the retail method of inventory to establish a continuing gross margin figure, as well as to verify if a profit has been achieved. By illustrating the relationship between sales volume, cost of merchandise sold, given expenses, and the operating profit, the example that follows shows the application of the data collected through this method of inventory valuation. (For ease of comprehension of this system, the same figures are used as in the preceding calculation of gross margin to the operating profit.)

	Net sales		Cost		Retail	% of Sales
					$425,000	100%
	Opening book inventory		$49,000			
+	Purchases	+	240,000			
	Total mdse. handled	=	$289,000			
–	Closing book inventory	–	60,250			
	Gross cost of mdse. sold	=	$228,750			
–	Cash discounts	–	13,000			
			$215,750			
+	Workroom costs	+	1,000			
	Net cost of mdse. sold	=	$216,750	–	216,750	– 51%
	Gross margin				$208,250	49%
–	Operating expenses			–	191,250	– 45%
	Net profit			=	$17,000	4%

THE EFFECT SHORTAGES AND OVERAGES HAVE ON GROSS MARGIN

After the closing book inventory is compared to the physical inventory and the resulting shortage or overage is calculated, buyers need to understand the impact this has on their gross margin. Shortages, the most common occurrence, will cause gross margin to decrease. The reason for this is that there are fewer products to sell; therefore, every other piece of product in inventory now costs more. With cost of goods increasing, gross margin decreases. For an overage, which is rare, the retail value of inventory has increased. The cost of goods sold decreases; each piece of product now costs less and gross margin will increase. (Refer to the profit and loss statement in Chapter 1.)

CASE STUDY 1
RETAIL METHOD OF INVENTORY

Two years ago, Ms. Carol, the misses' sportswear buyer, agreed with management that a separate petite sportswear department should be created. Because of increasing sales, she felt that petite sportswear had outgrown its status as a classification and deserved, in its own right, to become a separate department. Ms. Carol continued as the buyer for the newly created department, and with her enthusiastic and skillful attention, the impressive sales increases continued for the first year. The second year, however, the sales increases were minute. Ms. Carol now questioned if the category should remain a separate department or be reincorporated into the misses' sportswear department. To make an appropriate judgment, she requested the following data for analysis. The department had an opening inventory of $750,000 at retail that carried a 53% markup. During this period, the gross purchases of $570,000 at retail were priced with a 56.1% markup. The freight charges were $9,600. The merchandise returned to vendors amounted to $14,000 at cost and $30,000 at retail. Transfers from the misses' sportswear department were $3,500 at cost and $7,600 at retail. Transfers to the misses' sportswear department were $8,000 at retail, with an agreed cost of $3,700. The gross sales were $720,000; customer returns and allowances were $30,000. The markdowns taken were 12%, and employee discounts were 1%.

As Ms. Carol determined the gross margin achieved by the petite sportswear department, she weighed this against the 46.1% gross margin of the misses' department. Should this "new" department continue as a separate entity? Why? Justify your decision with a mathematical comparison of the performance of the petites versus misses' sportswear departments.

CASE STUDY 2
CONTROLLING SHORTAGES

Gary Abbott, the buyer for The Gift Shop, received the shortage report at the end of the Fall season. This report revealed that the overall department shortage for this six-month period was 1.3%, or 0.2% less than the previous season. Mr. Abbott was delighted to notice this decline in shortage, small as it was. As he analyzed the results of the individual stores, he found that Store 01 had a shortage of 1.2% while Store 09 had a 5.0% shortage.

Because the store uses a bar code scanning system to take inventory, the accuracy of the amount of inventory taken is ensured. However, Mr. Abbott reviews the figures for each store before trying to determine the causes of the vast shortage differences. He refers to the following data:

	Store 01			Store 09		
	Cost	*Retail*	*MU %*	*Cost*	*Retail*	*MU %*
Opening inventory		$450,000	52%		$300,000	52%
Purchases (including freight)	$142,500	$300,000		$71,250	$150,000	
Reductions		$7,000			$4,000	
Sales		$375,000			$150,000	
Shortage		1.2%			5%	

Store 01 had a physical inventory figure of $363,500, and Store 09's physical count was $288,500. Other differences between these two stores are:

1. Store 01 is one of the oldest existing branches of the chain, while Store 09 is the newest branch, having been opened one year ago.

2. Store 01 is located in a high-income area, while Store 09 is in a medium-income-bracket location.

3. Store 01 is one of the most profitable units of the chain, and because of its high productivity, it enjoys a commensurate sales force.

4. Since 09 is so young, it has been staffed with a minimum permanent sales organization supplemented by part-time employees.

Mr. Abbott takes three steps:

- He decides (though can computers ever be wrong?) to first determine the closing book inventory from the given figures.

- Having done that, he adjusts the physical count to the book inventory to determine the shortage percentage.

- Having satisfied himself as to the accuracy of the shortage percentage, he attempts to determine the possible causes.

If you were the buyer, what causes would you investigate more thoroughly in order to decrease shortages, and why? What effect, if any, would the large shortage percentage of Store 09 have on the overall department net profit?

SIX-MONTH PLANNING AND COMPONENTS

## CHAPTER 5

"The best way to predict the future is to create it."

PETER DRUCKER

"Knowledge comes by taking things apart, analysis. But wisdom comes by putting things together."

JOHN A. MORRISON

OBJECTIVES

- Understand and recognize the elements of a six-month merchandise plan.

- Gain knowledge and ability to plan sales.

- Calculate changes in sales as percentages.

- Understand importance of turnover.

- Calculate GMROI.

- Understand inventory planning methods:

  - Stock-sales ratio method.

  - Weeks of supply method.

  - Basic stock method.

- Gain proficiency in planning markdowns.

- Develop skill in planning purchases at retail and at cost.

- Calculate open-to-buy figures.

- Understand the importance of and how to plan assortments and classifications.

KEY TERMS

assortment/classification planning

average retail stock/inventory

basic stock method

BOM (beginning of month) stock

EOM (end of month) stock

GMROI (gross margin return on investment)

merchandise plan

on order

open-to-buy (OTB)

planned purchases/planned receipts

| retail (4-5-4) fiscal calendar | stock keeping unit (SKU) | turnover/turn |
| six-month seasonal dollar merchandise plan | stock-to-sales method | weeks of supply method |

KEY CONCEPT FORMULAS

Average retail stock

$$\text{Average retail stock/inventory} = \frac{\text{Planned sales for period}}{\text{Turnover rate}}$$

$$\text{Average retail stock/inventory} = \frac{\left(\begin{array}{c}\text{Sum of beginning} \\ \text{inventories}\end{array} + \begin{array}{c}\text{Ending inventory} \\ \text{for given period}\end{array}\right)}{\text{Number of inventories}}$$

$$\textbf{GMROI} = \frac{\text{Gross margin \%} \times \text{Turnover}}{100\% - \text{Markup \%}}$$

or

$$\textbf{GMROI} = \frac{\text{Gross margin \$}}{\text{Average inventory at cost \$}}$$

$$\textbf{Number of weeks of supply} = \frac{\text{\# Weeks in time period}}{\text{Turnover for the time period}}$$

Open-to-Buy (OTB)

$$\text{OTB} = \text{Planned purchases for the month} - \begin{array}{c}\text{Outstanding orders to} \\ \text{be delivered that month}\end{array}$$

$$\begin{array}{c}\text{OTB for balance} \\ \text{of month}\end{array} = \begin{array}{c}\text{Planned purchases} \\ \text{for month}\end{array} - \begin{array}{c}\text{Merchandise} \\ \text{received to date}\end{array} - \begin{array}{c}\text{Merchandise} \\ \text{on order}\end{array}$$

$$\begin{array}{c}\text{OTB for} \\ \text{balance} \\ \text{of month}\end{array} = \begin{array}{c}\text{Planned} \\ \text{EOM} \\ \text{stock}\end{array} + \begin{array}{c}\text{Planned} \\ \text{sales for} \\ \text{balance} \\ \text{of month}\end{array} + \begin{array}{c}\text{Planned} \\ \text{markdowns} \\ \text{for balance} \\ \text{of month}\end{array} - \begin{array}{c}\text{Actual} \\ \text{stock-} \\ \text{on-hand}\end{array} - \begin{array}{c}\text{On} \\ \text{order}\end{array}$$

Planned purchases

$$\begin{array}{c}\text{Planned monthly} \\ \text{purchases at} \\ \text{retail}\end{array} = \begin{array}{c}\text{Planned} \\ \text{EOM} \\ \text{stock}\end{array} + \begin{array}{c}\text{Planned sales} \\ \text{for month}\end{array} + \begin{array}{c}\text{Planned} \\ \text{markdowns} \\ \text{for month}\end{array} - \begin{array}{c}\text{Planned} \\ \text{BOM} \\ \text{stock}\end{array}$$

$$\begin{array}{c}\text{Planned monthly} \\ \text{purchase at cost}\end{array} = \text{Planned retail purchases} \times (100\% - \text{Planned markup \%})$$

Seasonal markdowns

$$\text{Planned total seasonal dollar markdowns} = \text{Planned total seasonal sales \$} \times \text{Total seasonal markdown \%}$$

$$\text{Total seasonal markdown \%} = \frac{\text{Total dollar seasonal markdowns}}{\text{Total seasonal sales \$}} \times 100$$

Stock ratios

$$\text{Stock-to-sales ratio} = \frac{\text{Retail stock at given time in the period}}{\text{Sales for the period}}$$

$$\text{BOM stock} = \text{Planned monthly sales} \times \text{Stock-to-sales ratio}$$

$$\text{BOM stock} = \text{Basic stock} + \text{Planned sales for the month}$$

$$\text{Planned stock} = \text{Average weekly sales} \times \text{Number of weeks of supply}$$

$$\text{Sales increase \% or decrease \%} = \frac{\text{This year (TY) planned sales} - \text{Last year (LY) actual sales}}{\text{LY actual sales}} \times 100$$

Seasonal planned sales $= \text{LY sales \$} + \text{Dollar increase}$

$\text{Dollar increase} = \text{LY sales \$} \times \text{Planned increase \%}$

or

Seasonal planned sales $= \text{LY sales \$} - \text{Dollar decrease}$

$\text{Dollar decrease} = \text{LY sales \$} \times \text{Planned decrease \%}$

$$\textbf{Turnover} = \frac{\text{Net sales for period}}{\text{Average retail stock for the same period}}$$

Profit in retailing is determined largely by maintaining a proper proportion between sales, inventories, and prices. The buyer is responsible for purchasing product that reflects customer demand and also remains within the financial limits set by management. For each department, a sales goal is forecast, and the size of the inventory necessary to meet these goals is planned. A budget that coordinates these sales and stocks is called a **merchandise plan**, which can be calculated in dollars or units. In this chapter, we focus on dollar planning. It schedules planned sales month by month, the amount of stock planned for each of these months, the amount of projected reductions, and the amount of receipts necessary to drive the business. The budget is prepared in advance of the selling period to which it applies. It typically covers a six-month period, for example, Spring season (beginning of fiscal month of February to end of fiscal month of July) or Fall season (beginning of fiscal month of August to end of fiscal month of January).

The information in this budget permits the merchandiser to determine the amount of purchases required. In no way does the dollar merchandise plan address the issue of what merchandise should be purchased. The development of an assortment that reflects customer demands is another important aspect of the total planning process.

Because of the quantitative nature of this book, this chapter focuses on the dollar mathematics used in this process; concepts and principles are briefly defined and discussed for better comprehension.

Although the dollar merchandise plans used by different stores vary considerably in scope and detail, when properly planned and administered, the sales, stocks, markdowns, turnover, and projected cumulative markup percentage (i.e., the original retail price of the total merchandise handled minus the cost) are the indispensable figures that should result in a satisfactory gross margin/net profit.

The main reason for planning purchases is to assist the buyer in making purchases at the proper time and in the correct amounts so that the stock level is in ratio to sales. Consequently, the dollar merchandise plan also provides a control figure called **open-to-buy (OTB)**. This figure represents the dollar amount of merchandise the buyer may receive during the balance of a given period, without exceeding the planned stock figure at the end of the period under consideration. Because of the benefits that result from this process, most large and many small retailers are committed to comprehensive planning activities. The dollar merchandise system of planning and control discussed in this chapter is designed to protect a store's major investment, that is, its inventory. A relationship exists between the amount of stock that is necessary to drive sales, limit markdowns, and maximize gross margin.

As the art of this merchandising technique is broad in scope and requires an in-depth examination, this subject must be included in any study related to buying for retail.

Six-Month Seasonal Dollar Merchandise Plan

As a device for unifying merchandising operations, the objectives of the dollar plan are:

- To achieve the planned gross margin and net profit by providing an instrument that plans, forecasts, and controls the purchase and sales of merchandise.

- To research previous results in order to repeat and improve prior successes and to avoid failures.

- To integrate the various merchandising activities involved in determining the purchases necessary to achieve the sales plan.

THE PROCEDURE OF DOLLAR PLANNING BY FACTOR

As previously discussed, there are several factors involved in the merchandise plan. We will begin by discussing each factor and the formulas related to them. This will culminate in formulating a six-month merchandise plan at the end of the chapter.

5.1 Planning Net Sales

The planning of net sales is most significant, as it is the driving force of the profit and loss statement (Chapter 1). The net sales plan is the basis for establishing the stock, markdown, and purchase figures needed for the business. Thus, it must be calculated first. However, its calculation requires the greatest skill and judgment because its accuracy depends on detailed investigation and analysis.

Step 1: Carefully forecast future total dollar sales volume for the entire period by:

    a. Reviewing and analyzing past sales performance for the same time period allowing for any changes in the calendar due to holiday shifts or weather impact. The **retail (4-5-4) fiscal calendar**, shown in Figure 24, is the guide that buyers use to compare retail sales from one time period to another. The calendar comprises the two retail seasons, Spring (February to July) and Fall (August to January). The retail week starts on Sunday and ends on Saturday, which is why the beginning of the month may not be the first day. Each month begins on the first fiscal Sunday for the reporting month. The calendar also reflects three years, the past year, which the sales plan is based on, the current year, and the next year, as planning is done at least six months in advance. In analyzing the retail calendar, buyers will need to shift sales accordingly; for example, Easter is on April 5 in 2015, in 2016 it falls on March 27, and in 2017, Easter occurs on April 16. This is a three-week shift in sales planning that a buyer must take into account. It is named the 4-5-4 calendar, as the second month of a quarter (March, June, September, and December) will have five weeks versus four weeks in the other months. In a five-week month, more sales will be planned for the extra week and potentially more stock will be needed as well.

Figure 24. Retail 4-5-4 Calendar for 2015–2017

NATIONAL RETAIL FEDERATION
2015-2017 RETAIL SALES REPORTING and
4-5-4 MERCHANDISING CALENDAR

* Fiscal Year 2017 is a 53-week year.

** Gray shaded boxes indicate a Sales Release Date. Black shaded boxes indicate the following holidays: Valentine's Day, Presidents Day, Easter, Mother's Day, Memorial Day, Father's Day, Independence Day, Labor Day, Rosh Hashanah, Yom Kippur, Columbus Day, Halloween, Election Day, Veterans Day, Thanksgiving, Christmas, New Year's Day, and Martin Luther King Day.

b. Considering factors that may cause a change in sales. These factors include:

- Current sales trends. In retail, businesses shift in importance from season to season or year to year. Merchandise managers work with buyers to shift sales and purchase dollars to businesses that are performing well and meeting sales plans and take away from those departments or classifications that are down trending. Being able to change plans should result in a more profitable plan, maximize sales, and minimize markdowns.

- Previous rate-of-growth patterns. Buyers need to look at history but focus on the future as well.

- Economic conditions. Apparel and accessory retail is dependent on customers' disposable income. Therefore, consumer confidence in the economy has an impact on how this disposable income is spent.

- Local business conditions/mall vacancies.

- Fashion factors.

- Influencing conditions within and outside of the store or department (e.g., changes in store concepts, market direction, competition, etc.).

While the formulas are straightforward, it is the analysis of the preceding factors that take thought, reasoning, and time.

c. Establishing, for the time period, in this case a season, a percentage of estimated sales change after analyzing the sales performance and current conditions that cause sales changes. Then calculate the total dollar sales volume for the period. These formulas are used every day by retailers and can be utilized for any time period: year, season, quarter, month, week, or day.

Next we look at formulas involved in planning sales before moving on to Step 2.

Calculating Percentage of Sales Increase or Decrease When Last Year's Actual Sales and This Year's Planned Sales Are Known

Percentage of sales increase $=$ This year (TY) planned sales

$-$ Last year (LY) actual sales

$=$ Sales increase

$= \dfrac{\text{Sales increase}}{\text{LY actual sales}} \times 100$

$=$ % Sales increase

CONCEPT

PROBLEM If last year's actual sales were $2,000,000 and this year's planned sales are $2,200,000, what is the percentage of sales increase?

SOLUTION

Percentage of sales increase	=	$2,200,000	TY planned sales
	−	$2,000,000	LY actual sales
	=	$200,000	Sales increase

$$\frac{\$200,000 \text{ Sales increase}}{\$2,000,000 \text{ LY sales}} \times 100$$

| | = | 0.10, or 10% |
| **Percentage of sales increase** | = | 10.0% |

There are circumstances under which the sales volume of a department or classification is reduced because of a decreased demand or downward trending. The concept for a decrease in sales is the same as for an increase in sales.

PROBLEM The sales of the boot classification declined significantly because of the current fashion emphasis. Consequently, the shoe buyer planned sales for this category at $500,000 this season, although last year's actual sales amounted to $650,000. What was the planned percentage of sales decrease for this classification?

SOLUTION

$$\text{Percentage of sales decrease} = \frac{\text{TY planned sales} - \text{LY actual sales}}{\text{LY actual sales}} \times 100$$

	=	$500,000	TY planned sales
	−	650,000	LY actual sales
	=	$150,000	Sales decrease

$$= \frac{\$150,000 \text{ Sales decrease}}{\$650,000 \text{ LY actual sales}} \times 100$$

| **Percentage of sales decrease** | = | 23.1% |

Calculating a Total Planned Seasonal Sales Figure When Last Year's Sales and the Planned Percentage of Increase Are Known

CONCEPT

Seasonal planned sales	=	Last year (LY) sales × Planned increase %
	=	Dollar increase
	=	LY sales + Dollar increase

PROBLEM

If last year's seasonal sales are $2,000,000 and there was a planned 10.0% sales increase, what are the seasonal planned sales for this year?

SOLUTION

Seasonal planned sales	=	$2,000,000	LY sales
	×	10.0%	Sales increase
	=	$200,000	Sales increase
		$2,000,000	LY sales
		+ 200,000	Sales increase
TY seasonal planned sales	=	$2,200,000	

Step 2: With a six-month plan, once a seasonal sales plan is calculated, each month's contribution can be planned. To set the individual monthly sales goals, use the seasonal distribution of the previous year's sales for the same period as a guideline. The six-month sales percentages will add up to 100%. When adjusting the planned monthly sales increase or decrease, the three essential processes that influence a buyer's judgment are:

- Considering the department's past experience with respect to the normal percentage distribution of sales for the planning period.

- Comparing the monthly percentage distribution to industry performance (see Figure 25).

- Adjusting monthly sales figures due to shifting dates of certain holidays (especially Easter), planned special promotions, weather impact from the previous year, and other merchandising strategies (Figure 26).

Figure 25. Typical Conventional Department Store's Monthly Sales Distribution

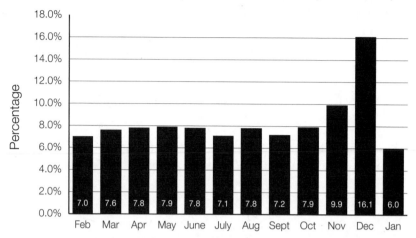

Feb	Mar	Apr	May	June	July	Aug	Sept	Oct	Nov	Dec	Jan
7.0	7.6	7.8	7.9	7.8	7.1	7.8	7.2	7.9	9.9	16.1	6.0

Source: U.S. Department of Commerce, Bureau of the Census: Combined Annual and Revised Monthly Report

Figure 26. Daily Flash Sales by Store

Daily Flash Sales
Daily Flash Sales for Wednesday 2/20/2013   Date: per 09 wk 2 day 4

*****PLAN NUMBERS REPRESENT AN END-OF-WEEK CUMULATIVE TOTAL*****

		(3) TODAY	(4) PTD ($1000)				(5) STD	
LOC	TY	LY	TY	LY	PLAN	PCT	TY	PLAN
(1) DEPT 220 BELTS								
(2) 01 NY	3680	2147	40	37	55	7.5+	277	284
02 BR	301	403	4	3	5	7.8+	32	22
03^ FM	0	0	0	0	0	0.0+	0	0
04^ ST	0	0	0	0	0	0.0+	0	0
05 BC	61	506	5	5	8	6.1-	38	36
06 SH	216	207	5	4	5	27.5+	31	28
07 CP	0	0	0	0	0	0.0+	0	0
08 NM	719	243	7	5	8	36.3+	57	46
09 GC	471	276	5	4	5	38.4+	32	27
10 PG	402	77	2	2	2	25.6+	13	8
11 CH	695	343	5	3	5	38.4+	34	31
12 WP	322	320	6	5	7	1.4+	41	42
13 WF	293	859	3	5	6	46.2-	21	27
14 TC	185	237	3	4	5	9.6-	22	23
16 KP	265	306	4	3	4	16.0+	22	21
17 WG	177	170	2	2	2	12.4+	17	14
20^ VV	0	0	0	0	0	0.0+	0	0
21* FA	0	580	0	6	7	102.9-	12	35
22* FR	0	0	0	0	0	0.0+	0	0
24 FN	0	0	0	0	0	0.0+	0	0
25* MI	50	0	3	0	6	100.0+	25	29
TOT-CMP	7787	6094	90	83	117	8.4+	638	609
TOT-ALL	7837	6674	94	90	130	4.5+	675	673
PCT	17.4+		4.5+					

*****PLAN NUMBERS REPRESENT AN END-OF-WEEK CUMULATIVE TOTAL*****

		TODAY	PTD ($1000)				STD	
LOC	TY	LY	TY	LY	PLAN	PCT	TY	PLAN
DEPT 231 SCARVES								
01 NY	4822	4191	59	64	81	8.6-	316	301
02 BR	122	59-	2	2	0	35.8+	13	3
03^ FM	0	0	0	0	0	0.0+	0	0
04^ ST	0	0	0	0	0	0.0+	0	0
05 BC	661	488	8	6	10	24.8+	43	33
06 SH	478	740	6	7	9	14.8-	35	32
07 CP	0	0	0	0	0	0.0+	0	0
08 NM	368	848	7	6	11	27.0+	55	40
09 GC	407	155-	4	3	5	29.8+	24	18
10 PG	56	44	1	0	0	131.2+	4	1
11 CH	571	82	5	6	7	11.6-	35	22
12 WP	73	602	10	6	10	72.4+	53	38
13 WF	170	315	3	4	5	33.1-	19	21
14 TC	85	483	3	3	5	17.3-	18	20
16 KP	485	311	4	4	5	10.4+	22	23
17 WG	26	465	3	3	4	5.3-	19	15
20^ VV	0	0	0	0	0	0.0+	0	0
21* FA	0	57	0	1	2	100.0-	4	7
22* FR	0	0	0	0	0	0.0+	0	0
24 FN	0	0	0	0	0	0.0+	0	0
25* MI	349	0	4	0	0	100.0+	23	0
TOT-CMP	8324	8356	113	113	152	0.2+	658	567
TOT-ALL	8673	8413	117	115	154	2.5+	685	574
PCT	3.0+		2.5+					

*****PLAN NUMBERS REPRESENT AN END-OF-WEEK CUMULATIVE TOTAL*****

		TODAY	PTD ($1000)				STD	
LOC	TY	LY	TY	LY	PLAN	PCT	TY	PLAN
MGM 105 DRESS ACCESSORIES								
01 NY	13709	12232	162	163	223	0.6-	1038	1008
02 BR	1001	1376	16	15	20	3.9+	122	97
03^ FM	0	0	0	0	0	0.0+	0	0
04^ ST	0	0	0	0	0	0.0+	0	0
05 BC	1324	2362	20	20	30	2.3+	151	129
06 SH	1284	1786	23	21	27	12.9+	152	136
07 CP	0	0	0	0	0	0.0+	0	0
08 NM	2636	2871	29	29	44	0.7-	231	215
09 GC	1163	687	14	13	17	13.8+	96	80
10 PG	874	519	7	5	8	24.1+	44	38
11 CH	2751	821	19	17	22	8.0+	139	110
12 WP	968	1248	27	21	30	32.0+	176	151
13 WF	1043	2045	11	17	21	33.4-	83	100
14 TC	921	1389	12	13	17	10.3-	88	80
16 KP	1504	1352	13	11	15	22.1+	86	80
17 WG	616	1008	9	11	12	11.5+	63	58
20^ VV	0	0	0	0	0	0.0+	0	0
21* FA	0	1847	0	17	23	101.1-	41	114
22* FR	0	0	0	0	0	0.0+	0	0
24 FN	0	0	0	0	0	0.0+	0	0
25* MI	634	0	13	0	16	100.0+	102	85
TOT-CMP	29794	29696	363	355	486	2.2+	2470	2282
TOT-ALL	30428	31543	376	372	525	0.9+	2613	2481
PCT	3.5-		0.9+					

*****PLAN NUMBERS REPRESENT AN END-OF-WEEK CUMULATIVE TOTAL*****

		TODAY	PTD ($1000)				STD	
LOC	TY	LY	TY	LY	PLAN	PCT	TY	PLAN
DEPT 252 SOCKS								
01 NY	6382	6578	76	82	81	7.6-	334	386
02 BR	368	313	3	3	0	0.3-	22	7
03^ FM	0	0	0	0	0	0.0+	0	0
04^ ST	0	0	0	0	0	0.0+	0	0
05 BC	1017	1673	12	13	10	2.0-	52	54
06 SH	754	1002	13	11	9	18.5+	56	52
07 CP	0	0	0	0	0	0.0+	0	0
08 NM	1348	1133	16	15	11	6.2+	77	85
09 GC	839	1000	12	11	5	7.1+	51	44
10 PG	38	27	1	1	0	16.0-	6	7
11 CH	802	516	8	7	7	21.8+	35	33
12 WP	1129	775	13	13	10	0.4-	59	62
13 WF	399	958	6	9	5	35.7-	25	42
14 TC	469	429	6	6	5	4.2+	22	24
16 KP	335	772	4	6	5	26.2-	19	31
17 WG	307	515	4	5	4	15.3-	17	21
20^ VV	0	0	0	0	0	0.0+	0	0
21* FA	0	296	0	3	2	100.0-	5	21
22* FR	0	0	0	0	0	0.0+	0	0
24 FN	0	0	0	0	0	0.0+	0	0
25* MI	534	0	13	0	0	100.0+	23	45
TOT-CMP	14187	15691	175	181	152	3.7-	776	848
TOT-ALL	14721	15987	179	184	154	3.2-	805	914
PCT	7.9-		3.1-					

*CMP = comp stores

Calculating Sales on the Basis of Sales Achieved per Square Footage

Retailers also plan sales based on how productive the space is that is allocated to a specific department. Departments that generate higher sales dollars per square foot usually have a more prominent position in the store and a larger allocated space.

$$\text{Sales \$ per square foot} = \frac{\text{Sales \$}}{\text{Square footage}}$$

CONCEPT

The men's department has annual sales of \$4,000,000 and a department size of 10,000 square feet. What are the dollars per square foot generated for the men's department?

PROBLEM

$$\text{Sales \$ per square foot} = \frac{\$4,000,000}{10,000} = \$400$$

SOLUTION

Planning Sales Practice Problems

1. In the children's department, the August sales were planned at $247,500 because of additional promotional events. The actual sales for this month last year were $225,000. What is the percentage increase in planned sales for August of this year?

2. For the Spring period, the handbag department's total seasonal sales volume for last year was $750,000. If there is an 8% increase this year, what is the dollar amount of sales planned?

3. For Spring, there is a 4.7% increase planned for the contemporary department. Last year's Spring sales were $456,000. What is the dollar sales plan for this Spring?

4. After reviewing the sales for Holiday, the gift department is being planned up by 1.5%. Holiday sales were $52,000. What is the sales plan for the gift department?

5. Last year's Fall sales in missy sportswear were $895,000. For this year, a 3.4% decrease is being planned. What is the Sales $ plan for this Fall?

6. The suburban stores for Retailer A did not perform well during the Summer season; therefore, a decision was made to plan the sales down 2.7% for this coming Summer. Last year's Summer sales were $3,600,000. What is the new sales plan for the suburban stores?

7. The men's business department exceeded the Fall plan by 4.1%. If the Fall sales plan was $2,500,000, what sales did men's business achieve?

8. If actual sales in men's were $2,602,500 and last year's sales were $2,500,000, what is the percentage change in sales?

9. The denim department reported Fall sales for this year of $23,800. Last year's sales were $25,450. Calculate the percentage change in the denim department's Fall sales.

10. During August, sales for a sporting goods store are planned at $900,000, which is 15% of the planned season's total sales. Calculate the monthly sales for the balance of the season if sales are planned as follows:

August	15%	November	18%
September	14%	December	25%
October	16%	January	12%

11. For April, the small leather goods department sales are $18,000, which represents 15.0% of the total season's sales. Calculate the total Spring season sales and the monthly sales for the balance of the season if the percentages of monthly sales are as shown:

February	12.0%	May	27.0%
March	14.0%	June	23.0%
April	15.0%	July	9.0%

12. A small retailer is planning a 10% reduction in sales due to competition from a major new department store. If last year's sales were $500,000, what sales figure should be planned for this year?

13. After a detailed analysis of sales by classification, the hosiery buyer determined a decline in the panty hose category. Last year's sales for this category were $75,000. This year, the sales for this classification are planned at $60,000. What is the percentage of sales decline?

14. Seasonal sales for last year were $855,000, and this year the merchandise manager planned for a sales increase of 8%. What is the estimated planned dollar sales figure for this year?

15. If actual sales for last year were $855,000, and this year's planned sales are $923,400, calculate the percentage of sales increase for this year.

16. The missy dress department has yearly sales of $425,000. The department is 1,000 square feet. Calculate the sales per square foot achieved in the missy dress department.

17. The jewelry department covers 1,600 square feet. Its sales for last year totaled $890,000. Calculate the dollars per square foot generated in the jewelry department.

18. The shoe department accounts for 2,700 square feet in a store and achieved sales per square foot of $800. Calculate the total sales for the shoe department.

19. The housewares department sales per square foot are $365 and the department has a square footage of 1,350. Calculate the total sales for the housewares department.

5.2 Turnover/GMROI

Inventory, which has a limited selling period and depreciates over time, can be a retailer's largest asset and thus needs to be carefully managed. As merchandising policies of retail stores differ, there is no absolute formula for developing the variety of a stock assortment. However, the planning phase of stock investment is accomplished through the dollar plan. In the planning and control of dollar stocks, every merchandiser's objective is to:

- Maintain adequate assortments (i.e., reasonably complete from a customer's viewpoint).

- Regulate the dollar investment of stocks in relation to sales in order to obtain a satisfactory balance between these two factors.

- Plan inventory assets carefully to avoid taking excessive markdowns, which will impact profitability.

Daily computerized sales reports provide the buyer with information on actual performance and any variance from planned performance. This information requires analysis for appropriate action and decisions. These computerized reports provide the basis for dollar control of inventories. This report helps alert the merchandiser to the most current sales position to make any revisions deemed necessary.

After planned monthly sales are established, the amount of dollar stock that is required to be on hand at the beginning of each month (**BOM stock**) and/or the end of each month (**EOM stock**) must be determined. The EOM stock for a particular month is the same as the BOM stock for the following month; for example, if $230,000 is the EOM stock for February, this same figure is the BOM stock for March.

When planning inventory, it is important to understand that differences exist in planning fashion and basic assortments. Fashion product is trendy, brought in on a bi-monthly or monthly basis, and an outdate needs to be set for this product (Chapter 2). Basic product are consumer staples, such as basic five-pocket denim jeans, hosiery, and so on. A buyer needs a consistent amount of inventory on hand and reorders stock as it sells. Basic stock models are formulated on a store-by-store basis for basic product because each store in the chain may sell different sizes or colors in a given time period. Almost every department sells a mix of basic and fashion product, which will vary by product category. Buyers need to plan basic merchandise classifications first to reserve purchase dollars for the inventory necessary and for reorders to fill in sales.

There are variations in the methods of calculating individual monthly stock figures. Before discussing these possible techniques, it is essential to examine turnover because it represents the degree of balance between sales and stocks. The rate of stock turnover measures the velocity with which merchandise moves into and out of a department or store. **Turnover (turn)**, or rate of stock turnover, is an important merchandising figure and a productivity measure. It indicates the number of times that an **average retail stock (inventory)** has been sold and replaced during a given period, that is, the number of times goods have been turned into money, and, subsequently, money turned back into goods. Turnover is expressed as a rate, not a percentage. Although turnover is a resultant figure, it can be planned and controlled and is calculated for a month, quarter, season, or year.

DETERMINING THE TURNOVER FIGURE

Every retailer should understand the importance of turnover to make better use of capital investment and control inventories, and, ultimately, realize optimum profits. It acts as an index to efficient merchandising. Successful stock planning does not begin with turnover but results in achieving the desired rate of stock turnover. This term indicates the number of times that an average stock is sold for a given period of time, which, unless otherwise stated, refers to a period of one year. However, turnover may be computed on a monthly, quarterly, or seasonal basis. The actual number of stock turns varies with the type of merchandise and price. Depending on the retailer, merchandise in lower price ranges may turn more rapidly than in higher ranges; apparel and accessories turn more rapidly than home furnishings, for instance. Fashion merchandise should turn faster than basic merchandise, which will have a slower turn.

Turnover is important to a merchandising operation because it:

- Stimulates sales by presenting fresh merchandise to the customer.

- Reduces markdowns by keeping the flow of new goods constant, thereby curbing the accumulation of large amounts of older stock.

- Lowers cost of goods sold because the "open-to-buy" position permits the buyer to take advantage of special prices and offerings.

- Decreases interest, merchandise taxes, and other operating expenses as a percentage of net sales.

The stock turnover rate can be calculated on either a unit or dollar basis, but for the purposes of this text, the dollar basis is examined.

Calculating Turnover When Average Retail Stock and Sales for the Period Are Known

The dollar figures of stock turn can be determined on either a cost or retail basis. Generally, in stores that use the retail method of inventory, the rate of stock turn is determined on a retail basis. Essential for accuracy, however, is that both sales and inventory be calculated on the same foundation.

CONCEPT | $$\text{Turnover} = \frac{\text{Net sales for period}}{\text{Average retail stock for the same period}}$$

For the year, the infants' department had net sales of $2,000,000. The average retail stock during this period was $500,000. What was the rate of stock turn?

PROBLEM

SOLUTION

Turnover rate for the period $= \dfrac{\$2{,}000{,}000 \text{ Net sales}}{\$500{,}000 \text{ Average retail stock}}$

Turnover $= 4.0$

Calculating Average Retail Stock When Planned Sales and Turnover Are Known

CONCEPT

Average retail stock $= \dfrac{\text{Planned sales for period}}{\text{Turnover rate}}$

PROBLEM

The women's slipper department planned sales of $2,000,000 with a stock turn of 2.5 as the goal. What should be the average stock carried for the period under consideration?

SOLUTION

Average retail stock for period $= \dfrac{\$2{,}000{,}000 \text{ Planned sales}}{2.5 \text{ Turnover rate}}$

Average retail stock for period $= \$800{,}000$

By understanding the relationship of the average stock, planned sales, and turnover, and by substituting the known factors of the basic formula, the unknown can be calculated (e.g., Net sales = Stock turnover × Average stock at retail).

Calculating Average Retail Stock When Monthly Inventories Are Known

Because the determination of the average inventory directly affects the rate of stock turn, stores and retail establishments need a common method to determine the average stock amounts so that the comparison of stock turns can be meaningful. Under the retail method of inventory, an average retail stock is the sum of the retail inventories at the beginning of each year, season, month, or week. This is added to the ending inventory for a specific period and then divided by the number of inventories used. This is the most accurate and commonly used method because a monthly book inventory figure is available through the retail method of inventory. For example, to obtain an average retail stock figure for a year, the 12 stock inventories at the beginning of each month are added to the ending inventory and the total sum is divided by 13. If the stock turnover rate is computed for a shorter period than one year, the same principle is applied (e.g., for determining a six-month turnover rate, add the 7 stock-on-hand figures and divide by 7). As turnover is cumulative and usually expressed in two decimal places, the turnover rate, which has been computed for a period of less than a year, can then be converted to an equivalent annual rate.

In addition, an average stock figure can be calculated in cost as well as retail dollars. The method of finding an average monthly inventory at cost is exactly the same as determining the average stock at retail. For reasons that should be apparent, it is incorrect to mix cost figures with those at retail in the same turnover calculation, so when this type of figure is desired, only the cost inventory figures are used.

CONCEPT

$$\text{Average retail stock} = \frac{\left(\begin{array}{c}\text{Sum of beginning} \\ \text{inventories}\end{array} + \begin{array}{c}\text{Ending inventory} \\ \text{for given period}\end{array}\right)}{\text{Number of inventories}}$$

PROBLEM

Find the average retail stock and the turnover for this period:

	Sales		BOM stock	Ending inventory
February	$3,400	February		$22,400
March	4,200	March		23,800
April	4,600	April		26,500
May	4,400	May		27,600
June	5,500	June		30,000
July	4,000	July		26,000
August	5,400	August		31,000
September	6,000	September		32,400
October	5,800	October		29,800
November	7,500	November		35,000
December	10,000	December		37,500
January	3,000	January		20,000
Total	$63,800			$342,000
		January EOM		$22,000

Sum of 12 BOM stocks	=	$342,000
+ Ending inventory	=	+ 22,000
	=	$364,000

$$\text{Average retail stock} = \frac{\$364{,}000 \text{ (Sum of 13 figures)}}{13 \text{ (Number of inventories)}}$$

Average retail stock for one year = $28,000

After calculating an average stock figure, the formula of net sales for the period under consideration divided by the average stock is applied to determine the turnover rate. For example:

$$\text{Turnover rate} = \frac{\$63{,}800 \text{ (Sum of 12 monthly sales figures)}}{\$28{,}000 \text{ (Average retail stock for the period)}}$$

Turnover rate = 2.28

This same method is used to calculate an average retail stock for a shorter period. The next problem applies the formulas for average inventory and turnover. It illustrates how to determine the average retail stock for a quarter and how to convert the turnover to an annual rate. This will be an approximate annual rate, as not all of the quarters turn equally, but it is a good estimate.

For the first quarter the junior sportswear department had the following sales and inventory figures. Calculate the turnover for the first quarter.

	Sales	Stock-on-hand (book inventory)	
February	$12,000	$48,000	
March	10,000	45,000	
April	9,000	40,000	
April EOM		47,000	
Total sales	$31,000	$180,000	Sum of inventories

SOLUTION

Average stock	=	$\dfrac{\$180,000}{4}$	Sum of inventories Number of inventories
	=	$45,000	
Stock turn rate	=	$\dfrac{\$31,000}{\$45,000}$	Net sales for period Average stock for same period

First-quarter turnover rate =   0.69 for 3 months or 1/4 year

Approximate annual rate =   0.69 $\times$ 4 = 2.76

It is important to understand in calculating turnover why actual net sales and average inventory are used. Actual net sales are what is collected from customers during a given period of time and relate to the net sales in the profit and loss statement (Chapter 1). Average inventory is used for the following reasons:

- Not all merchandise is on the selling floor at the same time. There is back stock of product that will be filled in when product sells down. This product is included in the total inventory figures controlled by a buyer.

- Merchandise is receipted throughout the month. Basic product is being filled in regularly, and fashion product may be delivered two times a month or more frequently.

- Vendors may ship product early or late with a buyer's approval.

- Book inventory differs from physical inventory as discussed in Chapter 4.

Turnover is one of the most important retail metrics a buyer will use and monitor regularly. Therefore, a buyer needs to understand how to increase turnover as well as understand the impact it has on gross margin. In order to increase turnover, buyers need to increase sales, most likely by taking markdowns, or decrease their inventory levels. Reduction of inventory will be achieved by selling more product or ordering less merchandise. By increasing net sales, gross margin, for all intents and purposes, should increase (Chapter 1). Turnover is sometimes used synonymously with sell through percentage (Chapter 2). The formulas are similar using sales and inventory. Sell through is a snapshot in time, usually week to week. Turnover is cumulative and more accurate over a longer period of time when retail sales fluctuate and inventory levels are changing.

DETERMINING GROSS MARGIN RETURN BY DOLLAR INVENTORY

While retailers have stock turn goals to judge the efficiency of the balance between sales and stocks, when money is tight greater emphasis is placed on the relationship between the inventory investment, or working capital, and its ability to produce gross margin dollars. The objective is to produce a maximum gross margin from a minimum dollar amount investment.

The ratio of productivity of each dollar invested in inventory is similar to a share of stock, and the productivity of this dollar is equivalent, to some degree, to earnings per share. Stock turnover influences and affects the utilization of money invested in inventory. The more times money is converted into sales and gross margin, the greater the return per dollar of inventory. Today, the frequency of this "reinvestment" is an increasingly significant factor. The measurement of the efficiency of investment in inventory is referred to as **gross margin return on investment**, which is commonly known as **GMROI** (pronounced *jimroy*). This element is used by financial analysts to measure capital turnover.

Merchandisers in retailing are responsible for a successful stock turnover and, consequently, give it much focus. Both stock turn and GMROI are involved with inventory productivity, and the relationship between these two elements is that the calculation of stock turn utilizes an average inventory at retail, while GMROI uses an average inventory at cost.

The following example illustrates this concept:

Net sales	=	$1,200,000	
Gross margin	=	$480,000	
Average inventory (retail)	=	$480,000	
Average inventory (cost)	=	$240,000	
a. Stock turn	=	$\dfrac{\$1,200,000}{\$480,000}$	Net sales Average inventory at retail
	=	2.5	
b. GMROI	=	$\dfrac{\$480,000}{\$240,000}$	Gross margin Average inventory at cost
	=	$2.00	

This is the simplest level of calculating GMROI. It is apparent that as more sales and gross margin dollars are generated, without increasing inventory, GMROI will increase.

It is more practical to think of GMROI in terms commonly used in merchandising. These factors, which can be managed and influenced, are:

- Markup percentage.
- Gross margin percentage.
- Turnover.

Another way to think of the calculation is:

$$\frac{\text{How much is made on a sale} \times \text{How long it takes to sell it}}{\text{How much was paid for it}}$$

This results in the following calculation:

CONCEPT

$$\text{GMROI} = \frac{\text{Gross margin \% } \times \text{ Turnover}}{100\% - \text{Markup \%}}$$

PROBLEM

The year-to-date results of the intimate apparel department are:

Gross margin: 40%

Turnover: 2.5

Markup: 50%

What is the GMROI achieved by this department?

SOLUTION

$$\text{GMROI} = \frac{\text{Gross margin \% } \times \text{ Turnover}}{100\% - \text{Markup \%}}$$

$$= \frac{40\% \text{ GM } \times \text{ 2.5 Turnover}}{100\% - 50\% \text{ MU}}$$

$$= \frac{0.40 \times 2.5}{1.0 - 0.50}$$

$$= \frac{1}{0.50}$$

$$\text{GMROI} = \$2.00$$

The buyer made $2.00 for every dollar invested in inventory at cost.

The GMROI result is identical for either calculation, but the second example shows the relationship of the components and demonstrates how future results can be improved using the important retail calculations.

With the increasing use of computerized spreadsheets, gross margin dollars and average inventory are already calculated and cumulative markup percentage is given, so buyers can use a simplified version of the GMROI formula:

CONCEPT

$$\text{GMROI} = \frac{\text{Gross margin \$}}{\text{Average inventory at cost}}$$

PROBLEM

For the first quarter, the junior sportswear department had the following gross margin figures with a cumulative markup of 55.0%. Calculate the GMROI for the first quarter.

	Sales	Stock-on-hand (book inventory)	Gross margin $
February	$12,000	$48,000	$6,000
March	$10,000	$45,000	$4,500
April	$9,000	$40,000	$4,000
April end		$47,000	

SOLUTION

Gross margin $ = $6,000 + $4,500 + $4,000 = $14,500

$$\text{Average inventory} = \frac{\$48,000 + \$45,000 + \$40,000 + \$47,000}{4} = \frac{\$180,000}{4} = \$45,000$$

Average inventory at cost = Average inventory $ × (100% − Markup %)

= $45,000 × (100 − 55%)

= $45,000 × 45% = $20,250

$$\textbf{GMROI} = \frac{\text{Gross margin \$}}{\text{Average inventory at cost}} = \frac{\$14,500}{\$20,250} = \$0.72$$

The key to successful retailing is achieving more dollar sales without a corresponding increase in inventory. Through the determination of turnover, the stock level that produces an optional sales level can be measured. The calculation of GMROI shows the profitability or cash flow that these sales produce.

Another calculation and comparison that needs to be made is the resulting gross margin percentage for a given time period and how it relates to the cumulative markup percentage.

CONCEPT

$$\text{Gross margin \%} = \frac{\text{Gross margin \$}}{\text{Net sales \$}} × 100$$

PROBLEM

Calculate the first-quarter gross margin percentage for the junior sportswear department from the previous example.

SOLUTION

$$\text{Gross margin \%} = \frac{\$14,500}{\$31,000} × 100$$

= 46.77, or 46.8%

Note that there is a difference between the cumulative markup percentage of 55% and the resulting gross margin of 46.8%. The factor that accounts for the difference is the amount of markdowns taken. As we discussed in Chapter 2, if there are no markdowns or reductions taken, then markup and gross margin would be equal. However, once markdowns/reductions are taken, the two figures are no longer equal, and any loss in planned gross margin dollars needs to be addressed. In order to recoup gross margin, a buyer would need to increase sales or negotiate a lower cost (increasing markup as well). As you can see, the answer for any buyer is the same, no matter what the formula: increase sales, negotiate the best possible cost prices, and keep inventory under control!

Calculating Average Retail Stock, Turnover, and GMROI Practice Problems

20. Calculate the turn for the accessories department for the Fall season if the average inventory is $3,209,600 and the sales are $2,360,000.

21. Calculate the yearly turn for the missy sportswear department if the average inventory is $2,400,000 and the sales are $7,920,000.

22. A shoe department has net sales of $2,500,000 for the year. The average stock carried during this period was $1,000,000. What was the annual rate of stock turn?

$$\frac{2500,000}{1000000} = 2.5$$

23. The net sales for the petite sportswear department were $99,900 for the Spring season. The turn was 1.85. What was the average inventory for this department for Spring?

$$\frac{Sales}{TO}$$

$54000

24. The net sales for the fragrance department were $345,000 for the fourth quarter. The turn was 1.15. What was the average inventory for fragrances for the fourth quarter?

25. The net sales in the neckwear department were $240,000, with a stock turnover of 3.0. Find this department's average stock at retail.

26. What amount of average stock should be carried by a costume jewelry department with net sales of $920,000 for the year and a stock turn of 4.0?

27. What is the average stock of a department with annual sales of $1,350,000 and an annual stock turn of 4.5?

28. A housewares department has an average inventory of $112,000 at retail, with a stock turnover of 2.0. What are the department sales for the period?

29. The average inventory for the girls' department for Spring was $23,700 and the Spring turn was 1.26. What were the Spring sales for girls?

TO × Stock = $29862

30. The sales for October were $8,000; the stock on October 1 at retail value was $24,000; the stock on October 31 was $28,000. What was the stock turn for the month?

31. Calculate the turnover for men's ties for June if June beginning inventory was $23,500 and July beginning inventory was $19,800. June sales were $8,640.

32. Calculate the jewelry turnover for May if May beginning stock was $214,500 and June beginning stock was $194,600. May sales were $51,135.

$$TO = \frac{Sales}{Stock}$$

51135 | 214500
       | 194600
       _____
       409100/2
       = 204550

.25

33. Find the average stock from an activewear department's inventory figures:

BOM January	$62,000	BOM July	$120,000
BOM February	$64,000	BOM August	$78,000
BOM March	$70,000	BOM September	$78,000
BOM April	$74,000	BOM October	$68,000
BOM May	$88,000	BOM November	$64,000
BOM June	$100,000	BOM December	$60,000
		BOM January next year	$62,000

34. Determine the seasonal stock turnover on the basis of the following information for girls' 4–6X:

	Beginning retail inventory	Sales
August	$60,000	$20,000
September	$68,000	$25,000
October	$47,000	$15,000
November	$50,000	$20,000
December	$70,000	$26,000
January	$38,000	$10,000
January end	$32,000	

116000

.7
365000

$52142.9

=2.2

35. Calculate the seasonal turnover using the following figures from an outer-wear department:

Net sales	$347,500
Inventory beginning August	$85,000
Inventory beginning September	$105,000
Inventory beginning October	$150,000
Inventory beginning November	$250,000
Inventory beginning December	$290,000
Inventory beginning January	$180,000
Inventory end January	$100,000

36. Departmental net sales for the second quarter were $48,000. During the year these beginning inventories were recorded:

Date	Inventory value (retail)
May	$36,500
June	$41,500
July	$32,000
July end	$34,000

Find:

   a. The average stock for the year.

   b. The annual rate of turn.

37. Calculate the turn for the year given the following information:

	Sales	Beginning inventory
February	$1,250	$8,600
March	1,000	7,400
April	1,025	6,900
May	1,400	8,150
June	1,100	7,650
July	900	7,500
August	1,500	7,400
September	1,700	7,600
October	1,800	7,700
November	1,900	8,800
December	2,200	9,400
January	800	7,400
January end		8,000

Spring { February – August }

fall { September – January }

16575 _____

7884.61 /13

8,000 _____

(2.1)

38. Use these numbers for the Fall season:

	Sales	Beginning inventory	GM $
April	$13,250	$88,100	$7,900
May	$17,500	$93,600	$9,800
June	$13,400	$87,700	$7,200
June end		$87,000	

MU % for the quarter is 68.2%.

Find:

  a. Total sales for the quarter.

  b. Average inventory for the quarter.

  c. Average inventory at cost for the quarter.

  d. Total GM $ for the quarter.

e. Turn for the quarter.

f. GMROI for the quarter.

g. GM % for the quarter.

39. The following is the third-quarter information for men's denim:

	Sales	BOM inventory	GM $
August	$1,425	$9,490	$655
September	$1,580	$9,840	$690
October	$1,520	$9,650	$640
End October		$9,800	

MU % for the quarter is 59.8%.

Find:

a. Total sales for the quarter.

b. Average inventory for the quarter.

c. Average inventory at cost for the quarter.

d. Total GM $ for the quarter.

e. Turn for the quarter.

f. GMROI for the quarter.

g. GM % for the quarter.

40. Use these numbers for the Fall season:

	Sales	Beginning inventory	GM $
August	$10,500	$58,000	$5,600
September	$11,900	$66,000	$6,800
October	$11,000	$62,000	$5,900
November	$12,600	$72,000	$7,200
December	$14,800	$80,000	$7,700
January	$9,500	$52,000	$4,300
January end		$60,000	

MU % for the season is 61.7%.

Find:

a. Total sales for the season.

70300

b. Average inventory for the season.

$ 64285.7

c. Average inventory at cost for the season.

2

d. Total GM $ for the season.

$37500

e. Turn for the season.

sales / stock

70300 / 64285.7   [1.09]

f. GMROI for the season.

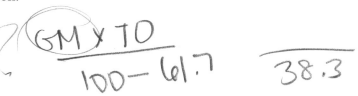

$$\frac{GM \times TO}{100 - 61.7} \quad \overline{38.3}$$

g. GM % for the season.

41. The men's furnishings department for a mass market retailer had the following performance for the period under consideration:

- 32.0% Gross margin.
- 2.8 Turnover.
- 52.7% Markup.

What GMROI was achieved?

$$\lceil all \downarrow cost\% \frac{gross M \times TO}{47.3}$$

[1.9]

42. The same men's furnishings buyer (in problem 41) made some promotional purchases for an annual store event that increased the markup to 55.8%, with the other factors being constant. What GMROI resulted from this strategy?

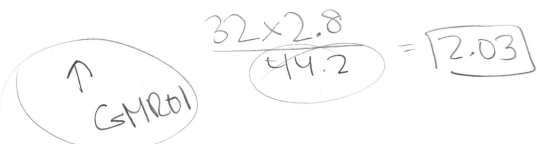

$$\uparrow GMROI \quad \frac{32 \times 2.8}{44.2} = [2.03]$$

43. During the last Fall season, the active sportswear department achieved a 45.9% gross margin with a stock turn of 2.1. The markup was 60.3%. During this Fall season, the gross margin was increased to 50.5%. Compare the GMROI performance from last year to this year.

44. The misses' sportswear department achieved a 38.1% gross margin and had a 69.5% markup, with a stock turn of 2.5. What was the resultant GMROI for this department?

5.3 Stock/Inventory Planning Methods

It is common to plan monthly stock figures for the beginning of the period by a **stock-sales ratio method**. This technique, illustrated in the following examples, indicates the relationship between stock-on-hand at the beginning of the month and the retail sales for the same month.

SETTING INDIVIDUAL FIRST-OF-MONTH STOCK FIGURES BY THE STOCK-SALES RATIO METHOD

After planned monthly sales figures are established, the amount of dollar stock that is required on hand at the beginning of each month (BOM stocks) and the end of each month (EOM stocks) must be determined. This relationship is referred to as a stock-sales ratio. Generally, the BOM stock-sales ratio is used to balance planned monthly stocks with the planned monthly sales. Stock-to-sales ratios will vary based on merchandise classifications. For basic product in a size intensive department (e.g., shoes, bras), the stock-to-sales ratio will be greater than in a department where size is not an issue (e.g., handbags, small leather goods). Use of this ratio provides the buyer with how much stock is necessary to sell one unit of product. Standard stock-sales ratios in departments can be established by evaluating the actual past stock-sales ratio performance of a department. This has proven to provide the proper relationship. Additionally, researched guidelines of data showing typical monthly stock-sales ratios are available and can be used as a source of information in planning monthly stock proportions. Because monthly stock-sales ratio proportions vary according to location, customer type, and so on, the best source of information in establishing a proper ratio for each individual month is a store's own records.

Calculating Stock-Sales Ratio When Retail Stock and Sales for a Given Period Are Known

CONCEPT

$$\text{Stock-sales ratio} = \frac{\text{Retail stock at given time in the period}}{\text{Sales for the period}}$$

PROBLEM

On February 1, the boys' wear department had a retail stock of $120,000. The planned sales for this month were $20,000. Find the stock-sales ratio for February.

SOLUTION

$$\text{Stock-sales ratio} = \frac{\$120,000 \text{ BOM stock}}{\$20,000 \text{ February sales}}$$

Stock-sales ratio = 6.0

Calculating BOM Stock When Planned Sales and Stock-Sales Ratio Are Known

CONCEPT	BOM stock = Planned monthly sales × Stock-sales ratio
PROBLEM	The fabric department planned sales of $40,000 for July. Experience in the department showed that an 8.2 stock-sales ratio was successful. What should be the planned BOM stock for July?
SOLUTION	BOM July stock = $40,000 Planned July sales × 8.2 Stock-sales ratio **BOM stock** = $328,000

A relationship exists between turnover and stock-to-sales; the formulas are inverse. Therefore, fashion merchandise categories should have a faster turn and lower stock-to-sales ratio, while basic-oriented merchandise will have a higher stock-to-sales ratio and slower turnover.

SETTING STOCK FIGURES BY THE WEEKS OF SUPPLY METHOD

The **weeks of supply method** plans the inventory needed for the beginning of a month, based on a calculated number of weeks of supply and the average sales for a period of time. The number of weeks of supply that is to be "on hand" depends on the planned turnover figure for the specific time period and is used as a guide to set the inventory. This technique of stock planning is best used to plan fashion merchandise inventory, but it can be used to plan basic commodities as well. Weeks of supply is discussed in Chapter 2 as an analytical method when a buyer may need to take markdowns or reorder product. That uses weeks of supply in a reactive method when you have either too many or too little weeks of supply and inventory will either surpass or not reach the outdate set.

According to the 4-5-4 calendar (Figure 24), the following is the relationship between weeks and months for the retail year:

Time period	Number of months	Number of weeks
Year	12	52
Season	6	26
Quarter	3	13
Month	1	4 or 5

Note that because the stock size is in direct relation to the average planned weekly sales, it can result in an excessive stock condition at peak selling periods or in dangerously low stocks during the slower months.

Calculating the Number of Weeks of Supply

CONCEPT

$$\text{Number of weeks of supply} = \frac{\text{Weeks in time period}}{\text{Desired turnover for time period}}$$

PROBLEM

Department #32 has a planned stock turnover of 1.5 for the six-month period. Determine the number of weeks of supply needed to achieve the desired turnover.

SOLUTION

$$\text{Number of weeks of supply} = \frac{26 \text{ Weeks}}{1.5 \text{ Turnover}}$$

Number of weeks of supply = 17.33, or 17.3

Finding Planned Stock Given Turnover and Weekly Rate of Sales

CONCEPT

Planned stock $ = Average weekly sales $ × Number of weeks of supply

PROBLEM

A department has an average weekly sales rate of $9,800 and a planned turnover rate of 1.5 for the six-month period. Calculate the amount of stock to be carried.

SOLUTION

Step 1: Find the number of weeks of supply given the turnover and the supply period.

$$\text{Number of weeks of supply} = \frac{26 \text{ Weeks}}{1.5 \text{ Turnover}}$$

Number of weeks of supply = 17.33, or 17.3

Step 2: Find planned stock given the average weekly sales and the number of weeks of supply.

Planned stock = $9,800 Average weekly sales × 17.3 Number of weeks of supply

Planned stock = $169,540

SETTING BEGINNING OF THE MONTH (BOM) STOCK FIGURES BY BASIC STOCK METHOD

Another approach to balancing stocks and sales is the **basic stock method**, which is primarily used for basic commodity merchandise. This model provides the minimum amount of basic stock that remains constant on a monthly basis and buys back the sales each month. For this model, a buyer needs to know his or her average inventory levels, which are derived simply from the planned sales and turnover. For example, if the anticipated six-month sales total of $960,000 and a turnover of 2.0 is desired for the season, average inventory can be calculated by applying the following formula:

$$\text{Average inventory} = \frac{\$960,000 \quad \text{Sales}}{2.0 \quad \text{Turnover}}$$

Average inventory = $480,000

The buyer also needs to know his or her average monthly sales planned in order to derive the basic stock necessary.

Calculating Average Monthly Sales

Planned sales

February	$110,000
March	150,000
April	160,000
May	180,000
June	210,000
July	150,000
Total sales	$960,000

$$\text{Average monthly sales} = \frac{\$960,000 \text{ Total sales}}{6 \text{ Months}}$$

Average monthly sales = $160,000

Finding a Basic Stock Given the Average Monthly Sales and the Average Inventory

The average inventory minus the average monthly sales produces a basic stock at retail. For example:

Average inventory	=		$480,000
− Average monthly sales	=	−	160,000
Basic stock	=		$320,000

Finding a BOM Stock When a Basic Stock and Planned Sales for the Month Are Known

The calculated basic stock figure is then added to each month's planned sales to determine the BOM amount for the month.

BOM stock = Basic stock + Planned sales for the month

In an accessories department that has planned a turnover of 2.0 for the Fall season, the estimated sales are as follows:

August	$28,000	November	$36,000
September	$30,000	December	$40,000
October	$32,000	January	$26,000

Calculate the BOM stocks using the basic stock method.

Step 1: Determine average monthly sales.

August	$28,000
September	30,000
October	32,000
November	36,000
December	40,000
January	+ 26,000
Total for the season	$192,000

$$\text{Average inventory} = \frac{\$192,000}{6 \text{ Months}}$$

Average monthly sales = $32,000

Step 2: Calculate average inventory.

$$\text{Average inventory} = \frac{\$192,000 \text{ Sales}}{2.0 \text{ Turnover}}$$

Average inventory = $96,000

Step 3: Find basic stock.

Basic stock at retail	=	Average inventory	$96,000
	−	Average monthly sales	− 32,000
		Basic stock =	$64,000

Step 4: Calculate BOM stock by adding basic stock to monthly planned sales.

BOM stock =	*Monthly sales*		*Basic stock*		*BOM stock*
August	$28,000	+	$64,000	=	$92,000
September	$30,000	+	$64,000	=	$94,000
October	$32,000	+	$64,000	=	$96,000
November	$36,000	+	$64,000	=	$100,000
December	$40,000	+	$64,000	=	$104,000
January	$26,000	+	$64,000	=	$90,000

Calculating Stock-Sales Ratio
Practice Problems

45. What is the planned stock-sales ratio in the handbag department when beginning of the month stock is planned at $19,000 and planned sales are $9,100?

46. Planned sales in the costume jewelry department for April are $130,000, and the planned stock-sales ratio is 2.4. What should be the stock figure for the beginning of April?

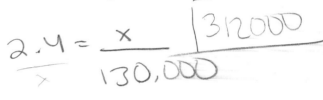

47. The outerwear department buyer decided that a stock-sales ratio of 5.5 for February would be appropriate. If February's sales were planned at $12,000, how much stock should be carried for February BOM?

48. The glove department's stock at the beginning of March was $67,500, with sales for the month at $15,700. What was the stock-sales ratio for March?

49. Calculate the stock-to-sales ratio for April if the BOM stock is $68,000 and the sales for April are $7,000.

50. Calculate the stock-to-sales ratio for the shoe department in October if sales are $178,000 and the inventory for October is $3,100,000.

51. The bra department has a planned stock-to-sales ratio for August of 14.5 and planned sales of $27,100. Find the stock for August.

52. The tie department has a planned stock-to-sales ratio of 6.0 and planned sales of $12,900. Find the average inventory for June in the department.

Finding Weeks of Supply
Practice Problems

53. A junior sportswear department has an average weekly sales figure of $110,000 and a planned turnover of 0.92 for the quarter. Calculate the amount of stock to be carried using the WOS method.

(weeks/turn) × sales

13 / .92 = 1554347.7

54. A missy sportswear department has an average weekly sales figure of $196,000 and a planned turnover of 3.47 for the year. Calculate the amount of stock to be carried using the WOS method.

52 weeks

14.98 × 196000

2937175.6

55. Using the WOS method, calculate the amount of stock that should be carried in the junior dress department if sales per week are $15,000 and the turnover is 1.6 for the six-month Spring season.

26 / 1.6 = 16.25

243750

56. The boys' department has an average weekly sales figure of $33,500 and a planned turnover of 1.45 for the Fall season. Calculate the amount of stock to be carried using the WOS method.

57. The hosiery department sells control-top panty hose at a rate of 576 pairs per week at a retail price of $4.50 per pair. Calculate the amount of stock that should be carried to achieve a turnover of 1.4 for the six-month season in this category.

58. A stationery store has sales of $18,000 per week and a planned turnover of 1.25 for a six-month period. Calculate the amount of stock that should be carried in this store.

59. A handbag department plans a stock turn at 2.9 for a twelve-month period. What figure represents the number of weeks of supply needed to achieve the desired turnover?

60. A cold weather accessories department has an average weekly sales figure of $14,500 and a planned turnover rate of 2.2 for the six-month period. Calculate the amount of stock to be carried.

Using Basic Stock Method
Practice Problems

61. The men's pants department has yearly sales of $4,800,000 and an annual stock turn of 2.0. Calculate the basic stock that needs to be carried in the men's pants department.

62. The hosiery department has Fall season sales of $52,800 and a planned seasonal turnover of 1.25. October sales are planned at $9,540. Calculate October stock that needs to be carried based on the basic stock method.

63. The bra department has planned Fall season sales of $254,100 and a planned seasonal turnover of 1.10. December sales are planned at $46,790. Calculate December BOM that needs to be carried based on the basic stock method.

64. Calculate the basic stock figure of a men's suit department that has annual sales of $1,650,000 and an annual stock turn of 1.6.

65. For May, the gift department had planned sales of $180,000. For the Spring season, the department's planned sales were $900,000, with a planned stock turnover of 2.25. Determine the BOM figure for May using the basic stock method.

66. The small leather goods department had planned the following figures for the Fall season:

Planned total sales for season: $102,000

Planned turnover for season: 2.0

Planned sales for November: $26,000

Calculate the November BOM figure for this department using the basic stock method.

67. The men's shirt department has Spring season sales of $88,200 and a planned seasonal turnover of 1.60. The sales planned by month are as follows:

February $8,880

March $13,320

April $15,540

May $16,872

June $25,596

July $7,992

Calculate the BOM stock needed for each month based on the basic stock method.

PLANNING MARKDOWNS

In dollar planning, markdowns are important because they reduce the total value of the stock available for sale. In Chapter 2, we discussed why markdowns are an important tool for a buyer to drive sales. Careful planning of markdowns assists in controlling the amount of markdowns taken, which in turn helps increase net profit figures. The amount of planned journalized markdowns to be taken is expressed both in dollars and as a percentage of planned net sales. Because the dollar markdowns vary greatly, the percentage data is more significant for comparison between past and present performance. The percentage of markdowns also varies with different lines of merchandise, different months, different seasons, and different retail channels of distribution. The planned markdown figure is usually based on a normal amount determined from experience.

It is common when planning markdowns for a season to:

Step 1: Set the total markdown amount (stated as a percentage of the total season's sales) for the entire period by:

a. Reviewing and analyzing past markdown performance for the same period and for the entire period under consideration.

b. Considering factors that may affect a change in markdowns, for example, additional coupons or promotions planned.

$$\text{Total seasonal markdown \%} = \frac{\text{Total dollar markdowns}}{\text{Total net sales}} \times 100 \qquad \text{CONCEPT}$$

Step 2: Convert the planned markdown percentage of sales to a total dollar figure for the season.

$$\text{Planned total seasonal dollar markdowns} = \text{Planned total seasonal sales} \times \text{Total seasonal markdown \%} \qquad \text{CONCEPT}$$

Step 3: Apportion total dollar planned markdowns by month. (Note that the distribution of monthly markdown goals does not necessarily mean that markdowns and sales will be in the same proportion during each of the months of the season.)

EXAMPLE

Last year, net sales for the season in the swimwear department were $100,000. The total amount of markdowns taken during the entire period was $45,000. The buyer, on reviewing the performance of the department and in preparation for planning markdowns for the same period this year, decided that the $45,000 markdown figure taken previously was normal and compared favorably to standard markdown percentages established for this type of merchandise. Consequently, last year's dollar markdown amount was converted to a percentage:

$$\text{Markdown \%} = \frac{\$45{,}000 \text{ LY markdown}}{\$100{,}000 \text{ LY net sales}} \times 100$$

$$\text{Markdown \%} = 45\%$$

The total planned sales figure established by the buyer for the season under consideration was set at $110,000. Because a repetition of the percentage of markdowns was desired for the forthcoming season, the dollar amount of markdowns to be taken was determined by:

$$\begin{array}{c}\$110{,}000 \\ \text{Planned sales}\end{array} \times \begin{array}{c}45\% \text{ Planned} \\ \text{markdowns}\end{array} = \begin{array}{c}\$49{,}500 \text{ Planned total markdown} \\ \text{for the season}\end{array}$$

The amount of $49,500 would then be apportioned by dollars to the individual months of the period.

PLANNING MARKUPS

Although markup planning and calculations are discussed in Chapter 3, it is necessary to understand that after the initial markup has been carefully planned, the buyer will have to constantly manipulate the actual markup to date in relation to the markup on additional purchases for the season in order to obtain the planned seasonal markup percentage. To "protect" profitability, the gross profit figure, including an estimated shortage amount, can be calculated easily as in the following example, which shows the facts that should be considered:

1. For the Spring season, a department has planned:

    - Sales at $2,000,000.

    - Markdowns at $600,000 (30%).

    - Shortages at $40,000 (2%).

2. The department came into the period under consideration with an opening inventory at retail of $500,000 and a cumulative markup for the period of 58%.

3. A closing inventory of $500,000 at retail is projected for the end of the Spring period.

4. Management projects a desired gross margin of 48.5% for the Spring period.

5. Based on a 48.5% gross margin, the cumulative markup (Stock + Purchases) is calculated:

    a. $$\begin{array}{c}\text{Cumulative} \\ \text{MU \%}\end{array} = \frac{48.5\% \text{ Gross margin} + (30\% \text{ Markdowns} + 2\% \text{ Shortages})}{100\% \text{ Sales} + 32\% \text{ Reductions}}$$

    $$= \frac{80.5\%}{132\%}$$

    $$= 60.98\%/61.0\%$$

b. The markup percentage required on new purchases to meet desired goals is determined by the following method:

$$\text{Total retail mdse. requirements} = \text{Net sales} + \text{Markdowns} + \text{Shortages} + \text{Closing retail inventory}$$

	$2,000,000	Net sales
+	600,000	Markdowns
+	40,000	Shortages
+	500,000	Closing retail inventory

Total retail mdse. requirements = $3,140,000

$$
\begin{aligned}
\text{Cost} &= \text{Total retail mdse. requirements} \times (100\% - \text{MU \%}) \\
&= \$3,140,000 \times (100\% - 61\%) \\
&= \$3,140,000 \times 39\% \\
&= \$1,224,600
\end{aligned}
$$

$$
\begin{aligned}
\text{New purchases at retail} &= \text{Total retail mdse. requirements} - \text{Opening inventory} \\
&= \$3,140,000 - \$500,000
\end{aligned}
$$

New purchases at retail = $2,640,000

$$
\begin{aligned}
\text{New purchases at cost} &= \text{New purchases at retail} \times (100\% - \text{Cumulative MU \%}) \\
&= \$2,640,000 \times (100\% - 58\%) \\
&= \$2,640,000 \times 42\% \\
&= \$1,108,800
\end{aligned}
$$

$$
\begin{aligned}
\text{Markup \% on new purchases} &= \frac{\$2,640,000 \text{ Retail (new purchases)} - \$1,108,800 \text{ Cost (new purchases)}}{\$2,640,000 \text{ Retail}} \times 100 \\
&= 58\%
\end{aligned}
$$

Planned gross profit percentage is determined by the following method:

Given:

Dollar sales (from plan)	=	$2,000,000
Dollar markdown (from plan) (30%)	=	$600,000
Anticipated shortage percentage	=	2%

$$
\begin{aligned}
\text{Anticipated dollar shortage} &= \text{Planned shortage \%} \times \text{Total planned dollar sales} \\
&= 2\% \times 2,000,000
\end{aligned}
$$

Anticipated dollar shortage = $40,000

Planned markup % on Planned stock + Purchases = 61.0%

Cost or complement % on Planned stock + Purchases = 39.0%

Cost of planned sales:

Planned markdown	=	$600,000 × 0.39	=		$234,000
Planned shortage	=	$40,000 × 0.39	=	+	15,600
Planned sales	=	$2,000,000 × 0.39	=	+	780,000
Total cost of planned sales			=		$1,029,600
Planned dollar sales			=		$2,000,000
Cost of planned sales			=	−	1,029,600
Planned dollar gross profit			=		$970,400

Planned gross profit percentage $= \dfrac{\$970,400}{\$2,000,000} \times 100$

Planned gross profit percentage = 48.5%

5.4 Open-to-Buy and Purchase/Receipt Planning

One objective of planning is to assist the buyer in proper timing and in purchasing the correct amounts of goods. Therefore, when the planned sales, stocks, and markdowns have been determined, the amount of monthly purchases is automatically calculated by a formula. **Planned purchases**, which is more accurately termed **planned receipts**, refers to the dollar amount of merchandise that can be brought into stock during a given period. Store reports frequently identify these figures as receipts. Generally, purchases are preplanned at retail value for each month and then converted, by formula, to a cost figure by applying the planned markup.

CALCULATING PLANNED MONTHLY PURCHASES AT RETAIL

CONCEPT

Planned monthly purchases at retail	=	Planned EOM stock
	+	Planned sales for month
	+	Planned markdowns for month
	=	Total merchandise requirements
	–	Planned BOM stock
	=	Planned purchase amount

PROBLEM

From the following planned figures for the lingerie department, calculate the planned purchase amount for June:

Planned stock beginning June	$638,000
Planned sales for June	$100,000
Planned markdowns for June	$35,000
Planned stock for beginning July (end June)	$640,000

SOLUTION

Planned June sales		$100,000
+ Planned EOM stock (beg. July)		640,000
+ Planned June markdowns	+	35,000
Total merchandise requirements	=	$775,000
– Planned BOM stock (June 1)	–	638,000
Planned monthly retail purchases	=	$137,000

CONVERTING RETAIL PLANNED PURCHASES TO COST

The planned purchase figure at retail must be established first before the planned purchase figure at cost is determined by conversion.

CONCEPT

$$\text{Planned monthly purchase at cost} = \text{Planned retail purchases} \times (100\% - \text{Planned markup \%})$$

PROBLEM

The planned retail purchases for June were $137,000 and the planned markup percentage was 55.0%. Calculate the planned purchase amount at cost.

SOLUTION

$$\text{Planned purchases} = \$137,000 \text{ Planned retail purchases} \times (100\% - 55\% \text{ Planned MU})$$

$$= \$137,000 \times 45\%$$

$$= \$61,650$$

Planned purchases at cost $= \$61,650$

The planning purchases/receipts formula should look familiar. It is similar to finding the maintained book inventory formula; the components are the same. This version of the formula tells a buyer the amount of money he or she has to spend on purchases; the previous formula plans and forecasts where the book inventory will be for the end of the current month/beginning of next month.

Based on the previous examination of the procedures, elements, and computations that relate to the creation of a dollar plan, analyze Figures 27–31, which are examples of typical **six-month seasonal dollar merchandise plans.** The formats differ, yet there are certain common metrics found on all reports: net sales, markdowns, gross margin, inventory levels, and receipts. Buyers need to learn how to analyze the reports and formulate strategies to drive their businesses. These forms are included to help you become familiar with their differences and similarities. In large retailers, these reports are normally available online for the buyer to view at any time. These reports assist buyers and divisional merchandise managers in making decisions on how many retail dollars are available for the required purchases—also known as planned receipts. It is common for a general merchandise manager and/or planner to contribute to the planning function.

Figure 27. Worksheet for Annual Merchandise Plan

$(000)															
SALES ($)	FEB.	MARCH	APRIL	MAY	JUNE	JULY	SPRING	AUG.	SEPT.	OCT.	NOV.	DEC.	JAN.	FALL	ANNUAL
00 PLAN							2007								
13 ACT.	1817	3396	3476	3066	3041	2070	16865	2303						2303	19168
13 PLAN	1643	3265	3207	3238	3034	1608	15996	2231	4095	3071	3161	4233	1681	18471	34467
12 ACT.	1427	2619	2550	2701	2742	1438	13478	1766	3157	2322	2112	3077	1457	13891	27368
11 ACT.	1224	2250	2065	2366	2447	1379	11730	1725	2536	1842	1847	2620	959	11530	23260
10 ACT.	1115	2018	1947	1977	1951	1170	10177	1451	2159	1412	1377	1988	833	9221	19399

SALES % CHG.	FEB.	MARCH	APRIL	MAY	JUNE	JULY	SPRING	AUG.	SEPT.	OCT.	NOV.	DEC.	JAN.	FALL	ANNUAL
04P/05A															
03P/04A	27.3	29.6	36.3	13.5	10.9	43.9	25.1	30.4	−100.0	−100.0	−100.0	−100.0	−100.0	−83.4	−30.0
02P/03A	15.1	24.7	25.8	19.9	10.6	11.9	18.7	26.3	29.7	32.3	49.7	37.6	15.3	33.0	25.9
01P/02A	16.6	16.4	23.5	14.2	12.1	4.3	14.9	2.4	24.5	26.0	14.3	17.4	52.0	20.5	17.7
00P/01A	9.8	11.5	6.1	19.7	25.4	17.9	15.3	18.9	17.5	30.4	34.1	31.8	15.1	25.0	19.9

EOM STOCK	FEB.	MARCH	APRIL	MAY	JUNE	JULY	AVG. SPRING	AUG.	SEPT.	OCT.	NOV.	DEC.	JAN.	AVG. FALL	AVG. ANNUAL
00 PLAN							10513								
13 ACT.	7449	9578	9714	8979	8518	7581	8337	10555							
13 PLAN	8971	9703	9586	8712	7410	6950	8241	11613	12270	11810	11256	9000	8431	10190	9390
12 ACT.	7204	8802	9009	8225	6474	6105	7339	7577	8098	8536	8138	5959	6538	7279	7401
11 ACT.	5389	5986	6182	6056	5261	5140	5477	6122	6120	6460	6692	5368	5551	5922	5742
10 ACT.	5349	6188	5614	4691	4069	4481	4916	4578	5285	5031	4998	4057	4323	4679	4822

EOM − WKS OF SUPPLY	FEB.	MARCH	APRIL	MAY	JUNE	JULY	TURNOVER SPRING	AUG.	SEPT.	OCT.	NOV.	DEC.	JAN.	T.O. FALL	T.O. ANNUAL
00 PLAN							1.95								
13 ACT.	9.8	13.0	15.7	14.9	13.1	10.5	2.02	13.3							
13 PLAN	12.1	13.6	16.1	15.2	12.4	9.8	1.94	14.5	17.3	18.1	17.7	14.9	12.1	1.81	3.67
12 ACT.	12.0	15.2	17.6	16.6	13.2	11.0	1.84	13.0	15.0	18.1	16.6	13.0	10.5	1.91	3.70
11 ACT.	10.8	11.2	13.0	14.0	12.3	10.9	2.14	12.8	12.6	15.9	16.2	13.6	11.4	1.95	4.05
10 ACT.	11.8	14.1	14.4	13.3	11.4	11.5	2.07	11.9	15.4	15.7	15.1	12.4	10.6	1.97	4.02

NET RECEIPTS	FEB.	MARCH	APRIL	MAY	JUNE	JULY	SPRING	AUG.	SEPT.	OCT.	NOV.	DEC.	JAN.	FALL	ANNUAL
00 PLAN															
13 ACT.	2728	5525	3611	2331	2580	1133	17909	5276						5276	23185
13 PLAN															
12 ACT.	3080	4217	2756	1918	992	1069	14032	3238	3677	2760	1714	898	2036	14323	28355
11 ACT.	2290	2846	2261	2240	1652	1258	12547	2707	2534	2183	2079	1296	1142	11942	24489
10 ACT.	2442	2857	1373	1054	1330	1581	10637	1549	2866	1158	1345	1047	1099	9064	19700

MARKDOWN ($)	FEB.	MARCH	APRIL	MAY	JUNE	JULY	SPRING	AUG.	SEPT.	OCT.	NOV.	DEC.	JAN.	FALL	ANNUAL
00 PLAN															
13 ACT.	395	380	456	773	797	448	3249	452						452	3700
13 PLAN															
12 ACT.	165	533	342	628	743	122	2533	314	488	479	578	996	31	2885	5418
11 ACT.	250	233	294	228	649	162	1816	253	365	489	362	1002	90	2560	4376
10 ACT.	216	216	350	252	504	292	1830	168	223	315	366	450	204	1725	3555

MARKDOWN %	FEB.	MARCH	APRIL	MAY	JUNE	JULY	SPRING	AUG.	SEPT.	OCT.	NOV.	DEC.	JAN.	FALL	ANNUAL
00 PLAN															
13 ACT.	21.7	11.2	13.1	25.2	26.2	21.6	19.3	19.6						19.6	19.3
13 PLAN															
12 ACT.	11.6	20.3	13.4	23.2	27.1	8.5	18.8	17.8	15.5	20.6	27.4	32.4	2.1	20.8	19.8
11 ACT.	20.4	10.3	14.3	9.6	26.5	11.7	15.5	14.7	14.4	26.6	19.6	38.2	9.4	22.2	19.8
10 ACT.	19.4	10.7	18.0	12.8	25.8	25.0	18.0	11.5	10.3	22.3	26.6	22.6	24.5	18.7	18.3

A13 – RTW C DRESSES
A13 – RTW C DRESSES

Figure 28. Six-Month Merchandise Plan (by Store)

SALES

STORE	FEBRUARY PLAN	L Y	MARCH PLAN	L Y	APRIL PLAN	L Y	MAY PLAN	L Y	JUNE PLAN	L Y	JULY PLAN	L Y	TOTAL SEASON PLAN	L Y	STORE
01	27.8	26.5	43.9	40.4	57.6	55.0	79.0	75.5	46.1	43.5	26.8	25.4	281.2	266.3	01
02	43.8	42.3	59.5	55.8	84.1	81.3	120.1	116.0	61.2	58.4	39.2	37.9	407.9	391.7	02
03	44.3	42.8	56.7	53.6	84.7	81.8	123.2	118.9	69.3	65.7	43.8	42.4	422.0	405.3	03
05	14.9	14.1	23.8	22.2	33.2	31.7	48.8	46.6	27.5	26.3	15.6	15.0	163.8	155.9	05
07	10.8	10.5	15.0	14.3	18.6	18.1	29.3	28.3	17.7	17.1	9.8	9.4	101.2	97.7	07
08	18.8	18.1	32.1	30.3	39.1	37.7	59.4	57.2	33.9	32.6	20.3	19.4	203.6	195.3	08
09	10.8	10.3	13.9	12.9	19.0	18.2	31.9	30.5	20.3	19.3	11.0	10.5	106.9	101.7	09
12	23.3	22.2	27.3	25.5	47.4	43.8	77.5	72.0	44.5	41.3	31.1	28.9	251.1	233.7	12
13	28.0	26.2	34.1	31.6	60.1	56.1	96.3	89.7	52.8	49.4	31.2	29.1	302.5	282.1	13
14	7.3	6.6	8.4	7.5	10.5	9.5	21.8	19.5	13.3	12.0	6.5	5.9	67.8	61.0	14
15	10.1	8.7	12.5	10.4	20.2	16.9	35.6	30.7	24.9	22.2	16.1	14.6	119.4	103.5	15
16	17.2	15.8	21.5	19.5	32.1	29.5	52.8	48.2	30.2	27.9	17.3	15.9	171.1	156.8	16
17	1.4	1.4	2.2	2.2	3.7	3.6	5.8	5.7	4.3	4.2	4.1	4.0	21.5	21.1	17
18	12.0	11.2	15.1	13.7	24.9	23.3	43.9	40.1	18.4	17.0	15.2	14.0	129.5	119.3	18
19	14.3	13.6	16.9	15.6	23.0	21.7	40.3	38.0	25.5	24.0	14.7	13.8	134.1	126.7	19
20	10.8	9.7	14.6	12.9	14.4	13.4	34.5	31.4	23.7	21.6	10.9	10.0	108.9	99.0	20
21	6.1	5.5	11.6	10.2	8.9	8.3	17.9	16.3	17.0	15.5	9.9	9.0	71.4	64.8	21
TOT	301.7	285.5	409.1	378.6	581.5	549.9	918.1	864.6	530.6	498.0	323.5	305.2	3064.5	2881.8	TOT

STOCK

STORE	FEBRUARY PLAN	L Y	MARCH PLAN	L Y	APRIL PLAN	L Y	MAY PLAN	L Y	JUNE PLAN	L Y	JULY PLAN	L Y	TOTAL SEASON PLAN	L Y	STORE
01	58.0	42.8	72.0	50.1	88.0	73.4	116.0	99.2	80.0	77.7	72.0	59.8	69.0	51.6	01
02	94.0	95.5	99.0	70.6	121.0	94.8	159.0	152.3	110.0	106.6	99.0	87.3	95.0	63.1	02
03	79.0	73.3	108.0	63.5	132.0	110.0	174.0	169.6	120.0	146.9	108.0	105.9	102.2	73.1	03
05	36.0	24.3	54.0	37.6	66.0	49.6	87.0	41.8	60.0	46.0	54.0	30.3	51.0	25.0	05
07	29.0	19.5	36.0	29.4	44.0	42.0	58.0	39.4	40.0	38.5	36.0	31.4	27.0	20.9	07
08	44.0	31.3	63.0	33.8	77.0	49.7	102.0	56.7	70.0	47.7	63.0	48.9	58.0	35.5	08
09	29.0	23.0	45.0	30.5	55.0	48.6	73.0	44.5	50.0	53.8	45.0	36.2	43.0	20.3	09
12	65.0	49.3	76.0	42.6	94.0	70.5	123.0	115.0	85.0	87.5	77.0	47.9	74.0	40.0	12
13	72.0	53.0	81.0	50.0	99.0	67.1	130.0	107.7	90.0	72.7	81.0	60.0	77.0	54.7	13
14	15.0	12.2	27.0	21.6	33.0	21.2	44.0	24.3	30.0	25.5	27.0	26.2	26.0	16.9	14
15	33.0	18.1	41.0	25.8	49.0	38.1	65.0	40.9	45.0	49.7	40.0	37.1	38.0	29.2	15
16	44.0	34.3	54.0	35.5	66.0	53.1	87.0	73.9	60.0	63.7	54.0	49.0	52.0	43.2	16
17	7.0	8.6	9.0	11.0	11.0	13.8	15.0	21.5	10.0	16.8	9.0	13.7	9.0	5.7	17
18	33.0	25.3	41.0	39.7	50.0	50.4	65.0	63.9	45.0	59.8	41.0	42.5	39.0	31.7	18
19	40.0	26.0	40.0	33.5	49.0	46.1	65.0	69.7	45.0	71.9	40.0	38.4	39.0	33.8	19
20	29.0	24.0	32.0	31.4	39.0	43.6	51.0	51.5	35.0	50.3	32.0	35.9	30.0	31.8	20
21	18.0	12.8	22.0	37.1	27.0	35.8	36.0	28.2	25.0	38.6	22.0	26.8	21.0	15.8	21
TOT	725.0	573.3	900.0	643.7	1100.0	907.8	1450.0	1200.1	1000.0	1053.7	900.0	777.3	850.0	592.3	TOT
PL. RCPTS.	476.7		609.1		931.5		468.1		430.6		273.5		3189.5		PL. RCPTS.
*MD	125.0	126.3	70.0	52.0	113.0	117.2	285.0	264.6	172.0	195.6	45.0	32.3	810.0	788.0	*MD

TOTAL SEASON		PLAN	L Y		PLAN	L Y	DEPT. NUMBER: _____
MARKUP %		58.0	57.4	GM & DISC %	50.6	49.9	DEPT. NAME: MS. BUDGET COORDINATES
MD & ED %		26.9	27.8	TURNOVER	3.1	3.5	BUYER: _____

* (EXCLUDING ED)

Figure 29. Six-Month Merchandise Plan

		AUGUST		SEPTEMBER		OCTOBER		NOVEMBER		DECEMBER		JANUARY		SEASON		FEBRUARY	
		SALES	BOM STOCK	SALES	BOM STOCK	SALES	BOM STOCK	SALES	BOM STOCK	SALES	BOM STOCK	SALES	BOM STOCK	SALES	AVER STOCK	SEASON T.O.	BOM STOCK
CHAIN	LY PLAN	365.8	576	348.8	790	306.4	704	376.5	612	310.0	607	130.9	278	1836.4	595	3.09	321
T.O.	LY PLAN	0.63		1.04		1.48		2.08		2.59		3.09		3.09			
O.T.B.	LY PLAN																
M.D.$	LY PLAN	64.8		46.3		37.8		70.8		59.2		75.1		354.0			
M.D.%	LY PLAN	17.72		13.36		12.33		18.80		19.10		57.40		19.28			
MU: PUR	LY PLAN	50.40		49.73		48.80		50.07		44.64		48.61		49.64			
MU% S&P	LY PLAN	50.12		49.69		49.20		49.49		49.26		49.07		49.07			
SHORT%	LY PLAN	2.07		2.04		2.08		2.18		2.15		2.18		2.11			
G.P.$	LY PLAN	147.2		143.6		124.3		149.9		115.5		20.6		701.0			
G.P.%	LY PLAN	40.24		41.40		40.55		39.80		37.25		15.76		38.17			
BEG SEAS STK MU%	LY PLAN	49.80															

Figure 30. Total Corporate Six-Month Plan

SPRING 2013 — Total Corporate Six-Month C-1 Plan

CLASS	FEB BOM	FEB SALE	FEB MD	FEB REC	MAR BOM	MAR SALE	MAR MD	MAR REC	APR BOM	APR SALE	APR MD	APR REC	MAY BOM	MAY SALE	MAY MD	MAY REC	JUN BOM	JUN SALE	JUN MD	JUN REC	JUL BOM	JUL SALE	JUL MD	JUL REC	AUG BOM	TOTAL SALE	AVE. STOCK	TURN	RETAIL	LCC
EARS R.PLAN																														
ACT.	533	58	42	115	548	100	25	120	543	105	25	126	539	135	35	135	504	125	35	215	559	180	50	130	459	703	526	1.34	841	210
P.PLAN	533	58	42	115	548	100	25	120	543	105	25	126	539	135	35	135	504	125	35	215	559	180	50	130	459	703	526	1.34	841	210
LY	371	60	4	66	365	90	4	140	398	85	8	207	406	113	5	232	564	99	20	116	534	145	9	106	323	592	423	1.40	867	217
STRAN R.PLAN																														
ACT.	268	31	2	61	296	50	10	40	276	55	10	57	268	70	15	85	268	60	10	98	296	90	20	64	250	356	275	1.30	405	101
P.PLAN	268	31	2	61	296	50	10	40	276	55	10	57	268	70	15	85	268	60	10	98	296	90	20	64	250	356	275	1.30	405	101
LY	301	34	0	0	256	48	2	47	245	50	2	83	259	69	4	114	282	61	2	106	308	89	0	68	241	351	270	1.30	418	105
FASHI BASIC R.PLAN																					202	90	20	183	275					
ACT.	170	21	3	93	239	45	10	24	208	45	10	40	193	55	10	54	182	50	10	85	207	75	15	66	183	291	197	1.47	362	91
P.PLAN	170	21	3	93	239	45	10	24	208	45	10	40	193	55	10	54	182	50	10	85	207	75	15	66	183	291	197	1.47	362	91
LY	119	18	3	9	103	36	3	59	118	31	3	91	165	46	3	130	229	38	6	32	206	50	3	34	119	219	151	1.45	355	89
COLO R.PLAN																														
ACT.	114	17	4	0	93	15	5	117	190	20	5	23	188	30	10	0	148	30	10	16	124	35	10	20	99	147	137	1.08	176	44
P.PLAN	114	17	4	0	93	15	5	117	190	20	5	23	188	30	10	0	148	30	10	16	124	35	10	20	99	147	137	1.08	176	44
LY	114	24	10	59	143	34	3	135	240	39	4	55	248	49	4	40	230	39	8	79	266	52	6	47	266	237	215	1.10	415	104
GOLD R.PLAN																														
ACT.	170	8	2	0	160	25	10	79	204	20	10	44	218	20	10	0	188	25	10	15	168	40	15	30	143	143	179	0.80	168	42
P.PLAN	170	8	2	0	160	25	10	79	204	20	10	44	218	20	10	0	188	25	10	15	168	40	15	30	143	143	179	0.80	168	42
LY	26	5	0	42	58	16	1	41	81	20	1	107	160	11	14	22	145	19	3	43	223	43		106	116	114	116	0.99	361	90
FASHI R.PLAN												102				214								64						
ACT.	172	26	3	118	261	60	15	98	284	50	20	210	424	60	20	68	412	55	20	60	397	75	30	40	322	326	325	1.00	594	149
P.PLAN	172	26	3	118	261	60	15	98	284	50	20	210	424	60	20	68	412	55	20	60	397	75	30	40	322	326	325	1.00	594	149
LY	301	33	6	38	291	59	8	122	301	52	10	86	304	61	12	112	315	42	11	44	283	42		16	224	289	288	1.00	418	105

Figure 31. Purchase Planning

	Planned	
Planned purchases for October based on *planned* figures	$20,000	Planned Sales
	+ 42,000	Planned EOM Stock
	+ 500	Planned Markdowns
	$62,500	Total Merchandise Requirements
	– 40,000	Planned BOM Stock
PLANNED PURCHASES—	22,500	

	Revised	
Planned purchases for October based on *revised* figures	$22,000	Revised Sales
	+ 42,000	Planned EOM Stock
	+ 500	Revised Markdowns
	$64,500	Total Merchandise Requirements
	– 40,000	Revised BOM Stock
ADJUSTED PLANNED PURCHASES—	$24,500	

As a guide to merchandising, the real value of dollar planning is that the figures projected for each element reflect goals that are reasonably attainable. Because the buyer is responsible for interpreting and achieving the projected figures, it is essential that the buyer be involved in the preparation of the figures. Also, a buyer who has helped to set these guidelines will be more inclined to use them. Once completed, a dollar plan must be adjusted to actual conditions and results during the season under consideration.

Adjusting the Planned Purchases

During the season, as merchandising activities are performed, the actual results are checked against the planned figures. Sometimes this reveals the need to adjust the original planned figures either for a specific month or for the balance of the season because of a deviation from the planned sales, markdowns, or receipts. A buyer is responsible for reacting to the various situations that may arise by department or category. For example, if sales and/or markdowns are actually larger than planned, purchases must be greater than planned to achieve the level of stock planned. The buyer may need to secure additional receipts if they can be delivered on a timely basis. Conversely, if these factors are actually less than planned, in order to maintain purchases placed, buyers need to increase sales most likely by increasing markdowns. The other option is to revise purchases downward. Figure 31 illustrates the variation between planned figures and actual results.

Explanation of Merchandise Reports

The elements that affect gross margin and profit are included in a merchandise report, as well as the stock and sales trends. It is a guide to the six-month projections, shows the current performance, and enables the buyer to make necessary decisions and adjustments. The annotated information in Figure 32 is numbered (1) to (8), and the following information corresponds to those numbers:

1. WEEK ENDING and WEEK NO.: Example: FEB 05 is WEEK NO. 01.

2. NET SALES (in 100s): This category is divided into the following two sections:

   a. WEEKLY: Figures that show the sales of TY, PLAN, and LY. Example:

      WEEK ENDING FEBRUARY 05

TY	$62.5
PLAN	$68.8
LY	$62.7

   b. CUMULATIVE: Cumulative sales for the period for TY, PLAN, LY, and % CHG (percentage change) for existing stores, but also excluding any new store(s). Example:

      WEEK ENDING FEBRUARY 12

TY	$122.7
PLAN	$123.8
LY	$123.5
% CHG	– 0.7%
EXCLUDE NEW STORE:	– 4.6%

3. MARKUP % CUMULATIVE SALES: Markup on all merchandise handled, season-to-date, before the adjustments of cash discounts for TY and LY. Example:

   WEEK ENDING FEBRUARY 05

Opening: TY	38.2%
LY	37.8%

4. MARKDOWNS—CUMULATIVE INCLUDING EMPLOYEE ALLOW-ANCE: Markdowns both in DOLLARS and % (of change) for TY and LY. Example:

   WEEK ENDING FEBRUARY 05

	DOLLARS	%
TY	$3.6	5.7%
LY	$6.6	10.5%

5. STOCK-ON-HAND: Merchandise in stock for TY, PLAN, and LY. Example:

   WEEK ENDING FEBRUARY 05

TY	$1,954.2
PLAN	$1,450.0
LY	$1,498.8

Figure 32. Merchandise Statistics Report

MERCHANDISE STATISTICS REPORT

DEPT ___

CURRENT WEEK
SALES, MARKDOWNS, STOCK,
GROSS MARGIN DATA ESTIMATED

SPRING 20___

(1) WEEK ENDING	WK NO	NET SALES WKLY TY	WKLY PLAN	WKLY LY	CUM TY	CUM PLAN	CUM LY	% CHG	EXCL NEW STORE % CHG	MKUP % CUM TY	MKUP % CUM LY	MD $ TY	MD $ LY	MD % TY	MD % LY	STOCK TY	STOCK PLAN	STOCK LY	PLATFORM REC TY	PLATFORM REC LY	OUTST ORD TY	OUTST ORD LY
OPENING										38.2	37.8					1748.3	1400.0	1455.1			394.5	126.9
FEB 05	01	62.5	68.8	62.7	62.5	68.8	62.7	-.4	-3.6	33.2	37.3	3.6	6.6	5.7	10.5	1954.2	1450.0	1498.8	74.7	118.0	360.2	131.6
FEB 12	02	60.2	55.0	60.6	122.7	123.8	123.5	-.7	-4.6	36.3	37.1	27.6	10.2	27.5	8.3	1865.6	1450.0	1544.7	197.9	101.9	175.3	127.3
FEB 19	03	86.4	55.0	48.3	209.1	178.8	189.8	23.1	18.6	36.2	37.1	54.8	-47.1	26.2	27.7	1853.7	1450.0	1601.3	105.5	48.5	106.7	153.2
FEB 26	04	69.5	66.2	63.2	278.0	245.0	233.0	19.6	16.0	37.6	37.0	76.3	-29.5	27.4	12.6	1888.1	1450.0	1598.4	125.9	77.7		
PLAN 4								5.2	-.3	37.8	37.8	16.0		7.8								
MAR 05	05	63.1	55.0	41.5	341.7	360.8	274.5	24.5	18.1	37.8	36.9	82.8	-1.2	16.3	-2.6	1901.9	1500.0	1816.5	62.1	82.0	159.3	121.3
MAR 12	06	52.1	55.0	43.9	393.6	355.0	316.5	26.7	17.0	37.7	37.0	82.8	54.0	16.0	10.7	1853.5	1500.0	1809.2	13.9	81.3	204.9	127.0
MAR 19	07	55.2	55.0	47.6	449.0	410.0	369.9	22.7	16.1	37.8	37.0	122.8	73.7	27.4	20.1	1888.7	1500.0	1554.5	122.3	29.5	156.4	330.9
MAR 26	08	62.4	75.0	76.9	511.5	485.8	442.8	15.6	6.9	37.1	37.1	38.8	78.0	60.1	17.6	1913.1	1500.0	1524.7	7.3	52.2	164.9	340.2
APR 02	09	48.1	63.5	68.8	557.5	546.5	511.6	9.0	2.8	37.8	37.2	33.4	91.2	80.1	17.8	1870.2	1500.0	1593.2	4.4	150.5	259.8	352.2
PLAN 9								7.2	-.1	37.6	37.6	34.6		6.2								
APR 09	10		60.0	51.5		688.5	583.5			37.0	37.0	169.6		19.4			1600.0	1461.2	CUR ORD	-58.5	215.1	422.2
APR 16	11		48.0	40.5		656.5	610.5			37.1	37.1	114.8		18.8			1600.0	1515.5	105.4	10.0	416.2	
APR 23	12		85.0	44.8		721.5	654.5			36.9	36.7	144.2		22.8			1600.0	1458.0	18.9	54.5	459.9	
APR 30	13		85.2	92.2		604.7	746.7	7.8	2.0	36.9	36.9	173.7		23.3			1600.0	1401.0	64.5	193.2		
PLAN 13										38.1		49.0		6.1								
MAY 07	14		145.1	151.4		944.8	898.1				37.1	188.9		18.8			1550.0	1281.2	26.7	234.0		
MAY 14	15		75.0	71.0		1824.6	969.7				36.9	153.7		15.6			1550.0	1383.7	160.8	517.1		
MAY 21	16		95.0	71.2		1119.8	1040.9				36.7	151.0		14.5			1550.0	1483.4	169.5	497.3		
MAY 28	17		100.0	90.5		1219.8	1131.4	7.8	2.0	36.2	36.9	168.3		14.9			1550.0	1561.7	172.5	603.4		
PLAN 17												63.6		5.2								
JUN 04	18		80.0	76.1		1299.8	1204.6				36.9	182.9		15.2			1500.0	1615.5	142.0	530.6		
JUN 11	19		105.8	181.5		1465.6	1306.1				37.6	181.8		13.9			1500.0	1699.1	162.8	405.1		
JUN 18	20		84.0	75.0		1489.6	1361.0				36.9	188.7		13.7			1500.0	1700.4	76.2	494.0		
JUN 25	21		85.0	76.6		1572.6	1457.6				36.9	172.7		11.8			1500.0	1799.2	148.7	200.6		
JULY 02	22		75.0	73.5		1647.6	1531.0	7.6	1.8	36.4	36.8	167.9		11.0			1500.0	1777.9	45.0	251.0		
PLAN 22												75.0		4.6								
JULY 09	23		60.0	88.8		1707.6	1599.4				36.8	140.1		8.8			1500.0	1722.8	-16.1	266.9		
JULY 16	24		55.0	47.7		1762.6	1647.0				36.4	141.3		8.6			1500.0	1622.4	-38.1	289.9		
JULY 23	25		60.0	52.6		1822.6	1699.8				36.9	128.8		7.8			1500.0	1608.5	15.6	368.5		
JULY 30	26		54.0	43.8		1876.6	1743.5	7.6	1.8	36.5	36.7	112.7		6.5			1500.0	1582.5	32.8	402.1		
PLAN 26												84.4		4.5								

(6) PLATFORM RECEIPTS — CUR ORD / NXT ORD / FUT ORD

STATISTICS BELOW ON FISCAL MONTH BASIS

COST PURCH & DISC EARNED INCL LOAD TO 6.6%

(8)	4 WEEKS TY	4 WEEKS PLAN	4 WEEKS LY	9 WEEKS TY	9 WEEKS PLAN	9 WEEKS LY	13 WEEKS TY	13 WEEKS PLAN	13 WEEKS LY	17 WEEKS TY	17 WEEKS PLAN	17 WEEKS LY	22 WEEKS TY	22 WEEKS PLAN	22 WEEKS LY	28 WEEKS TY	28 WEEKS PLAN	28 WEEKS LY
GROSS MARKDOWN MMO AFTER SHTG %	17.5	29.7	41.6	30.5	30.6	22.6		30.9	18.8		31.6	24.1	32.2		26.5	32.4		28.7
Disc Earned %	6.6	6.0	4.7	6.0	6.0	5.6		5.6	6.2		5.8	8.1	5.7		5.9	5.7		5.7
Alteration %	.1	.1	.4	.1	.1	.1		.1	.1		.1	.1	.1		.1	.1		.1
Gross Margin %	24.0	35.6	46.2	36.5	36.3	28.7		36.6	25.2		37.3	30.1	37.8		32.3	38.0		34.3
Gross Margin %	67.0	87.3	107.5	200.2	200.3	146.7		294.6	136.2		355.0	340.7	622.8		394.8	713.3		597.8
SELECTIVE DATA																		
Cash Disc to BOM V P %	.8	.2	.8	.8	.4	.8		.8	.8		.8	.8	.6		.6			.3
Stock Turn	.2	.2	.3	.8		.3		.2	.5		.8	.7	.8		1.0	1.3		1.1
Transactions	123.3		13.3	22.0		25.6						62.0			84.9			96.6
% Chg	-6.2			-22.3														
Avg Sales Chk	24.70	19.36	19.47	27.49		19.57						19.67			19.47			19.16
Ret % to Gr Sales	8.2	8.1	7.9			7.8						7.3			7.3			7.7
Setting Salary		6.8	4.3			9.0						9.1			9.1			9.6
Direct Pub																		
Gr Lineage $	18.2	9.9	16.2			39.6						101.7			137.0			140.3
Rebates $	2.5		2.5			30.6						91.5			110.2			119.2
Net Lineage %	2.7	4.3	1.4			1.7						1.5			1.2			1.2
Direct Mail $		4.6	-3.4			-5.1						-5.3			-2.8			.4

WEEKS SUPPLY — 22.0 | 18.0 | 20.7 | 20.7

6. PLATFORM RECEIPTS: Merchandise received TY and LY for the reported end of week. Example:

WEEK ENDING FEBRUARY 05

TY	$74.7
LY	$118.0

7. OUTSTANDING ORDERS: Amount of open orders. Example:

WEEK ENDING FEBRUARY 05

TY	$394.5
LY	$126.9

8. STATISTICS BELOW ON FISCAL MONTH BASIS: Comparison of operational factors that affect ultimate profit, such as GROSS MARGIN, STOCK TURN, DISCOUNTS EARNED, and so on, for TY over LY. Example:

9 WEEKS—GROSS MARGIN AFTER SHORTAGE %

TY	30.5%
PLAN	30.6%
LY	22.6%

Now we will apply the concepts to Figure 32.

PROBLEM

Buyers use reports to plan future sales and stock levels. Use Figure 32 from "WEEK ENDING DATE FEB 05 TO APR 30," columns (2a) "NET SALES: WEEKLY: TY/PLAN/LY, " (3) MARK ON % CUM, and (5) "STOCK-ON-HAND: TY/PLAN/LY" to answer the following questions.

1. Calculate the percentage change by which current sales in March were above or below last year's sales. What is the percentage change for this year to plan for March?

2. Based on this information, how would you evaluate the planned sales for April?

3. What was the opening cumulative markup percentage for this department? What percentage change was this over LY?

4. Season-to-date, which week ending had the largest dollar sales TY? What was the dollar amount of those sales? Which week ending had the best sales increase percentage for the season TY over LY?

1. Total March sales for this year are:

   $63.1 + 52.1 + 55.2 + 62.4 + 48.1 = $280.9

   Total March sales for last year are:

   $41.5 + 43.9 + 47.6 + 76.9 + 68.8 = $278.7

   % change $= \dfrac{\$280.9 - \$278.7}{\$278.7} \times 100 = \dfrac{\$2.2}{\$278.7} \times 100 = +0.8\%$

   Total March sales for plan are:

   $55.0 + 55.0 + 55.0 + 75.0 + 63.5 = $303.5

   % change $= \dfrac{\$280.9 - \$303.5}{\$303.5} \times 100 = \dfrac{-\$22.6}{\$303.5} \times 100 = -7.4\%$

2. April's planned sales are:

   $60.0 + 48.0 + 85.0 + 85.2 = $278.2

   Based on the current trend to plan regarding sales for March, April sales may not be met and potentially should be forecasted to be a decrease. Buyers do need to take into account when Easter occurs. Easter can shift March and April monthly sales for up to four weeks. Buyers need to review the two months of sales (March and April) combined and plan future months accordingly.

3. The opening CMU % is 38.2% for this year versus 37.8% for last year. The difference is 0.4% change higher for this year.

4. Week 3 in February, week ending Feb. 19, produced $86.4 in sales, the highest year-to-date. This week also produced the highest sales percentage increase versus last year:

   $\dfrac{\$86.4 - \$48.3}{\$48.3} \times 100 = \dfrac{\$38.1}{\$48.3} \times 100 = 78.9\%$

Planned Purchase Practice Problems

68. Calculate the planned purchase dollars for August if:

    August sales are $370.

    August markdowns are $106.

    August BOM inventory is $2,666.

    August EOM inventory is $2,463.

69. What will be the receipt dollars for December if:

    December BOM stock is $12,000,000.

    December sales are $4,320,000.

    December markdowns are $2,240,000.

    December EOM stock is $9,600,000.

70. The missy sportswear department has sales for March planned at $580,000, and March planned markdowns are $174,000. March planned BOM stock is $2,300,000, and March EOM stock is planned at $2,900,000. What are the planned March purchase dollars?

71. Calculate the receipt dollars for June if:

     June sales are $560,000.

     June MDs are 30%.

     June BOM is $1,400,000.

     July BOM is $1,100,000.

72. Find the planned purchases for June given the following information:

Planned June sales	$52,000
Planned June markdowns	$19,500
Planned stock June BOM	$150,000
Planned stock July BOM	$155,600

73. Calculate the planned July purchases at cost using the following figures:

Planned July sales	$70,000
Planned July markdowns	$38,500
Planned stock July BOM	$210,000
Planned stock July EOM	$250,000
Planned markup	57%

74. Note the following figures:

Planned September sales	$18,000
Planned September markdowns	$4,900
Planned stock beginning September	$49,200
Planned stock beginning October	$50,400
Planned markup	61.5%

Determine:

    a. The planned September purchases at retail.

    b. The planned September purchases at cost.

    c. The turnover for September.

75. The hosiery department has an initial markup of 64%. The planned sales for April are $10,000 and $12,000 for May. The desired BOM stock-sales ratio for April is 7.0 and 6.5 for May. The planned markdowns for April are $3,000.00.

Calculate:

    a. The planned April purchases at retail.

    b. The planned April purchases at cost.

76. The following figures are from a shoe department:

Planned stock November BOM	$110,000
Planned stock December BOM	$147,000
Planned November markdowns	$16,000
Planned November sales	$38,000
Actual stock November BOM	$120,000
Actual November sales	$41,000

Find:

    a. The original planned purchases.

    b. The adjusted planned purchases.

77. The petite sportswear department had the following seasonal planned figures for October:

	Dollars	Percentages
Sales	$120,000	
Markdowns		45%
BOM stock	$336,000	
EOM stock	$308,000	
Markup		60.0%

Determine:

    a. The planned purchases at retail.

    b. The planned purchases at cost.

78. The children's clothing department had projected the following figures for January:

- Sales of $46,000.
- Stock-sales ratio of 6.0.
- Reductions of $32,000.
- EOM inventory of $290,000.

What are the planned retail purchases for January?

79. A men's accessories department had the following figures planned for December:

Planned sales	$400,000
Planned markdowns	$95,000
Planned stock (December)	$900,000
Planned stock (January)	$600,000

However, the following figures reflect the actual performance:

Actual sales	$375,000
Actual stock (January BOM)	$620,000

Find:

    a. The original planned purchases.

    b. The adjusted planned purchases.

5.5 Open-to-Buy Control

Merchandise control results from effective use of data that is available through the dollar planning process. In purchasing merchandise, a buyer is guided by the sales, timing, and quantity goals established in the six-month seasonal dollar plan. To provide an even tighter control on the amount of merchandise received in a specific period, and to achieve as precisely as possible the sales and stock plans, the buyer refers to a merchandising figure called open-to-buy. This term, abbreviated OTB, denotes the amount of unspent (i.e., order limit) money that is available for purchasing merchandise that will be delivered during a given period. Usually, it is calculated on a monthly basis and indicates that the buyer has not yet spent all of the planned purchases or receipts for the period in question. It represents the difference between the planned purchases for a period and the merchandise orders already placed for that period. Unfilled orders, generally known as open orders, or "**on order**," should be charged to those months during which delivery is expected so that the buyer is able to control and time buying activities to correlate with selling activities. The purpose of this control is to identify the deviations between actual results and planned goals so that the buyer can take corrective measures when needed. After following up with vendors on order deliveries, if the vendor is unable to ship certain product, a buyer needs to adjust his or her on-order and receipt dollars down. In order to stay on the inventory plan, a buyer may need to secure product from other sources if available. If additional merchandise is to be shipped, then receipt dollars need to be increased.

The planned purchase figure for a particular month indicates the sum available to purchase goods during that month, but this figure does not indicate the distribution of the money throughout the month. Experienced buyers attempt to distribute purchases over the entire month to:

- Reorder or replace fast-selling goods.

- Fill in stocks on basic replenishment merchandise.

- Compete advantageously when buying special purchases and/or new fashion items/trends as they become available.

- Test offerings of new resources.

Information showing current developments helps ensure that all the planned factors will proceed according to plan. Consequently, large retailers commonly generate a separate open-to-buy report. The typical report (see Figure 33) contains information that covers:

Figure 33. Open-to-Buy Monthly Report

CO P1, MD A, RD 4, DG 026 SUITS — Open-to-Buy Report — (CGMRTO) PAGE: 58 09:50 AM

THIS WEEK (JUN:3/5) #24		Last Month (MAY)	Current Month (JUN)	JUN :1/5 #22	JUN :2/5 #23	JUN :3/5 #24	JUN :4/5 #25	JUN :5/5 #26	JUL :1/4 #27	CURR. MO. (MTD)	Next Month (JUL)	2 Nxt Month (AUG)	3 Nxt Month (SEP)
$ NET SALES	LAST YEAR	0	0	0	0	0	0	0	0	0	0	0	0
	PLAN	10,000	5,000	950	1,000	1,000	1,050	1,000	0	1,950	0	8,000	20,000
	ACTUAL	3,801	5,249	558	0					558			
	% PLAN: LY	0	0	0	0	0	0	0	0	0	0	0	0
	% ACT.: LY	0	0	0	0					0			
	% ACT.: PLAN	(62)		(41)	(100)					(71)			
$ STOCK/SALES	LAST YEAR			0.0	0.0	0.0	0.0	0.0	0.0	0.0			
	ACTUAL			9.4	0.0								
$ MARKDOWNS	LAST YEAR	0	0	0	0	0	0	0	0	0	0	0	0
	PLAN	2,000	5,000	950	1,000	1,000	1,050	1,000	0	1,950	0	0	1,000
	HOME OFF.	0		0	0					0			
	P.O.S.	0		0	0					0			
	TOTAL	0		0	0					0			
MARKDOWNS/ SALES	% LAST YEAR	0	0	0	0	0	0	0	0	0	0	0	0
	% PLAN	20	100	100	100	100	100	100	0	100	0	0	5
	% ACTUAL	0		0	0					0			
# NET SALES	LAST YEAR	0	0	0	0	0	0	0	0	0	0	0	0
	PLAN	68		10	0					10			
	ACTUAL		0.00	0.0	0.0	0.0	0.0	0.0	0.0				
# STOCK/SALES	LAST YEAR	0.00		9.2	0.0					0.00			
	ACTUAL												
# AVERAGE SALE	LAST YEAR	0.00	0.00	0.00	0.00	0.00	0.00	0.00	0.00	0.00	0.00	0.00	0.00
	PLAN	55.90	55.80	55.80	0.00					55.80			
	ACTUAL	0.00	0.00	0.00	0.00	0.00	0.00	0.00	0.00	0.00	0.00	0.00	0.00
# AVERAGE STOCK	LAST YEAR		57.05	57.05	57.07	0.00							
	PLAN	58.55											
	ACTUAL												
	LAST YEAR	0	0	0	0	0	0	0	0	0	0	0	0
	PLAN	22,000	10,000	5,249	4,680						15,000	15,000	30,000
	ACTUAL	6,558	5,249	5,249									
$ RECEIVED NOT SHIPPED			0	0	0	0	0	0	0	0	0	0	0
$ SHIPMENTS		2,568	0	0	0	0	0	0	0	0	0	0	0
MARKUP	% LAST YEAR	0	0	0	0	0	0	0	0	0	0	0	0
	% PLAN	32	32	0						32		35	35
	% ACTUAL	35											
# RECEIVED NOT SHIPPED			0	0	0	0	0	0	0	0	0	0	0
# SHIPMENTS		48	0	0	0					0			

	CURR. MO. (MTD)	JUL	AUG	SEP
# OPEN-TO-RECEIVE	0	0	0	0
# ON ORDER				
# OPEN TO BUY	0	15,000	15,000	30,000
$ OPEN-TO-RECEIVE	0	0	23,160	16,400
$ ON ORDER	0	0	0	0
% MARK UP	0	0	0	0
$ OPEN TO BUY	0	15,000	23,160	16,400
$ CUM. OPEN-TO-BUY	0	15,000	38,160	54,560

- **Sales, including:**
  - Plans for month.
  - This month to date.
  - Adjusted plan for month.
- **Markdowns, including:**
  - Season-to-date at BOM in dollars.
  - Season-to-date at BOM in percentage to sales.
  - Month-to-date.
- **Stocks, including:**
  - First of month.
  - Balance for current month.
  - Receipts to date (additions).
  - On hand today.
- **Open-to-buy, including:**
  - Planned EOM stock.
  - Adjusted EOM stock.
- **Outstanding orders, including:**
  - For delivery by month.
- **Purchases, including:**
  - Plan for month.
  - Adjusted plan for month.
  - Plan for next month.
- **Cumulative markup, including:**
  - Plan for month.
  - Actual to date.

Because it is critical to be able to determine at any time the dollar amount still available to purchase future merchandise, a computerized report (see Figure 34) controls the merchandising facts planned and identifies deviation between planned goals and the actual reports so that necessary corrective measures can be taken. Generally, it is prepared on a weekly basis.

Explanation of Open-to-Buy Reports

Figure 34 illustrates the information that is contained in a typical OTB report (e.g., sales, stocks, markdowns, outstanding orders, and open-to-receive). The report format and frequency of issuance can vary with organizational size and needs. This particular report shown gives the reviewer an opportunity to analyze the department's performance by individual store or on a combined all-store basis. The annotated information in Figure 34 is numbered (1) to (9), and the following information corresponds to those numbers:

1. Date: Published date of the report. Example: 10/10/13.

2. WEEK 01 OF 04: Week of the month being viewed.

3. DEPT 736 BRIDGE SUITS: Department number and name.

4. Branch store listing: Listing of all the stores by location. Example: Store NY (left-hand column). At the bottom of the sheet is the total (T) section, which designates the total for all stores.

Figure 34. Open-to-Buy Report

5. SALES: Net sales (in 1,000s) by store, and the percentage change, which indicates the variance of CURRENT sales figures from PLAN's and LY's actual sales. This category is divided into the following sections:

a. CURRENT WEEK: Sales in dollars and percentages by store, for the current week. Example:

For Store NY, CURRENT WEEK:

	Dollars	Percentages
TY	$18.6	
PLAN	$14.4	29%
LY	$22.2	– 16%

These figures show that for the current week, Store NY had net sales of $18.6, which was 29% ahead of PLAN, but 16% behind LY.

b. LAST WEEK: Sales in dollars and percentages by store, for the prior week. Example:

For Store NY, LAST WEEK:

	Dollars	Percentages
TY	$9.7	
PLAN	$14.2	– 32%
LY	$24.2	– 60%

These figures show that for LAST WEEK, Store NY had net sales of $9.7, which was 32% under PLAN, and 60% behind LY.

c. 2 WKS AGO: Sales in dollars and percentages by store, for prior two weeks. Example:

For Store NY, 2 WKS AGO:

	Dollars	Percentages
TY	$23.3	
PLAN	$14.2	64%
LY	$17.0	37%

These figures show that for 2 WKS AGO, Store NY had net sales of $23.3, which was 64% ahead of PLAN, and 37% over LY.

d. PRIOR 4 WKS: Total sales in dollars and percentages by store, for prior four weeks. Example:

For Store NY, PRIOR 4 WKS:

	Dollars	Percentages
TY	$24.2	
PLAN	$28.5	– 15%
LY	$26.5	– 9%

These figures show that for PRIOR 4 WKS, Store NY had net sales of $24.2, which was 15% under PLAN, and 9% behind LY.

e. MTD (month-to-date): Total sales in dollars and percentages by store, for fiscal month. Example:

For Store NM, MTD:

	Dollars	Percentages
TY	$3.8	
PLAN	$4.3	– 12%
LY	$8.5	– 55%

These figures show that for MTD, Store NM had net sales of $3.8, which was 11% under PLAN, and 55% behind LY.

f. STD (season-to-date): Total net sales in dollars and percentages by store, from beginning of season to the current date. Example:

For Store BR, STD:

	Dollars	Percentages
TY	$13.1	
PLAN	$5.4	143%
LY	$15.8	– 17%

These figures show that for MTD, Store BR had net sales of $13.1, which was 145% ahead of PLAN, but 17% behind LY.

g. OCT $, NOV $, DEC $: Planned sales in dollars for the present month and the next two months, compared to the same months LY. Example:

For Store BC:

	OCT	NOV	DEC
PLAN	$6.0	$6.6	$8.0
LY	$1.8	$1.8	$3.3

6. STOCKS: Retail dollar value of stock currently received, which is planned by the month. This category is divided into the following sections:

a. LAST WK: Dollar value of stock LAST WK compared to PLAN and LY amounts for the same week. Example:

For Store NY, LAST WK:

TY	$141.5
PLAN	$177.3
LY	$272.0

b. CURRENT WK: Current week's dollar value of stock compared to PLAN and LY amounts for the same week. Example:

For Store NY, CURRENT WK:

TY	$126.7
PLAN	$166.4
LY	$289.7

c. OCT $, NOV $, DEC $: Comparison of the PLAN EOM with LY's stock dollars for the current month and the next two months. Example:

For Store NY:

	OCT	NOV	DEC
PLAN	$166.4	$142.1	$99.3
LY	$270.4	$283.9	$305.3

d. WKS OF STOCK: This subcategory is divided into two sections:

    i. WKS OF STOCK ONPLN: Number of weeks merchandise should last based on planned sales. This figure indicates how many future weeks of planned sales will be covered by the current week's stock. Example:

        For Store NY: 11 (weeks)

    ii. WKS OF STOCK ON TRD: Weeks of stock adjusted for actual versus planned sales performance. Example:

        For Store NY: 8 (weeks)

7. ORDERS: Commitments by retail value of merchandise ordered. This category is divided into the following sections:

a. PRIOR MOS. PAST DUE: Alerts the buyer to past-due orders, TY versus LY. Example:

For Store NY:

TY	$37.0
LY	$17.2

b. OCT $, NOV $, DEC $: Orders due for the current month and the next month. Example:

For Store NY:

OCT	NOV	DEC
$76.9 TY	$27.0 TY	
$117.2 LY		

c. FUTURE $: Figures for orders that would be due in future months, subsequent to the current month, and the next two months. Blank spaces indicate no future commitments.

d. TOTAL $: Figures that are the total of orders due for the present month and next two months. Example:

For Store NY:

TY	$103.9
LY	$117.2

e. STOCK AND ORDERS (S & O): Figures, which are a combination of the stock with the total orders, used to compare TY figures to LY figures. Example:

For Store NY:
TY	$230.7
LY	$406.9

8. MARKDOWNS: Dollar reductions taken. This category is divided into the following sections:

   a. CURRENT WEEK: Markdowns for the current week, comparing TY to LY. Example:

   For Store NY:
TY	$8.0
LY	$0.3

   b. MTD: Total dollar reductions taken month-to-date, comparing TY to LY. Example:

   For Store NY:
TY	$8.0
LY	$0.3

   c. STD: Total dollar reductions taken season-to-date, comparing TY to LY. Example:

   For Store NY:
TY	$27.7
LY	$43.3

   d. STD % SLS: Total reductions expressed as percentages of sales, comparing TY to LY. Example:

   For Store NY:
TY	21.9%
LY	32.0%

9. OPEN TO REC: Comparison of the planned and actual receipts at a given point in time during the month. It lists by month the retail dollar amount of merchandise open to be bought and received and is calculated by subtracting the month's orders from the month's planned receipts (i.e., planned purchases) figure. Positive numbers indicate money still available, while negative numbers show an overextended or overbought condition. The overbought condition occurs when the month's orders placed exceed that month's planned receipts. Example:

   For Store NY:
OCT	NOV	DEC
– $23.7 TY	$13.4 TY	$28.3 TY
$65.1 LY	$40.4 LY	$28.3 LY

CALCULATING RETAIL OPEN-TO-BUY AT THE BEGINNING OF A MONTH

CONCEPT

OTB = Planned purchases for the month – outstanding orders to be delivered that month

PROBLEM

A buyer has planned January sales of $60,000, with an opening January stock planned at $250,000, a closing stock of $280,000, and markdowns planned at $40,000. If the orders that have already been placed for January delivery amount to $80,000 at retail, what is the buyer's January open-to-buy?

SOLUTION

January EOM stock	$280,000	
+ January sales	+ 60,000	
+ January markdowns	+ 40,000	
Total merchandise requirements	= $380,000	
– January BOM stock	– 280,000	
January planned purchases	= $100,000	
– January on order	– 80,000	
January OTB at retail	= $20,000	

When the retail open-to-buy for any period is established, it can be converted to a cost open-to-buy figure. For example, $30,500 retail open-to-buy is converted to a cost figure by multiplying the retail open-to-buy by 100% (minus the planned markup percentage).

CALCULATING RETAIL OPEN-TO-BUY DURING THE MONTH

If the buyer wishes to calculate the OTB figure at a certain time during the period, the calculations may be based on the predetermined planned purchases, or the open-to-buy figure may be determined for the balance of the period using the planned closing stock figure. The problems that follow illustrate these calculations.

OTB for Balance of Month Based on Predetermined Planned Purchases

CONCEPT

OTB for balance of month =

    Planned purchases for month

– Merchandise received to date

– Merchandise on order

= OTB for balance of month

The merchandise plan shows that the planned purchases for September amount to $17,000. The store's records indicate that from September 1 to September 15 the department received $8,300 worth of new goods and there is an order of $700 for September delivery. What is the open-to-buy for the balance of the month?

	September planned purchases	$17,000
–	Merchandise received	– 8,300
–	On order	– 700
	September OTB balance	$8,000

OTB for Balance of Month Based on Planned Closing Stock

OTB for balance of month =

    Planned EOM stock

+ Planned sales for balance of month

+ Planned markdowns for balance of month

= Total merchandise requirements

– Actual stock-on-hand

– On order

= OTB for balance of month

On September 15, an infants' department has a stock of $26,000 and merchandise on order amounting to $700. The planned sales for the balance of September are $8,000, with planned markdowns for the balance of the month at $500. The stock planned for September 30 is $31,800. What is the OTB for the balance of the month?

	Planned sales for balance of month		$8,000
+	Planned markdowns for balance of month	+	500
+	Planned EOM stock	+	31,800
	Total merchandise requirements	=	$40,300
–	Actual stock-on-hand	–	26,000
–	On order	–	700
	September OTB balance		$13,600

Calculating Retail Open-to-Buy Practice Problems

80. What is the open-to-buy remaining if planned purchases are $64,000 and actual purchases are $57,500?

81. A buyer has written orders for merchandise for September delivery totaling $98,000. The planned receipt budget for September was $92,100. Does the buyer have any receipt dollars left to spend for September, and if so, by how much?

82. Calculate the remaining OTB balance given the following information:

February BOM	$1,060
February sales	$550
February MDs	$248
March BOM	$1,340
February receipts on order	$875

83. The men's buyer has June sales of $890,000 and June markdowns of $338,000. June BOM is $2,100,000 and July BOM is $1,750,000. The on order for June is $940,000. Calculate the remaining OTB for June.

84. What is the OTB for a department that has planned purchases of $71,500 and outstanding orders of $74,000?

85. The actual stock at the beginning of April is $316,000, with on order in April amounting to $88,000. Sales are planned at $75,000, with markdowns estimated to be 35.0%, and the stock for April EOM is planned at $312,000. What is the OTB for this month?

86. On March 13, stock-on-hand is $76,300, with planned sales for the balance of the month at $9,000; remaining markdowns are $2,800. Merchandise on order comes to $5,000, and the planned April BOM stock is $70,000. Find the balance of the OTB for March.

87. The May portion of a six-month plan for a swim department is as follows:

Planned May sales	$37,500
Planned May markdowns	25%
Planned May BOM stock	$166,000
Planned June BOM stock	$159,000
Planned markup	59%

    a. What are the planned May purchases at retail?

    b. On May 1, the buyer is notified that $38,000 worth of goods (retail value) is on order. What is the OTB at cost for May?

88. Find the OTB balance for December when on December 10 the stock-on-hand is $265,000 and the planned sales for the balance of the month are $101,000. Markdowns are planned at $31,000, and planned inventory for December 31 is $150,000, with outstanding orders totaling $21,500.

89. Research and Discussion: Describe how a buyer may use turnover and stock-sales ratio figures in planning a future departmental operation.

90. Research and Discussion: Are turnover and stock-sales ratio related? Explain.

91. Research and Discussion: Does an increased turnover rate always mean that the department is functioning more effectively and profitably? Explain.

5.6 Six-Month Seasonal Dollar Merchandise Plan

Now that we have covered the components that are used in the six-month merchandising plan, it is time to put all the factors together to formulate one. Buyers begin the planning process well in advance of buying for the next season. For example, the women's sportswear buyer will be purchasing product for the Spring selling season in August and September of the current year. Therefore, the Spring merchandise plan must be completed based on the final Spring results from the previous season and before going to market. These plans will guide the buyer in discussions with vendors and deciding on what merchandise needs to be purchased. We will be working in dollars, but this can also be compiled using units. Beginning with last year's sales figures and the increase or decrease planned for sales, a buyer will then forecast markdowns based on a planned promotional schedule, then beginning of month stock levels, and lastly receipts. This plan is sometimes called an "open-to-buy" plan, as it is monitored constantly during the season. It provides buyers with a sales and markdown trend in season that they need to react to and adjust all factors in their plans accordingly. It is, in fact, a buyer's "report card"; did I make the plan set or not? Figure 35 represents the Spring six-month plan for an activewear department. Last year's results are as follows:

- Net Sales amounted to $4,500.0 M. (Note that all sales on all reports are in millions of dollars. The reports are truncated to fit on one page.)

- Cumulative markup percentage was 68.5% and markdowns for the season were $1,914.0, representing a journalized markdown percentage of 42.5%, which resulted in a gross margin of 55.1%.

- Turn for the season was 0.96.

You will formulate the six-month plan for next year's Spring season in Case Study 4 at the end of this chapter.

Figure 36 represents another version of a yearly plan that reflects sales, markdowns, gross margin, and turnover, this time for a fashion jewelry department. Last year's results set the plan for the buyer. The projected/actual column tells the buyer how he or she is doing against the plan set. This allows the buyer to take actions to improve the business where necessary. Once a fiscal month ends, the numbers become actual, and the next year's plan is based on that. This version of the merchandising plan is broken out into two seasons and there is a quarterly summary at the bottom of the report.

Figure 35. Six-Month Merchandising Plan for Women's Activewear

Department		FEBRUARY	MARCH	APRIL	MAY	JUNE	JULY	AUGUST	SEASON TOTAL
Women's Activewear									
SPRING		FEBRUARY	MARCH	APRIL	MAY	JUNE	JULY	AUGUST	SEASON TOTAL
SALES $	Sales % to total								
	Last Year	685.0	790.0	650.0	800.0	950.0	625.0		4,500.0
	Plan								
	% Inc/Dec								
	Revised								
	Actual								
STOCK-SALES RATIO	Last Year	6.1	5.8	6.7	6.3	5.7	6.9		
	Plan								
BOM STOCK $ (Retail)	Last Year	$ 4,200.0	4,600.0	4,350.0	5,000.0	5,400.0	4,300.0	4,800.0	4,664.3
	Plan								
	Revised								
	Actual								
MARKDOWNS $	Last Year	$ 229.0	288.0	254.0	348.0	420.0	375.0		1,914.0
	Plan								
	% to Sales								
	% by Month								100.0%
	Revised								
	Actual								
PURCHASES $ (Retail)	Last Year	$ 1,478.0	828.0	1,554.0	1,548.0	270.0	1,500.0		7,178.0
	Plan								
	Revised								
	Actual								

SEASON TOT.	LAST YEAR	PLAN	ACTUAL
Sales	$4,500.00		
CMU %	68.5%		
Markdown %	42.5%		
Gross Margin %	55.1%		
Average Stock	4,664.3		
Turnover	0.96		

Figure 36. Annual Merchandising Plan for Fashion Jewelry

Fashion Jewelry Spring

	Feb Proj/ACT '15	Feb Plan '15	Feb LY Act '14	March Proj/ACT '15	March Plan '15	March LY Act '14	April Proj/ACT '15	April Plan '15	April LY Act '14	May Proj/ACT '15	May Plan '15	May LY Act '14	June Proj/ACT '15	June Plan '15	June LY Act '14	July Proj/ACT '15	July Plan '15	July LY Act '14	Tot/Season Proj/ACT '15	Tot/Season Plan '15	Tot/Season LY Act '14
Seasonal Sales %	13.9%	14.0%	14.0%	15.3%	13.8%	13.3%	15.9%	14.7%	15.4%	20.6%	21.8%	21.8%	15.5%	17.5%	16.1%	18.9%	18.2%	19.5%			
Turn	0.12	0.10	0.08	0.14	0.09	0.07	0.15	0.10	0.08	0.18	0.14	0.12	0.13	0.12	0.09	0.15	0.12	0.11	0.86	0.66	0.90
CMU %	74.60%	75.42%	73.97%	74.86%	75.44%	75.05%	74.06%	75.42%	74.33%	74.25%	75.34%	74.21%	74.48%	75.31%	74.87%	74.45%	75.39%	74.02%	74.44%	75.38%	74.26%
BOM Stock	4937	4819	4107	4712	5042	4506	4361	5092	4537	4646	5437	4559	4945	5209	4367	4759	5018	4495	5322	5526	4476
Sales	575	478	348	633	471	330	657	504	383	852	746	542	640	597	400	780	623	485	4137	3419	2488
Markdowns	252	220	190	437	189	68	261	139	96	220	246	165	216	196	60	207	162	93	1593	1152	672
Shortage	246	200	150																246	200	150
Receipts	802	1021	1087	719	710	429	1203	988	501	1371	764	515	670	602	588	1550	1293	559	6315	5378	3679
GM $	365	306	208	364	309	231	419	346	280	576	501	360	422	401	284	528	430	335	2674	2293	1698
MD %	43.8%	46.0%	54.6%	69.0%	40.1%	20.6%	39.7%	27.6%	25.1%	25.8%	33.0%	30.4%	33.8%	32.8%	15.0%	26.5%	26.0%	19.2%	38.5%	33.7%	27.0%
STD Sales $	575	478	348	1208	949	678	1865	1453	1061	2717	2199	1603	3357	2796	2003	4137	3419	2488	4137	3419	2488
Sales % Chg to LY	65.2%	37.4%		78.2%	40.0%		75.8%	36.9%		69.5%	37.2%		67.6%	39.6%		66.3%	37.4%		66.3%	37.4%	
STD GM $	365	306	208	729	615	439	1148	961	719	1724	1462	1079	2146	1863	1363	2674	2293	1698	2674	2293	1698
STD GM %	63.5%	64.0%	59.8%	60.3%	64.8%	64.7%	61.6%	66.1%	67.3%	63.5%	66.5%	67.3%	63.9%	66.6%	68.0%	64.6%	67.1%	68.2%	64.6%	67.1%	68.2%

Fashion Jewelry Fall

	Aug Proj/ACT '15	Aug Plan '15	Aug LY Act '14	Sept Proj/ACT '15	Sept Plan '15	Sept LY Act '14	Oct Proj/ACT '15	Oct Plan '15	Oct LY Act '14	Nov Proj/ACT '15	Nov Plan '15	Nov LY Act '14	Dec Proj/ACT '15	Dec Plan '15	Dec LY Act '14	Jan Proj/ACT '15	Jan Plan '15	Jan LY Act '14	Tot/Season Proj/ACT '15	Tot/Season Plan '15	Tot/Season LY Act '14
Seasonal Sales %	22.9%	25.0%	24.6%	17.4%	17.6%	17.0%	20.7%	23.4%	19.4%	38.4%	44.6%	48.3%	40.4%	45.8%	44.7%	8.4%	9.5%	17.2%			
Turn	0.18	0.16	0.14	0.12	0.10	0.09	0.12	0.12	0.10	0.21	0.21	0.23	0.25	0.25	0.22	0.06	0.06	0.09	0.99	0.94	0.88
CMU %	74.42%	75.49%	75.14%	74.43%	75.47%	78.75%	74.42%	75.39%	73.99%	74.44%	75.34%	77.58%	74.42%	75.37%	74.91%	74.31%	75.36%	73.65%	74.43%	75.39%	75.87%
BOM Stock	5322	5526	4476	5303	5384	4476	6573	6473	4739	7500	7122	4964	7728	7284	5559	5475	5300	4688	5543	5350	4853
Sales	948	855	612	720	603	424	855	800	483	1590	1525	1201	1670	1566	1111	346	325	428	6129	5674	4259
Markdowns	309	255	160	231	196	68	324	325	117	800	680	680	1093	957	825	141	214	307	2898	2627	2157
Shortage																					
Receipts	1238	968	772	2221	1888	755	2106	1774	825	2618	2367	2476	510	539	1065	555	589	900	9248	8125	6793
GM $	648	583	420	477	407	319	553	529	327	1045	1010	779	963	945	625	221	192	234	3907	3666	2704
MD %	32.6%	29.8%	26.1%	32.1%	32.5%	16.0%	37.9%	40.6%	24.2%	50.3%	44.6%	56.6%	65.4%	61.1%	74.3%	40.8%	65.8%	71.7%	63.7%	64.6%	63.5%
STD Sales $	948	855	612	1668	1458	1036	2523	2258	1519	4113	3783	2720	5783	5349	3831	6129	5674	4259	6129	5674	4259

Top section:

	Proj/ACT '15	Plan '15	LY Act '14	Proj/ACT '15	Plan '15	LY Act '14	Proj/ACT '15	Plan '15	LY Act '14	Proj/ACT '15	Plan '15	LY Act '14	Proj/ACT '15	Plan '15	LY Act '14	Proj/ACT '15	Plan '15	LY Act '14
Sales % Chg to LY	54.9%	39.7%		61.0%	40.7%		66.1%	48.7%		51.2%	39.1%		51.0%	39.6%		43.9%	33.2%	
STD GM $	648	583	420	1125	990	739	1678	1519	1066	2723	2529	1845	3686	3474	2470	3907	3666	2704
STD GM %	68.4%	68.2%	68.6%	67.4%	67.9%	71.3%	66.5%	67.3%	70.2%	66.2%	66.9%	67.8%	63.7%	64.9%	64.5%	63.7%	64.6%	63.5%

Total

	1st Quarter			2nd Quarter			3rd Quarter			4th Quarter			Tot/Year		
	Proj/ACT '15	Plan '15	LY Act '14	Proj/ACT '15	Plan '15	LY Act '14	Proj/ACT '15	Plan '15	LY Act '14	Proj/ACT '15	Plan '15	LY Act '14	Proj/ACT '15	Plan '15	LY Act '14
Sales %	45.1%	42.5%	42.6%	54.9%	57.5%	57.4%	41.2%	39.8%	35.7%	58.8%	60.2%	64.3%			
Turn	0.40	0.29	0.24	0.46	0.37	0.32	0.41	0.37	0.33	0.55	0.55	0.55	1.86	1.62	1.45
CMU %	74.66%	75.41%	74.09%	74.26%	75.36%	74.43%	74.43%	75.45%	75.75%	74.43%	75.37%	75.92%	74.43%	75.39%	75.31%
Average Stock	4664	5098	4427	4918	5298	4474	6175	6126	4664	6562	6264	5016	5523	5620	4640
Sales	1865	1453	1061	2272	1966	1427	2523	2258	1519	3606	3416	2740	10266	9093	6747
Markdowns	950	548	354	643	604	318	864	776	345	2034	1851	1812	4491	3779	2829
Shortage															
Receipts	2724	2719	2017	3591	2659	1662	5565	4630	2352	3683	3495	4441	15563	13503	10472
GM $	1148	961	719	1526	1332	979	1678	1519	1066	2229	2147	1638	6581	5959	4402
MD %	50.9%	37.7%	33.4%	28.3%	30.7%	22.3%	34.2%	34.4%	22.7%	56.4%	54.2%	66.1%	43.7%	41.6%	41.9%
YTD Sales $	1865	1453	1061	4137	3419	2488	6660	5677	4007	10266	9093	6747	10266	9093	6747
Sales % Chg to LY	75.8%	36.9%		66.3%	37.4%		66.2%	41.7%		52.2%	34.8%		52.2%	34.8%	
YTD GM $	1148	961	719	2674	2293	1698	4352	3812	2764	6581	5959	4402	6581	5959	4402
YTD GM %	61.6%	66.1%	67.8%	64.6%	67.1%	68.2%	65.3%	67.1%	69.0%	64.1%	65.5%	65.2%	64.1%	65.5%	65.2%
GMROI	0.97	0.77	0.63	1.21	1.02	0.86	1.06	1.01	0.94	1.33	1.39	1.36	4.57	4.19	3.79

Note: All sales are in millions.

5.7 Assortment/Classification Planning

After the six-month plan is completed, buyers will analyze the individual classifications that comprise their total business. Understanding what has sold and what the future trends are will aid in this classification planning.

Assortment/classification planning segments a department's business based on related product categories. The department's total sales are broken down into individual classifications or product segments that will be needed for the time period. In most departments, buyers have both fashion and basic product categories. Basic product will need to be set up with a model stock assortment by size and color for each individual store based on selling history. Each store in a given region will sell different styles and sizes at different rates. Once the model stock is set up, purchase dollars need to be reserved for reorders to fill in to stock. Fashion merchandise is planned after basic stock. Fashion product may be "on trend" only for a season and must be planned accordingly. Buyers also need to consider floor space and fixture capacity when developing a merchandise plan.

There are many different ways in which a retailer may breakdown its departments into classes and subclasses. Different classification models can include:

- Vendor or label—for example, brand name product and private label product may be in separate classes within a given department.

- Fabrication—for example, handbags can be classified in the following manner: leather, vinyl, canvas, straw, nylon, or fabric.

- Garment type—in missy sportswear, classifications planned can include knit tops, woven tops (shirts), sweaters, dress pants, denim, shorts, jackets, dresses, and so on.

- Silhouette—for a denim buyer, there can be classes for five-pocket jeans that are replenishment basics, fashion denim, cropped denim, trouser, boot-cut, skinny, and so on.

- Pricing—good or opening price, better or moderate price, best.

- Color—white, black, fashion colors, basic colors, prints.

Buyers will review by classification the amount of product ordered versus the sales generated, gross margin achieved, and amount of markdowns taken. Product categories where sales outperformed the receipt inventory and at above average gross margin should be planned up for the upcoming season. Merchandise that did not sell through well will need to be replaced with newer styles and/or trends. This type of analysis is an ongoing process for buyers.

There are different ways to analyze an assortment/classification plan. The following examples represent just three of the ways that an assortment plan can be constructed.

The first step for a buyer is to break down the department's total sales plan into the respective classes. Figure 37 is an example of a classification analysis, in dollars, for a fashion jewelry department. Using the sales, gross margin, and receipt dollars as well as percentage comparisons attained this year, the buyer can plan next year's classes.

CONCEPT

$$\text{Classification sales percentage to total} \quad = \quad \frac{\text{Classification sales}}{\text{Total department sales}} \times 100$$

PROBLEM

Calculate the percentage to total sales for each classification for this year from Figure 37.

SOLUTION

$$\text{Necklaces \% to total sales} \quad = \quad \frac{\$551,500}{\$6,129,000} \times 100 = 9.0\%$$

$$\text{Earrings \% to total sales} \quad = \quad \frac{\$3,371,000}{\$6,129,000} \times 100 = 55.0\%$$

$$\text{Rings \% to total sales} \quad = \quad \frac{\$245,000}{\$6,129,000} \times 100 = 4.0\%$$

$$\text{Bracelets \% to total sales} \quad = \quad \frac{\$551,500}{\$6,129,000} \times 100 = 9.0\%$$

$$\text{Boxed jewelry \% to total sales} \quad = \quad \frac{\$1,410,000}{\$6,129,000} \times 100 = 23.0\%$$

The second step is to calculate the receipt percentage to total for each class for this year.

CONCEPT

$$\text{Classification receipt percentage to total} = \frac{\text{Classification receipts}}{\text{Total department receipts}} \times 100$$

PROBLEM

Calculate the percentage to total receipts by classification for this year from Figure 37.

SOLUTION

$$\text{Necklaces \% to total receipts} \quad = \quad \frac{\$925,000}{\$9,248,000} \times 100 = 10.0\%$$

$$\text{Earrings \% to total receipts} \quad = \quad \frac{\$4,625,000}{\$9,248,000} \times 100 = 50.0\%$$

$$\text{Rings \% to total receipts} \quad = \quad \frac{\$463,000}{\$9,248,000} \times 100 = 5.0\%$$

$$\text{Bracelets \% to total receipts} \quad = \quad \frac{\$1,110,000}{\$9,248,000} \times 100 = 12.0\%$$

$$\text{Boxed jewelry \% to total receipts} \quad = \quad \frac{\$2,125,000}{\$9,248,000} \times 100 = 23.0\%$$

Figure 37. Dollar Classification Plan for Fashion Jewelry, Fall 2015: Sales/Receipts August–January

Class	TY Tot Book Receipts $	TY AUR* RECEIPTS	TY Tot Sales $	TY AUR SALES	TY Tot GM $	Tot GM %	TY Tot Sales Units	TY Tot Sell Through %	TY Tot RCPT Units
Necklaces	$925,000	$47.93	$551,500	$37.01	$352,700	64.0%	14,900	77%	19,300
Earrings	$4,625,000	$32.99	$3,371,000	$27.63	$2,158,000	64.0%	122,000	87%	140,200
Rings	$463,000	$35.08	$245,000	$30.06	$147,000	60.0%	8,150	62%	13,200
Bracelets	$1,110,000	$38.28	$551,500	$27.71	$344,500	62.5%	19,900	69%	29,000
Boxed Jewelry	$2,125,000	$25.00	$1,410,000	$18.93	$902,000	64.0%	74,500	88%	85,000
	$9,248,000	$32.26	$6,129,000	$25.60	$3,904,200	63.7%	239,450	84%	286,700
TOTAL Jewelry	$9,248,000	$32.26	$6,129,000	$25.60	$3,904,200	63.7%	239,450	84%	286,700

*AUR means average unit retail.

*RCPT means receipts.

The buyer will then compare the receipt percentage to the percentage of sales. The classifications where sales exceed receipts at a gross margin equal to or above the department's gross margin should be planned up. Conversely, if there was too much inventory and the sales percentage to total sales was below inventory levels, those classes may be planned down depending on the gross margin achieved.

Based on comparison of sales and receipts for each class given in the preceding calculations, a buyer would plan as follows:

- Earrings should be planned up. Sales exceeded receipts: 55% of total department sales versus 50% of the receipts. Gross margin was 64.0%, which exceeded the department total of 63.7%, and sell through for the season was 87%, which was above the department's overall sell through.

- Boxed jewelry should be planned up as well. Sales and receipts were both 23% to total. Gross margin was 64.0% above the department's total, and this classification had the highest sell through percentage, 88%.

- Necklace sales were 9% to total versus receipts of 10%, and sell through was below the department at 77%. You may think about planning this classification down. The one aspect that may lead a buyer to plan this department flat or slightly less in receipts is that the gross margin was above the department average. If necklaces are trending up as a fashion statement, that should be taken into consideration as well.

- Bracelets should definitely be planned down. Sales were 9% of the total and receipts were 12% to total. Gross margin and sell through were both below the departmental averages.

- Rings should be planned down as well. Sales were below receipts: 4% versus 5%. Gross margin and sell through were also below the department total.

Armed with this information, the buyer would then use the plan set to develop the amount of units and dollars to purchase by classification for the next season. If fashion jewelry is being planned up 5% for the next year in sales, the buyer should plan an equivalent increase in inventory based on the original retail selling price (retail value of inventory). In Figure 38, the assortment plan for fashion jewelry, the Fall season receipt plan is broken out by classification. The plan is based on the average retail price by classification. As you can see, earrings have been planned up to represent 54% of the total inventory for the Fall season.

After the total class is planned, the buyer then breaks down each class into subclasses or style categories based on previous selling history and trend.

Figure 38. Merchandise Assortment Plan for Fashion Jewelry

Fall in store Classification/Style	Size Range	MSRP Range	Avg. Retail	Total # Units	Total Retail	Classification %
Necklaces	One Size					
Chain		$35.00–$65.00	$50.00	3,595	$179,728	18.5%
Collar and Short		$30.00–$60.00	$45.00	2,699	$121,438	12.5%
Pendant		$25.00–$55.00	$40.00	10,006	$400,258	41.2%
Statement		$40.00–$80.00	$60.00	4,501	$270,077	27.8%
Total			**$46.70**	**20,801**	**$971,500**	**10.0%**
Earrings	One Size					
Chandelier		$28.00–$44.00	$36.00	16,742	$602,715	11.5%
Drop		$28.00–$44.00	$36.00	54,594	$1,965,375	37.5%
Hoop		$24.00–$32.00	$28.00	52,410	$1,467,480	28.0%
Stud		$24.00–$30.00	$27.00	44,646	$1,205,430	23.0%
Total			**$31.12**	**168,391**	**$5,241,000**	**54.0%**
Rings						
Stackable	5,6,7,8,9	$20.00–$50.00	$35.00	2,696	$94,355	24.4%
"Gem"	5,6,7,8,9	$25.00–$50.00	$37.50	6,002	$225,059	58.2%
Basic	5,6,7,8,9	$20.00–$36.00	$28.00	2,403	$67,286	17.4%
Total			**$34.84**	**11,100**	**$386,700**	**4.0%**
Bracelets	One Size					
Bangle		$29.00–$48.00	$38.50	7,494	$288,534	37.3%
Beads		$24.00–$42.00	$33.00	4,993	$164,766	21.3%
Charm		$26.00–$50.00	$38.00	3,603	$136,918	17.7%
Stretch		$25.00–$36.00	$30.50	6,011	$183,331	23.7%
Total			**$35.00**	**22,101**	**$773,550**	**8.0%**
Boxed Jewelry	One Size					
Holiday Theme		$25.00	$25.00	51,484	$1,287,108	55.3%
Earrings		$25.00	$25.00	18,620	$465,500	20.0%
Necklaces/Earrings Set		$25.00	$25.00	13,965	$349,125	15.0%
Pins		$25.00	$25.00	9,031	$225,768	9.7%
Total			**$25.00**	**93,100**	**$2,327,500**	**24.0%**
Grand Total			**$30.75**	**315,494**	**$9,700,250**	**100.0%**
					5.0% increase	

Subclass/style category $ = Classification $ × Subclass/style category %

The total planned purchases for earrings are $5,241,000. The four subclasses of earrings the buyer will be purchasing and the percentage to total earrings for Fall are:

Chandeliers   11.5%

Drops   37.5%

Hoops   28.0%

Studs   23.0%

Calculate the total receipt dollars at retail for each subclass/style category.

Chandeliers = $5,241,000 × 11.5% = $602,715

Drops   = $5,241,000 × 37.5% = $1,965,375

Hoops   = $5,241,000 × 28.0% = $1,467,480

Studs   = $5,241,000 × 23.0% = $1,205,430

Based on the average retail price, the buyer can then project the approximate number of units needed by subclass/style category.

$$\text{Planned units to be purchased} = \frac{\text{Subclass retail \$}}{\text{Average unit retail price}}$$

Calculate the number of units to be purchased for the subclass/style categories of earrings if the average initial retail price is:

Chandeliers and Drops $36.00

Hoops $28.00

Studs $27.00

$$\text{Chandeliers} = \frac{\$602,715}{\$36.00} = 16,742$$

$$\text{Drops} = \frac{\$1,965,375}{\$36.00} = 54,594$$

$$\text{Hoops} = \frac{\$1,467,480}{\$28.00} = 52,410$$

$$\text{Studs} = \frac{\$1,205,430}{\$27.00} = 44,646$$

The process will be repeated for each classification in the department and the buyer can take this plan to market to assist in making the purchase.

The last example provided for assortment planning indicates how many stock keeping units (SKUs) are being planned for each category in a women's sportswear department. A **stock keeping unit (SKU)** is the product identification for a vendor/label, style, size, and color being sold by a retail store. Once buyers know the amount of product that they need to purchase, they can break down the total purchase into styles, sizes, and colors by product category. The analysis is similar to what was discussed earlier. A comparison needs to be made between units received and units sold. Any SKU that sold well should be updated and replaced for the next year. If a style, size, or color did not sell well, then a buyer would choose to replace it with a new item. Figure 39 represents the Women's Sportswear Outlet Fall SKU Analysis. Looking at the sweater category, the decision was made to increase the number of SKUs from 19 in 2015 to 20 in 2016. For 2015, sweater sales outperformed the amount receipted and represented 25.6% to total sales, versus 22% of the receipts.

As you can see, there are many different ways to analyze a department's business. Computer reporting is very sophisticated, and buyers can analyze down to the style, size, and color level by store. Learning how to analyze the data will take time and experience.

Figure 39. Women's Sportswear Outlet Fall SKU Analysis

TOTAL FALL SEASON									AVG SELLING RTL	
Silhouette	# of SKUS FALL 2015	RECOMMENDED # of SKUS FALL 2016	SALES UNITS	RCPT UNITS	SALES $$	RCPT $$	GP $	GP %		UNIT ST %
KNITS	20	20	39.2%	35.8%	29.7%	27%	$247,177	60.8%	$38.67	55.0%
			10,507	19,091	$406,315	$857,793				
Represented 19% of total sales										
11 SKUs produced 81% of knit business										
Best Sellers : RS74192CO-SEQUIN TANK CO- (black, white, pink)			sales:	2993 units	$72K	96% unit S/T	JULY			
4855600-L/S TOP- (black, milk)			sales:	1367 units	$70K	78% unit S/T	AUG			
SWEATERS	19	20	23.6%	20.4%	25.6%	22%	$205,288	58.5%	$55.41	58.4%
			6,335	10,844	$350,999	$685,251				
Represented 20% of total sales										
12 SKUs produced 79% of business										
Best Sellers : 4855200-L/S SWEATER- (black, milk, palm)			sales:	1794 units	$96K	76% unit S/T	AUG			
SHIRTS	16	16	11.2%	12.3%	10.7%	11%	$93,279	63.9%	$48.48	45.7%
			3,009	6,578	$145,876	$352,768				
Represented 14% of total sales										
8 SKUs produced 84% of shirt sales										
Best Sellers : U2576505-BUTTON DOWN SHIRT- (black, white)			sales:	1212 units	$53K	81% unit S/T	AUG			
SKIRTS	2	5	3.9%	3.5%	4.6%	4%	$43,300	68.2%	$60.62	56.7%
			1,047	1,848	$63,466	$126,803				
Represented 4% of total sales										
Best Sellers : 4855401-SKIRT - (black)			sales:	718 units	$53K	90% unit S/T	AUG			

(continued)

Figure 39. Women's Sportswear Outlet Fall SKU Analysis (continued)

Silhouette	# of SKUS FALL 2015	RECOMMENDED # of SKUS FALL 2016		SALES UNITS	RCPT UNITS	SALES $$	RCPT $$	GP $	GP %	AVG SELLING RTL	UNIT ST %
PANTS	18	16		11.5%	14.3%	12.1%	16%	$103,197	62.4%	$53.70	40.5%
				3,082	7,607	$165,499	$498,274				
Represented 23% of total sales											
10 SKUs produced 80% of pants business											
Best Sellers : 4855300-STRIPE PANT - (denim)				sales:	840 units	$55K	84% unit S/T	AUG			
DENIM	2	4		2.9%	4.3%	3.5%	5%	$29,747	61.3%	$62.25	33.8%
				780	2,310	$48,556	$159,619				
Represented 2% of total sales											
Dk Vint outsold Med Vint 2.5:1 in dollars											
JACKETS	8	5		4.3%	6.0%	8.5%	11%	$72,928	62.8%	$100.88	36.3%
				1,152	3,175	$116,211	$344,841				
Represented 14% of total sales											
Best Sellers : 4855510-1 BTTN BOUCLE JKT - (Chocolate)				sales:	472 units	$62K	59% unit S/T	SEPT			
DRESSES	2	2		3.4%	3.4%	5.3%	5%	$36,620	50.4%	$80.56	49.6%
				901	1,815	$72,589	$154,884				
Represented 3% total sales											
TOTAL SKUs	87	88	0	26,813	53,268	$1,369,510	$3,180,233	$728,862	53.2%	$51.08	50.3%
VAR TY/LY SKUs	1	0	0	100%	100%	100%	100%				
COMMENTS:											

3RD QTR

Silhouette	# of SKUS FALL 2015	RECOMMENDED # of SKUS FALL 2016			SALES UNITS	RCPT UNITS	SALES $$	RCPT $$	GP $	GP %	AVG SELLING RTL	UNIT ST %
2015	JUL	AUG	SEPT	TOT Q3	% to total		2016	JUL	AUG	SEPT	TOT Q3	% to total
								Recommended # SKUS				
KNITS	7	2	3	12	24%		KNITS	6	3	3	12	23%
SWEATERS	2	3	5	10	20%		SWEATERS	3	3	5	11	21%
SHIRTS	2	5	2	9	18%		SHIRTS	3	4	2	9	17%
SKIRTS	1	1	0	2	4%		SKIRTS	1	2	1	4	8%
PANTS	2	4	4	10	20%		PANTS	3	3	4	10	19%
DENIM	2	0	0	2	4%		DENIM	2	0	0	2	4%
JACKETS	1	2	2	5	10%		JACKETS	1	1	1	3	6%
DRESSES	1	0	0	1	2%		DRESSES	1	0	0	1	2%
TOTAL	18	17	16	51			TOTAL	20	16	16	52	

4TH QTR

Silhouette	# of SKUS FALL 2015	RECOMMENDED # of SKUS FALL 2016			SALES UNITS	RCPT UNITS	SALES $$	RCPT $$	GP $	GP %	AVG SELLING RTL	UNIT ST %
2015	OCT	NOV	DEC	TOT Q4	% of total		2016	OCT	NOV	DEC	TOT Q4	% of total
								Recommended # SKUS				
KNITS	4	2	2	8	22%		KNITS	4	2	2	8	22%
SWEATERS	5	2	2	9	25%		SWEATERS	3	3	3	9	25%
SHIRTS	0	5	2	7	19%		SHIRTS	3	2	2	7	19%
SKIRTS	0	0	0	0	0%		SKIRTS	1	0	0	1	3%
PANTS	3	2	3	8	22%		PANTS	3	3	0	6	17%
DENIM	0	0	0	0	0%		DENIM	2	0	0	2	6%
JACKETS	1	1	1	3	8%		JACKETS	1	1	0	2	6%
DRESSES	0	1	0	1	3%		DRESSES	0	1	0	1	3%
TOTAL	13	13	10	36			TOTAL	17	12	7	36	100%

CASE STUDY 1
OPEN-TO-BUY

It is the beginning of the third week in April. Mr. Johnston, the handbag buyer for a women's specialty store in California, studies the position of this department as he approaches the second quarter of the Spring season.

Before Mr. Johnston analyzes the actual results of the season-to-date performances, he examines the classification reports for the department to ascertain if the composition of his stock is in balance with the sales records. He finds that the leather handbag category—in which the price lines are highest—has fewer unit sales, which result in a high dollar inventory. The "fashion" fabrication of the season—sisal and straw, combined with new styling—has caused an out-of-proportion increase in unit sales of this group when compared to the sales of previous years. This trend has surpassed even Mr. Johnston's originally high expectations of this fashion. Additionally, the weather, which has turned unusually warm for this time of year, has been a catalyst to this vigorous selling in the Spring–Summer look. On the six-month merchandise plan, the season-to-date figures for the department are shown in Figure 40.

Figure 40. Six-Month Merchandising Plan

Department Name _____   Department No. _____

<table>
<tr><td rowspan="7" style="text-align:center">SIX-MONTH
MERCHANDISING
PLAN</td><td></td><td></td><td>PLAN
(This Year)</td><td>ACTUAL
(Last Year)</td></tr>
<tr><td colspan="2">Workroom Cost</td><td></td><td></td></tr>
<tr><td colspan="2">Cash Discount %</td><td></td><td></td></tr>
<tr><td colspan="2">Season Stock Turnover</td><td>2.0</td><td></td></tr>
<tr><td colspan="2">Shortage %</td><td></td><td></td></tr>
<tr><td colspan="2">Average Stock</td><td>$530,000</td><td></td></tr>
<tr><td colspan="2">Markdown %</td><td>5.0%</td><td></td></tr>
</table>

SPRING 2013		FEB.	MAR.	APR.	MAY	JUNE	JULY	SEASON TOTAL
SALES $	Last Year							
	Plan	80,000	120,000	145,000	300,000	315,000	100,000	$1,060,000
	Percent of Increase							
	Revised							
	Actual	78,194	119,873					
RETAIL STOCK (BOM) $	Last Year							
	Plan	350,000	550,000	650,000	700,000	650,000	450,000	
	Revised							
	Actual	325,312	552,100	651,325				
MARKDOWNS $	Last Year							
	Plan (dollars)	3,000	5,000	5,000	8,000	16,000	16,000	53,000
	Plan (percent)							
	Revised							
	Actual	3,000	5,000					
RETAIL PURCHASES	Last Year							
	Plan							
	Revised							
	Actual							
	Outstanding Orders				$160,000	50,000		
ENDING STOCK JULY 31	Last Year							
	Plan	360,000						
	Revised							
	Actual							

Comments

Merchandise Manager _____   Buyer _____

Controller _____

As Mr. Johnston examines these figures, he considers the following facts:

- The February and March sales are almost on target for the plan, but the post-Easter sales sagged. (Mr. Johnston estimates that there will be a 10% decrease in sales from the plan during the first quarter because the sales before Easter were slightly off and have been decreasing since that time.) A 5% increase is required over planned sales for the second quarter to achieve, if not surpass, the total seasonal planning goals in relation to sales, markdowns, and turnover.

- Unless immediate action is taken, the lowered actual sales to date will result in a higher than planned May 1 inventory figure.

- Both the dollar amount in the inventory and the outstanding orders in the straw category are entirely too low to generate possible sales increases because the demand for this merchandise has exploded. (This requires instant correction.)

- The sales at the beginning of the third week for the month are $60,000, and the inventory figure is $795,000.

To accomplish the second-quarter objectives (i.e., to attain the originally planned figures regarding sales, markdowns, and turnover), what actions must Mr. Johnston take? What are the alternatives, if any? What adjustments do you recommend? Justify your suggestions mathematically.

CASE STUDY 2
PLANNING FOR EFFECTIVE BUYING

You were recently promoted to the position of buyer for the hosiery department in a large specialty store. Your market is about to open, and in anticipation of this you must be prepared with certain dollar goals for the coming season.

It is the policy of your store that the buyer be responsible for the formulation of the departmental dollar six-month plan. You know that if this plan is to be of value, the figures established must be ones that you can actually achieve. You also know that despite your inexperience you will have to be prepared to explain and justify the plans and strategies you will use as guidelines when merchandising for the period under consideration.

Where shall you begin? You know a sound basis for future planning is to analyze the past results of your "new" department. So before you develop your plan for Fall, you decide to review the following figures, which show the performance achieved by the hosiery department for Fall of last year.

Month	BOM stock	Sales	Markdowns
August	$455,500	$75,000	$2,000
September	$850,000	$205,000	$2,000
October	$550,000	$135,000	$7,500
November	$600,500	$135,000	$7,500
December	$850,000	$230,000	$8,300
January	$440,000	$120,000	$24,000
February	$454,000		
Total	$900,000		$51,300
Turnover for period	1.5		
Markdown %	5.7%		

Your divisional merchandise manager (DMM) informed you that though the sales increases for the Fall season of last year had been greater than planned, there were other areas in the overall operation that needed improvement.

You are aware of the following facts: The nationwide economy is moving briskly; top management has planned on an overall storewide sales increase of 7%; legwear has had a strong surge of sales for the first six-month period (sales were planned with a 15% increase but actually were ahead 23% over the year before); fashion influences of long, leggy looks with slits in dresses and skirts continue as important apparel looks; the rising trend for legwear in the Spring season, after four dismal years, also saw the revival of body suits, which has stabilized to a fair contribution of total sales. The textured hosiery introduced in the Spring retailing at 20% higher retail prices is expected to create big business.

Your DMM requested a meeting with you to discuss your projected goals for the six months before they are finalized. You want to address the following issues in preparation of your meeting:

- How should the LY figures be used in preparation for your plan for the Fall season of this year?

- It would seem as if the sales trend in your department lends itself to a further increase of sales. Why must you estimate as accurately as possible (neither too high nor too low) the amount of sales you can generate during this season?

- As the buyer, what three strategies can you plan in order to achieve the sales gain you propose?

- Having set your projected sales figures, you now want to adjust your stocks to the proper size in order to achieve the planned monthly sales figures. Your DMM gave you August 1 stock figures of $460,000 and February 1 stock figures of $450,000. He told you to work out the BOM stock figures for each of the other months in your six-month plan. There are three approaches to planning the amount of stock necessary for projected sales figures. Which will you choose? Why?

- After you have determined all BOM stock figures for the entire period, what measurement will tell you how well you balanced your stock and sales for the entire period?

- In addition to planning sales and stocks, the markdown amounts are to be included. The typical markdown percentage in the industry for a hosiery department is 8%. The amount taken by your predecessor was 5.7%. In planning the amount of reductions for the entire period, how will you plan the markdowns on your current plan? In dollars? In percentages? Higher? Lower?

- Because your predecessor achieved a turnover of only 1.5, and the typical turnover in the industry for your department is 3.7, you realize that this was one of the "areas that needs improvement." How can you show an increased turnover on the dollar plan you are going to submit at present?

It is September 15. The following table shows the figures of your six-month plan. Should you make any revisions in your plan in light of the fact that your department for August had a 10% decrease in planned sales? If so, why and what revision(s) would you make? If not, why not?

	Aug.	Sept.	Oct.	Nov.	Dec.	Jan.	Seasonal total
Sales	$100.00	$235.00	$165.00	$165.00	$265.00	$150.00	$1,080.00
LY	$175.00	$205.00	$135.00	$135.00	$130.00	$120.00	$900.00
Plan	$100.00	$235.00	$165.00	$165.00	$265.00	$150.00	$1,080.00
Actual	$90.00						
Revised							
BOM stock	$460.00	$840.00	$525.00	$655.00	$860.00	$410.00	
LY	$455.50	$850.00	$550.00	$600.50	$850.00	$440.00	
Plan	$460.00	$840.00	$525.00	$655.00	$860.00	$410.00	
Actual							
Revised							
Outstanding orders					$200.00	$250.00	$450.00

From this information, calculate the OTB figure for November. What could cause the OTB figure for September to change after it is established? Can you convert an overbought condition to an OTB position? If so, how? If not, why not?

During the course of the six-month period, as you review your actual sales performance, should the actual results be compared to last year's sales or to the planned sales figures, or to both, in order to have a meaningful comparison? Explain your answer.

CASE STUDY 3
DOLLAR PLANNING AND CONTROL

The sales performance of the luggage department in a sporting goods store last Fall was:

August	$80,000	November	$140,000
September	$90,000	December	$160,000
October	$100,000	January	$120,000

Total seasonal sales = $690,000

As the six-month merchandising plan for this department was being formulated for this Fall season, the following decisions were made:

1. An 8% sales increase could be attained this year with the introduction and addition of a new classification of carry-on travel luggage that is well priced and of exceptional value.

2. The planned BOM stock-sales ratio for each month this year would be the same as last year—i.e., August 3.3, September 3.1, October 2.9, November 2.5, December 2.2, January 2.6—with an ending retail inventory for the period of $288,000.

3. The planned total reductions for last year were 11.6% and were distributed with 7% in August, 9% in September, 18% in October, 12% in November, 26% in December, and 28% in January.

Compute:

- The planned monthly retail receipts (purchases) for each month.

- The planned average stock and the planned stock turnover.

CASE STUDY 4
FORMULATING A SIX-MONTH PLAN

When the buyer for the activewear department started to develop the merchandise plan for the Spring season, she reviewed the six-month plan in Figure 35. The numbers that were achieved represent the department's performance last year for a fast-selling and up-trending department. The buyer was given the following information to plan the upcoming Spring season:

Planned sales   +   4.0%

Planned markdown %   45.1%

Planned turnover   0.98

Cumulative markup %   68.7%

For next Spring, the buyer has to take into account a shift in Easter selling. Last year, Easter occurred on the first Sunday in April; therefore, pre-Easter sales happened the last two weeks in March. This year, Easter falls in the third week of April.

Based on the sales success this department has experienced over the last two years, the buyer is concerned about keeping that trend going.

Acting as the buyer for the activewear department, formulate the six-month plan:

a.   Calculate each month's percentage of sales for last year.

b.   Calculate the total season sales planned. What will the planned sales be by month taking into account the Easter shift?

c.   Calculate the planned markdown dollars and percentage by month.

d.   Calculate the BOM stock needed by month.

e.   Calculate the receipt dollars needed to achieve the BOM stock.

f.   Does this plan achieve the desired turnover necessary?

g.   How will a buyer achieve the increased cumulative markup percentage? What is the potential effect on gross margin given the higher markdown percentage?

h.   How should the buyer address her concern regarding sales potentially slowing down?

INVOICE MATHEMATICS: TERMS OF SALE

CHAPTER **6**

"For every minute spent organizing, an hour is earned."

BENJAMIN FRANKLIN

OBJECTIVES

- Identify and recognize the different types of discounts.

- Calculate net cost.

- Identify and understand the different types of dating terms.

- Calculate discount and net payment dates.

- Identify and recognize the different types of shipping terms.

KEY TERMS

advanced dating

anticipation

cash discount

dating

discount date

discount period

DOI dating

EOM dating

extra dating

FOB city or port of destination

FOB factory

FOB retailer

list price

loading

net cost

net payment date

net terms

postdating

prepaid

quantity discount (QD)

regular/ordinary dating

ROG dating

terms of sale

trade discount

6.1 INVOICE MATHEMATICS: TERMS OF SALE

The buyer should be able to identify and recognize the different types of discounts offered, as well as understand the different types of dating and shipping terms involved in buying goods, because much of the secondary negotiating between vendors and retail buyers revolves around these three factors.

When retail buyers select merchandise, they not only agree on the cost price, but they also negotiate other factors that influence final cost. These conditions of the sale that are agreed on when the merchandise is purchased are called **terms of sale**. These terms deal with discounts granted, dating for payments, transportation arrangements, and shipping charges. When the discounts granted are deducted from the billed cost, **net cost** remitted to the vendor is the resultant figure. When shipping charges are to be paid by the retailers, they are added to the net cost that is due to the vendor, and the final or total amount to be sent to the vendor is determined. Lack of familiarity with terms of sale is a serious handicap because one of the best ways to improve gross margin and profits is to lower the cost of goods, assuming other factors remain constant. Consequently, any factor that will increase the ever-significant gross margin figure is essential.

DIFFERENT TYPES OF DISCOUNTS

A discount is a deduction (expressed as a percentage or in dollars) off the quoted or billed cost of the merchandise. Discounts are granted by a vendor to a purchaser for various negotiated terms. While discount practices and schedules vary from one industry to another, and from firm to firm, and even within different merchandise classifications, there are three basic types of discounts. Generally these discounts are taken in the following order: (1) trade discounts, (2) quantity discounts, and (3) cash discounts. These three types of discounts are examined in the following sections.

Trade Discount
Trade discount is a percentage or a series of percentages deducted from the **list price** (i.e., the theoretical retail price recommended by the manufacturer). The price that a buyer pays for merchandise is determined by deducting this trade discount percentage from the list price. It is a means of establishing the cost price of the goods. The number and/or amount of trade discounts varies according to the classification of the purchasers (i.e., retail stores, jobbers, other middlemen, or industrial buyers) and the amount of marketing services performed by that group. For example, a flashlight manufacturer quotes trade discounts to general retailers at 35%, department stores at 40%, chain stores at 45%, and wholesalers at 50%.

Trade discounts are deducted regardless of when the invoice is paid. In merchandise lines that customarily offer trade discounts, the list price minus the trade discount(s) is a way of quoting the cost. In some cases, this type of discount is quoted as a single percentage (e.g., $100 list price, less 45%), or it is offered as a series of discounts (e.g., $100 list price, less 30%, less 10%, less 5%). Generally, the apparel and accessory industries do not use the trade discount approach to determine the cost of an item; usually cost prices are quoted directly (e.g., style #332 costs $18.75 each, or socks cost $120/dozen). Trade discounts deducted from an established list price provide a vendor with a mechanism for changing cost easily. For example, when a supplier shows and describes merchandise through a catalog, the price change is done expeditiously by printing new price lists with a change in the discount. It is a device whereby the various middlemen in the channels of distribution can get larger and/or more discounts than retailers either because of the functional services they provide for the manufacturer or because of the larger quantities that they purchase. On the same item, a wholesaler might receive discounts of 40% and 10%, while the retailer may receive a discount of 40% only.

Billed cost = List price – Trade discount(s)

CONCEPT

Trade discounts on a lawn mower that "lists" at $200 are 25%, 10%, and 5%. Find the billed cost.

PROBLEM

	Price	Discount	Discount amount	Resultant figure
Lawn mower list	$200.00	0.25	$50.00	$150.00
1st discount	$150.00	0.10	$15.00	$135.00
2nd discount	$135.00	0.05	$6.75	$128.25

SOLUTION: *Spreadsheet format*

List price	=	$200	
Less 25%		$200.00	List price
	–	50.00	($200 × 25%) = 1st discount
		$150.00	(discounted price)
Less 10%		$150.00	
	–	15.00	($150 × 10%) = 2nd discount
		$135.00	(discounted price)
Less 5%		$135.00	
	–	6.75	($135 × 5%) = 3rd discount
		$128.25	(final price)
Billed cost	=	$128.25	

SOLUTION: *Arithmetic format*

Note that even though the list price is $200, it is common practice for the retailer to use the billed cost and the appropriate markup percentage to calculate the retail price of the merchandise.

Quantity Discount

Quantity discount (QD) is a percentage off the billed cost given by a vendor when a stipulated quantity is purchased, and it is deductible regardless of when invoices are paid. Usually, the purchase of a large amount of goods is involved. Depending on custom and practice within individual industries, this kind of discount is offered either when the stipulated quantity is purchased or for accumulated purchases over a specified period of time. The amount of discount is based on a sliding scale (i.e., the larger the purchase, the greater the percentage of quantity discount). A quantity discount is offered as an incentive for buyers to commit to purchasing large amounts of goods. This is a legal practice under specific provisions of the Robinson-Patman Act of 1936, federal legislation regulating wholesale pricing. Additionally, it is the buyer's responsibility to judge the merits of savings through this quantity discount against the risks of tying up more than the normal planned amount of open-to-buy money and buying only what the retailer can realistically sell through.

CONCEPT

Quantity discount $ = Billed cost $ × Quantity discount %

Net billed cost $ = Billed cost $ – Quantity discount $

PROBLEM

A cookware manufacturer's established price schedule is:

- A minimum initial order of $500 receives a 1% QD.

- An initial order of $1,250 receives 1.5%.

- An initial order of $2,500 receives 2%, and so on.

On an order of assorted cookware amounting to $2,000, use this discount schedule to determine:

a. The quantity discount.

b. The net cost of this order.

SOLUTION: Spreadsheet format

Item	Billed cost	Quantity discount	Discount amount	Net cost
Cookware	$2,000	0.015	$30	$1,970

SOLUTION: Arithmetic format

Quantity discount = $2,000 Billed cost × 1.5% Quantity discount

$2,000 × 1.5%

Quantity discount	=	$30
Billed cost	=	$2,000
Quantity discount	–	30
Net cost	=	$1,970

Cash Discount

Cash discount, the most common kind of discount, is a stated percentage of the billed cost allowed by a vendor if payment of the invoice amount is made within a stipulated time. The full utilization of cash discounts is another approach to decreasing the total cost of merchandise that results in an increased profit potential. Although any invoice or bill must be paid within some specified time, the intent of the cash discount is to offer the purchaser an incentive to make an early payment. The vendor sacrifices a fraction of the cost that is due in order to receive payment more rapidly. Cost prices that are subject to quantity and/or trade discounts may also be subject to cash discounts. Eligibility for a cash discount is contingent on the time element only. The cash discount percentage is not only written on the purchase order but also on the vendor's invoice (e.g., 8/10 EOM terms refers to an 8% discount if the invoice is paid within 10 days after the end of the fiscal month.)

CALCULATING NET COST

Billed Cost and Cash Discount Are Known

Cash discount $ = Billed cost $ × Cash discount %

Net cost $ = Billed cost $ − Cash discount $

CONCEPT

The cost of a sweater is $60. The cash discount earned is 12%. What is the net cost paid to the manufacturer?

PROBLEM

Item	Billed cost	Discount	Discount amount	Net cost
Sweater	$60	0.12	$7.20	$52.80

SOLUTION:
Spreadsheet format

Cash discount = $60.00 Billed cost × 12% Cash discount

$60.00

× 12%

Cash discount = $7.20

Billed cost = $60.00

− Cash discount − 7.20

Net cost = $52.80 (Amount to be remitted per unit purchased)

SOLUTION:
Arithmetic format

List Price Is Quoted and Cash Discount Is Given

When the cost of goods is stated by quoting a list price with a series of trade discounts, and the buyer is also eligible for a cash discount, the amount to be paid is determined by calculating the billed cost first and then deducting the cash discount.

CONCEPT

Net cost $ = List price $ − Trade discount(s) $ − Cash discount $

PROBLEM

The list price of a lawn mower is $200 less 25%, less 10%, less 5%. There is a 2% cash discount offered for payment within 10 days. What is the amount to be remitted if the cash discount is earned?

SOLUTION:
Spreadsheet format

	Price	Discount %	Discount amount	Discounted price	Cash discount	Cash discount amount	Net cost
Lawn mower list	$200	0.25	$50.00	$150.00			
1st discount	$150	0.10	$15.00	$135.00			
2nd discount	$135	0.05	$6.75	$128.25	0.02	$2.57	$125.68

SOLUTION:
Arithmetic format

List price		$200.00		$200.00	List price
Less 25%	×	25%	−	50.00	1st dollar discount
		$50.00		$150.00	
Less 10%		$150.00		$150.00	discounted price
	×	10%	−	15.00	2nd dollar discount
		$15.00		$135.00	
Less 5%		$135.00		$135.00	2nd discounted price
	×	5%	−	6.75	3rd dollar discount
		$6.75		$128.25	
Billed cost				$128.25	Billed cost
			×	2%	Cash discount
				$2.57	Cash discount
				$128.25	Billed cost
			−	2.57	Cash discount
Net cost				$125.68	Amount remitted

Quantity and Cash Discounts Must Be Considered

When the purchase is large enough to become eligible for a quantity discount, and a cash discount is offered, the amount to be paid is calculated by first deducting the amount of the quantity discount and then deducting the cash discount.

Net cost \$ = Billed cost \$ − Quantity discount \$ − Cash discount \$

A cookware manufacturer has established price schedules of:

- A minimum initial order of \$500 receives 1% QD.

- An initial order of \$1,250 receives 1.5%.

- An initial order of \$2,500 receives 2%, etc.

In addition, there is a 3% cash discount offered for payment made within 10 days. Based on this discount schedule, what is the net cost for a \$2,000 order of assorted cookware if it is paid within 7 days?

Item	Order	Quantity discount	Discount amount	Discounted price	Cash discount	Cash discount amount	Net cost
Cookware	\$2,000	0.015	\$30	\$1,970	0.03	\$59.10	\$1,910.90

Quantity discount	=	\$2,000.00 Billed cost × 1.5% QD	
	=	\$2,000.00	
	×	1.5%	
Quantity discount	=	\$30.00	
Cost	=	\$2,000.00	Billed cost
	−	30.00	QD
Cost	=	\$1,970.00	
Cash discount	=	\$1,970.00	
	×	3%	Cash discount
Cash discount	=	\$59.10	
Net cost	=	\$1,970.00	
	−	59.10	Cash discount
Net cost	=	\$1,910.90	

List Price Is Quoted and Quantity Discounts and Cash Discounts Are Allowed

When the cost of goods for some types of merchandise is stated by quoting a list price with a series of discounts, and the buyer is granted a quantity discount and is also eligible for a cash discount, the amount to be remitted to the vendor is calculated by:

- First, deducting the series of trade discounts to find the billed cost.

- Second, determining the eligibility for the quantity discounts offered and deducting the percentage of dollar amount from the calculated billed cost.

- Third, subtracting the cash discount from this amount.

The reason for this order is that when merchandise is quoted with trade discounts, the cost price of the goods must be established first. Only then can the buyer determine if the amount purchased satisfies the quantity specified for the quantity discount, regardless of when the invoice is paid. After this cost price is calculated, the cash discount is then subtracted—but only if payment is made within the stipulated time. Savings realized by these discounts alone have an impact on the department's profit margin and should be thoroughly understood for what they are and how they are calculated to determine the remitted cost price.

CONCEPT

$$\text{Net cost \$} = \text{List price \$} - \text{Trade discount(s) \$} - \text{Quantity discount \$} - \text{Cash discounts \$}$$

PROBLEM

A silverware buyer purchases 75 pairs of sterling salt and pepper shakers directly from a manufacturer who quotes the list price of this item for $125 less 25%, 10%, and 5%. The vendor's price schedule is as follows:

- A minimum order of $4,000 receives a 3% quantity discount.

- An initial order of $4,500 receives a 4% quantity discount.

- An initial order of $5,000 receives a 7% quantity discount.

In addition, there is a 2% cash discount offered for payment made within 10 days. What is the net cost of this order if it is paid in 8 days?

SOLUTION:
Spreadsheet format

Item	List price	Quantity	Billed cost									
Sterling S+Ps	$125	75	$9,375									

			Discount	Discount amount	Net cost	Quantity discount	Quantity discount amount	Discounted cost	Cash discount	Cash discount amount	Net cost remitted
Total list price	$9,375	0.25	$2,343.75	$7,031.25							
1st discount	$7,031.25	0.1	$703.13	$6,328.12							
2nd discount	$6,328.12	0.05	$316.41	$6,011.71	0.07	$420.82	$5,590.89	0.02	$111.82	$5,479.07

List price: $125 × 75 pairs		=	$9,375.00
– 1st trade discount 25%		×	25%
		=	$2,343.75
Total list price		=	$9,375.00
– 1st $ discount		–	2,343.75
1st discounted price		=	$7,031.25
		=	$7,031.25
– 2nd trade discount 10%		×	10%
		=	$703.125
1st discounted price		=	$7,031.25
– 2nd $ discount		–	703.13
2nd discounted price		=	$6,328.12
		=	$6,328.12
– 3rd trade discount 5%		×	5%
		=	$316.41
2nd discounted price		=	$6,328.12
– 3rd $ discount		–	316.41
Billed cost		=	$6,011.71
		=	$6,011.71
– Quantity discount 7%		×	7%
		=	$420.82
Billed cost		=	$6,011.71
– Quantity discount $		–	420.82
		=	$5,590.89
– Cash discount 2%		×	2%
Cash discount		=	$111.82
Billed cost		=	$5,590.89
– Cash discount		–	111.82
Amount remitted		=	$5,479.07

SOLUTION:
Arithmetic format

NET TERMS

Net terms is the expression used to refer to a condition of sale if a cash discount is neither offered nor permitted. When an item is sold under these conditions, it is expressed as a "net" arrangement; there are no additional payment discounts allowed. This is the most common term used currently in the industry.

PROBLEM

A buyer purchases an item costing $500 with net terms. The invoice is dated October 5 and the bill is paid within 30 days. What is the amount of the bill that was paid?

SOLUTION

Billed cost of $500 with net terms means no cash discount is allowed, so $500 is paid.

DATING

Dating is an agreement between the supplier and retailer whereby a specified time period for payment of an invoice is arranged. Dating arrangements vary within any particular industry and from one industry to another. Dating usually implies a cash discount and is expressed as a single term of sale (e.g., 2/10). This means that the buyer will deduct a 2% cash discount from the billed cost if the payment is remitted to the manufacturer on or before the stipulated 10-day period. For example:

Industry	*Common dating practice*
Ready-to-wear	8/10 EOM
Jewelry	2/10, net 30
Home furnishings	2/10, net 30

EOM dating will be described later in this section. In the jewelry and home furnishings examples, "2/10, net 30" means that a 2% discount off the billed cost is permitted if the invoice is paid within 10 days following the date of invoice. If payment isn't made in the 10-day discount time period, the payment of the net amount (i.e., total amount of billed cost) is required between the 11th and the 30th day following the date of the invoice.

PROBLEM

An invoice, dated March 1, for 10 folding chairs at a cost of $24 each carries terms of 2/10, net 30. If the bill is paid on any day from March 1 to March 11, 2% may be deducted. How much should be paid if the invoice is paid on March 8?

Each chair		$24.00
× Quantity	×	10
Total cost	=	$240.00

		$240.00	Billed cost
	×	2%	Cash discount
Cash discount	=	$4.80	

		$240.00	Billed cost
	−	4.80	Cash discount
Net cost	=	$235.20	

However, if the bill is paid on or after March 12, the full amount of $240 is due, as listed in the following payment schedule:

Cash discount period		Net period	
Date of invoice	*Last date for cash discount*	*First date for net payment*	*Last date for net payment*
March 1	March 11	March 12	March 31

In dating that allows a 10-day **discount period**, the last day for the net payment can be determined by adding another 20 days to the last discount day (i.e., date). For example:

Starting with a March 1 invoice date

+ 10	Discount days
March 11	**Last discount date**
+ 20	Net payment days
March 31	**Last net payment date** (traditional calendar)

or

Last net payment date = March 1 invoice date + 30 days = March 31

Different Types of Dating

There are many different types of dating used in all industries. As stated before, variations can even occur within a particular industry. Generally, the nature of the goods influences the prevalent dating practices. For example, some segments of the apparel industry offer a relatively high cash discount (e.g., 8%) to induce purchasers to take advantage of the savings for early or prompt payment. This is vital in an industry composed of many small businesses that are frequently undercapitalized. From the standpoint of the purchaser (i.e., retailer) who utilizes the cash discount privileges, the cost of the merchandise is considerably reduced, which has potential implications for increased profits. In determining when to pay an invoice, the buyer must be able to distinguish between the discount date and the net payment date. The **discount date** is the date by which the invoice may be paid to take advantage of the discount granted, and the **net payment date** is the date by which the invoice must be paid to acquire a favorable credit rating and avoid possible late penalties.

The previous explanations and problems pertaining to the time period of payment reflect customary, accepted US practices that are associated with the various types of invoice-payment dating. However, in buyer versus seller markets, and in certain other economic conditions (e.g., a recession), adherence to these rules can, and frequently does, change. For example, when economic conditions are not favorable, a retailer may be prone to disregard or possibly extend the traditional negotiated time period. Under these conditions, the vendor usually makes exceptions and concentrates on invoice payment rather than the strict observance of dating. Nonetheless, the most important negotiation is to set a specific date for payment of an invoice and then be able to calculate the exact payment date. Even though there are different numbers of days in each month, to simplify payment calculations, many businesses base their calculations on a 30-day month. Businesses that want to take advantage of all possible days in the payment period often prefer using the traditional calendar. Since individual arrangements can vary, for the purpose of the identification and application of the various types of dating, the problems and illustrations used in this text calculate the discount and net payment dates based on a 30-day month.

Regular (or Ordinary) Dating

Regular or **ordinary dating** is one of the most common kinds of dating. The discount period is calculated from the date of the invoice, which is usually the same date that the merchandise is shipped.

PROBLEM	What payment should be made on an invoice for $500 dated November 16, carrying terms of 4/10, net 30?

SOLUTION	If paid on or before November 26 (November 26 is 16 + 10 days):

Billed cost	$500
– Cash discount ($500 × 4%)	– 20
Remitted	= $480

If paid between November 27 and December 17 (i.e., the 20-day net payment period), no discount is permitted, and the full $500 is remitted. The vendor reserves the right to charge carrying fees after the expiration of the net payment period. The exercising or bypassing of this option is done on a case-by-case basis and depends on individual factors (e.g., credit history, the relationship of the vendor with the retailer, etc.).

Extra Dating

Extra dating (written as an X) is calculated from the date of the invoice, with a specified number of extra days granted during which the discount may be taken. Consequently, 2/10–60X means that the bill may be paid in 10 days, plus 60 extra days (i.e., a total of 70 days), from the date of the invoice in order to earn the 2% discount. The full amount is due after the expiration of the 70 days, and the customary, though often unstated, 20-day additional net payment period follows. This extended time to pay an invoice is used in certain markets, such as swimwear and coats. Both of these merchandise categories are set up in the store before the majority of sales happen. For example, swimwear is set up in stores in April. But the peak selling time for swimwear is June and July. Therefore, if the buyer negotiates extended payment time, it will give the retailer time to sell product in order to pay the bills.

An invoice dated March 16 has a billed cost of $1,800 and terms of 3/10–60X. Determine:

   a.   The final date for taking the cash discount.

   b.   The cash discount earned if the bill is paid on June 14.

   c.   The amount due if paid in full on April 17.

   d.   The last date for net payment.

   a.   Final date for cash discount:

   March 16 through 31 = 15 days

   April (entire month) = 30 days

   May 1 through 25 = 25 days

   End of cash discount period: May 25 = 70 days

   Cash discount allowable through May 25 only.

   b.   No cash discount is earned if the bill is paid on June 14.

   c.   Eligible for cash discount:

   $1,800   Billed cost

   −   54   ($1,800 × 3% Cash discount)

   $1,746   Amount due

   $1,746   Amount due if paid in full on April 17

   d.   Last date for net payment:

   20 days after May 25 = June 14

   Last date for net payment: June 14

EOM Dating

EOM dating (end of month) means the cash discount period is computed from the end of the fiscal month in which the invoice is dated, rather than from the date of the invoice itself. Thus, 8/10 EOM (invoice dated April 1, for example) means that the time for payment is calculated from the end of fiscal month of April based on the 4-5-4 calendar. Additionally, an 8% cash discount may be taken if the bill is paid by May 10, that is, 10 days after the end of April. Again, an implied 20-day net period occurs from May 11 through May 31, during which the retailer may pay the bill in full.

Note that, traditionally, under EOM dating only, invoices dated on or after the 25th of any month are considered to be part of the next month's transactions. For example, a bill with 8/10 EOM dated on August 26 is considered a September 1 bill, and the discount period extends to October 10. Of course, arrangements of this kind vary. It is common to apply this concept for invoice dates after the 25th of a month to other types of dating as well.

PROBLEM

An invoice for $1,000 dated March 17 has terms of 8/10 EOM.

    a.   What is the last date for deducting the 8% cash discount?

    b.   What amount will be due if the bill is paid on that date?

SOLUTION

    a.   Discount date = April 10 (10 days after the end of March)

        Last date for 8% discount: April 10

    b. $1,000   Billed cost

        – 80   ($1,000 × 8% Cash discount)

        $920   Amount due

        $920   Amount due if paid in full by April 10

If this invoice was dated March 26 through March 31 (using the traditional calendar), the discount date of payment would be May 10.

ROG Dating

ROG dating (receipt of goods) means that the discount period is calculated from the date the goods are delivered to the retailer's premises, rather than from the date of the invoice. This type of dating is often requested by buyers located a considerable distance from the market (or shipping point). These retailers typically receive bills a few days after shipment but may not get delivery of the merchandise itself for a considerably longer time. Therefore, 5/10 ROG, for example, means that the bill must be paid within 10 days after receipt of goods to earn the cash discount.

An invoice for $100 is dated April 4 and carries terms of 5/10 ROG. The goods arrive at the store on May 7.

a. What is the last date that the discount may be deducted?

b. How much should be remitted if payment is made on that date?

a. Date goods were received + 10 days

    May 7 + 10 days = May 17

    Last date for discount: May 17

b. $100 Billed cost − $5 ($100 × 5% Cash discount) = $95

    $95 Amount due on or before May 17

DOI Dating

DOI dating (date of invoice) means that the discount period is calculated from the date the invoice is received by the retailer. This type of dating is used for basic replenishment merchandise that is receipted throughout the month.

The denim buyer received an invoice for the five-pocket denim jeans reorder in the amount of $12,000 on September 1. The terms on the order are 8/40 DOI.

a. When does the payment need to be made in order for the discount to be taken?

b. How much should be paid on that date?

a. Date goods were received + 40 days

    September 1 + 40 days = October 11

    Last date for discount: October 11

b. $12,000 Billed cost − $960 ($12,000 × 8% Cash discount) = $11,040

    $11,040 Amount due on or before October 11

Advanced Dating or Postdating

Advanced dating or **postdating** (seasonal discount) is a type of dating that indicates the invoice date is advanced so that additional time is allowed for payment to be made and, ultimately, for the cash discount to be deducted. The discount period is then calculated from this advanced date agreed on by the buyer and the seller. Generally, this type of dating is used by manufacturers to persuade buyers to buy and/or receive goods earlier than they would normally. It is also requested by purchasers who are momentarily short of cash. Consequently, if a shipment was made on February 10, and the invoice date was May 1, terms of 2/10 would mean that payment was due on or before May 11 to qualify for a 2% cash discount. (Note: On invoices with advanced dating or postdating, the payment of the invoice at net is delayed until the last day of the month in which the cash discount is earned, after which it is considered overdue.)

PROBLEM | An invoice for merchandise shipped on August 18 is postdated October 1 and carries terms of 3/10, net 30. When does the discount period expire?

SOLUTION | The terms mean that 3% may be deducted if payment is made on or before October 11. The full amount is due at the end of the customary net period on October 31, using the traditional calendar.

Net Payment Dates

Net payment dates refer to that date by which an invoice must be paid with no additional payment discount. This date is expressed as n/30 or "net 30." It is considered overdue—and may be subject to an interest charge—if paid after the net payment period. Of course, there are variations for determining the final net payment date of an invoice (see Figure 41). The net payment date is determined by the agreed-on type of cash discount dating. The commonly used practices are:

- Regular dating: The full amount of the invoice is due exactly 30 days from the date of invoice.

- Extra, EOM, and ROG dating: The net payment date of the invoice is determined by adding 20 days from the expiration of the cash discount period.

- Advanced dating or postdating: The payment of the net invoice is delayed until the last day of the month in which the cash discount is earned.

Figure 41. Summary of Discount Dates

Type of dating	Invoice date	Last date eligible for discount	Net amount paid between dates below	Bill past due if paid on or later than
1. Regular (2/10 or net 30)	11/16	11/26	11/27 through 12/17	12/18
2. Extra Dating (X) (3/10–90X)	6/7	9/17	9/17 through 10/7	10/8
3. End of Month (EOM) (8/10 EOM)	4/29	6/10	6/11 through 6/30	7/1
4. Receipt of Goods (ROG) (5/10 ROG; Rec'd 4/16)	4/4	4/26	4/27 through 5/16	5/17
5. Advanced dating/Postdating (3/10 net 30 as of 10/1)	8/18	10/11	10/12 through 10/31	11/1

Deadline dates used in this chart are based on a 30-day month.

ANTICIPATION

Anticipation is an extra type of cash discount that is usually calculated at the prevailing prime rate of business interest and is subject to change based on economic conditions. This extra discount is not utilized in the industry currently as in the past. Anticipation could be permitted by vendors when an invoice is paid prior to the end of the cash discount period and, again, is subject to change based on economic conditions.

LOADING

Loading is a rare practice of a vendor intentionally increasing the amount of an invoice to a price that would allow a theoretically greater cost discount, but that results in the retailer paying the net amount that the vendor quotes. The standardized cash discount percentage arbitrarily set by top management does not reflect the true cash discount allowed by the vendor. When loading is practiced, the retailer may request that the vendor bill a "loaded" cost that is then adjusted by the required cash discount percentage to achieve the true net cost. In other cases, the store will make the adjustments statistically when the invoices are processed.

PROBLEM

A manufacturer quotes the cost of an item at $30 with terms of 3/10, n/30. The buyer desired an 8% cash discount. What is the "loaded" cost?

SOLUTION

Net cost of invoice	=	$30 Billed cost – 3% Cash discount
	=	$30 – $0.90 (3% × $30)
	=	$29.10
Loaded cost	=	$\dfrac{\$29.10 \text{ Net cost}}{92\% \ (100\% \ - \ 8\% \text{ Loaded discount})}$
	=	$31.63

SHIPPING TERMS

As with dating, shipping charges vary in different industries and in different situations. They are expressed as free-on-board (FOB) at a designated location. The place that is designated defines the point to which the vendor or retailer pays transportation charges and assumes risk of loss or damage and the legal title to the merchandise being shipped to the destination. Because the factors that determine the total cost of goods include inward freight charges, it is important that the retailer negotiate advantageous shipping terms as a means of reducing the total cost of goods. The buyer should apply ethical but firm pressure on merchandise resources for appropriate and favorable terms of sale and discounts. The most common arrangements are:

- **FOB retailer.** Vendor pays transportation charges to the retailer's store or warehouse and, unless otherwise agreed on, bears the risk of loss until goods are received by the retailer.

- **FOB factory.** Purchaser (retailer) pays transportation charges from factory to purchaser's premises and, unless otherwise agreed on, bears the risk of loss from the time the goods leave the factory.

- **FOB city or port of destination.** Vendor pays the transportation charges to a specified location in the city of destination, and then the purchaser pays delivery charges from that point to the purchaser's premises. Unless otherwise agreed on, the risk of loss passes from seller to buyer when goods arrive at the specified location in the city of destination.

- **Prepaid.** Vendor pays transportation (freight) charges to the retailer's store or warehouse when the merchandise is shipped from vendor's premises. The FOB agreement, made at the time of sale, determines whether the vendor or purchaser pays the freight charges.

Discount Practice Problems

1. The Robner Electronic Company lists a top-of-the-line answering machine for $175. The trade discount offered is 30%. What is the billing price?

2. A guitar manufacturer sells electric guitars at $450 less 30% and 10%. What is the net cost to the buyer?

3. Dealer A sells stereo sets for $975 with a 30% trade discount. Competitor B offers a similar model at $760 with a 15% discount. Which is the better buy for the customer? By how much?

4. The quantity discount schedule of a china importer is 0.5% discount on orders for $1,000, 1% discount on orders for $1,500, 1.5% discount on orders for $2,500, and 2% discount on orders for $3,000. A retailer's order of bone china luncheon sets amounted to $2,800. No other discounts were allowed on this particular group. How much should the retailer pay the importer?

5. As an incentive, a supplier of motorbikes offers an additional 10% quantity discount on orders of more than 5 bikes. The normal trade discount offered by the supplier is 40% and 10% on the suggested list price of $250 each. How much would a retailer remit if 8 bikes are purchased?

6. Determine the final dates on which a cash discount may be taken on invoices dated May 15 for the different terms listed. Assume that the merchandise is received in the stores on June 2.

    a. 8/10, net 30.

    b. 2/10 EOM.

    c. 2/10–60X.

    d. Net 30.

    e. 3/10 ROG.

7. An electronics retailer buys 3 color TV sets that list for $725 each and is billed with trade discounts of 20% and 10%. Terms are 4/10, n/30.

    a. What is the actual net cost of each TV?

    b. If the invoice is dated November 16 and paid on November 26, what amount should be remitted?

8. Your department receives an invoice dated October 10 in the amount of $6,750. How much must be paid on November 10 if terms are:

   a. 10/10, net 30.

   b. 10/10 EOM.

   c. Net.

9. Merchandise that amounts to $650 at cost is shipped and invoiced on August 29. Terms are 4/10 EOM. Payment is made on September 26. How much should be remitted?

10. A buyer purchased 75 ginger jar lamps at a list price of $40 each. The trade discounts were 20% and 5%, with terms of 2/10, net 30. The lamps were shipped and billed on October 18 and were received October 22. The bill was paid on October 31. What amount was paid?

11. An invoice dated March 2 carries terms of 3/10–60X. When does the discount period expire? Explain.

12. Goods are invoiced and shipped on July 1 and received on July 15. Terms are 5/10 EOM, and the invoice is for $5,600. Payment is made on August 10. How much should be remitted?

13. An invoice for $3,290, dated April 26, covering merchandise received May 19, carries terms of 8/10 EOM, ROG. It is paid on June 10.

    a. How much should have been remitted?

    b. What would have been remitted had ROG not been included? Why?

14. Goods that are invoiced on July 26 are received on August 10. Indicate the final discount date and the final date for net payment if terms are:

	Final discount date	Final net payment date
3/10 EOM	_____	_____
2/10, net 30	_____	_____
1/20–30X	_____	_____
8/10 EOM as of Sept. 1	_____	_____
8/10 EOM, ROG	_____	_____

15. The bra buyer received a reorder of 600 bras that totaled $6,300 at cost. The invoice was received on May 10 with terms of 8/40 DOI. What is the date that this order needs to be paid by? What will be the total cost paid by that date?

16. A reorder of white bath towels was received on June 20. The order was for 1,000 towels at a billed cost of $4.80 per towel. The terms on the order were 2/10 DOI. When is the latest date the order can be paid by and the cost that will be paid on that date?

CASE STUDY 1
TERMS OF SALE

Mr. Williams, the silverware buyer for a specialty store located in San Francisco, decides to review his vendor analysis report before making his forthcoming season's purchases. The report shows that among the top six resources, there are three relatively strong and three relatively weak suppliers in relation to the gross margin each generated. Mr. Williams realizes that some important aspects of his job as buyer are negotiating trade discounts, quantity discounts, cash discounts, and dating, as well as transportation charges. Because any and/or all of these factors can increase the essential gross margin figure, he examines copies of past orders to determine the terms of sale on previous purchases. He discovers that some suppliers granted all his requests pertaining to discount and dating elements, certain vendors negotiated these factors only after an initial order was placed, and a considerable number allowed only the absolute minimum discount that prevailed in the market.

Because business conditions have been less than favorable, Mr. Williams feels that the success of the next season depends on his ability not only to select the most desirable items from his key resources but also to negotiate with those vendors who offer the most advantageous terms of sale in order to help maintain or improve the gross margin performance.

The first classification he shops in the market is sterling flatware. He had, and continues to have, strong sales in one well-advertised national brand that is distributed and can be bought directly from the manufacturer or from a jobber (i.e., middleperson). Customarily, Mr. Williams places his order for these goods with the manufacturer because he is able to view the complete line of patterns and buy any quantity he needs. Additionally, he has developed a rapport with one of the salespeople who has served him. This salesperson would rush special orders, call Mr. Williams about special promotions, and so on. Consequently, during market week, Mr. Williams visits the manufacturer's showroom, shops the entire line, gets delivery dates, and inquires about the current terms of sale, which are:

- Trade discounts from list price: 40%, less 25%.

- Quantity discounts offered: None.

- Cash discount: 2/10, n/30.

- FOB: Factory/shipping charges, running 0.5%.

When Mr. Williams returns to the store, he studies his open-to-buy for this category and decides to purchase:

- 15 sets of Pattern A: List price $175 for each 5-piece place setting, 40-piece service.

- 10 sets of Pattern B: List price $200 for each 5-piece place setting, 40-piece service.

- 8 sets of Pattern C: List price $225 for each 5-piece place setting, 40-piece service.

He is interrupted in his calculations by his assistant, who informs him that the salesperson of an out-of-town jobber would like to speak with him. This particular supplier has tried for several seasons to get the store as an account. In the past, Mr. Williams had used local jobbers, often for immediate shipment of various items when his stock would become "low" on fast-moving items, but he had not done business before with this particular firm. Mr. Williams invites the salesperson into his office and, during their conversation, Mr. Williams senses the salesperson's eagerness to open an account with him now. He deduces this because of all the concessions the salesperson is willing to offer the store. Because this jobber carries the same brand of silverware Mr. Williams has just seen at the manufacturer's showroom, he asks the prices, terms, and other pertinent details. They are:

- Trade discount from list price: 40%, less 20%, less 5%.

- Quantity discount: An additional 1% for orders over $10,000; 1.5% for orders over $15,000; and 2% for orders over $20,000.

- Cash discount: 2/10–60X, anticipation allowed.

- FOB store.

With which resource should Mr. Williams place his order—the manufacturer, the jobber, or a combination of both? Justify your choice mathematically.

CASE STUDY 2
RESOURCES INFLUENCED
BY TERMS OF SALE

Mrs. Lawrence is the owner of a three-store shoe chain called TRED-RITE. The merchandise featured in these stores, which are located in small strip malls, could be described as fashion forward at moderate to high prices. The strength of her operation is the services offered to customers combined with merchandise that has a unique twist.

Mrs. Lawrence has developed an extensive mailing list over the fifteen years of the store's existence. Periodically throughout the year, she sends out a direct-mail brochure, which has successfully produced more business because of the items featured.

In April, as she covers the market for the Fall season, she is on the lookout for a promotional item to be selected and promoted in this year's Christmas mailing piece.

She finally decides on a very trendy, attractive slipper that can be worn outdoors. It is a lamb's wool-lined scuff with a leather suede upper, made in China. The slipper has a one-inch platform with a hard sole, available in this season's four most desirable fashion colors. It would be priced at $55 and represents exceptional value. This item is being offered by X-Cel Co., an importer from which Mrs. Lawrence has bought consistently because this resource has had superior sales performance. Their deliveries and terms have been exactly as negotiated, and their offerings are synonymous with good value. The X-Cel Co. has quoted on this particular item a landed cost of $30 per pair, requiring a minimum order of 3,000 pairs, with terms of n/30, FOB store. The mailing date for this Christmas brochure is set for October 15, and X-Cel Co. has agreed on an October 1 complete delivery date. Mrs. Lawrence is confident about the item, but she questions her stores' capacity to meet the demand of this quantity in a relatively short selling period.

Mrs. Lawrence saw in the market a similar, though not identical, branded slipper manufactured by a medium-size local factory, quoted with a cost of $31.50. This resource does not require a minimum quantity, yet guarantees shipment of sufficient quantities as needed (by the response to the brochure), with prompt delivery throughout the holiday season and the life of the "mailer." The terms for this resource are 5/10 EOM, anticipation allowed, FOB store. This resource will set a delivery date of September 26 and, should Mrs. Lawrence write the order for 3,000 pairs, will ship half the order by September 26 and then the balance by November 1.

With which resource should Mrs. Lawrence negotiate? Would the terms offered by each vendor affect the profitability of this purchase? How? Explain mathematically.

GLOSSARY OF CONCEPT FORMULAS

Billed Cost

Billed cost = List price − Trade discount(s)

Billed cost = # Units purchased × Invoice cost

Book Inventory

$$\text{Book inventory at retail} = \text{Physical inventory} + \underset{\text{(Total merchandise handled)}}{\text{Net retail purchases}} + \text{Other stock additions} - \text{Net sales} - \text{Markdown differences} - \text{Other deductions from stock}$$

$$\text{Book inventory at cost} = \text{Opening retail book inventory} \times \left(100\% - \text{Cumulative markup \% achieved on stock} + \text{Purchases} \right)$$

Build/Percentage Change/Trend

$$\text{Build/percentage change/trend} = \frac{\text{This year sales} - \text{Last year sales}}{\text{Last year sales}} \times 100$$

$$\text{Build/percentage change/trend} = \frac{\text{This year sales} - \text{Planned sales}}{\text{Planned sales}} \times 100$$

Cost (Markup Formulas)

Cost $ = Retail $ − Markup $

Cost $ = Retail $ × (100% − Markup %)

$$\text{Cost \%} = \frac{\text{Cost \$}}{\text{Retail \$}} \times 100$$

Cost % = Retail % − Markup %

Cost % = 100% − Markup %

$$\text{Cumulative markup \%} = \frac{\text{Cumulative markup \$}}{\text{Cumulative retail \$}} \times 100$$

Cost of Goods Sold

$$\begin{array}{c}\text{Total cost} \\ \text{of goods} \\ \text{sold \$}\end{array} = \begin{array}{c}\text{Billed} \\ \text{cost \$}\end{array} + \begin{array}{c}\text{Inward freight} \\ \text{charges \$}\end{array} + \begin{array}{c}\text{Workroom} \\ \text{costs \$}\end{array} - \begin{array}{c}\text{Cash} \\ \text{discount \$}\end{array}$$

$$\text{Cost of goods sold \$} = \text{Cost of goods sold \%} \times \text{Net sales \$}$$

$$\text{Cost of goods sold \%} = \frac{\text{Cost of goods sold \$}}{\text{Net sales \$}} \times 100$$

Customer Returns and Allowances

$$\begin{array}{c}\text{Customer returns} \\ \text{and allowances \$}\end{array} = \begin{array}{c}\text{Total of all refunds or credits} \\ \text{to the customer on individual} \\ \text{items of merchandise \$}\end{array} \times \begin{array}{c}\text{Number of units} \\ \text{actually returned}\end{array}$$

$$\begin{array}{c}\text{Customer returns} \\ \text{and allowances \%}\end{array} = \frac{\text{Customer returns and allowances \$}}{\text{Gross sales \$}} \times 100$$

$$\begin{array}{c}\text{Customer returns} \\ \text{and allowances \$}\end{array} = \text{Gross sales \$} \times \begin{array}{c}\text{Customer returns} \\ \text{and allowances \%}\end{array}$$

Department's Net Sales

$$\begin{array}{c}\text{Department's net sales} \\ \text{\% of total store sales}\end{array} = \frac{\text{Department's net dollar sales}}{\text{Store's total net dollar sales}} \times 100$$

Gross Margin

$$\text{Gross margin} = \text{Net sales} - \text{Total cost of goods sold}$$

$$\text{Gross margin \$} = \text{Gross margin \%} \times \text{Net sales \$}$$

$$\text{Gross margin \%} = \frac{\text{Gross margin \$}}{\text{Net sales \$}} \times 100$$

$$\text{GMROI} = \frac{\text{Gross margin \%} \times \text{Turnover}}{100\% - \text{Markup \%}}$$

or

$$\text{GMROI} = \frac{\text{Gross margin \$}}{\text{Average inventory at cost \$}}$$

$$\text{Gross margin \%} = \frac{\text{Net sales \$} - \text{Total cost of goods sold \$}}{\text{Net sales \$}} \times 100$$

or

$$\text{Gross margin \%} = \frac{\text{Gross margin \$}}{\text{Net sales \$}} \times 100$$

$$\begin{array}{c}\text{Gross} \\ \text{margin \%}\end{array} = \frac{\text{Maintained markup} + \text{Cash discounts} - \text{Alteration costs}}{\text{Net sales}} \times 100$$

Gross Sales

$$\text{Gross sales} = \frac{\text{Total of all the prices charged to}}{\text{consumers on individual items}} \times \frac{\text{Number of units}}{\text{actually sold}}$$

$$\text{Gross sales \$} = \frac{\text{Net sales \$}}{(100\% - \text{Customer returns and allowances \%})}$$

Markdown

$$\text{Markdown \$} = \text{Original or present retail price \$} - \text{New retail price \$}$$

$$\text{Markdown \$} = \text{Percentage off} \times \text{Present retail price \$}$$

$$\text{Total markdown \$} = \text{First total \$ markdown} + \text{Second total \$ markdown}$$

$$\text{Planned markdowns \$} = \text{Net sales \$} \times \text{Markdown \%}$$

$$\text{Markdown \%} = \frac{\text{Markdown \$}}{\text{Net sales}} \times 100$$

$$\text{Markdown \%} = \frac{\text{Markdown \$}}{\text{Total dollar sales of group's final selling prices}} \times 100$$

$$\text{Markdown cancellation} = \text{Higher retail \$} - \text{Markdown price \$}$$

$$\text{Net markdown \$} = \text{Gross markdown \$} - \text{Markdown cancellation \$}$$

$$\text{Planned total seasonal dollar markdowns} = \frac{\text{Planned total}}{\text{seasonal sales \$}} \times \frac{\text{Total seasonal}}{\text{markdown \%}}$$

$$\text{Total seasonal markdown \%} = \frac{\text{Total dollar seasonal markdowns}}{\text{Total seasonal sales \$}} \times 100$$

$$\text{Total seasonal markdown \%} = \frac{\text{Last year (LY) total markdown \$}}{\text{LY total sales}} \times 100$$

Markup

$$\text{Markup \$} = \text{Retail \$} - \text{Cost \$}$$

$$\text{Markup \% on retail} = \frac{\text{Markup \$}}{\text{Retail \$}} \times 100 \quad \text{or} \quad \frac{\text{Retail \$} - \text{Cost \$}}{\text{Retail \$}} \times 100$$

$$\text{Markup \% on cost} = \frac{\text{Markup \$}}{\text{Cost \$}} \times 100 \quad \text{or} \quad \frac{\text{Retail \$} - \text{Cost \$}}{\text{Cost \$}} \times 100$$

$$\text{Cumulative retail markup \% on entire purchase} = \frac{\text{Total markup \$}}{\text{Total retail \$}} \times 100$$

or

$$\text{Cumulative retail markup \% on entire purchase} = \frac{\text{Total retail \$} - \text{Total cost \$}}{\text{Total retail \$}} \times 100$$

$$\text{Purchase balance} = \frac{\text{Total planned (pieces,}}{\text{retail, cost, or markup \%)}} - \text{Purchases to date}$$

$$\text{Initial markup \%} = \frac{\text{Gross margin \%} + \text{Retail reductions \%}}{100\% + \text{Retail reductions \%}}$$

$$\text{Initial markup \%} = \frac{\text{Gross margin \$} + \text{Retail reductions \$}}{\text{Sales \$} + \text{Retail reductions \$}} \times 100$$

$$\text{Initial markup \%} = \frac{\text{Gross margin} + \text{Alteration costs} - \text{Cash discount earned} + \text{Retail reduction}}{\text{Sales (100\%)} + \text{Retail reductions \%}}$$

$$\text{Markup \% on retail} = \frac{\text{Markup \$}}{\text{Retail \$}} \times 100 \quad \text{or} \quad \frac{\text{Retail \$} - \text{Cost \$}}{\text{Retail \$}} \times 100$$

$$\text{Markup \% on cost} = \frac{\text{Markup \$}}{\text{Cost \$}} \times 100 \quad \text{or} \quad \frac{\text{Retail \$} - \text{Cost \$}}{\text{Cost \$}} \times 100$$

$$\text{Maintained markup \%} = \frac{\text{Net sales} - \text{Gross cost of goods sold}}{\text{Net sales}} \times 100$$

$$\text{Maintained markup \%} = \frac{\text{Gross margin} - \text{Cash discounts} + \text{Alteration costs}}{\text{Net sales}} \times 100$$

$$\text{Maintained markup \%} = \text{Initial markup \%} - \text{Retail reduction \%} \times (100\% - \text{Initial markup \%})$$

$$\text{Cumulative markup \% on entire purchase} = \frac{\text{Total markup \$}}{\text{Total retail \$}} \times 100$$

Net Cost

$$\text{Net cost \$} = \text{Billed cost \$} - \text{Cash discount \$}$$

$$\text{Net cost \$} = \text{List price \$} - \text{Trade discount(s) \$} - \text{Cash discount \$}$$

Net Profit

$$\text{Net profit} = \text{Net sales} - \text{Cost of goods sold} - \text{Operating expenses}$$

$$\text{Net operating profit or net profit} = \text{Gross margin} - \text{All operating expenses}$$

$$\text{Net profit \$} = \text{Net profit \%} \times \text{Net sales \$}$$

$$\text{Net profit \%} = \frac{\text{Net profit \$}}{\text{Net sales \$}} \times 100$$

Net Sales

$$\text{Net sales \$} = \text{Gross sales \$} - \text{Customer returns and allowances \$}$$

Number of Weeks of Supply

$$\text{Number of weeks of supply} = \frac{\text{\# Weeks in time period}}{\text{Turnover for the time period}}$$

Open-to-Buy (OTB)

$$\text{OTB} = \begin{array}{c}\text{Planned purchases}\\\text{for the month}\end{array} - \begin{array}{c}\text{Outstanding orders to be}\\\text{delivered that month}\end{array}$$

$$\begin{array}{c}\text{OTB for balance}\\\text{of month}\end{array} = \begin{array}{c}\text{Planned purchases}\\\text{for month}\end{array} - \begin{array}{c}\text{Merchandise}\\\text{received to date}\end{array} - \begin{array}{c}\text{Merchandise}\\\text{on order}\end{array}$$

$$\begin{array}{c}\text{OTB for}\\\text{balance}\\\text{of month}\end{array} = \begin{array}{c}\text{Planned}\\\text{EOM}\\\text{stock}\end{array} + \begin{array}{c}\text{Planned}\\\text{sales for}\\\text{balance}\\\text{of month}\end{array} + \begin{array}{c}\text{Planned}\\\text{markdowns}\\\text{for balance}\\\text{of month}\end{array} - \begin{array}{c}\text{Actual}\\\text{stock}\\\text{on hand}\end{array} - \begin{array}{c}\text{On}\\\text{order}\end{array}$$

Operating Expenses

$$\text{Operating expenses} = \text{Direct expenses} + \text{Indirect expenses}$$

$$\text{Operating expenses \$} = \text{Operating expenses \%} \times \text{Net sales \$}$$

$$\text{Operating expenses \%} = \frac{\text{Direct and indirect expenses in dollars}}{\text{Net sales \$}} \times 100$$

Planned Purchases

$$\begin{array}{c}\text{Planned monthly}\\\text{purchases at}\\\text{retail}\end{array} = \begin{array}{c}\text{Planned}\\\text{EOM}\\\text{stock}\end{array} + \begin{array}{c}\text{Planned}\\\text{sales for}\\\text{month}\end{array} + \begin{array}{c}\text{Planned}\\\text{markdowns}\\\text{for month}\end{array} - \begin{array}{c}\text{Planned}\\\text{BOM}\\\text{stock}\end{array}$$

$$\begin{array}{c}\text{Planned monthly}\\\text{purchase at cost}\end{array} = \text{Planned retail purchases} \times (100\% - \text{Planned markup \%})$$

$$\text{Purchase balance} = \begin{array}{c}\text{Total planned (pieces,}\\\text{retail, cost, or markup \%)}\end{array} - \text{Purchases to date}$$

Retail

$$\text{Retail \$} = \text{Cost \$} + \text{Markup \$}$$

$$\text{Retail \%} = \text{Cost \%} + \text{Markup \%}$$

$$\text{Retail \$} = \frac{\text{Cost \$}}{\text{Cost \%}} = \frac{\text{Cost \$}}{100\% - \text{Markup \%}}$$

$$\text{Average retail stock/inventory} = \frac{\text{Planned sales for period}}{\text{Turnover rate}}$$

$$\text{Average retail stock/inventory} = \frac{\text{Sum of beginning inventories + Ending inventory for given period}}{\text{Number of inventories}}$$

$$\text{Retail reduction \%} = \frac{\text{Initial markup \%} - \text{Maintained markup \%}}{\text{Sales (100\%)} - \text{Initial markup \%}}$$

Sales

$$\text{Sales increase \% or decrease \%} = \frac{\text{This year (TY) planned sales \$} - \text{Last year (LY) actual sales \$}}{\text{LY actual sales \$}} \times 100$$

$$\text{Seasonal planned sales} = \text{LY sales \$} + \text{Dollar increase}$$

$$\text{Dollar increase} = \text{LY sales \$} \times \text{Planned increase \%}$$

or

$$\text{Seasonal planned sales} = \text{LY sales \$} - \text{Dollar decrease}$$

$$\text{Dollar decrease} = \text{LY sales \$} \times \text{Planned decrease \%}$$

Sell Through Percentage

$$\text{Sell through \%} = \frac{\text{Units sold in a week (Sunday–Saturday)}}{\text{Beginning units on hand for a week (Sunday)}} \times 100$$

Shortage or Overage

$$\text{Shortage (or overage) \$} = \text{Closing book inventory at retail \$} - \text{Physical inventory count at retail \$}$$

$$\text{Shortage \%} = \frac{\text{Shortage \$}}{\text{Annual net sales \$}} \times 100$$

$$\text{Planned dollar shortage} = \text{Planned shortage percentage} \times \text{Planned net sales \$}$$

Stock Ratios

$$\text{Stock-to-sales ratio} = \frac{\text{Retail stock at given time in the period}}{\text{Sales for the period}}$$

$$\text{Planned stock} = \text{Average weekly sales} \times \text{Number of weeks of supply}$$

$$\text{BOM stock} = \text{Planned monthly sales} \times \text{Stock-sales ratio}$$

$$\text{BOM stock} = \text{Basic stock} + \text{Planned sales for the month}$$

Turnover

$$\text{Turnover} = \frac{\text{Net sales for period}}{\text{Average retail stock for the same period}}$$

Weeks of Supply

$$\text{Weeks of supply} = \frac{\text{Beginning units on hand for a week (Sunday)}}{\text{Units sold in that week (Sunday–Saturday)}}$$

GLOSSARY OF TERMS

Additional markup Adjustment that raises the price on merchandise already in stock.

Advanced dating A type of dating in which the invoice date is advanced so that additional time is allowed for payment. If a seasonal discount has been offered, advanced dating is often put in place so that the additional cash discount may be applied.

Allowance to customer A partial refund or credit compensating for a merchandising deficiency, such as missing buttons, dry cleaning, and so on.

Alteration and workroom costs A charge to a selling department when it is necessary to put merchandise in condition for sale (e.g., assembling, polishing, making cuffs).

Anticipation A discount earned by retailers, under certain conditions, for the payment of invoices prior to the expiration of the cash discount period.

Assortment planning (classification planning) Segmentation of a department's business based on related product categories.

Average cost The proportioning of different cost amounts that can carry retail prices that achieve the desired markup percentage.

Average dollar per sale or transaction (ADT) The retail sales an associate secures divided by the number of transactions.

Average retail Price that will achieve a desired markup percentage.

Average retail stock/inventory Sum of retail inventories at the beginning of each year, season, month, or week.

Average stock The total of BOM dollar inventory figures divided by the number of stocks considered.

Averaging or balancing markups The adjustment of the proportions of goods purchased at different markups. A composite of the relationship between all cost and retail for a department or grouping of goods during a specified time.

Averaging retails The proportioning of different retail prices on purchases that may have two or more costs to achieve a desired markup percentage.

Balance sheet A statement that summarizes the total assets, liabilities, and net worth of a business.

Basic stock method Stock size using a constant basic stock figure with a turnover rate.

Billed cost The manufacturer's price for goods offered to a retailer.

BOM stock The beginning of the month stock figure in dollars.

Book inventory (maintained inventory) Statistical records that show the value at retail of goods on hand at a given time.

Build A figure that provides the comparison as a percentage change between two periods of time. Also referred to as percentage change, acceleration, or trend.

Cash discount A percentage or dollar amount deducted from the cost of goods for conformance to prearranged terms of payment of an invoice between the vendor and retailer.

Charge-back Form on which the amounts of merchandise returned to resources by retailer for credit or refund is recorded.

Closing book inventory The value of merchandise in stock at the end of an accounting period. It can be expressed in cost or retail.

Closing physical stock/inventory The retail value of aggregate retail prices of a stock determined by a physical count at the end of a designated time period.

Complement The difference between 100 and any number less than 100 (e.g., the complement of 60 is 40).

Compounding markdowns An additional reduction to a markdown offered to the customer at point-of-sale (e.g., coupons).

Contribution or controllable margin The technique that evaluates the buyer's performance based on those expenses that are direct, controllable, or a combination of direct and controllable expenses. It is the amount a department contributes to indirect expenses and profit.

Controllable expenses Many, but not all, direct expenses are controllable. See *Direct expenses*.

Cost The amount a retailer pays a resource for purchases.

Cost complement The amount paid for a purchase, which can be calculated when dollar markup is subtracted from retail.

Cost of goods (merchandise) sold (COGS) The cost of merchandise that has been sold during a given period.

Cumulative markup The markup percentage achieved on all goods available for sale from the beginning of a given period. It is the markup in dollars or percentages obtained on the accumulated inventory at the beginning of the given period, plus the markup of all the new purchases received season-to-date.

Customer allowance The amount of reduction in price the customer has been given before a sale has been made.

Customer returns Dollar amount value returned to retailer by customer for credit or refund.

Customer returns and allowances Dollar amount value of credits or refunds when customers return merchandise to the retailer.

Dating An agreement specifying the time period for payment of an invoice.

Debit memo form A record of an accounting debt.

Department A grouping of related merchandise for which common records are kept.

Direct expenses Expenses that exist only within a given department and cease if that department is discontinued (e.g., department advertising).

Discount date The date by which an invoice must be paid to take advantage of the discount granted.

Discount period The period of time when a buyer can deduct discounts negotiated from the invoice.

DOI (date of invoice) dating Payment terms based on the invoice date.

Dollar merchandise plan A "road map" indicating projected sales, stocks, markdowns, and purchases, as well as the desired markups, usually prepared biannually in advance of the selling season.

EDP (electronic data processing) The planned conversion of factors (as by the computer) into storable form to achieve a desired result.

Employee discount A percentage deducted from a regular retail price as a courtesy to employees of a retail organization and is considered a "retail reduction."

EOM End of month. Usually designates dollar value of stock at the end of a month.

EOM dating Computation of the cash discount period from the end of the month in which the invoice is dated rather than from the date of the invoice itself.

EOM stock End-of-month stock. Usually designates dollar value of stock at the end of a month.

Everyday Low Price (EDLP) or Everyday Value Price (EDVP) Pricing strategies used by retailers to provide a lower value price to the consumer.

Expenses The overhead of doing business (e.g., salaries, rent, advertising, delivery, utilities).

Extra dating A specific number of days granted during which a discount may be taken.

Final profit and loss statement The basic profit factors (i.e., sales, cost of goods, and expenses) are developed in detail so that every transaction is clearly seen.

Final selling price Price received when an item is sold. Also called *new retail price*.

Flash report Daily report indicating sales amount.

FOB (free-on-board) A way of expressing who is responsible for payment of transportation and the point at which title is transferred.

FOB city or port of destination An arrangement in which the vendor pays transportation charges to a specific city or destination.

FOB factory An arrangement in which the retailer pays transportation.

FOB retailer An arrangement in which the resource pays transportation.

GMROI (gross margin return on investment) The relationship between the average inventory at cost and gross margin. Gross margin divided by average inventory at cost.

Gross margin The remainder after subtracting total cost of goods sold from the total retail amount of sales. Also called *gross profit*. The difference between net sales and the cost of goods sold.

Gross markdown Original price reduction.

Gross sales Retail value of total initial sales prior to deduction of dollar amount returned by customers.

Income statement See *Profit and loss statement*.

Indirect expenses Expenses that consist of some store expenses, which are prorated to all selling departments on the basis of sales volume.

Initial cumulative markup A departmental goal used in planning monthly and/or seasonal markups, expressed as a dollar amount or percentage.

Initial markup or original markup The difference between the cost of goods and the original retail price. The first price placed on merchandise for resale. Planned markups specified on orders for merchandise; a projected markup goal.

Initial or original retail The first price placed on merchandise for sale before any markdowns are taken.

Inventory (n.) Synonymous with the term "stock."

Inventory (v.) To actively count and record quantities of merchandise.

Invoice A bill presented by a vendor to a retailer for goods purchased.

Inward freight The amount charged for transporting merchandise to designated premises (e.g., trucking, freight, postage, etc.). Charges are paid by either vendor or retailer according to an agreement between them at the time of purchase.

Journal or purchase record Consolidated listing of purchases by invoice amounts, transportation charges, discounts, vendors, and so on.

List price A theoretical retail price set by manufacturers.

Loading Intentionally increasing the amount of the invoice to a price that would allow a theoretically greater cash discount, but which results in paying the net amount that the vendor quotes.

LY Last year.

Maintained book inventory See *Book inventory*.

Maintained markup (MMU) The difference between the cost of goods and the actual selling price of the merchandise sold.

Markdown (MD) A reduction in retail price. The lowering or reducing of any retail price on one item or group of items. The difference between the original or present retail price and the new retail price. Taken in dollars or as a percentage. Can be expressed as a percentage as well as a dollar amount.

Markdown cancellation The restoration of a markdown price to the former retail.

Markdown journalization The depreciation in value that a retailer journalizes based on markdowns taken.

Markdown percentage Markdown expressed as a percentage of net sales.

Markup (MU) The difference between cost and retail price, expressed either in dollars or as a percentage.

Markup cancellation A downward price adjustment that offsets an original inflated markup.

Markup percentage Markup expressed as a percentage of net sales.

Merchandise loans Goods given temporarily to another department or division for purposes other than resale, such as display.

Merchandise plan A combination of a dollar merchandise plan and an assortment plan.

Merchandise transfers Goods "bought or sold" internally, from one department to another, for purposes of resale to the ultimate consumer.

Net What remains when nothing more is to be taken away.

Net cost When no additional discounts are earned on merchandise purchased.

Net loss When the operating expenses are greater than the gross margin.

Net markdown Difference between gross markdown and markdown cancellation.

Net payment date The date by which an invoice must be paid to acquire a favorable credit rating and avoid late penalties.

Net period Span of time between expiration of eligibility for a cash discount and start of the penalty period.

Net profit The difference between gross margin and operating expenses. Also called *net operating profit*.

Net sales The sales total after customer returns and allowances have been deducted from gross sales.

Net terms A condition of sale in which a cash discount is neither offered nor permitted.

New retail price See *Final selling price*.

On order Unfilled orders, also known as open orders.

Opening book inventory The value of merchandise in stock at the beginning of an accounting period. It can be expressed at retail or at cost.

Opening inventory The retail value of merchandise in stock.

Open-to-buy (OTB) The amount of unspent money available for purchasing merchandise.

Operating expenses Disbursals incurred in running an organization. There are two types, direct and indirect.

Operating income In retailing, this is the net sales.

Ordinary dating See *Regular dating*.

Outdate The last date that a buyer plans for merchandise to be available for sale to a customer.

Overage Dollar difference between book stock figure and physical count when the latter is the larger of the two.

Percentage change Comparison between two different points in time. See *Build*.

Permanent (physical) markdown Merchandise price is changed permanently on the price ticket, therefore reducing the inventory value.

Perpetual inventory See *Book inventory*.

Physical inventory The retail dollar value of all goods physically present in a periodic stock count.

Planned purchases Also known as planned receipts, the dollar amount of merchandise that can be brought into a stock during a given period.

Planned receipts See *Planned purchases.*

Point-of-sale (POS) markdown Temporary markdown taken either in percentage off or dollars off when an item is being sold.

POS Point-of-sale.

Postdating See *Advanced dating.*

Prepaid Payment of transportation charges by vendor when merchandise is shipped.

Prestige price zone Refers to the high price lines in a stock assortment.

Price change form Form on which markdowns, markdown cancellation, additional markups, and markup cancellation, or any price change made, is recorded.

Price changes Any change in the price of merchandise.

Price line A predetermined retail figure or a specific price point that is aimed at a specific customer market segment.

Price lining The predetermination of retail prices at which an assortment of merchandise will be carried.

Price range The spread from highest to lowest price lines.

Price zone Series of price lines likely to appeal to one group of a store's customers. These can be referred to as volume, promotional, or prestige price zones.

Profit The dollar amount remaining after costs and expenses are paid.

Profit and loss statement Statement prepared periodically by either department, store, or organization that summarizes the basic merchandising factors that affect profit results. Also called an *income statement.*

Promotional price zone Refers to the lower price lines in a stock assortment.

Purchase record A form used to preserve information about merchandise bought.

Quantity discount (QD) A percentage deduction from billed cost allowable when the dollar or unit amount on an order for goods (or a cumulative figure for a period of time) falls within certain predesignated limits.

Reduction Anything that lowers the ultimate price that the retailer receives for merchandise, including markdowns, customer returns and allowances, and shortages.

Regular dating Discount date calculated from date of invoice. Also called *ordinary dating.*

Remit or remittance Payment.

Retail Price at which stores offer merchandise for sale.

Retail (4-5-4) fiscal calendar Accounting calendar used to plan retail metrics from one time period to another.

Retail merchandising The science of offering goods to the ultimate consumer at the right price, in the right form, at the right location, and at an appropriate time.

Retail method of inventory An accounting system used in retail stores that values merchandising at current retail prices that can then be converted to cost value by markup formula.

Retail price The price at which goods are ultimately sold to the consumer.

Retail reduction Markdowns plus stock shortages and employee discounts.

Return to vendor (RTV) Amount of merchandise returned to a vendor for refund or credit.

ROG dating Receipt of goods used in dating terms to denote the beginning of a discount period.

Sales volume Indicates in dollars how much merchandise has been sold.

Season letter A code letter indicating the date of an item's entry into stock.

Sell through percentage (ST%) Formula that calculates how fast or slow merchandise is selling, usually calculated on a week-to-week basis.

Shortage Dollar difference between closing book inventory and physical inventory count figures, when the former is the larger of the two.

Shrinkage Lessening of retail value of stock-on-hand, generally due to theft or breakage. See *Shortage.*

Six-month seasonal dollar merchandise plan A budget scheduling the planned month-by-month sales, the amount of stock planned for each of these months, and the projected reductions.

Skeletal profit and loss statement A quick method to determine profit or loss at any given time.

Stock Goods on hand at a given time, expressed as a unit or dollar amount.

Stock keeping unit (SKU) Product identification for a vendor/label, style, size, and color being sold by a retail store.

Stock-to-sales ratio The proportion between the BOM stock figure and the dollar amount of sales for the same month.

Terms of sale Arrangement between merchandise source or vendor and retailer relative to time period of invoice, cost of merchandise, shipping charges, and transportation arrangements.

Total cost of goods purchased Combined cost of merchandise purchased and inward freight charges.

Total cost of goods sold Results from subtracting cash discounts and adding alteration and workroom costs to the gross cost of merchandise sold (total merchandise handled less the cost of the closing inventory).

Total merchandise handled Opening inventory at cost plus new purchases at cost plus inward freight, or the sum of the opening inventory that is all merchandise available for sale plus the total cost of the purchases.

Trade discount A percentage or series of percentages deducted from a list price, thereby determining cost price.

Transfer Change of ownership of merchandise between departments or stores.

Turnover (turn) The number of times the average retail stock has been sold and replaced.

TY This year.

Units per sale or transaction (UPT) A figure based on the average number of units sold by the associate divided by the number of transactions.

Vendor A merchandise resource such as a manufacturer, importer, jobber, distributor, and so on.

Vendor analysis An investigation of the profitability of each vendor's products sold by a retailer.

Volume The retail value of sales for a given period, usually expressed annually. See *Sales volume*.

Volume price zone A series of price lines generally in the middle price lines, where the largest percentage of sales occur.

Weeks of supply (WOS) (used in markdown calculations) The calculation to determine how many weeks of product are left to sell out completely.

Weeks of supply method A method of planning stock size on a weekly basis.

Workroom charges A charge to a selling department when it is necessary to put merchandise in condition for sale (e.g., assembling, polishing, putting on cuffs, etc.). See *Alteration and workroom costs*.

SELECTED ANSWERS

CHAPTER 1: MERCHANDISING FOR A PROFIT

Operating Income

1. 5.0%
3. $905,000
5. (a) $44,700; (b) $253,300
7. $2,488,640
9. (a) $635,380; (b) Sales are the same for this year as last year.
11. $180,000
13. Casual sneakers, $40,500; athletic sneakers, $28,800
15. Small leather goods, $570,000; handbags, $630,000
17. 9.1%

Cost of Goods Sold

19. $2,677.50
21. $18,252
23. (a) $33,400; (b) $2,672; (c) $32,548
25. $59,045.00
27. (a) $1,374.00; (b) $1,420.26

Gross Margin

29. $194,800, 38.2%
31. $62,060, 44.3%

Operating Expenses

33. (a) TY: $178,000, 36.0%
    Plan: $170,000, 32.9%
    LY: $177,000, 39.3%
    (b) TY vs. Plan: −4.3%
    TY vs. LY: +10.0%

Skeletal Profit and Loss Statements

35. COGS: $735,500, 57.0%
    GM: 43.0%
    Expenses: $450,700, 34.9%
    Profit: 8.1%
37. Net sales: $2,140,000, 100%
    COGS: $1,605,000, 75.0%
    Expenses: 26.9%
    Loss: –$40,000, –1.9%
39. (a) COGS: $9,000; (b) Expenses: 41.25%, or 41.3%
41. Expenses: $38,400, 48.0%
43. Net sales: $220,000, 100%
    COGS and GM: $110,000, 50.0%
    Expenses: $104,500
45. COGS: 52.9%
    GM: $40,000, 47.1%
    Expenses: $38,300, 45.1%
    Profit: 2.0%
47. COGS: $622,400, 47.9%
    GM: $677,600, 52.1%
    Expenses: $499,000, 38.4%
    Profit: $178,600, 13.7%

Final Profit and Loss Statements

49. Profit: $3,000, 1.62%; Gross margin: $85,000
51. Net sales: $222,200, 100%; COGS: $120,600, 54.3%; GM: $101,600, 45.7%;
    OE: $98,000, 44.1%; Profit: $3,600, 1.6%

CHAPTER 2: RETAIL PRICING AND REPRICING OF MERCHANDISE

Retail Pricing

3. $67.00
5. $599.99
7. $20.75
9. $22.00
11. $35.40
13. $25.20, 70.0%
15. $79.00, 53.0%

Markup

17. $40.94
19. $121.50
21. $9.14
23. (a) $28.70; (b) $14.94; (c) $7.70
25. $34.00
27. $99.34; Strategies: $99.00/$99.99/$100.00
29. $14.91; Strategies: $14.99/$15.00

Cumulative Markup for a Purchase

31. 48.7%
33. 68.1%
35. (a) Vendor A: $29.25 or $175,500, 54.2%; (b) Vendor B: $28.00 or $201,600, 57.1%; (c) CMU: 55.7%
37. (a) Crew neck: $47.50 or $570,000, 60.1%; (b) V-neck: $57.50 or $460,000, 64.6%; (c) CMU: 62.0%

Cumulative Markup Applications

39. (a) $25.00; (b) $10.83
41. (a) $69.99; (b) $30.94
43. $5,440 overspent; you have no retail dollars left

Repricing of Merchandise/Markdowns

45. $29.01
47. $22.77 MD, $46.23
49.

	MD $	Total MD $	MD % to customer
(a)	$10.01	$12,762.75	33.4%
(b)	$39.01	$18,724.80	26.2%
(c)	$49.02	$17,157.00	24.6%
(d)	$39.05	$28,116.00	56.6%

Planned and Actual Markdowns

51. 49.4%
53. 40.0%
55. $153,300
57. (a) $17,405; (b) $3,595 underspent
59. $2,880 under plan; actual MD % 52.9%
61. Answers will vary.

Compounding of Markdowns

63. (a) $31.86; (b) 46.0%; (c) 85.2%

Point-of-Sale Markdowns

65. (a) $1,150.90; (b) $2,249.10; (c) 51.2%
67. (a) $3,175.00; (b) $9,525.00; (c) 33.3%
69. (a) $55,206; (b) $86,694; (c) 63.7%; (d) $6,206 overspent

Permanent Markdowns

71. (a) $5,200.00; (b) $11,296.90; (c) 46.0%
73. (a) $116,750.50; (b) $226,554.25; (c) 51.5%

Weeks of Supply, Sell through %, and Build

75. (a) WOS: 15.0, ST %: 6.7%
    (b) WOS: 9.3, ST %: 10.7%, Build: 50.0%, MD % to customer: 20.0%, MD % to journal: 25.0%
    (c) WOS: 10.0, ST %: 10.0%, Build: –16.7%
    (d) WOS: 3.8, ST %: 26.7%, Build: 140.0%, MD % to customer: 50.0%, MD % to journal: 100.0%

CHAPTER 3: BASIC MARKUP EQUATIONS USED IN MERCHANDISING DECISIONS

Initial Markup Concepts

1. 51.4%
3. 60.5%

Calculating Initial Markup

5. 53.0%
7. 53.8%
9. 50.4%

Cumulative Markup

11. 63.7%
13. (a) 55.3%; (b) 54.9%
15. 50.1%

Maintained Markup

17. 37.3%
19. 48.9% for both
21. 13.4%

Average Costs

23. (a) $7,020; (b) $2.93
25. $1,774.50
27. $36.57

Average Retail

29. $67.00
31. $68.03, Pricing strategies: $68.00/$68.50/$69.00

Average Markup Percentage

33. 63.5%
35. 55.4%
37. (a) $33.39; (b) 53.1%; (c) 58.3%

CHAPTER 4: THE RETAIL METHOD OF INVENTORY

Maintaining a Perpetual Book Inventory Figure

1. $62,875.00
3. $851,000
5. (a) $48,000; (b) $22,080
7. $102,000
9. $3,346; answers will vary
11. (a) $1,547,000; (b) $560,014
13. $311,000

Shortages and Overages

15. (a) $238; (b) 2.1%; (c) 3.0%
17. 2.8%
19. $185,000 shortage, 2.7%
21. 2.6% shortage

23. 3.1% overage
25. $595
27. (a) $2,528,000; (b) $128,000 shortage; (c) 2.3% shortage

CHAPTER 5: SIX-MONTH PLANNING AND COMPONENTS

Planning Sales

1. 10.0%
3. $477,432
5. $864,570
7. $2,602,500
9. −6.5%
11. Total Spring season sales: $120,000

February	$14,400
March	$16,800
April	$18,000
May	$32,400
June	$27,600
July	$10,800

13. −20.0%
15. 8.0%

Sales per Square Foot

17. $556.25
19. $492,750

Calculating Average Retail Stock, Turnover, and GMROI

21. 3.30
23. $54,000
25. $80,000.00
27. $300,000.00
29. $29,862
31. .40
33. $76,000
35. 2.10
37. 2.10
39. (a) $4,525; (b) $9,695; (c) $3,897.39; (d) $1,985; (e) .47; (f) $0.51; (g) 43.9%
41. $1.90
43. LY: $2.42, TY: $2.67; $0.25 improvement

Calculating Stock-Sales Ratios

45. 2.1
47. $66,000
49. 9.7
51. $392,950

Finding Weeks of Supply

53. $1,554,300 or $1,551,000
55. $243,750 or $244,500
57. $48,133.44 or $48,211.20
59. 17.93, or 17.9

Using Basic Stock Method

61. $2,000,000
63. $235,440
65. $430,000
67. February $49,305
     March $53,745
     April $55,965
     May $57,297
     June $66,021
     July $48,417

Planned Purchases

69. $4,160,000
71. $428,000
73. $63,855
75. (a) $21,000; (b) $7,560
77. (a) $146,000; (b) $58,400
79. (a) $195,000; (b) $190,000

Calculating Retail Open-to-Buy

81. –$5,900 overspent; the buyer has no receipt dollars left to spend
83. –$62,000 overspent
85. $9,250
87. (a) $39,875; (b) $768.75

CHAPTER 6: INVOICE MATHEMATICS: TERMS OF SALE

Discounts

1. $122.50
3. Competitor B, $36.50 difference
5. $972.00

Dating

7. (a) $522.00; (b) $1,503.36
9. $624.00
11. May 11
13. (a) $3,026.80; (b) $3,026.80
15. June 18, $5,796

INDEX

Page numbers in italics refer to figures.

A

additional markups, 89
advanced dating, 347–348
allowances, customer. *See* Customer
  returns and allowances
alteration and workroom costs, 6, 13
annual merchandise plan worksheet,
  281
anticipation, 349
assortment planning, 314
average dollars per sale or transaction,
  191
average inventory, 246–249
average retail stock, 226, 242–246
averaging costs, 151–152
averaging markups, 150–163
  by cost averaging, 151–152
  defined, 150
  with known retail and planned
    markup, 155–156
  principles, 150–151
  by retail price averaging, 153–154
averaging retail, 153–155

B

balance sheets, 30
balancing markups. *See* Averaging
  markups
basic stock method of stock planning,
  266–268

(B-continued, right column)

beginning of month (BOM) stock, 241,
  266–268
billed cost, 12
book inventory
  calculating at retail, 180
  calculating at stock, 181
  defined, 176
  formulas, 174
book stock, 179, 204
branch price change form, *108*
build, 107
buyer evaluation, 48
buyer's price change worksheet, *186*

C

cash discounts
  anticipation type, 349
  in cost of goods sold calculation, 13
  dating and, 342
  defined, 6
charge-back to vendor forms, *189*
classification planning, 314–315
closing physical stock, 177
comparable store sales, 12
compounding of markdowns, 95, 115
computer price change entry, *187*
contribution operating statement, *17*
controllable and noncontrollable
  expenses, 16
controllable margin, 16

cost of goods (merchandise) sold, 12–13
    decreasing, for improved profits, 337
    defined, 12, 13, 217
    formulas, 13–14
    retail method of inventory valuation, 217–219
cost complement, 70
cost percentage, 54
costs, averaging, 151–152
credit slip, POS, *100*
cumulative markup, 71–73, 276
customer returns, 5
customer returns and allowances, 7–11
    defined, 5, 7–8
    formulas, 2, 9

D

daily exception selling price report, *191*, 191
daily flash sheets, *234*
date, discount, 344
dating, 342–348
    advance dating, 347–348
    common practices, 342
    different types of, 343–348
    DOI dating, 347
    EOM dating, 346
    extra dating, 345
    regular dating, 344
    ROG dating, 346–347
    summary of types and examples, 348
debit memo form, *189*
department store typical monthly sales, *234*
direct expenses, 6, 36
discount date, 343, *348. See also* Dating
discounts, employee, 61, 102, 195
discounts, trade, 334–335
discounts, types of, 334–337
district flash sales forms, *194*
DOI dating, 347
dollar inventory, 246–250
dollar merchandise plan, 228

dollar planning
    case study, 330
    markdowns in, 275–276
    markups in, 276–278
    objectives of, 228
    procedure, 228

E

employee discounts, 61, 102, 195
end of month (EOM) dating, 346
end of month (EOM) stock, 241
errors, clerical, 205
everyday low price or everyday value price, 56–57
exception selling price report, daily, 191, *191*
expenses, controlling, case study, 50
expenses, operating. *See* Operating expenses
expenses, reducing, 47
extra dating, 345

F

final profit and loss statements, 33–36
flash sales forms, district, *194*
flash sheets, daily, *234*
FOB shipping charges, 349
forms, retail method of inventory, 182–195
    buyer's price change worksheet, *186*
    charge-back to vendor forms, *189*
    daily exception selling price report, *191*
    debit memo form, *189*
    district flash sales by group, *194*
    district flash sales by store, *194*
    outstanding transfer list form, *184*
    price change entry, *187*
    price change forms, 186–187
    purchase records, 182–184
    return to vendor authorization and worksheet, *190*
    sales and productivity report, *192*
    sales reports, *191–194*
    shipment summary, *185*

specific departments by
classification form, *188*
weekly sales challenge recap, *193*
free-on-board shipping charges, 349
freight inward, 6, 13

G

GMROI, 226, 247–250
gross margin, 14–16
   defined, 5, 36
   determining, by dollar inventory,
     246–250
   formulas, 3, 14
   retail method of inventory
     valuation, 217–219
   return on investment (GMROI),
     226, 247–250
   on stock plus purchases,
     calculating, *217*
gross profit. *See* Gross margin
gross profit percentage, planning,
   277–278
gross sales, 3, 5, 7

I

income, operating. *See* Net sales
income statements. *See* Profit and loss
   statements
indirect expenses, 6, 15–16
individual first-of-the-month stock
   figures, 263–264
individual item pricing, 58
initial markup, 131–135
   calculating, 62–63
   defined, 131
   factors in considering, 131–132
   method for establishing, 132–133
   percentage formulas, 130, 134–135
   sample problems, 141–143
inventory
   average, 243–249
   control, 174
   investment efficiency, 247
   physical, 176–177
   retail method of. *See* Retail method
     of inventory

inventory turnover. *See* Turnover, stock
invoice payment date. *See* Dating
inward freight, 6, 13

J

journal of purchase record, *183*
justification of pricing strategy, 127

K

key performance indicators (KPIs),
   11–12

L

linear foot, sales per, 12
loading, 349
loss, physical merchandise, 205

M

maintained inventory. *See* Book
   inventory
maintained markup, 137–140
   defined, 137
   percentage formulas, 130, 140
margin, gross. *See* Gross margin
margin results, buyer, 48
markdowns, 90–102
   amount of, 90–91
   cancellations, calculating, 100–101
   causes of, 91–92
   compounding, 95, 115
   defined, 90
   dollar calculations, 95–98
   formulas, 54
   journalization, 99–102
   net, calculating, 101–102
   percentage, calculating, 98
   permanent, 103–105
   planned amount, calculating,
     97–98
   planning, 275–276
   point-of-sale (POS), 103–105
   purposes of, 91
   receipt, POS, *100*
   second markdown, calculating,
     95–96
   timing of, 92–93

markup dollar calculations
    cost calculations, 62
    vs. percentage calculations,
        164–165
    retail price calculations, 61
markup percentage equations, 68–77
    on cost, 68–70
    cumulative markups, 76–77
    vs. dollar calculations, 164–165
    formulas, 130
    on a group of items with varying
        prices or costs, 75–76
    with individual cost and individual
        retail, 72–73
    initial markups, 133
    maintained markup, 137–139, 140
    on retail using retail method of
        inventory, 68
markups
    additional, 89
    averaging or balancing, 150–157
    cancellations, 89
    case studies, 166–171
    cumulative markup, 71–73, 276
    formulas, 54, 130
    initial markup, 131–135
    maintained markup, 137–139
    percentage vs. dollar calculations,
        164–165
    planning, 276–278
merchandise plan, 280
merchandise plan worksheet, annual,
    281
merchandise statistics reports,
    285–289, 287
merchandising, profitable pricing in, 30
merchandising for profit case study,
    49–52
monthly sales distribution, department
    store, 234

N
net cost, 337–341
    all formulas, 3
    billed cost and cash discount
        formula, 337

list price and cash discount
        formula, 338
    list price and quality discount
        formula, 339
    quantity and cash discount
        formula, 336
net loss. See Net operating profit
net operating profit
    defined, 5, 31
    formulas, 31
    inventory valuation and, 219
    results, buyer, 48
net payment dates, 344
net profit. See Net operating profit
net sales, 9–11
    defined, 5–6, 9
    formulas, 2–3
    shortages and overages as
        percentage of, 207
    volume, comparing percentages
        of, 31
net terms, 342
number of weeks of supply, 265

O
on order, 296
opening book inventory, 178
open-to-buy (OTB)
    case study, 324
    defined, 228, 296
    formulas, 226
    reports, 299
    reports, explanation of, 299–303
    retail calculating, beginning of
        month, 304
    retail calculating, during month,
        304–305
operating expenses
    defined, 5, 36
    direct expenses, 36
    formulas, 3
    indirect expenses, 36
operating income. See Net sales
operating profit, net. See Net operating
    profit
ordinary dating, 344

original markup. *See* Initial markup

OTB. *See* Open-to-buy (OTB)

outdate, 106

Outstanding Transfer List Form, *184*

overage, 177. *See also* Shortages and
overages

P

payment dates, net, 344

percent change formula, 96–97

performance, sales, 11–12

permanent markdowns, 104–105

perpetual book inventory, 178–179

physical inventory, 176

    in calculating shortages or
overages, 174

    company averages, 267

    count sheet, 177

plan, annual merchandise worksheet,
281

plan sales comparison, 11

planned gross profit percentage,
277–278

planned purchases, 279–289

    adjusting, 285

    case study, 327–329

    at cost, calculating, 280

    formulas, 226, 279, 280

    monthly purchases at retail, 279

    purpose of, 279

    six-month seasonal dollar
merchandise plans, 303–305

planned receipts. *See* planned
purchases

planning sales, 229–236

planning stocks. *See* Stock planning

point of sale (POS) markdown,
100–101

POS credit slip, *100*

POS markdown receipt, *100*

postdating, 347–348

prestige price zone, 57

price, retail, 58, 59, 61, 153–155

price change entry, *187*

price change forms, 186–188

price change printout, *108*

price change procedures, 108

price change worksheet, buyer's, *186*

price lining, 56–58

    price line reports, 59

    report by classification, *60*

    strategy advantages, 59

    structure chart, *57*

price range, 56

price zone, 57

pricing, 56–62

    case studies, 125–127

    factors influencing, 59

    factors relationship, 59

    formulas, 54–55

    price line structuring, 56–58

    profit and, 47

profit, net. *See* net profit

profit and loss statements, 30–36, *34*

    analysis case study, 51

    basic format of, 30

    components of, 35–36

    final, 33–34

    skeletal, 31–32

profits

    approaches to increasing, 45–47

    calculations, use and importance
of, 4

    merchandising for, case study,
49–52

    pricing factors and, 78

    repricing and, 109

promotional price zone, 57

purchase planning. *See* planned
purchases

purchase records, 182–184, *183*

R

receipt of goods (ROG) dating,
346–347

receipts, planned. *See* planned
purchases

records, purchase, 182–184, *183*

reductions, price. *See* Markdowns

regular dating, 344

reports, merchandise statistics,
285–286, *287*

reports, price line, 59, *60*

repricing, 90, 93, 109

retail fiscal (4-5-4) calendar, *230*

retail method of inventory, 174–223

    advantages of, 216

    book inventory calculations, 180–182

    case studies, 221–223

    cost of goods sold and gross margin, finding, 217–219

    defined, 175

    forms used in, 182–195

    formulas, 174

    limitations of, 216

    net profit calculation, 219

    principles of, 176

retail open-to-buy (OTB)

    calculating, beginning of month, 304

    calculating, during month, 304–305

    formulas, 304–305

retail price, 5–6, 58–59, 130

retail pricing. *See* pricing

retail reduction, 102

retail store function, 4

return to vendor authorization and worksheet, *190*

returns, customer. *See* Customer returns and allowances

ROG dating, 346–347

S

sales, gross. *See* Gross sales

sales, year-to-date, 11

sales and productivity report, *191*

sales increase percentage, 231–232

sales per square or linear foot, 12

sales performance, 11–12

sales planning, 229–236

sales reports, 191, *191–192*

    daily exception selling price report, 191, *191*

    district flash sales by group, 191, *194*

    district flash sales by store, 191, *194*

    sales and productivity report, *192*

    weekly sales challenge recap, *193*

sales results, buyer, 48

sales volume. *See* Net sales

sales volume, basic, 5

same store sales, 12

seasonal markdowns, 227, 275

seasonal planned sales

    annual merchandise plan worksheet, *281*

    formula, 227

    six-month merchandise plans, *282–283,* 326

sell through percentage, 12, 55, 107, 122–124

shipment summary, 185, *185*

shipping terms, 349–350

shortages and overages

    average annual shrink percentage, *204*

    calculating, 206–207

    causes of, 205

    controlling, case study in, 207

    formulas, 206–207

    overview, 204

    reports, *204*

shrinkage, 177, 204

six-month merchandise plans, 228, *282–284, 311, 325*

six-month seasonal dollar merchandise plans, 310

skeletal profit and loss statements, 31–32

specific departments by classification form, *188*

square foot, sales per, 12

statistics reports, merchandise, *287*

stock, average retail, 242–244

stock keeping unit (SKU), 320, *321, 322*

stock planning

    basic stock method, 266–268

    methods of, 263–278

    stock-to-sales ratio method, 263–264

    week's supply method, 264–265

stock plus purchases gross margin, 217–219
stock ratios, 227
stock turnover. *See* Turnover, stock
stock-on-hand, 174–175
stock-to-sales ratio, 263–264
store function, 5
strategy, case study in pricing, 127

T

terms of sale, 334
terms of sale case studies, 355–357
total corporate six-month plan, *284*
trade discounts, 334–335
transfer of goods, 184–185
turnover/turn, stock, 241–250
    average retail stock and, 242
    determining, 242–246
    formulas, 227, 242–243
    importance of, 241
    as KPI, 11
    rate, calculating, 245

U

unfilled orders, 296
units per sale or transaction, 191

V

volume, sales. *See* Net sales
volume price zone, 57

W

weekly sales challenge recap, *193*
weeks of supply markdown criteria, 106
weeks of supply, number of, 226
week's supply stock planning, 264–265
workroom costs, 6, 13
worksheet, annual merchandise plan, *281*

Y

year-to-date sales, 11